Selling the Church

STUDIES IN LEGAL HISTORY

Published by the University of North Carolina Press
in association with the American Society for Legal History
Thomas A. Green and Hendrik Hartog, editors

ROBERT C. PALMER

Selling the Church

The English Parish in Law,

Commerce, and Religion,

1350–1550

The University of North Carolina Press

Chapel Hill and London

Publication of this work was made possible in part
through a grant from the Joseph H. Smith Memorial Publication
Fund of the American Society for Legal History.

Designed by Heidi Perov
Set in Centaur and Goudy Text by Keystone Typesetting, Inc.
Manufactured in the United States of America

Library of Congress Cataloging-in-Publication Data
Palmer, Robert C., 1947–
Selling the church : the English parish in law, commerce,
and religion, 1350–1550 / Robert C. Palmer.
p. cm. — (Studies in legal history)
Includes bibliographical references and index.
ISBN 0-8078-2743-6 (alk. paper)
1. Church and state—England—History. 2. Parishes—England—
History. 3. Leases—England—History. 4. Benefices, Ecclesiastical—
England—History. 5. Reformation—England. I. Title. II. Series.
KD8700 .P35 2002
274.2′05—dc21   2002003831

06   05   04   03   02   5   4   3   2   1

TO S. F. C. MILSOM

CONTENTS

Tables

Figures

ACKNOWLEDGMENTS

I have accumulated the usual academic debts in writing this book, but particularly to the staff of the Public Record Office and to Tom Green, who has administered encouragement and criticism in equal doses. The personal debts, however, are just as significant. I wrote this book while I was participating in a restructuring of the University of Houston; I was president of the U.H. Faculty Senate in 1998. Intense participation in academic politics and working on the book thus exacted a double cost on my children, who were then adolescents. My gratitude to my wife, Patricia Rochford Palmer, and to my children, Ned and Elspeth, is thus all the more heartfelt, and I hope eventually they come to think this product worth the time I invested in it. I have dedicated the book to Professor S. F. C. Milsom, whom I first met in 1973 at a seminar at the Institute for Historical Research. His jurisprudential perspective has served me as a constant inspiration to search out the conceptual orientations in legal history.

Selling the Church

From 1529 to 1540 Henry VIII reformed the English parish from a commercial enterprise into a pastoral institution; in the process he reformed and transformed English society. This reformation concentrated on the parish, not on the forms of popular piety, the doctrine of transubstantiation, or the relationship of works or faith to individual salvation. For more than a century and a half before 1529, the parish had been a subject of commerce. Rectors and perpetual vicars leased out their parishes as well as their tithes. Often thus absent, they could avoid their parishioners and improve their standard of living by pursuing education, engaging in administration, taking a different ecclesiastical position, following their own interests. Chaplains, the poorest and least educated of the clergy, were the curates who cared for parish needs; and they were often hired by lay lessees. Henry VIII transformed that kind of clergy and parish in 1529. By statutory action the revenue from the parish increasingly from 1529 to 1540 commanded the presence of the rector himself; thus a more educated, substantial clergyman was present in the parish. Parishioners found themselves suddenly armed with new mechanisms for enforcing late medieval clerical ideals. These mechanisms radically altered traditional allocations of social power. The parish under Henry VIII became an organization more oriented to spiritual needs and more regulated by the crown. The complex of changes involved a reordering not only of power relations between laity and clergy, but also of the context for parish life: the handling of and control over much of the agricultural surplus of England, the means available for managing and exploiting land, the avenues available for pursuing spiritual ends. These changes amounted to a transformation of rural and urban communities in every county of England.

The decade after 1529 required a redefinition of the patterns of life, and that redefinition merged the national and the local in intricate ways. At the national level the fall of Cardinal Wolsey, the rise of Thomas Cromwell, Henry VIII's divorce and his marriage to Anne Boleyn, and the king's assumption of the headship of the church all indicated an assertive monarchy that was completing

the assumption of the comprehensive, self-confident governmental power begun after the Black Death of 1348. Those same events also symbolized the
transformation of life taking place in the locality. Bishops found themselves
completely subordinated to the crown, but in a better position to regulate
parish life. Inserting the rector back into the parish altered the economic,
educational, and religious context of parish life. The rector's wealth and education became critical elements in many parishes. The dynamics of parish life,
however, now included parishioners who had been statutorily empowered to
supervise their clerics to ensure their residence in the parish and to keep them
from engaging in commercial activity. Moreover, the monasteries and religious
houses rapidly disappeared from the countryside; people had to view their
religious life and the clerical order differently. Personal conflicts and varied
traditions shaped the changes in different ways in each parish. No matter how
idiosyncratic the local relationships were, however, the context of parish life was
one set by the institutionalized rules of the church and the state; those rules
changed rapidly after 1529. The events around the king necessarily reverberated
in mundane parish life.

Law wove the local situation together with the events instituted in London
and Westminster. In some ways over the preceding century and a half, the
English government had progressively undermined the capacity of the church to
regulate social behavior. After 1348 and the death of upwards of a third of the
English population, the king's government had increasingly accepted responsibility for the workings of society.[1] National governance of localities came
primarily through the law courts, both the courts of common law and soon also
the more expeditious prerogative courts. The prerogative courts—most importantly, chancery and king's council or star chamber—were usually most effective
at correction of individual injustices or the implementation of particularized
governmental initiatives aimed at temporary phenomena. The common law
courts, however, managed the basic long-term structure of society. Any rule at
common law set parameters that society would thereafter either follow or
develop new means to circumvent. The common law courts, primarily king's
bench and common pleas, increasingly protected the full range of commercial

---

1. Palmer, *English Law in the Age of the Black Death, 1348–1381* (hereafter cited as *ELABD*).
Subsequent treatments do not seem to require any adjustment. The quasi-evolutionary, biologi-
cal approach to the changes espoused by Ormrod and Musson does not actually deal with the
scale of change: Musson and Ormrod, *Evolution of English Justice*. Ibbetson's attempt to write a
solely doctrinal history severs the law from its context in society and government: Ibbetson,
Historical Introduction.

arrangements, including arrangements concerning the economic elements of the parish. The most important manifestation of this phenomenon was the legal protection of the rector's ability to sell his parish for a term of years. The common law virtually promoted the commercialization of the parish; the greater parameters of royal governance generally made the governance powers of the church seem more anomalous. Probably without seeing the irony, Henry VIII used those same courts that had made parishes into items of commerce as his instrument for making the parish more into a pastoral institution and for regulating the clergy and the parish community.

Law was an effective governance mechanism because it provided a set of empirically reinforced assumptions that constituted what people were willing to accept as natural. The ordinary protections of property, persons, and commercial relations had been developed before the time of anyone living in the sixteenth century; English subjects thus assumed that they were natural, enduring, reliable. Moreover, continuing enforcement of those protections made the assumption about the reliability of their civilization reasonable in ways that would have been unlikely in the early fourteenth and improbable in the twelfth century. Each generation added onto people's automatic assumptions about what could be relied upon from government. Those assumptions together with the actual performance of government enabled ordinary governance; they also allowed the monarch to use the powerful mechanisms of the law to enforce particular policies that would thus draw their power from the very processes that held society together. Henry VIII used the law masterfully to restructure basic elements of English society, particularly the parish and the clerical order, and to change those very assumptions about relations among people and about the manipulation of wealth.

This reformation of the English parish in 1529, because it used the law, was irretrievably just as much individual and local as institutional and national. The use of the law as the instrument of change dictated reliance on subjects to initiate litigation under the new statutes. This reformation was not an imposition of an administrative bureaucratic regime, but the provision of civil remedies that relied on hundreds of ordinary subjects to bring suits to enforce royal policy about clerical residence in parishes and against clerical involvement in commercial activity—and on juries willing to convict. Part of the motivation for and certainly part of the context of the litigation would be local politics, but the crown provided economic incentives and thus encouraged the litigation. Individuals functioned within a whole society; each person responded both to local situations and to national pressures of politics, religion, and economics. The willingness of a parishioner to sue his parish priest might arise from personal animosity. At the same time, however, such lawsuits against clerics carried critical economic consequences for both parties, mirrored traditional morals that criticized the absence of a rector, and enforced a national policy. Both people and the church functioned as but part of a social web structured by complex institutionalized rules. The institutions made England into more than a collection of individuals: England had long been both a community and a state.

Within a legal regime that had reinforced the commercialization of the parish, statute intruded to reorient the clergy by empowering the laity to enforce traditional expectations. The common law had developed effective indirect protections for leases. Rectors and perpetual vicars had taken advantage of those mechanisms to such an extent that leasing out the parish with its tithes, mortuary fees, church offerings, and the right to hire the actual parish priest had become normal. Statutory action in 1529 empowered the laity to make such rectors and vicars reside on their parish and at the same time to exclude them from the commercial world. Then, beginning in 1536, the dissolution of the religious houses eliminated the last major body of absentee clerical rectors who were not involved in education or service to the aristocracy. The handling of tithes, a great proportion of the agrarian surplus of the country, now had to function within a different social and legal context. Rectors and vicars had become subject to lay control and regulation at the same time that they found themselves almost prisoners in the rural parishes. The dynamics of parish, clerical, and economic life after 1540 were far different from the world of late medieval England.

That difference between late medieval England and later Tudor England was either a transformation or a revolution, but certainly not merely just evolutionary change. Historians are prone to conceptualizing change in terms of evolution, because dramatic events seldom happen unheralded. Evolutionary discourse, however, can dissolve complex, transforming events into a simple narrative. At both parish and national level, elements of continuity were prominent: most of the common law, chancery law, and church law remained the same; much of the church and royal administrative structure remained the same; most of the economic relationships and the rural rhythms for eking subsistence from the land remained the same. Nonetheless, the working of both parish and nation around those enduring laws, structures, relationships and rhythms was dramatically different. The king assumed overt and direct control of the church and thus unified in himself all governmental power. The laity found themselves with substantial power to enforce royal policy by regulating their clergy. The traditional allocation of wealth as between the clerical and lay orders of society collapsed. The government dissolved the religious houses and thus limited spiritual options and traditional mechanisms for provision of alms. Change here was sudden, dramatic, not predictable on the basis of prior events, but yet also substantially the result of prior events even from the late fifteenth century.

This study, oriented toward the English Reformation, rests on research on the common law as it related to clergy and the parish in both late medieval and Tudor England. Chapters 1–5 elaborate the ways in which the common law of late medieval England controlled the functioning of the parish and the ways in which litigation regulated, fortified, and interfered within that local community, particularly in regard to the leasing of parishes. Chapter 1 lays out the traditional allocations of power within the parish community. Traditional legal remedies established the ways in which individuals could call upon royal power to compel compliance with the rules dictated by the royal courts. Because litigation at Westminster was simultaneously personal confrontation in the locality, the remedies thus reflected and continually erected power structures within the parish. As early as 1495 the king's justices began to use those remedies to alter traditional society. They expanded their own powers over religious affairs and thus both empowered the king and reduced clerical influence.

The general view of the English parish from the point of view of the common law is the subject of Chapters 2 and 3. Chapter 2 elucidates the economic role of the parish. The rector accumulated much of the agrarian surplus of the parish through tithes, mortuary fees, and the produce of the glebe. That economic function was as important for the parish in society as was the religious function, because the collection of produce enabled efficient commercial activity. Regular common law litigation over those rectorial rights involved the crown in the everyday life of the late medieval English parish. When Henry VIII became head of the English church in the 1530s, he radically transformed traditional royal powers. Even Henry VIII, however, had to accommodate economic realities. He could not alter certain elements of traditional parish organization, because the parish was essential to the collection of the agrarian surplus that fed the towns. Certain commercial practices that were in fact detrimental to the religious life of the parish thus survived. Chapter 3 in a similar way sets out the breadth of other ecclesiastical matters that came into the king's court before the Reformation. In even central ecclesiastical functions, individual ecclesiastics resorted to common law mechanisms to resolve disputes and implement church decisions. At the same time the common law determined matters that church ideology might have allocated to the church courts. Most particularly, after 1495, John Fyneux, chief justice of the court of king's bench, initiated in various ways processes that undermined the power of church courts and thus ecclesiastical power over people's daily lives. That clerical power had been a mechanism for implementing church decisions about morality and church discipline, but it was also the most critical mechanism for legitimating the activity of the church in the governance of society. Fyneux, far from being a Lollard or a Lutheran, was only a particularly astute and able advocate of royal power; his thirty years as chief justice, however, quite effectively set the stage for the English Reformation. Fyneux disarmed the church. The church then was vulnerable when Henry VIII finally abandoned his attempt to govern the church through the medium of a cardinal and simply became head of the church in England. Chapters 2 and 3 examine broad issues of the interaction of church and state in England before 1529, but they also reveal why the first stage of the Reformation beginning in 1529 concentrated on the parish and why the church found itself unable to resist effectively.

Chapters 4 and 5 focus on a particular aspect of the late medieval parish: the leasing of parishes as whole economic units. Chapter 4 assesses the practice of leasing parishes. Prior to 1348 and the Black Death, absentee rectors used bailiffs as estate managers, a practice that meant that rectors had a continuing managerial role and interest in the parish. After 1348 and because of the common law mechanisms that reinforced the security of leaseholds, rectors and vicars sold their parishes for terms of years, both to ecclesiastics and to laymen. Some absenteeism had been institutionalized by the practice of permitting heads of religious houses to serve as rectors and by pluralism: the holding of more than a single position with care of souls. Even for rectors with a single position, however, leasing severed the rector or vicar from the activity of the parish. Selling the church for terms of years became common throughout England and was plausibly more important for producing rectorial absenteeism than pluralism. Chapter 5 examines the variety of disputes and consequences that resulted from leasing the parishes. While such leases were subject to the same range of problems as any lease, the practice of leasing parishes encountered particular problems: the income from the parish depended on faithful performance of religious duty, the rector's duty to repair parish buildings depended on the lessee's care of the premises, the activity of the bishop could interfere with either the lessor rector or the lessee. The practice of selling the church for a term was so central to the economy, despite being contrary to church law, that it presented an intractable problem for the church. Even Henry VIII was able to deal with it only partially.

Chapters 6, 7, and 8 deal with the way in which Henry VIII and Cromwell allowed parish leasing to continue, but remedied many of the abuses that accompanied the practice. They erected a clerical order different from its medieval antecedent: the Tudor church was subject to the king and in service to lay lords, the parishes, and education and was insulated from commercial endeavors and profit. Chapter 6 examines the statutes of 1529 that inaugurated the parish reformation by empowering the laity to enforce traditional ideals that priests should refrain from commerce and be resident on the parish. Those statutes, designed viciously to encourage prosecution by any person, were probably the means by which Cromwell proved his worth to the king, at a time when Henry VIII had been forthright with his concerns about the clergy. Chapter 7 examines the pattern of enforcement of the statutes of 1529 from 552 cases gathered from the courts of king's bench, common pleas, and exchequer of pleas in the first five and a quarter years. The litigation was designed to compel compliance, not to increase royal revenue: out-of-court settlement that deprived the crown of its share of a forfeiture was acceptable. Moreover, royal resources were available to private prosecutors, so that even suits with a low probability of success were feasible: many innocent clerics were thus prosecuted. Prosecution of the innocent made clerics less likely even to appear to infringe the statutory prohibitions. Clergy in the 1530s had fewer opportunities for enrichment; at the same time they were systematically harassed. Chapter 8 deals with the way in which the dissolution of the religious houses continued the policies of the statutes of 1529; the dissolution eliminated another large category of absentee clerical rectors. Two other major statutes, the statute of uses and the statute for the resumption of liberties, were related to the dissolution of the monasteries. Those statutes restructured both the ways in which people could manage their property and the ways in which governmental power was handled locally. In the wake of these changes that derived in significant part from the reform of the abuses arising from parish leasing, the court of king's bench reformed its procedures to redefine the boundaries between the king's common law and the church law that was now the king's church law. The attention, predictably, was on tithing. The nature of legal remedies ensured that the policy embodied in the statutes of 1529 remained effective through the reign of Henry VIII, unaffected by the shifting factions around the king. As continuing and effective royal policy, those statutes reformed the clergy and the parish community, not in doctrine, liturgy, or piety, but in the allocation of power within the parish. Any lay (or ecclesiastical) person could now wield the king's power to enforce traditional church ideals in ways that would enrich himself and at the same time construct a new noncommercial clerical order decisively subordinated to the laity. The ability to sell the church for terms of years continued, but at a much reduced frequency. Lay lessees even gained security in their parish leases, because their role in the accumulation of the agrarian surplus was critical to the survival of the towns. From 1348 until at least 1550, parish leases were central to the life of the parish, the problems of the church, and, finally, the current of Tudor reform.

This study thus departs in almost every way from the established historiographies of England under the early Tudors. It asserts a parish reformation beginning in 1529. Traditional historiography would assert that the English Reformation consisted of two main and distinct elements: a seizure by the central government of control over the church in the 1530s and then a change in popular piety late in the sixteenth century. Moreover, it departs from traditional historiographies in that it asserts that central and local concerns were irretrievably interconnected by the common law. Older historiographies often assumed a connection without examination; newer historiography prefers to deal either with local studies or studies of central government and politics. This study does not regard the law as something abstract or set apart from society. Law was the primary mechanism by which the state interfered in local social relations to allocate power, mediate disputes, implement initiatives. It was a mechanism of national and direct social importance and governance. Moreover, law was regulatory. Neither medieval nor Tudor England had an army of bureaucrats that could regulate society administratively. The law, nevertheless, was bureaucratic; that is, it had specialized functions, fixed rules, and a hierarchical structure of authority, all of which provided relatively predictable results. The justices were part of the government that made and occasionally changed the rules the courts enforced, and that enforcement allocated power between people and rights to things and thus changed patterns of interaction. Finally, the arguments here do not envisage either simply slow change or a radical change without precedent. Dramatically new elements were interwoven with major continuities to create a new institutional context for personal lives.

The new structure of personal life and exercise of power in the parish was the direct result of litigation, but litigation in Westminster Hall was also a parish event. The litigants at Westminster lived in a parish and confronted each other during litigation that lasted at times for years. Law suits were not just a brief explosion of aggravated emotion, but rather protracted, public confrontations that raised emotions, divided people, and changed lives in the parish. The plaintiff drew on the institutionalized and bureaucratic royal power of the law and did so for years at a time. One might like to have diaries of parishioners who commented on parish conflict, but such accounts would actually be less valuable than the litigation, because the anecdotes in diaries could be completely idiosyncratic even for the individual parish. Frequent litigation, however, indicates general phenomena; the power actually exercised by more than 400 plaintiffs in only five years was power available to literally everyone in the parish. Recognized access to that power changed relations even in parishes where no one sued. The conclusions here about reallocation of power within the parish, the regulation of the clergy, and the changed pattern of life are not inferential; the litigation itself is direct evidence not only of parish confrontation but also of the effective exercise of royal power in the parish to erect a different kind of clerical order in a different kind of parish.

This study nevertheless is itself far from comprehensive. It does outline both a third aspect of the English Reformation and the late medieval parish management style that makes that aspect of the Reformation comprehensible. It does not attempt to depict or reconceptualize the whole of the English Reformation. This study about the reformation of the English parish is unconcerned with Lutheran or Calvinist doctrine; it is concerned with law, economics, and power in the locality. Elements of this project do indeed point to broader parts of that larger framework that need reexamination. This study, however, has no such ambition: it simply argues the local component of the English Reformation in the 1530s. Moreover, the common law records are so voluminous that they can yield many times the data here utilized. In order to further research, I have included as much of the two major databases in the appendices as was feasible. The full version of the databases is on my website, currently under the University of Houston Department of History site at ⟨vi.uh.edu⟩. Finally, the dynamic of change in Tudor England described here is significantly different from that found in other scholarly studies, precisely because this major new body of evidence dictates the adoption of different assumptions. I have tried to handle in detail the critical points at which I disagree with other interpretations, but for specialists the treatment may still be too brief.

CHAPTER ONE

The Parish as a Governed Community

he parish of late medieval England was a much governed community. As a governance community of the church, the parish was
distinct from the manor, even though often coincident with it. The
church, and particularly the bishop, had governance rights within the parish,
but those rights the bishop shared overtly with the crown, the parish patron, the
rector, and the parishioners. These rights-holders were thus both external and
internal to the parish, and the interplay dictated the traditional perception of
parish dynamics. That traditional perception of the parish was the ordinary
language of discourse and thus set the ordinary ideals of clerical conduct. Late
medieval actual conduct diverged markedly from this traditional perception, as
succeeding chapters will show. Henry VIII after 1529 would bring actual conduct a fair way into line with these traditional perceptions, although in a
radically changed context.

Internal Parish Government

The allocations of power within the parish included both the vertical and the
horizontal elements characteristic of late medieval governance. The vertical
element was the rector, appointed by the bishop at the nomination of the
patron, and legally in charge of providing spiritual care to the parishioners. The
rector's position was managerial. He did not necessarily perform the religious
services himself, but he was responsible for making sure that the spiritual needs
of the parish were met and that the buildings belonging to the parish, including
the church chancel, were maintained. The rector also disposed of the various
revenue streams that constituted the economic aspect of the parish that, in the
end, supported both the parish and the international bureaucratic church organization. The horizontal part of internal parish government was the church
wardens, who were selected by the parishioners. They were responsible both for
certain parish endowments and activities and for the upkeep of part of the
church building, vestments, and church ornaments. The church wardens could

complain to the rector's superiors, of course, but otherwise did not control his activities. Since church wardens apparently only became a significant feature of the English parish after the Black Death, their presence provided a new governance dynamic at the local level. The varied interplay between the vertical and horizontal elements of the parish determined the character of the parish. The presence of both elements, however, ensured that the parish was not just a governed unit, but a governed community. That change in parish structure kept it current, so that the parish remained as vital a community as the other communities within which individuals lived: the communities of town and manor, the community of the county and diocese, and the broader community of the realm.

The rector, if resident, could dominate the parish. The rector did not have to be a priest, but he normally was.[1] He received the bulk of the parish income and the responsibility for running the parish. In some sense, the rector is best considered a manager who could but certainly need not have direct involvement with the spiritual care of his parishioners. If resident, he either performed the church services (mass, the liturgical hours of matins and vespers) in person or hired a chaplain to do so. He was responsible for the provision of the other sacraments: baptizing children, presiding over marriages, hearing confessions, performing the last rites for the dying. He managed the economic resources of the parish, economic resources that were often as significant as those that went to the lord of the manor. He received the parish tithes: a tenth of the parish produce, both from the lord's demesne lands and from the lands of the ordinary parishioners. Additionally, the rector normally had the sole benefit of lands attached to the church within the parish, often called the glebe lands, ranging from a few acres in some parishes to large estates in others. The rector claimed the traditional offerings from the parishioners as well as significant occasional profits, such as mortuary fees: often the second best animal or piece of movable property of a dead parishioner. In return, the rector was liable for both royal and ecclesiastical taxation and was responsible for repair of the church chancel. A resident and involved rector could be a powerful personal and economic force in a parish.

The rector, however, was often necessarily absent. Monasteries had their own large agricultural estates, but they also found support from the appropriation of parishes. If a monastery thus appropriated a parish, the head of the monastery or other religious house—whether abbot, abbess, prior, prioress, or master—

1. Swanson, *Church and Society*, 43.

became the rector of the parish. No one expected the abbot or prior to abandon the religious house and live in the parish. Instead, the rector appointed a perpetual vicar, who received a portion of the church revenue; the bulk of the revenue still went to the rector to support the religious house. The actual apportionment of revenue between rector and vicar, as well as all other elements of the relationship, was under the control of the bishop: when the rector was clearly not present, the vicar had to have the resources to manage the parish. Between a fifth and a third of England's nine thousand or so parishes were appropriated in this way; the number increased to about 3,300 by the Reformation.[2]

Just as parish revenue could support a religious house of monks or friars, the parish could supply the personnel needs of cathedrals and other large churches, as well as the needs of the bishop's administration. Cathedrals had relatively large staffs and proportionately large economic needs. Cathedral personnel were often prebendaries, that is, priests supported by a parish whose revenues were dedicated to endowing a position outside the parish. Prebendaries worked within cathedrals, with the bishop, in church courts; generally, they administered the church. Prebendaries likewise might require the services of a substitute within the parish on a regular basis.

Even when the administrative structure of the church did not dictate an absentee rector, the rector might necessarily be absent. The church was not only the institution of religion; it was also the institution of education. In late medieval England the church did not have the same monopoly of education that it had had in the early Middle Ages and had largely retained in the high Middle Ages. Still, however, the colleges of Oxford and Cambridge were clerical. One occupation of rectors was educational; some rectors were thus absent from the parish and used the parish revenue to attend university to obtain advanced degrees in theology, law, medicine. Likewise, a rector might have received his appointment to the parish from the king in return for service in the king's bureaucracy in the chancery, exchequer, or the courts. The revenue from the parish, in that case, directly supported the state bureaucracy by paying its personnel. Finally, a rector might occasionally go on pilgrimage or prosper and receive a license to hold more than one rectory, sometimes many more than one. Many parishes could thus have a rector who, for an extended time, was necessarily absent. Absentee rectors might appoint a temporary substitute.

Parish rectors were thus vital to the bureaucratic, religious, and cultural life

---

2. Ibid., 44. My figure assumes that institutional absentee rectors would in fact appoint a perpetual vicar, and that was not always true.

of England, but they were likewise central to the economic life of the country. In an agrarian society with a vital commercial life, the problem of gathering agricultural surplus together available to traders for transport to towns, cities, and merchants was critical. Traders could work easily with lords of manors and with monasteries, both of which would have, predictably, large amounts of agricultural produce that had to be converted into other forms of wealth. Rectors constituted a similar economic node: they controlled more than a tenth of the agricultural produce of the country, regularly extracting, accumulating, and making the produce available for commerce. Lords of manors and rectors of parishes simplified the task of traders in supplying urban needs; otherwise, traders would have had to bargain with dozens of local people in each village. The religious as much as the aristocratic rights of England simplified the economic development and survival of towns by collection of the agrarian surplus within manors and parishes.

Church wardens represented the parish as a community. The parish itself had no control over who would be rector or vicar. After the Black Death, however, parishioners began to participate more substantially and officially in the parish. Church wardens were the guardians of the goods and ornaments of the church; they were the official representatives of the parishioners. They were the people who normally sued or were sued for the parish as a community.[3] Their duties included the reporting of clerical or religious deficiencies to the ecclesiastical authorities.[4] The rector had responsibility for the upkeep and care only of the "ecclesiastical" part of the church building: that part of the church after the nave, including the sanctuary. The rest was the responsibility of the parish, which normally acted through its church wardens.

Church wardens, thus representing the horizontal, communal, lay side of the church, fit well within the context of the time. Edward III's accommodation with his bishops after the Black Death dictated certain substantial elements of royal control over the church.[5] Through the period of the Hundred Years War, roughly coincident with the Babylonian Captivity and the Great Schism, popular perceptions tended to regard papal policy as dictated largely by state politics. John Wycliff's heresy arose during the Babylonian Captivity, when the pope resided in Avignon and was subject to the influence of the French monarch. In both England and France, kings in fact exercised more control over the church.

3. Kumin, *Shaping of a Community*, 19–24; Ault, "The Village Church," 211–12.
4. Helmholz, "Usury," 378.
5. Palmer, *ELABD*, 28–53.

Wycliff's heresy was broader than mere lay control over the church, but lay control was a prominent part of the Lollard agenda.[6] Wycliff's message here was only an aggressive extension of the style of governance that grew in England after the Black Death. While the government attacked Lollardy, royal control over the church demonstrated the way in which heresy often only carried contemporary perceptions rather farther than orthodoxy permitted. The institution of church wardens was completely orthodox, not tainted with heresy. Still, as an active lay participation in the life of the parish, church wardens were not simply an anomalous growth, but rather a distinctive product of a society that increasingly demanded active lay involvement in religious life. Even if the institution flourished initially simply to provide for immediate parish management following the death of many clergy in the Black Death, the presence of church wardens would nonetheless still stimulate attitudes about the proper allocation of power within the parish. Allocation of power within the parish, of course, would eventually carry implications about the role of the laity in the church generally: fact feeds theory.

Still, conflict between church wardens and rectors was not endemic. Relatively little information has survived about church wardens, although there is much more than has yet been brought to light. The division of responsibility for the church buildings as well as the church wardens' responsibility for the goods and ornaments of the church should have generated substantial frictions even among well-intentioned people in well-run parishes. The lack of conflict was plausibly real. Rectors and church wardens constituted only the formal structure of the parish. Underneath that, the vital and actual operations of the parish worked much differently. Chapters 4 and 5 will thus examine the commercial relationship of leasing that characterized many parishes before 1529.

External Parish Government

External governance of the parish came through the two theoretically independent but actually interdependent court systems: the royal and the ecclesiastical. The king ran the royal governance structure, working through justices of the peace, coroners, the sheriff, and the sheriff's bailiffs at the county level and through the prerogative and common law courts at the central level. The king's law governed individual personal and real property, contractual relationships,

6. Lambert, *Medieval Heresy*, 232–36; Aston, *Lollards and Reformers*, 2–3.

commission of crimes and ordinary wrongs, labor relations, a plethora of interpersonal problems; most litigation on these matters began with local litigants who brought cases directly into the central courts. Those litigants at common law, however, were all parishioners, at times in disputes related to parish life. The common law protected also the rights of the patron to nominate the person whom the bishop would appoint as parish priest. Alongside this royal organization was the church organization that placed the pope, whether in Avignon or in Rome, at the apex of the ecclesiastical hierarchy as the foremost bishop, with Christendom divided further into dioceses headed by bishops. Dioceses were grouped together administratively into provinces under an archbishop and subdivided into archdeaconries, deaneries, and finally into parishes. Church governance as exercised in ecclesiastical courts involved doctrinal correctness, church property, probate of wills and testamentary causes, breaking of oaths, usury, individual morals relating to sexuality, marriage, vows: more generally, matters relating either to individual salvation or to the maintenance of the institutional structure of the church. At levels above the parish, church courts served as the means for regulating religious conduct. Matters of otherworldly salvation, however, intertwined with this-worldly affairs: sex, money, land, power. State and church remained independent structures, as dictated by the flexible resolution of the Investiture Controversy of the eleventh century. Still, as in any society, the independence of different governance structures was in many ways restricted to form. Centuries and necessity had forged processes and accommodations that bound England together under the monarch into a comparatively cohesive state.

The person principally responsible for supervising the parish was the bishop. Normally, only the bishop could appoint a person as rector; that is, only a bishop could commission a person to act as the legitimately constituted religious authority in the parish. The bishop thus was responsible for seeing to it that the person to be appointed was sufficiently qualified under church requirements. The bishop was likewise responsible for the enforcement of clerical morality and the running of the parish. A dedicated bishop would see to it that parishes were visited and examined periodically to discover and correct irregularities. If the parish resources were divided between a rector and vicar unfairly so that the vicar had inadequate resources, the bishop could redress that imbalance. For irregularities, the bishop could remove a rector, although few examples of removal have survived.[7] The bishop thus was the ultimate power

7. *Registrum Thome Bourgchier*, ed. Du Boulay, 287.

over the rector in his ecclesiastical capacity, even though he often acted through his various subordinates: officials, archdeacons, and deans.

If the bishop was the only person who could make a cleric into the rector of the parish, that power was not unlimited; the social power that an unrestricted right to appoint would have given bishops proved unacceptable in England. In most cases the bishop found himself constrained in selecting the person only he could appoint. Various people—abbots and priors, gentry, magnates, the king himself—held a property right called an advowson. The advowson right entitled the holder to nominate the person whom the bishop would examine and, if found qualified, appoint to a particular parish. That examination by the bishop might at times have been perfunctory prior to the Reformation, but thereafter it assumed a larger role.[8] The advowson right often attached to the lord's right to the manor, so much so that if the manor was divided by inheritance, for example, among three daughters, the various holders would often have the right to nominate at the proportionate vacancy—here, every third vacancy. Advowson rights greatly qualified the ability of the bishop to control his diocese: he could not appoint to the parishes only the most pious, the most obedient, the most efficient, or the most learned of the clergy he licensed to practice in his diocese, because for most appointments he was constrained to examine only the nominee presented by someone else. Advowson rights were essential elements of power for all concerned. For both king and pope, the ability to have a person appointed as rector was completely equivalent to the ability to hire that person for an essential administrative position or to train him in law, medicine, or theology. For ordinary lords with advowson rights, the right allowed them to provide positions for clerical relatives or dependents.

Once nominated and appointed, however, a rector was basically free from the control of the holder of the right of advowson. Royal wealth and power might normally ensure the loyalty of those the king preferred. Gratitude and family ties could bind a rector to other persons who nominated. Still, such ties fell short of control, because the patron only nominated. The only person who actually controlled the rector was the bishop. The laity who held rights of advowson—the wealthy and powerful—had a limited but important element of participation in parish life, a role that again was completely separate from devotion and dogma and tied directly to the parish as a generator of wealth and a resource for patronage.

8. Bowker, *Henrician Reformation*, 39.

Both internally and externally, then, the laity participated in the governance of the parish, even at the most obvious level of bureaucratic structures. The parish as an economic unit supported the ecclesiastical, educational, and state structures that gave order to medieval life; it also supported the monasteries that best embodied the conviction of medieval Catholics that God's grace enabled one to lead a more perfect life and thus to merit salvation. Church wardens were the overt instrument for the parishioners as a whole to participate in the upkeep and management of the church, while advowsons ensured for the magnates and the king some continuing ability to dictate the manner of person who succeeded to church positions. Still, the rector was the focus of the whole complex: his wealth, his appointment, his powers.

The Protection of Advowson Rights

Rights of advowson, the right to nominate the person whom the bishop would appoint to an ecclesiastical, revenue-producing position, produced substantial conflict and much litigation. Ecclesiastics and kings had fought out the basic structure in the twelfth century.[9] Following nearly two further centuries of intermittent friction, Edward III after the Black Death worked out with his bishops and magnates new accommodations and protective mechanisms.[10] Nothing really eliminated the basic problem. The king's courts year in and year out, century after century, handled the lawsuits that applied the accommodations in hotly contested and locally crucial disputes about the control of the resources that, although generated by the parishioners, ecclesiastical law dictated should be gathered into the rector's hands. The legal forms not only structured the exercise of power and expectations; they also forged continuously and effectively the precise borders and priorities between church and state, between churchmen and laity. Unlike persons, legal remedies were standard and enduring, available and relatively predictable decade after decade, well-crafted tools that in the hands of the lawyer could inflict heavy burdens on transgressors and thus determine the forms for social interaction. They continually reinforced and reforged the assumptions about "necessary" or "natural" divisions of power and allocations of wealth.

The primary common law court was the court of common pleas, situated at

9. Warren, *Henry II*, 483, 542–46; Morris, *The Papal Monarchy*, 557.
10. Palmer, *ELABD*, 28–56.

Westminster near London. From shortly after the Black Death until another explosion of litigation late in the sixteenth century, that court handled litigation sufficient to fill about two thousand sheepskin a year with case records. Each membrane contained from one to several dozen entries of process taken on cases. The court was not appellate; it handled the lawsuit at trial level, hearing lawyers' arguments at Westminster and sending individual questions to be answered by juries before justices on circuit. In every sense, it was a national court,[11] fed by attorneys who spent their working lives on horseback traveling from the far corners of England to Westminster and back. Most likely, more than 1 percent of England's adult male population were party to lawsuits just in the court of common pleas every year in the late fourteenth and early fifteenth centuries, while others functioned as jurors, summoners, pledges.[12] The intense interaction of the court of common pleas with the populace made the common law a powerful governmental tool.

The writs largely determined what kind of suits parties could bring at common law, and writs were nothing other than standard-form written orders. A prospective litigant (or his attorney) bought the appropriate writ from chancery in Westminster. The selection was vital. Today, a litigant in some sense can simply choose to sue and cite relevant law that will make the situation appropriate for the court to accord a remedy. In medieval England, litigation required the selection of the right writ: the writ purchased determined the allegations that plaintiffs could make.

The plaintiff purchased the original writ that both initiated the process and set the structure for the whole case. The chancery wrote it out and sent it to the sheriff of the relevant county. The sheriff performed the action ordered (such as summoning the defendant to appear in court) and recorded his actions on the back of the writ; he then returned the writ to the court empowered to hear the case. That returned writ gave the court jurisdiction: the power to hear the particular case. From then on, the court itself ordered the sheriff to take specific actions that would finally compel the defendant's appearance. If the defendant appeared in court before the parties settled or were worn out, their serjeants (highly skilled lawyers who held a monopoly of pleading in the court of

11. Table 2.

12. Palmer, *Whilton Dispute*, 6–8. The figure is based on the litigation in the 1330s. After the Black Death the absolute volume of litigation grew while the population fell drastically so that the amount of litigation per person probably doubled from the situation in the 1330s.

common pleas)[13] argued the case before the justices at Westminster and arrived at the central issue of law to be determined by the justices or of fact to be submitted to a jury. That issue had to be focused on the determination of the matter specified in the original writ. Alternatively, and increasingly by 1500, the defendant simply pleaded a general issue (such as "not guilty"), often merely by the submission of written instead of oral pleadings, and left the whole matter to be handled before the jury. After pleading, the court ordered the sheriff of the county to assemble a jury to meet before justices on circuit. The justices predictably arrived, presided over the jury's consideration of evidence, if any, and the giving of their verdict; the verdict was sent back to the justices at Westminster for judgment. Judgment before the justices at Westminster resulted in further orders to the sheriff for execution of judgment: putting the plaintiff on the land or compelling the defendant to perform an obligation or pay monetary damages. The original writ, the writ that thus began the whole case, not only gave the court power to hear the individual case but also set the limits for the whole succeeding process.

Two twelfth-century writs, although seldom used in the fourteenth century, still set the continuing late medieval law on certain aspects of advowsons. The writ of right of advowson[14] settled claims to the right itself: who was the person who could rightfully nominate to the bishop the person to be considered for the benefice?[15] Darrein presentment ("last presentment") handled a problem encountered with canon law, the body of law used by the church. Canon law determined that the parish's need for a rector was so great that, if the position remained vacant for six months, the bishop could appoint his own candidate. The danger was that both claimants to the advowson thus might lose the exercise of the right for a particular vacancy. Darrein presentment handled that problem by using an expeditious process to determine who had presented (nominated) to the bishop for that benefice last. Whoever had done it last

---

13. Baker, *Introduction to English Legal History* (hereafter cited as *IELH*), 179–82.

14. "The king to such a one, greetings. We order you to hold full right without delay to R of C concerning the advowson of the church of N which he claims to pertain to his free tenement that he holds of you in N by the free service of so much annually for all service, of which he deforces him. And if he does not do so, let the sheriff do it, lest I hear further complaint thereof for default of right." *Early Registers of Writs*, ed. de Haas and Hall, 126 (R.77) (retranslated; variations omitted).

15. Milsom, Introduction to *Novae Narrationes*, xxxix–xli.

would be allowed to nominate again, while slower litigation by the writ of right of advowson would work out who, in the future, would do so.[16]

These two writs, then, established the advowson as a property right governed by the common law of England. The common law yielded to canon law enough not simply to overrule it, but to devise a process for avoiding its consequences. Litigants only rarely used either the writ of right of advowson or the writ of darrein presentment after the early fourteenth century. Seldom-used writs often, as with these two, remained central to the law because they established rights then enforced and manipulated under other more flexible forms of litigation. Despite the revolutionary reforms of 1529, the property rights in advowsons protected by these writs continued unscathed into Reformation England. As with all property rights, however, their distribution in society determined their social meaning. Medieval monasteries had held many of the English advowson rights. After the dissolution of the monasteries, advowsons would represent a decidedly more lay influence on church benefices. Which sector of society holds a right to wealth, power, and patronage can often be as important as the nature of the right itself.

A different writ, the writ of prohibition, handled disputes between the king's court and church courts about jurisdiction, particularly about the right of church courts to handle cases concerning advowsons. The writ, issuing likewise out of chancery,[17] prohibited either the church court judge or the church court plaintiff from continuing in a case that belonged not in ecclesiastical court but in the king's court. One of the standard forms of the writ of prohibition concerned church court litigation about advowsons. Church courts at times understandably felt that they were the appropriate forum for such cases. When defendants arrived in church court they might well disagree and seek a writ of prohibition from the chancellor. Ignoring the prohibition could result in sub-

---

16. Ibid., xli–xliii. The form of the writ: "The king to the sheriff, greetings. If A. gives you security etc., then summon etc. twelve free and lawful men of the neighborhood of N. to be before our justices at Westminster on such a day ready to recognize by oath which patron in time of peace presented the last parson, who is dead, to the church of N. which is vacant as it is said, and the advowson of which the same A. says pertains to him. And meanwhile let them view that church; and make their names to be written down. And summon by good summoners B. who deforces him of that advowson to be there to hear that recognition. And have there the summoners and this writ." *Early Registers of Writs*, 127 (R.79) (variations omitted).

17. In the sixteenth century, prohibition process began more frequently without writ and directly out of king's bench, as had premunire process since the late fifteenth century.

stantial penalties, so that the writ was fairly effective: advowsons were in fact preserved for the consideration of the king's court.[18] The writ of prohibition, fashioned in the early thirteenth century to regulate a court system run by the external authority of the pope, found a similar role after the 1530s; but it then regulated the jurisdiction and internal workings of the *king's* church courts.

The effectiveness of the writs of prohibition was actually greater than has recently been thought. The process of consultation allowed for suspension of the writ of prohibition. The ecclesiastical court judge thus could consult with the chancellor and explain the situation; the chancellor might then permit him to continue with the case in ecclesiastical court. The chancellor issued the consultation and thus decided the jurisdictional issue solely on the basis of the libel (the plaintiff's statement of claim). That process would certainly have diminished the effect of the prohibition had it been conclusive. The writ of consultation issued from chancery, however, was conditional; it gave permission for the case to continue if the case was in fact as it had been portrayed to the chancellor.[19] Issuance of a writ of consultation did not prevent the defendant from bringing his suit based on a violation of the prohibition. The consultation would be cited in defense; but the issue at common law, notwithstanding the writ of consultation, was whether in fact the suit had contravened royal court jurisdiction.[20] While the process of consultation allowed the church to main-

---

18. Helmholz, *Canon Law*, 59–75, 83–85. The form of the writ: "The king to such a one, greetings. Whereas R. our cleric holds the church of N. from our advowson, you, claiming it from the advowson of H. of C., draw him into a plea thereof in court Christian, as we have heard from the report of many. Because it is manifest that we etc., we prohibit you from prosecuting that plea in court Christian until it has been discussed in our court whether the advowson of the same church pertains to us or to the abovesaid H., because pleas concerning advowsons to churches pertain to our crown and dignity." *Early Registers of Writs*, 136 (R119) (retranslated; variations omitted; extended).

19. *Early Registers of Writs*, 142–43 (R143, R144). When not explicitly conditional as in R143, the basis for the decision is carefully cited, as in R144.

20. Helmholz thinks that the consultation determined the issue. Helmholz, *Canon Law*, 59–76, 86–87. Had the consultation been determinative, consultation would have prevented a suit of attachment on the prohibition. Attachments on the prohibition, however, continued despite the issuance of a consultation order. Braban v. Richard Synkele vicar of Hallow, Worcestershire, CP40/456, m. 572; Mylot v. Waleys, CP40/519, m. 409; Alnthorp v. John Burnham, prior of Beaulieu, CP40/508, m. 102 (directly on the prohibition); Cartwright v. William, parson of Allesley, Warwickshire, CP40/507, m. 459d. Writs of consultation were issued on hearing from one side as were writs of prohibition, precisely because the subsequent suit on the prohibition

tain the jurisdictions the crown considered appropriate, it did not undermine the effectiveness of the writ of prohibition.

The writ *quare impedit* (why he impedes) protected the advowson primarily against impediments presented by the relevant bishop.[21] *Quare impedit* normally focused on the bishop when he resisted a king's court order concerning the appropriate person to nominate. One of the more frequent situations that lay behind the issuance of a writ of *quare impedit* was a papal provision. Popes since the thirteenth century had increasingly expanded occasions on which they could preempt the ordinary holder of an advowson and themselves nominate.[22] One such occasion was the death of an incumbent rector while on business before the pope: such a death was held to give the pope the right to nominate the successor. The pope's ordinary power over bishops allowed him likewise to command the bishop to convey to a certain cleric the first benefice that came available. A bishop thus caught between royal command and papal command might decline to obey the royal order; he would then become the defendant in *quare impedit. Quare impedit* litigation was frequent from the thirteenth century into the sixteenth century. Both the judges in church courts and the bishops who appointed rectors were targets of frequently used and effective suits that inflicted large penalties on those unwilling to abide by the common law protections of advowson rights; those suits protected the advowson rights of the king, magnates and knights, and abbots and priors. Unlike darrein presentment and the writ of right of advowson, the writs of prohibition and *quare impedit* were applications of coercive state authority coming to bear regularly in late medieval England to construct and maintain the boundaries between church and crown authority.

Under continued papal pressure, some English bishops had refused to yield to those processes (as well as other less frequently used procedures);[23] such resistance precipitated a further and more drastic conflict with Edward III in

---

would put in issue whether the suit was in fact one of the prohibited varieties. The consultation became definitive around 1500 when king's bench was in charge of consultation and ensured that consultation was part of a litigation process.

21. The form of the writ: "The king to the sheriff, greeting. Command B. that justly etc. he permit A. to present a suitable parson to the church of N. which is vacant and pertains to his gift, as he says, whereof he complains that the aforesaid B. unjustly impedes him, and if he does not do this, and if A. shall have given you security to prosecute his claim, then summon by good summoners etc." *Early Registers of Writs*, 50 (C.51).

22. Pennington, *Popes and Bishops*, 115–54.

23. Milsom, Introduction to *Novae Narrationes*, xli–xlvi.

the 1340s that resulted in the most crushing of the royal procedures: the premunire writ. After cornering and ruining two bishops in the conflict, and as a part of a more general restructuring of government after the Black Death, Edward III restored the fortunes of those two bishops and instituted premunire as a more regularized procedure for crushing future opposition.[24] The death of between a third and a half of the population within only two years was sufficient to prompt a restructuring that left the crown in control of a more extensive and, for a time, a more collegial government. The government now had greater control over the church.

A part of that cooperative involvement was the writ of premunire. Instead of a process that had simply jailed any papal provisor (a papal nominee for a benefice), the premunire statute mandated a sixty-day warning period within which the accused could appear before royal officials to explain his conduct. Recalcitrance could lead to a judgment that would treat the defendant as the king's enemy: the loss of lands and tenements, goods and chattels. The premunire statute handled the matter broadly and provided process against anyone who undermined king's court judgments by resort to papal or other ecclesiastical court processes. By the terms of the statute, premunire could handle problems beyond appointments to benefices.[25] Fourteenth-century premunire, however, almost always concerned such appointments; other matters were handled more moderately by writs of prohibition.[26]

Undermining the Governance Powers of the Church: Premunire

In the late fifteenth and early sixteenth century the government regularly provided access to the broader potential of premunire. After 1495 premunire prosecutions became relatively frequent. They also focused on the activities of English church courts rather than on papal incursions on English advowsons. Premunire thus undermined the ability of the English church to govern in society: it progressively eliminated English church court jurisdictions. This new aggressive stance was only part of a wider consolidation of power by the court of king's bench, because the justices had also established a regulatory function in regard even to the prerogative courts. The justices gave remedy to those who

24. Palmer, *ELABD*, 45–53.
25. Ibid., 32; Statute of Premunire, 27 Edw. III, c. 1; Coke, *Institutes*, Bk. 3, c. 54.
26. Martin, "Crown Policy and Anglo-Papal Relations."

had improperly been sued in king's council,[27] chancery,[28] and admiralty.[29] By statute in 1515, king's bench, already possessed of jurisdiction in error over the court of common pleas, obtained a similar jurisdiction over the exchequer of pleas.[30] King's bench thus became the dominant common law court. Limiting church court power by premunire was perhaps the most difficult initiative of king's bench, but not its only initiative. Extending royal power by undermining the governance power of the church was a genuine part of the English Reformation insofar as the Reformation was concerned with royal authority over the church. The expansion of king's bench power over ecclesiastical matters translated directly into common law regulation of parish life.

27. KB27/961, m. 74 (John Waltham v. Thomas Lunde, citing Magna Carta); KB27/965, m. 25 (Draper v. Claver); KB27/972, mm. 9, 92 (Upton v. Prior of Newstead by Stamford, citing Magna Carta); KB27/978, m. 26d (Thomas Morley v. John Trippam, citing Magna Carta); KB27/981, m. 104d (Florencius Bartam v. John Barowe, citing Magna Carta); KB27/992, m. 37 (Richard Belton cleric v. William Dregge, citing Magna Carta); KB27/993, m. 78 (William Fetiplace v. John Feld, citing statute of 1368, suing him before three of the king's councillors [bishop of Carlisle, Richard Emson, and Robert Southwell]; demurrer with adjournments for judgment for more than three years); KB27/994, m. 82, KB27/995, m. 3d (John Anne v. Hugh Frebody, citing statute of 1368 [KB27/1000, m. 37, Fyneux issues supersedeas on the exigent]); KB27/994, m. 34d (Henry Milborne v. John Thackeham, citing Magna Carta); KB27/997, m. 75 (Lawrence Streynsham v. Margaret Hoore, citing Magna Carta); KB27/999, m. 39 (Roger Vyseke v. William Fry, citing Magna Carta); KB27/999, m. 26d (Nicholas Speccote v. William Fry, citing statute of 1368); KB27/1001, m. 13d (rex) (indictment before jp's of Hampshire under Magna Carta provision); KB27/1001, m. 79d (William Gybbes v. John Huysshe, citing statute of 1368, suing him before Richard Emson); KB27/1005, m. 48, KB27/1006, m. 41 (John Stanley v. Humfrey Stanley, citing statute of 1368); KB27/1011, m. 33d, KB27/1018, m. 65, KB27/1020, m. 74, KB27/1021, m. 63d (Abbot of Bury St. Edmunds v. William Adams et al., suing him before king's council; verdict for plaintiff but judgment delayed for at least a year and a half afterwards); KB27/1016, m. 62d (Robert Brandon v. Edward Jenny et al., citing Magna Carta); KB27/1048, m. 75 (Thomas Butler v. Robert Fuller, citing Magna Carta, demurrer); KB27/1050, m. 47 (Edward Pomerey v. John Butland, citing statute of 1368).

28. KB27/963, m. 22d (John, William, and Thomas Fynche v. John Hay, citing statute of 1368); KB27/1082, m. 87 (John Parnell v. Geoffrey Vaughn, citing Magna Carta, suing him in chancery and having him imprisoned in Fleet Prison).

29. KB27/925, m. 88; KB27/973, m. 18d. See also CP40/1016, m. 664 (Christopher Hamond v. Elizabeth Burgh, citing statutes of 1389 and 1401); KB27/1042, m. 60 (John Rastell v. John Thetford, citing statutes of 1389, 1391, and 1401); KB27/1050, m. 6 (John Heron v. Richard Frende, citing statutes of 1389 and 1401); KB27/1084, m. 45 (John Gilbert v. Robert Barker, citing statutes of 1389 and 1401); CP40/1073, m. 267d (Robert Berker of London vintner v. John Gilbert armiger, citing statutes of 1389 and 1401).

30. Statute 7 Henry VIII, c. 7, section 22, not noted in Baker, *IELH*, 158.

The change in the use of premunire came not by accident, but by a change in the process of prohibition, consultation, and premunire associated with the appointment of John Fyneux as chief justice of the court of king's bench. Fyneux became chief justice of the court of king's bench in 1495, remained in that position for the next thirty years until his death, and in the course of his tenure earned the veneration of his colleagues.[31] Fyneux effectively replaced the chancellor in the prohibition process. Traditionally, both prohibition and premunire process had begun with a writ from chancery and were thus under the control of the chancellor, normally but not always a bishop.[32] In 1497, however, king's bench handled process on a prohibition in which the king's bench justices issued the consultation and thus permitted an ecclesiastical court to proceed in a case that had been prohibited. The church court had made an award against a woman when she was single; after she had married and died, it proceeded against her husband as executor. The justices of king's bench were unanimous that in this case the church court could proceed, but Fyneux went on to expound when prohibition process could issue.[33] His comments were more than just legal speculation, because by then he granted prohibitions himself and would also grant consultations.

As he did with prohibition procedure, Fyneux allowed premunire litigants to petition king's bench directly without approaching the chancellor. He did not even bother to use available procedures that would have veiled his innovation;[34] he simply held a hearing on whether the premunire process should issue. Premunire procedure was much more rigorous than procedure concerning a prohibition since it reached anyone even tangentially involved in a problematic case in church court and carried the penalty of being treated as an enemy of the king. Even under Henry VII, Fyneux in this way attacked litigation in church courts

31. Baker, Introduction to *Spelman*, 2:55–57.

32. As late as 1492 litigants still obtain their prohibitions from chancery. KB27/934, m. 26. See earlier, CP40/846, m. 330d (prohibition issued from chancery 3 April 1472).

33. YB Trin 12 Henry VII, pl. 2. See also KB27/1024, m. 86, for a consultation involving the justification that the church court case involved mortuary, not just the taking of an animal. The libel presented in this case seems to have been the primary factor that the court would consider in granting the consultation writ. John Guy carries over the medieval procedure in which the chancellor issued writs of prohibition into the law of the Reformation: Guy, Introduction to *Christopher St. German*, 32.

34. See Appendix 6. Using Bill of Middlesex procedure for premunire would have eliminated the two-month warning instituted by the premunire statutes, but the procedure was allowed nonetheless in the fifteenth century. YB M 2 Richard II, no. 45.

concerning tithes of great trees, defamation, trespass concerning church vestments and a candelabrum, debt and detinue against executors, breach of faith, problems with glebe lands, rectory leases, and annuities.[35] Fyneux expanded his concerns even further under Henry VIII. Moreover, Fyneux's activity in king's bench was effective: the caseloads of church courts plummeted.[36] While each of these premunire actions required a litigant, people willing to litigate were never in particularly short supply. A defendant in church court could have no stronger response than a premunire, and even a prohibition could not be summarily ignored without consequences. The common law even insisted on the right of the church court defendant to receive a copy of the libel against him so that he could know whether to apply for common law intervention.[37] The limiting factor was the king's bench hearing and thus what the court of king's bench was willing to allow.[38] Fyneux did not always side against church courts, but he did do so with sufficient regularity that litigants could expect a favorable reception in his court. The assumption by king's bench of the power to authorize premunire prosecutions imported direct regulatory power over the church courts into king's bench even under Henry VII; that authority only continued to expand under Henry VIII. At times, those assertions concerned matters that directly implicated the parish as such. At other times, as with king's bench jurisdiction in defamation, the new common law powers concerned matters at the heart of parish life.

Because prohibitions issued directly out of king's bench, the process of consultation also changed. The petitioner for a prohibition had to put himself under a bond to proceed in the case if the other side contested; thus church courts were insulated from more frivolous prohibitions. Nevertheless, when the church judge asked for consultation, the matter surely went directly into litiga-

35. Baker, Introduction to *Spelman*, 2:66–67.

36. Helmholz, *Roman Canon Law*, 26–27, 30–32; Wunderli, *London Church Courts*, 81.

37. KB27/109, m. 36. If the defendant in church court had a copy of the libel, the king's bench would have good grounds to consider whether to grant a prohibition or a premunire. It is likewise probable, however, that defendants would seek the process prior even to receiving the copy of the libel, since they would often know what the dispute was about, although they might not know how the case was going to be framed.

38. Appendix 6. No recorded hearing for issuance of premunire procedure failed. Issuance of the procedure, however, required an affirmative decision by the court, and that decision is recorded. When the court decided against issuance, as it must have done at some points, it seems that the hearing was simply not recorded.

tion, not a perfunctory issuance of an order that would allow the court to proceed subject to the possibility of later litigation. Only after the litigation in king's bench would the consultation order issue out to allow the church court to continue, and then, of course, the consultation order was conclusive. The new process contained some benefit for the church, but ensured a more rigorous process that inevitably undermined church governance power. That new process reflected a much more aggressive chief justice of king's bench, and John Fyneux remained in that position for thirty years. The consultation process applied only to prohibition procedure, not to premunire. Under Fyneux premunire was the preferred method for eliminating church court jurisdictions. Aggressive justices were completely involved in the realm of government and politics, since law was the primary instrument the state had to maintain or alter the fabric of society. Fyneux and his companion justices were aggressive in maintaining that the king's courts, not the church courts, would regulate the structure of society. The regulation of parishioners passed increasingly from church court to common law courts.

A premunire campaign thus put the church in a very vulnerable position. A premunire prosecution was a close rival to a prosecution for a felony. Moreover, premunire lay against not only the ecclesiastical court judge and the plaintiff in ecclesiastical court; premunire targeted also the lawyers, summoners, and even the supporters of an offending action. The liability, being targeted as an enemy of the king, would have had a discouraging effect on officials and lawyers who encountered a potentially problematic case. A premunire campaign, a continuing stream of even a few cases of premunire each year, had a ripple effect. Ecclesiastics without a strong personal interest in a case or an equally strong ideological commitment would back away from getting involved; avoiding danger altogether was much safer than waiting to capitulate after the premunire issued. Feelings could run high. In 1505 Bishop Nykke wrote: "The laymen be more bolder against the Church than ever they were. . . . I would curse all such promoters and maintainers of the praemunire in such cases as heretics and not-believers in Christ's Church."[39] Twenty-five years of sustained premunire pressure had taken its toll on the church; Henry VIII had then attempted to govern the church through Cardinal Wolsey: a different strategy toward the same goal of royal control of the church. Henry VIII chose to humble Wolsey himself with a premunire prosecution, the initial suit in a new and extraordinarily broad

39. Quoted in Haigh, *English Reformations*, 76.

attack on the upper clergy.[40] At the same time and as part of the same process of subordinating the church, although not as part of the attack on Wolsey himself, Parliament passed the statutes of 1529 that aimed to reform the parish-level churchmen, the main topic of this book. Henry VIII thus abandoned his strategy of trying to control the church through a fully empowered churchman, and returned to a strategy of direct control, a control raised to a new level because of his need for a divorce. Now a pragmatic monopoly of governance was insufficient; Henry needed to take the position of the pope to be able to control church law itself. Nevertheless, the royal need for a divorce or for the destruction of Wolsey did not exhaust royal aims in 1529: Henry VIII's church would be different not so much in doctrine as in rigor. That increased rigor toward the church, however, came after thirty years of assertion of royal power over the church by sustained institutional pressure, normally quietly, but with occasional virulent protests.

The church in late medieval Europe recognized its inability to dictate all actual practice; canon law often accepted local custom as modifications of general rules. Acceptance of local custom, however, was not necessarily an indication of inherent canon law flexibility and respect for local custom. The fact that canon law did in fact yield to "local custom," that is, often, to national laws, only showed that the church was at times unsuccessful in imposing its own perceptions of morality and right order on society, particularly in those matters that touched on the distribution of power and the allocation of valuable economic rights. The church was hardly powerless; the boundaries developed between church and state were the result of necessary mutual accommodation. Still, the church was likewise not a completely separate entity: at all levels many of the clergy had strong loyalties not only to the church but also to a king, a country, a magnate, and a family. The clergy did not have and had never been a monolithic interest, but had participated on all sides of each controversy. Both the church and church law developed in varied social and institutional contexts. Neither church nor state liked to accommodate the law of the other, but both had done so. Under Henry VII that grudging willingness to accommodate eroded, and Fyneux remodeled a mechanism forged to protect advowson rights into a mechanism to undermine the governance power of the church. Finally,

---

40. *Notebook of Sir John Port*, ed. Baker, 58–59. The Wolsey prosecution complained of the exercise of an interference with advowson rights instead of the broader jurisdictional issues that had characterized the premunire prosecutions run by Fyneux.

Henry VIII exhausted his willingness to accommodate the church: the king governed the church then simply as head of the church.

Litigation in the king's court established the ongoing accommodation essential to the functioning of the church within the context of the whole of English society. The continuing use of the writ of prohibition, *quare impedit*, and the occasional premunire campaign incorporated the outgrowth of church convictions about appropriate control of the church over church matters, of the individual ambition of churchmen avid for positions of wealth and preferment, of magnate insistence on retention of their sources of patronage, of royal insistence on the rights of the crown and the sources of wealth that paid royal administrators: the coincidence, then, of conviction, idealism, ambition, greed, pragmatism, and necessity. The control of church life and church resources was a process continually worked out, but along relatively consistent institutionalized lines until perhaps 1495, certainly 1529. At the center of those continuing frictions between church and state, between clergymen and laymen, however, was once again the rector of the English parish. The premunire case against Wolsey himself quite appropriately focused on Wolsey's interference in an appointment of a rector, the rector of Stoke Guildford in Surrey. That appointment was completely irrelevant to the royal need for a divorce, but at the heart of an equally pressing, long-term problem among king, pope, bishops, patrons, and parishioners.

CHAPTER TWO

The Parish as a Commercial Entity

The English parish, if only because of its economic assets, was central to the workings of English society. The parish was the governance unit that extracted and collected between a quarter and a third of the country's agricultural surplus.[1] That surplus was a lifeline for the towns and religious houses and provided them with essential foodstuffs. The value paid to the church for that surplus provided in significant part for the institutional church in general, but particularly for the universities and for the administrators who served the king, the pope, the bishops, and the church courts. Society had a great investment in securing the extraction of those resources, but the resources came at an obviously heavy price for the tillers of the soil. Tensions had resulted in customs and legal rules; the value of the assets had ensured that the workings of the parish were completely integrated into the society. The times at which the workings of the parish changed—in some degree after the Black Death but particularly from 1529 to 1540—were times that necessarily redefined the essential contexts of life for the countryside.

Agricultural parish assets consisted mainly of tithes, the produce from the glebe, and mortuary fees. Tithes constituted a tenth of the agricultural *produce*, and thus represented a much larger share of the agricultural *surplus*. The loss of such a large proportion of the surplus was a major detriment to the agriculturalist, but was paid at harvest time, a time of plenty. Glebe land, attached to the parish church and under the management and cultivation of the rector, was more valuable than other land precisely because it did not pay tithes: the produce went completely to the church. Mortuary fees were basically death

---

1. This estimate comes from work with Dyer's figures around 1300 in Dyer, *Standards of Living*, 110–18. His examples allow the requisite information to compare tithes to surplus, but do not account for glebe, mortuary, and compulsory church offerings. For tithes alone as a percentage of overall agricultural surplus, the appropriate figure would range between a fifth and a quarter. For grains alone, tithes would seem to account for a bit more than a third of the surplus, because of the necessity to retain some grain for seed. The exactions of the lord claimed a somewhat larger share of the surplus than did tithes alone.

duties. They constituted an income far inferior to tithes but still significant. Moreover, mortuary fees, unlike tithes, were levied at a time of emotional and economic crisis, when a family lost a critical member.

The contribution of this chapter is a study, through the examination of a wide variety of different situations, of the role that those parish assets of tithes, mortuary fees, and the produce of the glebe played in the life of the country and of the reason the parish was such a desirable commodity. Appreciation of that role requires a brief survey of the law about rights to those assets, but the focus here is the way in which those various revenue streams, merged in the rector's hands, were individually and collectively fully commercialized, subject to transactions and also to compelling expectations from the towns and cities. The commercial handling of essential agrarian surplus, based on practices built up over a century and a half, ultimately constrained what Henry VIII could do in the 1530s. Too much tampering with the traditional mechanisms for the production and distribution of food would have produced the explosive mix of conservative religious fears and real economic uncertainty. Thus, when the king reformed the parish in 1529 and thereafter, the custom of tithing nonetheless continued; and the mechanisms for the collection of the agrarian surplus proceeded without interruption, but with a different social meaning.

The common law records reveal little that is startlingly new about the economic assets of the parish; but they clarify the place of the parish resources in the complicated social fabric. The detail that follows in this chapter is thus only a relation of typical learning about the law of tithes, glebe, and mortuary. At another level, however, the legal records compel concrete consideration of the complexity of the manipulation of those resources: the way that the produce was actually handled, the importance of those assets to the broader society, the complex of interests and mechanisms that were inevitably involved in the allocation of a major part of the agrarian surplus of a preindustrial but commercial society. The purpose of the detail of this chapter is precisely to ponder not only the economic significance of tithes, glebe, and mortuary fees, but also the ways in which local people used the common law to give social meaning to the legal rules about that wealth.

Tithes

Tithes entered directly into the commercial life of the country and were not segregated somehow into a "spiritual" side of society. In fact, as Chapters 4 and

5 will show, the specifically spiritual aspect of tithing was problematic. The primary meaning of tithing was social and economic rather than religious. Tithes provided economic resources, not the basic foodstuffs that the rector and his family (relatives and servants) would actually consume within the parish. The agricultural produce collected by tithing entered the stream of commerce. Those who received tithes could have commercial agents; they could also lease out the tithes for terms of years. They had disputes about whether particular lands or goods were subject to tithing, whether particular grain was tithe grain or, say, produce of the glebe. Not only did disagreements about tithes result in ordinary agrarian disputes, but people also submitted to arbitration and its rigors in tithing matters as they did in other normal affairs of life. Even though rectors, particularly the heads of religious houses, occasionally allowed tithes to be commuted into annual fixed payments of money, those who produced crops normally paid in kind: the tenth sheaf set aside from the nine at harvest time. Rectories and manor houses were the two major collection points for agrarian surplus; but only in the payment were tithes at all religious. Once collected, tithes were, after all, simply wheat, oats, lambs, calves, fish, trees.

Medieval people were not joyous tithe payers anxious to impoverish themselves to enrich the church. A parishioner did not have to be hostile to the clerical order to avoid tithing. Tithing involved wealth; and desperation or ambition were much more frequent motives for tithe evasion than doctrinal differences, even when there were doctrinal differences. For medieval villagers, tithes in a bad year could mean the starvation of children, inability to rent additional acreage or buy cattle, inability even to donate money to a favored religious purpose other than the parish. Local customs could easily conflict with what a new rector coming from a different region might consider to be proper tithing rights; that conflict produced disputes about tithes from completely different roots. A new rector also might disagree with a previous rector's arrangements;[2] a rector's own arrangements might prove ambiguous, as with any commercial transaction. Ordinary estate management practices could result in confusion. The complex of custom, statute, and dispute resolution procedures apparent through the detail of litigation shows both the size of the resources at stake with tithing and the utilization of the ordinary social mechanisms applicable to the economic resources of late medieval England.

2. CP40/548, m. 94d. Instead of taking tithes at harvest time, a Wiltshire parson accepted the assignment of the whole harvest from a tenth of the land, which his servants then harvested. That arrangement was certainly not in accord with legal expectations.

Tithing of trees was a particularly contentious issue, surrounded by unusual commercial and social attention. Older trees were vital for major construction projects, for use as great beams and flooring planks; they were thus a scarce economic resource and the subject of many disputes. Parliament intervened in this area in 1376 and declared that only trees under twenty years old were tithable. Small trees and brush were *silva cedua* and tithable: they were more a crop.[3] That distinction made the timing of harvest critical: cutting nineteen-year-old trees was foolish. Distinguishing tithable trees from exempt trees, however, would be impossible prior to cutting unless the owner exercised im-probably careful management, simply because only at cutting could one count the tree rings. In many situations harvesting big trees would be a gamble. An inaccurate estimate would pit the strong economic interests of a church against equally strong economic interests of the normally wealthy owner. Such contro-versies called into play the full range of conflict management developed in late medieval England.

Local custom complicated the collection of tithes to trees. Custom could apparently even supersede the statute. One parishioner won an award of £105 against the vicar who had attempted to tithe older trees on the grounds that they had been tithed within time of memory. The jury found that they had not been tithed within time of memory; the selection of the issue for the jury, however, indicates that a custom that had developed since the statute would bind.[4] Cropping trees presented ambiguities. One parishioner cropped his trees, so that six to eight trees grew from a single trunk; he sold the trees from time to time according to acre, half-acre, or rod. With such an agricultural practice, one could well question whether the twenty years started with the growth of the trunk or of the resulting trees. The prior of Beaulieu as parson of Clophill, Bedfordshire, claimed a tenth of the trees on fifty acres as tithes and carried the suit into ecclesiastical court. The process went through the steps of prohibition and consultation and finally reached the king's court in 1388; the parishioner claimed damages of £1,000.[5] The prior of Barnwell, as the parson of Hatley St. George, Cambridgeshire, was supposed to go only to the manor house gate to receive the tithe of trees cut down. The prior and his helpers had instead actually gone in through an open gate, and Baldwin St. George sued the prior in 1386 for breach of close, the taking of timber and great trees, and injuries to his

3. Swanson, *Church and Society*, 212.

4. CP40/507, m. 565.

5. CP40/510, m. 449.

servants.[6] Both ecclesiastics and parishioners relied on a complex of local custom that applied both to what was subject to tithe and how the tithe could be claimed.

The wealth involved dictated similarly regularized division of tithes among clerics. By 1387 a custom in Salisbury diocese dictated that if a parson died after 25 March, the deceased parson's executors could have the year's tithes if they elected within ten days also to pay the taxes due from the church. The executor of the deceased parson in this case sued the succeeding parson for £66.67 worth of crops. The new parson claimed that all but £7 worth of the crops were his because the executor had not made his election within the ten-day period. The new parson claimed the remaining £7 of crops as the result of ecclesiastical court proceedings that had sequestered the deceased parson's goods for the purpose of repairing the chancel and the rectory houses and enclosures at a cost of £13.50.[7] In 1386, after the death of the archdeacon of Northampton, the succeeding archdeacon had proceeded to lease the parish of Cropredy, Oxfordshire, to a layman. The executor sued, claiming a custom that any deceased prebendary received the tithes of the prebend until the August following his death. Whether that actually was the custom in the area was an issue for a common law jury.[8] At a time when £10 in annual income could put one among the lesser gentry,[9] these tithes represented considerable wealth, which was handled like any other major economic resource.

The practical aspects of tithing—the quantity of material involved, normal estate-managing practices, or local custom—inevitably resulted in problems. John Nelme's claim of nine cartloads of crops (wheat, barley, oats, and beans) as tithes also involved the borders between Filton and Almondsbury.[10] Some tithing rights had been partitioned. In 1387 a parson in Devon explained that he and his predecessors had always had two-thirds of the tithable lambs from certain land and that he had received eight of the twelve tithable lambs from the plaintiff's reeve and shepherd.[11] In 1491 the lessee of the abbot of Bermondsey claimed a right to two-thirds of the tithes of Fyfield, Essex: eighteen cartloads of crops (wheat, barley, oats, peas, beans, and bullimong).[12] In 1495 a chaplain in

6. CP40/501, m. 317.
7. CP40/506, m. 355. C & S, 177.
8. CP40/501, m. 344.
9. Dyer, *Standards of Living*, 20–22.
10. CP40/799, m. 395; see also CP40/547, m. 658d.
11. CP40/505, m. 128.
12. CP40/915, m. 360.

charge of the rectory of Hartest and Boxted in Suffolk had to sue a mercer for £23.50. He had sold all the tithes to the mercer and granted him free ingress and egress and storage rights, but had not been paid. The tithes had amounted to 130 cartloads of wheat, barley, oats, and peas.[13] In 1480 a knight sued the prior of Bodmin for thirty-six quarters of grain. The prior explained that a third party had taken the sheaves that actually were tithes, threshed the crop into five quarters of grain, and delivered the grain to the knight for safekeeping, whereupon the prior's servant seized the grain.[14] The prior of Ipswich Holy Trinity divided the tithes within the rectory of Fritton, Norfolk, but then leased out the priory's two-thirds of the tithes to John Shelton, a knight, for twenty years.[15] The vicar of South Allington, Devon, had disposed of his tithes annually through an arrangement with a clothier of Salisbury, widely known as the vicar's agent. Although the agent heard of the vicar's death, he nonetheless sold 140 pounds of wool, tithes from South Allington, for £3. The bishop pursued the purchaser thereafter on the claim that the tithes had not belonged to the vicar because they were collected during the vacancy of the vicary.[16] Ecclesiastics partitioned tithes, leased them out, put them into safe keeping, sold and seized them. Tithes were part of ordinary commerce.

Arbitration proved useful in limiting the amount of litigation about tithes, just as it did with other disputes about commercial transactions. Arbitration burgeoned in the late fourteenth century, in part because submission to arbitration often avoided the complexities and costs of litigation, in part because the king's court had developed mechanisms for enforcing arbitration awards.[17] Osbert Hamelyn had thus submitted to arbitration in a dispute with the dean and chapter of Exeter Cathedral over tithes and other exactions. The arbitration had awarded that all suits should end and Osbert should pay the dean and chapter more than £21.50 for the litigation and the tithes. Osbert refused to abide by the award, so the dean and chapter proceeded to litigation in the king's court for the £100 specified in a bond as the penalty for noncompliance.[18] The penalty agreed upon in advance for not abiding by the arbitration award here was almost five times the eventual award. Osbert was the unusual party who failed to recognize the prudence of accepting the award instead of the penalty.

13. CP40/934, m. 118.
14. CP40/878, m. 435.
15. CP40/1069, m. 559.
16. CP40/993, m. 685d.
17. Palmer, *ELABD*, 96–99.
18. CP40/507, m. 308.

The common law had developed a mechanism for dictating conduct effectively and holding people to undertakings: the bonds were so punitive that most people simply complied and the courts did not need to get involved. Penal and performance bonds over the decades helped socialize people in a commercial society into the expectation of absolute performance of their duties, whether the duties were secular or religious.

Since tithes were often the subject of leases and leases were less well protected than freehold estates, lessees often demanded more complicated arrangements for the tithes, both to ensure their investment and to protect the food arrangements for various populations. In 1502 the rector of All Saints, Derby, leased the tithes of Quarndon chapel (grain, wool, and animals) to a gentleman for twelve years at £4 annually; the warranty for the lease was a performance bond for £20. The lessor excluded the lessee from the tithes for failure to pay the rent. The lessee explained that he had not paid because a previous lessee had taken thirteen tithable lambs: the default in payment of the rent was the lessor's fault even though not the lessor's own act. The jury had to decide whether the rector had been at all involved in the taking of the lambs and had thus violated his warranty. If he was involved, he would be obliged to pay the £20. If he was not involved, the lessee would have had to continue paying the rent to take advantage of the warranty.[19] Use of a performance bond to protect the lessee's right to the tithes was an effective way of securing a commercial transaction of agricultural produce, but the problems that arose from dealing with the wealth represented by tithes remained complicated. Moreover, a lease of tithes was particularly subject to the lessor's control since the lessee did not occupy a physical tenement, but only took the produce from third parties after harvest. The punitive nature of the performance bond helped secure what otherwise would have been a very insecure investment in essential agrarian produce.

Management of a parish involved all the varied activities of an agricultural estate. William de Humberston sued John Hertfeld in 1387 to account as his bailiff of the rectory of Harlow, Essex. Hertfeld allegedly administered the greater and lesser tithes, offerings, income, and proceeds, the horses, oxen, draught animals, cows, sheep, and pigs, as well as the crops: wheat, barley, beans,

---

19. CP40/974, m. 600. In a different case in 1509, the prior of Bath and John Fihilly, vicar of Carhampton, Somerset, put themselves under a performance bond of £40 to stand to the arbitration award of Roger Churche concerning their dispute about the tithes within the precinct of Dunster and Carhampton. Churche, the arbitrator, in 1511 sued the vicar for default. CP40/997, m. 347.

peas, and hay. He also was a receiver of money that amounted to about £7.75 from three people. Hertfeld denied having been bailiff, and so it was found by a jury. Nevertheless, he admitted accounting to Humberston in London before an assigned auditor. Perhaps the two were partners.[20] At the same time, Humberston sued Hertfeld for taking 20 quires of a missal, 240 velum skins, a processional, and 20 ells of woolen cloth worth £20. The jury in that case found Hertfeld guilty, but with damages of only £2.[21] In 1387 Robert de Weston, the rector of Wheatacre, Norfolk, likewise had to sue his bailiff, William Burman, for an accounting of his time of care of the offerings, income, minor tithes, wheat, rye, barley, peas and oats (sheaves and cleaned grain), malt, hay, straw, a wool altar cloth, horses, oxen, cows, sheep, carts, plows, a hairshirt, and the issue of a dovecote. The bailiff replied that he had already accounted before two named auditors, one of whom was himself a parson.[22] The rector, when resident in the parish, had to engage in ordinary estate management relationships.

Agreements about tithes, particularly between religious houses, produced jealously guarded rights. Around 1351, after litigation before the official of York, the archbishop of York had arbitrated a settlement between the prior of Malton and the rector of Wressle, Yorkshire, concerning the tithes of Brind and Newsholme. The parson kept the tithes, but had to pay £4 annually to the prior; default entailed a penalty of £5. That obligation, apparently, so depleted the resources of Wressle that the parish was appropriated to the priory of Drax. In 1388 the prior of Malton had to sue the prior of Drax in the king's court for six years' arrears, penalty, and interest as specified by the archbishop's award; the total then was £60.[23] Other exchanges of tithes for an annual rent found enforcement in Richard II's court fifty to a hundred years after the initial settlement.[24] In 1492 the court of common pleas even entertained a plea concerning an annual rent of £2.33 that had originated in a settlement between a monastery and the rector of Crick, Northamptonshire, in 1261.[25] Religious houses protected their rights, and often the king's court was the necessary jurisdiction.

Annual rents given in return for tithes only complicated matters. Monasteries and vicars often agreed to compound tithes into an annual rent, the

20. CP40/506, m. 114.
21. CP40/506, m. 258d.
22. CP40/506, m. 265.
23. CP40/509, m. 220.
24. CP40/511, m. 444; CP40/501, m. 319.
25. CP40/922, m. 428.

monastery retaining the tithes while the vicar received the annuity. The monastery benefitted by the increased agricultural productivity or a rising value of agrarian produce; the vicar's share remained set so that he suffered in inflationary times. If the annuity payment was in arrears, the vicar might easily think he could claim his rightful tithes. Such a complication could have been behind the abbot of Cirencester's premunire suit against the vicar of Shrivenham. The abbot objected to the vicar's suit in ecclesiastical court against a parishioner for tithes of wood and lambs, because it involved an annual rent. The jury in premunire returned a verdict for the abbot in the amount of £26.67, hardly as rigorous as one could expect in premunire.[26] Such agreements about tithes, however, wove rights to tithes into complex, long-standing relationships. Each new vicar had to figure out the complexities of the fiscal parish for himself, particularly if the vacancy that allowed his appointment had been created by the death of his predecessor.

The working of tithes could become even more complicated and draw in the patron who had the right of advowson. In 1507 the patron of the chantry of St. Leonard in Hazlewood, Yorkshire, intervened to ensure the well-being of the chapel. The current chantry priest was also the vicar of Tadcaster, and he had apparently been unable to enforce the tithing obligation for three years. Tithing, like other economic obligations, required enforcement. The patron intervened, agreeing to pay the priest £6 for the preceding three years and £2 annually thereafter. In return the patron received all the tithes, together with the right to prosecute in either secular or ecclesiastical court against anyone who had detained the tithes in the preceding three years.[27] The result was most likely the effective enforcement of tithing, but by the lay chantry patron instead of the seemingly ineffective chantry priest. These complications in handling tithes almost certainly only scratch the surface. Tithes were handled in every way that other produce was, but were enmeshed in greater complexities than other produce. The complex of the commercial handling of the produce in late medieval England is not yet well understood—the handling specifically of tithes, less so.

Outright opposition to tithing appeared at times, whether from religious convictions or from economic motives. The rector of South Hill, Cornwall, sued parishioners for building a ditch and dike around their property; the rector could not gather his tithes without danger, and the tithes (twenty-three cart-

26. CP40/519, m. 351.
27. CP40/997, m. 429.

loads of wheat, rye, oats, and hay) were spoiled and lost. Litigation in that case lasted at least from 1513 to 1515.[28] Thomas Knyll built an enclosure around his twenty acres in Devon with a wall five feet wide and eight feet high. His vicar sued him in 1534 for blocking his ingress and egress for taking tithes.[29] John Church of Tilmanstone, a husbandman, plowed down the ridge of land that divided the land that owed tithes to the parish of Eastry from the land that owed tithes to the parish of Tilmanstone. The prior of Christchurch, Canterbury, in 1507 sued him for £20 to compensate for the prior's impaired ability to ascertain which tithes belonged to him.[30] Whether such disputes about tithes indicated oversight, economic pressures, or heresy cannot be known.

In short, the tithes of England were not simply consumed in the parish rectory. The sheer quantity of agricultural produce involved was too large to suppose local consumption, and the produce of glebe or demesne lands would often have sufficed for immediate consumption. Tithes, rather, were collected and then converted systematically into money and entered immediately into the market. Tithing rights were the subject of all the normal processes devised for other economic resources: performance bonds, arbitration, leaseholds. The produce paid as tithes was just as manipulable as ordinary goods and just as prized. The flow of agricultural produce thus did not presume dozens of bargains in each village between traders and individual homesteads for the bulk of the produce. The surplus that remained in the hands of those who tilled the land most likely went to support village specialization: the needs of smiths, potters, carters, shepherds, thatchers, builders, and laborers. The agricultural surplus that supported towns and substantial commerce most easily would flow through lordships and rectories: easily collected by traders, fully commercialized, absolutely critical for the maintenance of social organization.

Glebe Lands

Glebe lands, which constituted the endowment of the rectory, were either a compact estate or dispersed strips of arable land scattered among the village fields and could include pasture and meadow land. Glebe land occasioned far fewer controversies than did tithing rights, probably because managing glebe lands did not require the extraction of economic resources from others. Still,

28. CP40/1002, m. 443; CP40/1003, m. 70; CP40/1005a, m. 92d; CP40/1006, m. 211.
29. CP40/1083, m. 187.
30. CP40/982, m. 190.

the glebe was a significant but not dominant part of the value of the parish. Rectors or their surrogates managed the glebe not as a specifically ecclesiastical resource, but merely as an economic resource. As an economic resource, however, it was particularly valuable. Glebe land, not subject to tithe because it was held by the rector himself, thus immediately had an effective yield to the holder of about 11 percent more than comparable land held by others. Since it was normally held in free alms and thus not subject to dues to a lord, its effective yield to the holder was probably something like 25 percent more than comparable lands in the hands of a villager.

The normal form of glebe and demesne was simply land, but such rectory endowments were highly varied. In 1469 members of the collegiate church of South Malling disagreed about which of them should control the four acres of glebe land in Ringmer, Sussex.[31] The perpetual vicar of East Tilbury, Essex, found that the parson, who was also the master of the college of Cobham, Kent, was three years in arrears on an annual rent owed the vicar; the vicar distrained for his money on the ten acres of glebe land in East Tilbury.[32] In 1505 the rector of Walkern, Hertfordshire, encountered problems with glebe land he had leased out: twenty-seven acres of land, six acres of meadow, and eight acres of pasture.[33] Swanson mentioned details of two parish's glebe lands: Trent, Somerset, with eighteen acres (1470); Harlow, Essex, with fifteen acres.[34] A lease of the rectory of Chesterton, Staffordshire, in 1494 detailed the church's glebe land: sixty-six acres, with thirty-nine acres in "The Great Field," an angle of land, five more acres in another field, and twenty-two acres of land in Owefeld.[35] The rector of Thame, Oxfordshire, in 1494 had glebe lands of three messuages, ten acres of arable land, twenty acres of meadow, and a hundred acres of pasture.[36] Some glebe was in the form of common of pasture. The rector of Marston, Yorkshire, had common of pasture in three hundred acres or more, which he then leased out in 1496.[37] The difference in glebe lands was only one part of the equation that made some parish rectories much more attractive than others.

Fertility, use, and location determined the actual value of the glebe, and those features varied considerably. The glebe lands that endowed a rectory

31. CP40/833, m. 547.
32. CP40/878, m. 343.
33. KB27/967, m. 72.
34. Swanson, *Church and Society*, 206–7.
35. CP40/974, m. 530.
36. CP40/978, m. 327.
37. CP40/942, m. 307.

could yield leasehold rents or trees as well as ordinary agricultural produce. The parson of Bledlow apparently had glebe that was simply forest. After a storm he took several hundred trees, prompting a rival claim from the prior of Ogbourne.[38] The rector of Bitton, Gloucestershire, was a canon of Salisbury Cathedral. In 1506 he leased out his glebe of four closes that the vicar had occupied, reserving access rights to the barn, for one year for £2.33. The lessee was John Coles, a merchant and citizen of Bristol.[39] The parson of Workington, Cumberland, controlled seven messuages and five carucates of land as glebe in 1397 and leased it to seven tenants as separate holdings.[40] The glebe found the same uses and was as varied as any other holding.

Rectors, like other landholders, had other property rights attached to their holding, such as hunting and fuel rights. The parson of Sparkford, Somerset, claimed that attached to his glebe land was the right to hunt there and, with permission, on the land of his neighbors who held heritably in fee simple. The lord of the manor nonetheless sued him in 1387 for hunting a hundred hares, a hundred rabbits, forty pheasants, and a hundred partridges in the lord's free warren over the course of three years.[41] The rector of Treeton, Yorkshire, claimed not hunting, but fuel rights as part of his glebe. His servants thus took three hundred hazel trees and three hundred hawthorn trees from Treetonwood as fuel for the rectory: they claimed they could take up to fifty cartloads. The lady of the manor challenged that right in 1391.[42]

The glebe was simply an endowment. Whether it yielded timber, game, rents, or the agricultural produce normal from arable land was of little consequence. It could vary in form and use because it was not designed necessarily to provide foodstuffs for consumption within the rectory as a self-sufficient tenement, but simply to provide economic value to support the parson. The glebe was, whatever its form and use, comparatively valuable, because it did not owe tithes. Glebe was also usually free from dues to the lord. Nevertheless, the value of the whole rectory was the aggregate of revenue sources. By the fourteenth century, English society was sufficiently commercial that the value of produce was much more significant than the form in which it appeared.

38. CP40/501, m. 318. The pleading was narrowed to concern just one tree so that the verdict would be less divisive, an ordinary tactic between parties who seemed to want to resolve an issue in a more amicable fashion.

39. CP40/982, m. 323.

40. CP40/548, m. 96.

41. CP40/506, m. 130.

42. CP40/520, m. 422d.

Mortuary Fees

Mortuary fees constituted a relatively unpredictable, very intrusive, and valuable right of the rectory. Mortuary fees were death duties, occasionally explained as final payments for tithes and obligatory offerings withheld or forgotten.[43] Unlike tithes, they burdened survivors economically at the very moment of both emotional trauma and financial insecurity. The value of mortuary fees depended both on the custom in the parish and on the wealth of the decedent. Some parishes, like Walton-le-Dale, had no mortuary fees at all; some paid on a sliding scale.[44] Some levied mortuary fees on wives and children; some, only on landholders. Although, in the usual case, mortuary fees would not rival tithes as a source of income, they could occasionally have exceeded the return from glebe lands. Ecclesiastical officials were careful to claim and protect these rights. People on the point of dying could attempt to diminish the economic impact of mortuary fees on their survivors; the survivors themselves tried to avoid the hardship of church exactions that coincided with their moments of greatest vulnerability. Parishioners, not necessarily hostile to clerics in general or to the duty of tithing in the abstract, reacted on their perceptions of their own needs in pressing circumstances.

The particular problem with mortuary fees was that for the most rural part of the population they coincided not only with death, but also with heriot, a death duty owed to a lord. The issue of mortuary fees came up in a controversy between the prior of Southwick and the parson of Colmer, Hampshire. The prior, as lord, complained about the taking of forty hares, sixty rabbits, sixty pheasants, and thirty partridges over the course of two years and also for the taking of a horse and an ox. The parson denied the hunting, but claimed the horse and ox as mortuary: in that parish the right to the second best animals of two dead parishioners. The prior claimed those two animals as the best animals of the tenants and thus the heriot duty since he was the lord of Colmer.[45] Nicholas Stucle, a knight, similarly admitted that he had a cow with a milking calf claimed by Katherine de Engayne. The dispute over the animals originated in Katherine's seizure of Thomas Cook of Upwood as her villein. When Cook died, the parson of Wistow, Huntingdonshire, took the cow and calf as mortuary and sold them to Nicholas for £0.35. The court ruled that if he had thus

43. KB27/1024, m. 86.
44. Haigh, *English Reformations*, 48.
45. CP40/506, m. 311d.

bought them, his possession was rightful; Katherine withdrew her suit.[46] The occasional horse, oxen, or cow as a mortuary fee was clearly a welcome and valuable right of the rectory. The coincidence of mortuary fees and heriot duty magnified the impact and generated disputes between manorial lord and parson.

Such a typical division between heriot and mortuary—the difference between the decedent's best and second best beast—obscures more complex local custom. The parson of Whimple, Devon, and William Westcote in 1410 disagreed about the possession of a mare. Westcote was the bailiff of the manor of Cobbaton, where a parishioner had died. For the parishioner's tenure of twenty acres of land, he had owed heriot to the manor's lord; the parson had accordingly taken the second best animal, a mare. The bailiff, however, pointed out that the parishioner had held a second tenement consisting of a messuage and thirty acres: each separate tenure on that manor owed heriot. The bailiff thus claimed also the second best animal, so that the parson could only have the third best animal as mortuary.[47] A similar prioritizing of rights seemed to apply in Moreton Pinkney, Northamptonshire. There the custom alleged in 1510 to preempt the rector's claim to an ox as the second best animal was that the lord of the tenement on which a person lived received the best animal of the deceased, but the lord of any other tenement that the deceased possessed received the next best animal before any mortuary fee. The rector in this situation disagreed about the custom, so the matter was left to be decided by a common law jury.[48] The same custom had applied in 1397 in Ambrosden, Oxfordshire.[49] The vicar of Aspatria, Cumberland, went to church court to retrieve a dead man's best animal, which he claimed as mortuary, but which Anthony Porter claimed as heriot because he was lord of the manor.[50] As with tithes, mortuary fees were the institutionalized extraction of wealth to support the church; the clergy collected these dues often without regard to the needs of the parishioners. The clergy needed those resources, but the collection of agricultural produce by the church also served the purposes of English towns.

When a tenant did not owe heriot—thus, often, when the tenure was free instead of villein—the rector could claim the best animal, but even that was subject to local custom. In the parish of Ewell, Surrey, the rector could claim

46. CP40/510, m. 254.

47. CP40/599, m. 204d.

48. CP40/997, m. 430.

49. CP40/545, m. 109d. The mortuary fee animal was to be brought to the church before the body.

50. KB27/1001, m. 1 Rex.

the best beast of a deceased parishioner. A defendant in a dispute about a horse and an ox, however, claimed that by the custom of the parish the deceased's executor could use the deceased's best animal or thing to perform his last will and testament. The king's court allowed a jury to determine what the parish custom actually was.[51] For certain families, then, mortuary fees were the only exaction levied at a death.

Mortuary rights often derived from persons instead of tenures. In 1506 Margaret Hyckys challenged the mortuary customs of Rockhampton parish, Gloucestershire. She sued Robert Burton, the parish priest, for taking two oxen. As to one of those oxen, Burton explained that he and his predecessors had always had by right of mortuary the second best animal of each parishioner aged twelve or more who died within the parish; he could seize the animal whenever and in whosesoever hands he found it. Burton had discovered the ox in Margaret's possession since she was the sole executor of her husband. The case went to the jury on the issue of that statement of the mortuary custom.[52] The vicar of Preston described a disputed custom in his whole parish except for that part of the parish called the Boroughhold in this way: "Each married man in the said parish, after the death of his wife who had received the sacraments of the church in the said parish of Preston within the year immediately before her death and who died in the said parish will give the second best animal which her husband had at the time of the death of his wife if he then had an animal. And if he did not have an animal, then he will give and pay another noble inanimate thing that the husband had at the time of the death of his wife in place of the animal in name of mortuary for the forgotten tithes and oblations of such wife to the vicar of the abovesaid church for the time being." The enforcement of that custom became the subject of a church court suit and then a prohibition.[53] In 1505 the king's bench handled a case arising from an arbitration award. Two parties had submitted performance bonds for £10 to stand to an arbitration award; the arbitrators awarded that one of the parties owed £0.50 as the mortuary for his wife.[54] Attaching mortuary to individuals was even more important

51. KB27/980, m. 72.

52. CP40/978, m. 605.

53. KB27/1024, m. 86.

54. KB27/975, m. 63. Another case indicated use of arbitration to determine disagreements about mortuary customs. Henry Peper, vicar of Ridge, Hertfordshire, disagreed with six of his parishioners about the parish mortuary custom. The parish belonged to the abbey of

in cities. John Randeby, a chaplain, sued the parson of St. Albans parish in London for taking a psalter worth £3. The parson cited the London mortuary custom: "whenever any person from outside should die within London, the rector of the parish church in which parish this should happen will have the best good thing (*optimam bonam rem*) which the deceased had within the said city at the time of his death." The administrator of the intestate cleric, so said Oudeby, had given him the psalter as principal mortuary according to the custom.[55] In very different situations, then, mortuary could apply to people, including married women, as distinct from tenures.

Mortuary fees, when combined with other circumstances, could prove explosive. The most notorious dispute over mortuary came in 1512 with Richard Hunne. Hunne was a London merchant and a Lollard. He had put his five-week-old baby boy to nurse outside his home parish in the parish of Whitechapel. When the baby died, the parson in church court claimed as mortuary the winding sheet that had found its way back into Hunne's hands. Hunne countered by getting Fyneux to issue a premunire. The process on that premunire continued through the rest of 1512, with Hunne appearing regularly to prosecute, but Cuthbert Tunsall, the church court judge, avoided the warning. When Hunne then went to vespers in Whitechapel on 27 December 1512, Henry Marshall, the parish priest, threw him out of church: "Hunne, thou art accursed and thou standest accursed, and therefore go thou out of the church, for as long as thou are in this church I will say no evensong nor service." Hunne thus brought a suit against him for defamation. Both the premunire and the defamation case proceeded thereafter without marked progress until both disappeared after the end of 1514.[56] The cases disappeared because the clerics had imprisoned Hunne at St. Pauls in October, where he was found in his cell dead by strangulation on 4 December; the clergy were suspected of his death. The clergy tried to preempt other process by posthumously finding Hunne a heretic, then exhuming and burning his body. An indictment of the clerics still fol-

---

St. Albans, and everyone was willing to submit to the arbitration of three people: the abbot himself, his official, and a knight. They put themselves under a £40 performance bond to stand to the award. In 1512 the vicar sued one of them on that performance bond; he replied that he was illiterate and that the bond when read to him had stipulated that if only two of the arbitrators in fact arbitrated, the knight had to be one of the two. CP40/999, m. 546.

55. CP40/503, m. 627.

56. The premunire: KB147/2/4/3, KB27/1004, m. 88, KB27/1006, m. 37. The defamation: KB27/1006, m. 36.

lowed, but that seemed to conclude in 1516.[57] Hunne's case was not symptomatic of widespread heresy, but does indicate the difficulty of the mortuary fee as well as the way in which local disputes wove into more general political initiatives, at this point the premunire campaign being waged in the courts. Hunne's case highlighted the problems of mortuary in a highly public way.

As might be expected of people who faced death and worried about their family, tenants at times seem to have tried to evade mortuary fees less obtrusively. In 1495 John Pepar sued the vicar of Huttoft, Lincolnshire, for taking six cows. The vicar claimed that the prior of Markby was rector of the parish and had always had the right to a parishioner's best animal when the parishioner died. The vicar admitted that as the prior's agent he had taken one cow as the mortuary due from Isabella Blake. Pepar claimed that the cow was his own, of which he had been possessed long before Isabella's death.[58] One could easily imagine that Isabella had tried to benefit a friend by giving him the cow when death approached or that she had given Pepar the cow in return for care.

Mortuary fees were by their nature unpredictable, depending on how many people in a parish died and the wealth of the deceased parishioners in a given year. From the perspective of the rectory, mortuary right probably meant at least an extra cow or ox each year; high mortality in a given year would have been, economically, a boon, particularly if the mortality occurred after harvest. An assessment of Brough under Stainmore, Cumberland, in 1344 found the parish was worth £53.33. The mortuary fees accounted for only 2 percent of that value (£1.13), whereas tithes of all kinds constituted 79 percent; offerings, 8 percent; demesne lands, 6 percent; fines, 4 percent.[59] For the families, however, mortuary right was exceedingly burdensome. When mortuary attached only to the tenure and thus usually only to the husband and father, many families lost their two best animals to heriot and mortuary at precisely the time that they were most insecure; confiscation of such resources probably often compelled a rapid new

57. Milsom, *Studies*, 145–47; Brigden, *London and the Reformation*, 98–103; Haigh, *English Reformations*, 78–80. On 6 December 1514 William Horsey, chancellor of the bishop of London; Charles Joseph of London, cleric and summoner; and John Spaldyng of London, yeoman and bellringer, were presented for Hunne's death of 4 December 1514 by strangulation. They tried to make it look as if Hunne had hanged himself. The indictment was taken into king's bench; the attorney general on 12 April 1516 by royal warrant asserted that Horsey was not guilty so that he was discharged from the Marshalsea. KB27/1019, m. 4 Rex. The pardon of John Spaldyng appears in KB27/1020, m. 1d Rex, dated 22 June 1516.

58. CP40/934, m. 337.

59. *Register of John Kirkby*, ed. Storey, 156–57.

marriage by the widow. When it attached to other people than the husband and father, mortuary fees constituted a continuing drain on the family economy. Not surprisingly, mortuary fees were one of the most frequent points of dispute in a parish.[60]

The ecclesiastical rights of tithe, glebe, and mortuary fees set the parish at the heart of the economic life of England. To the degree that the head of the parish enforced those rights effectively, the parish organization collected agrarian surplus in ways that facilitated commerce and supported urban life. To the extent that society grew to depend on the rector along with the manorial lord to collect agrarian produce, to that extent also the parish itself tended to become commercialized. The parish, of course, remained a religious and communal unit; but tithes, the produce of the glebe, and mortuary fees, once collected, were no different from other produce and were subject to the full range of commercial processes and social regulation common to other produce. The commercial importance of parish resources led to practices in late medieval England that tended to obscure the relationship between the sources of revenue and the provision of services, between the payment of tithes and the care of souls. The mere economic importance of the produce necessitated more efficient and, from the rector's point of view, more tempting mechanisms for management. The economic importance of the rectory's rights also necessitated royal regulation through the courts.

60. Bowker, *Secular Clergy*, 149–51.

CHAPTER THREE

The Common Law and the Mundane Church

When Henry VIII became supreme head of the English church and thus the head of English church courts, he greatly increased royal power. Nevertheless, Henry VIII's assumption of church governance was only possible because the monarchy had in fact been very involved in settling ecclesiastical disputes for centuries. The church had run its own elaborate set of courts, but the clergy were fully a part of their society. Both church and clergy relied on the king's system of courts. Since the church both as an institution and as individuals relied on the king's court for dispute resolution, the crown possessed the power to regulate the church. Enforcing or altering the rules that governed property, transactions, and conduct constituted regulation of society, a society of which the clergy were an integral part.

Common law involvement with the parish and the church in fact increased in late medieval England, but not simply as the imposition of royal control on an unwilling community. When a third to a half of the population died from the Black Death, the crown's determination to preserve social order resulted in a common law that was increasingly comprehensive. Thousands of plaintiffs each term enthusiastically used royal remedies to resolve disputes about relationships and resources. The resources of the rector were important for government, church, towns, and the universities; disputes about those resources came into the king's court. Local people, lay and ecclesiastical, brought into the king's court other disputes that the church would have considered more appropriate for determination in court Christian. The growth of royal power both created and reflected changed social attitudes.

The king thus not only regulated the church courts with legal remedies that supervised ecclesiastical jurisdictions, he also supervised the parish directly by the application of general rules in the course of ordinary litigation. Historians regularly discuss the former aspect of royal regulation, never the latter; it could easily seem that church courts and parish affairs were insulated from direct involvement of the royal courts. The relevant relationships, from that traditional perspective, were thus among deans, archdeacons, bishops, archbishops and papal courts, and the accompanying peculiar jurisdictions, as long as these courts did not intrude into areas of royal authority.[1] The world of litigation, however, was as porous as the real world. Marriage litigation in church courts, thus, might seem a matter of conscience, canon law, or salvation of souls; in fact, a suit in ecclesiastical court about marriage was often only a piece of a larger social dynamic among families played out also at the same time in king's court.[2] More strikingly, matters that might have appeared in ecclesiastical court could just as easily, under a different formal rubric, find their way into king's court. The common law was thus intricately involved with the resolution of disputes in the parish as well as in the village. Inconspicuous litigation regularly applied common rules of property, obligations, and wrongs to the affairs of the institutional church and to relationships within the parish about religious subject matter. This chapter documents, from a small sampling of the legal records, the mundane ways in which the church had come to use the king's court and had thus become dependent on and vulnerable to the crown.

When confronted with a problem, neither clergy nor laity were overly concerned about the niceties of jurisdictional boundaries: resolution of the problem was much more important than adherence to jurisdictional rules. Clearly, church courts did not reject litigants who formulated a claim of debt as a breach of faith in order to come within their jurisdiction. The writ of prohibition could stop the plaintiff, but the prohibition would only appear if the defendant considered it personally advantageous to object to having the suit settled in church court.[3] Church personnel often found royal courts more convenient than ecclesiastical courts for handling problems. The king's court acted on person and property, rather than on one's soul; in many contexts, that pragmatic approach was more effective. If neither party in king's court actively objected to the court's hearing the case, the justices did not intervene to throw the parties into church court. Ecclesiastics thus often put disputes into a form that would allow disagreements to be resolved by jury verdict at common law. Both in church court and in king's court, cases rarely advertised the fact that they were inappropriate. Moreover, most litigation is about applying pressure rather than

---

1. Thomson, *Early Tudor Church*, 125–38; Lander, "Church Courts and the Reformation," 34–55; Brigden, *London and the Reformation*, 199–203. Haigh highlights the premunire cases, church court claims of independence, and the transfers of jurisdiction over particular kinds of cases and the competition for debt litigation, without noticing the way in which ordinary litigation handled parish matters: Haigh, *English Reformations*, 72–87.

2. Palmer, "Contexts of Marriage," 42–67.

3. Helmholz, *Canon Law*, 77–99, 263–89.

about getting a judgment. The vast majority of cases ended by settlement or exhaustion without reaching judgment. The common law in fact was as central to the mundane life of the church as the church was to the mundane life of the English.

Church Reliance on the Common Law

The church could rely explicitly on the common law to provide for many of its needs. Indeed, it made arrangements about central ecclesiastical issues in forms that could only be enforced by the common law. The common law was relatively stable and offered the late medieval church the same kinds of advantages that the advanced property and contractual mechanisms of modern society offer modern religious institutions. Moreover, elements of the law were open to being used for collaborative resolution of difficult problems. The church was an integral part of society and made use of the same mechanisms that the laity used.

Performance bonds were all too tempting a device; the church used such bonds to impose this-worldly penalties that proved more coercive than excommunication. Performance bonds obligated a party to a specific sum in debt, payable unless that party performed a particular act or course of action. In 1497 the local bishop mediated a dispute between the abbot of Buildwas and the rector of Cound, Shropshire. Even though the resolution involved a wide variety of ecclesiastical subject matter, enforcement was left to the common law. The parties agreed that for the remainder of the time that they both held their benefices, the abbot would pay the rector £21.67 annually. In return, the rector leased to the abbot most of the tithes of his rectory together with a sufficient barn within the rectory and the tithes, offerings, wool, lambs, mortuaries, and hay in the vill of Cressage together with its glebe and chapel. The abbot on his side was responsible for finding a chaplain for the chapel and for its supplies. They each put themselves under a £40 performance bond; if either party defaulted, the other could sue for a debt of £40 already evidenced by a writing under seal. In 1503 the whole agreement fell apart over the sufficiency of the barn; the way was thus open for a suit to recover the whole £40 regardless of the actual damage incurred by an insufficient barn.[4] What the bishop had begun, the king's justices had then to enforce. The vicar of Stone, Kent, used a perfor-

4. CP40/962, m. 437.

mance bond of £40 to provide security for the payment of an annuity from his successor before surrendering his vicary into the hands of the ordinary to be conferred on his successor.[5] Performance bonds were likewise the mechanism of choice for rectors and vicars in managing their parish.[6] The performance bond was simply the most effective method of enforcement available; competent clergy would use the best means at hand.

In a similar way the church could use the performance bond at common law to enforce the resolution of a personal conflict between clergymen, a matter that, theoretically, might have been more suitably resolved within the church. The prior of Otterton and the vicar of Yarcombe, Devon, relied on arbitration reinforced by a performance bond to resolve the division of rights between rector and vicar. As part of the arbitration they agreed to relinquish all other actions against each other and not to vex each other. Default on that obligation was to incur a penalty of £10, if a panel of four law-worthy men of the parish confirmed the default. The prior finally alleged at law that in 1386 the vicar had managed to get a monk of Taunton Priory to obtain the priory of Otterton at farm from the king, thus expelling the prior, and that this had been found by the requisite panel of four men of the parish under oath.[7] The mechanism here was good, but the forfeiture was not set high enough to secure compliance.

Performance bonds could also enforce sexual regulation, a complex of matters that were at the core of much of ecclesiastical court jurisdiction and social influence. This regulation could occur completely outside ordinary church cognizance. Thomas Mees and John de Westhorp, a chaplain, in 1387 had put themselves to arbitration in a dispute over Mees's daughter. The chaplain, according to the arbitration award, would pay Mees £1.33 for wrongs that had occurred, but £13.67 if he had intercourse with or communicated in any suspect place with Mees's daughter. The chaplain succumbed to temptation after about two years, so that Mees sued him for the penalty.[8] Even a bishop could use the device to enforce morality. When Richard, bishop of Winchester, took it in hand to end a woman's career of running a house of prostitution, he did not manage the process through his own court. Edward Arnold of London, a gentleman, was willing to submit to a performance bond of £20 in 1510, the bond to be enforceable if she did not bear herself honestly or if she ran a

5. CP40/999, m. 449.
6. See below, Chapter 5.
7. CP40/505, m. 269.
8. CP40/521, m. 407.

brothel. The bishop sued Arnold in 1512 because the woman had opened a common brothel called The Swan in Southwark.[9] Instead of the imposition of spiritual penalties, the bishop relied on the performance bond for good behavior, even from an associate (relative?) who might be able to control the transgressor's conduct. In 1532 John Cook, a church court judge, had the sheriffs of London imprison a mercer of London until he agreed to a performance bond of £20 to abide by Cook's order that would sever the mercer's relationship with a woman.[10] Such performance bonds would, and did, come to the king's court for enforcement.

Ecclesiastics, like laymen, often used common law litigation to resolve intractable disputes in a somewhat collaborative manner. York Minster thus used the king's court to remedy problems arising from a lease. The Minster's treasurer had apparently leased a garden in Weston to the vicar of the local church. The vicar in turn had licensed some laymen to cut down certain trees and to take the furnishings of a house there. York Minster disagreed about what the vicar as lessee could legitimately license under the lease. It thus sued the laymen for the cutting down of sixty oak and one hundred ash trees, and the taking of wooden tables, doors, and windows. In the process of the case, however, plaintiff and defendants narrowed the pleading to focus on one tree and a door. This typical tactic allowed the main dispute to be decided by jury, but limited the actual judgment to a relatively small sum; once the facts and law had been settled, the parties could work out an appropriate arrangement among themselves.[11] Both York Minster and the lay licensees, however, found this an appropriate way to resolve a dispute that harnessed the king's court to resolve the basic dispute while avoiding resort to the king's court methods for enforcing judgments. Litigants, lay and clerical, used the law just as much as they were governed by it.

The sheer volume of litigation brought by the clergy made the court of common pleas one of the most important legal venues for handling the mundane problems of the church. A simple analysis of plea rolls of the court of common pleas gives some sense of the importance of the common law to ecclesiastics. The total amount of litigation in 1526 was something in the order of only 54 percent of the litigation in 1386. A count of parties most likely suing

9. CP40/1000, m. 541.

10. CP40/1077, m. 126.

11. CP40/508, m. 117. For another example of narrowing the subject matter to a relatively inconsequential portion of the whole claim, see Chapter 2 at note 38.

on their own behalf[12] finds that the various levels of ecclesiastics accounted for 15 percent of plaintiffs in 1386, 8 percent in 1465, and 10 percent in 1526. The actual number of clerical plaintiffs had fallen 64 percent by 1526, primarily because of the overall fall in the absolute volume of litigation. In debt litigation, clerical plaintiffs were somewhat more prominent than they were in overall litigation, with claims in a single term in 1386 running at £10,893, in 1465 at £8,421, and in 1526 at £4,112; in 1526 clerics still accounted for about 10 percent of the money claimed in debt. Cases of trespass followed generally the trend in debt. The decline in clerical plaintiffs that exceeded the overall decline in litigation occurred primarily in the realm of the clerics, vicars, and chaplains: religious houses tended to retain their share of litigation through the period. The reasons for the particular decline in common law litigation by rectors, vicars, and chaplains are not clear, but the church in the fifteenth century was still intent on achieving a more separate clerical order. The bishops obtained a charter from Edward IV that would have exempted clergy from major categories of common law litigation had it been implemented.[13] The church also asserted an ecclesiastical law that clerics should not resort to secular fora.[14] Even though clerical participation in the common law declined substantially during the fifteenth century, in 1526 the clergy still participated vigorously in common law litigation.[15]

These cases, thus, are far more than stray anomalies; clergy were prominent plaintiffs and defendants in king's court. Using litigation as one part of a larger strategy was typical, in both ecclesiastical and royal courts. All areas of church life appeared in the king's court. Clerical participation in the common law declined in the fifteenth century, but only somewhat more than lay participation. Clerics were no different from other people in being sufficiently inventive to use whatever means were available to attain their ends. The performance bond in particular was extremely popular as a coercive device; it rapidly became the preferred method of securing performance of duties after the Black Death. The punitive nature of the performance bond marked it as a governance device instead of an ordinary mechanism for the enforcement of agreements because

12. Clergy who sued as an executor, administrator, or a member of a group were excluded. Groups were often feoffees to uses and were thus functioning for others. The cases thus excluded constitute only about 5 percent of the whole body of litigation.

13. Rymer, *Foedera*, vol. 5, pt. 2, 111–13. For the continuing concern of the clergy with this charter, see Haigh, *English Reformations*, 76, 80–81.

14. KB27 / 1005, m. 64.

15. CP40 / 502; CP40 / 816; CP40 / 1051.

such bonds so strongly encouraged compliance with duties, but normally without recourse to actual litigation. Only the foolish, obstinate, or unfortunate
contravened them, so that the occasional case indicates a much larger social use,
whether for settlement of economic claims among clergymen or for ensuring
good behavior, securing marriages, or enforcing appropriate sexual conduct. To
be effective, the church relied increasingly on the common law. To the extent
that rectors, vicars, and chaplains diminished their activity at common law over
the fifteenth century, however, their interests would be less forcefully presented
to and present in the minds of the justices; the phenomenon is much the same as
the decline in clerical representatives to Parliament.[16] The agenda of a separate
jurisdictional order was a double-edged sword. The clergy used the common
law so much that they were also subject to it and dependent on it; they did not
use it enough to control it. Henry VII and Henry VIII thus found the clergy
vulnerable.

Common Law Regulation of the Church

The church, then, clearly relied on the common law for its own purposes, but
the common law also affirmatively resolved matters that could easily have been
considered ecclesiastical. The litigation concerning tithes, tithe leases, and mortuary fees in the previous chapter at one level demonstrates adequately the
degree to which the common law was intrinsic to church and parish life and
supervised or established its practices. Other kinds of supervision, however,
were equally assertive but struck closer to the power of the bishop. Matters
concerning the execution of a bishop's decrees, problems with a bishop's sequestration, endowments for providing religious services, and the wages of
chaplains and parish priests were all grist for the mill of the common law. The
common law quite simply was central to the running of the church of late
medieval England.

Various liabilities under a bishop's decree would seem appropriate for the
church courts, but the common law might nevertheless determine the issue.
Could a succeeding rector be held liable by church process for the proceeds due
a vicar according to a bishop's decree? In one case a vicar had complained to the
bishop of Norwich that the parish of Great Thurlow, Suffolk, yielded too little
to support him. The bishop appointed a commissioner to look into the matter,

16. Sayles, *King's Parliament of England*, 114–15.

and his inquest found that the vicar received no more than £4 annually. The commissioner decreed that a reapportionment take place so that the vicar would receive £8 annually.[17] By that time, however, the vicar had resigned. After six months the bishop appointed a new vicar and ordered the sequestration of rectory revenues to pay more than £4 arrears to the new vicar from the time of the vacancy. The sequestration prompted a suit at common law; the new corporate rector, the proctor and scholars of Godshouse College (later Christ's Church), Cambridge, sued the new vicar for the taking of 140 trees and 48 cartloads of varied crops in 1466. The new corporate rector claimed the produce, because they had not been rector at the time of the vacancy and thus should not be held liable to the sequestration.[18] The issue was one that would be important for the church, but the king's justices were the ones to determine that the college would not be liable if it had not then been rector.

The actions of executors and administrators of a decedent's estate were subjects for the common law, even though probate of a will or appointment of administrators was within the ecclesiastical sphere. Clearly administrators (those appointed to handle the estate of intestates) could sue and be sued at common law: administrators brought eight cases in a single term in 1386, forty-two cases in 1465, and twenty-five cases in 1526; the respective numbers for administrators as defendants are twenty-nine cases, twenty-five cases, and fourteen cases.[19] Likewise, however, the common law could determine the goods to which the administrator had access. John Chadwell had owned five hundred sheep, a pitchfork, and a sheep crook when he died intestate. The vicar general of the archbishop of York sequestered all his goods and appointed an administrator. The administrator took possession of the chattels, but was challenged. In the ensuing litigation in 1512, the issue was whether the decedent had had the sheep in his possession when he died.[20] The determination of the goods over which the church-appointed administrator had control thus here lay with the king's court and with the jury it would assemble. Clearly, a sequestration did not settle all dispute. In 1391 the court handled a case involving the sequestration of goods devised by will. The bequests had apparently ended up in the wrong hands; in response to a claim by the rightful recipients, the abbot of Westminster se-

17. Thomson has a nice series of such episcopal actions. Thompson, *Early Tudor Church*, 174–75.

18. CP40/825, m. 522.

19. CP40/502; CP40/816; CP40/1051.

20. CP40/1000, m. 527. I have accepted the recitation of the record, although it is quite likely that series of takings was only a formality of pleading, not a social fact.

questered the goods. Even after a writ of prohibition citing the king's court jurisdiction over cases concerning the detention of goods and chattels, the abbot refused to raise the sequestration, so the disregard of the prohibition itself formed the basis of suit in the court of common pleas.[21] The records of the common law are otherwise littered with cases involving wills. Executors brought 294 actions in a single term in 1386, 341 in 1465, and 327 in 1526; executors appeared as defendants in 101, 178, and 83 cases respectively in those same terms. Both as plaintiffs and as defendants, executors increased as a percentage in overall litigation.[22] Other cases came under allegations that a will containing instructions for feoffees to uses had been counterfeited to gain title to land or the forging of other documents: ten suits in only one term of 1526.[23] The jurisdictional hold that church courts had in the disposition of the goods of the dead was very narrow and interwoven with common law enforcement.

To a certain extent, the bishop's powers of sequestration were even at the disposal of the king's court. When an ecclesiastical person had no secular land, the sheriff might well be unable to act to coerce him into court; the king's justices could then order the bishop to sequester the appropriate goods. In 1390, for instance, the court ordered the bishop of Norwich to levy more than £92.50 owed to the prior of Lewes as arrears from an annual rent. The bishop responded that he had sequestered all the autumn fruits of the church of Feltwell, Norfolk. The proceeds were worth £13.67, but the bishop could not find buyers for the goods. The king's justices ordered him to find buyers and to continue to raise the rest of the arrears.[24] Even in matters of process, the king's court and the ecclesiastical courts had established careful linkages to provide justice, justice that was as important to ecclesiastics as it was to lay people.

While the bishop directed the priests of his diocese and the well-being of the parishes, the appropriate remuneration for a priest was not solely within the bishop's power. As early as the Ordinance of Laborers the king had taken an interest in the wages of chaplains, although he there deferred to the bishops.[25] Parliament under Henry V purported to limit such salaries: £5.33–6.00 for chaplains serving as parish priest; £4.67 for other chaplains.[26] Those "other

21. CP40/520, m. 170.

22. CP40/502; CP40/816; CP40/1051.

23. CP40/1051, mm. 112, 186, 253d, 310d, 313d, 314d, 353d, 370, 378d, 479d.

24. CP40/519, m. 104d.

25. Palmer, *ELABD*, 19.

26. Statute 2 Henry V, 2, c. 2; Swanson, *Church and Society*, 47; Heath, *English Parish Clergy*, 22.

chaplains" performed a variety of duties. Some hired priests were personal chaplains; such chaplains did not hesitate to use the king's court to secure their wages both before the statute and after it, but without particular reference to the statute. Henry Bakere of Stilton, Huntingdonshire, hired Thomas Crisp in 1388 to say mass, matins, vespers, and other prayers for one year for only £4.[27] Shortly after 1400, John Grey, a citizen of Exeter, hired William Sechevell as his personal chaplain at £5.33 annually.[28] Other hired priests were chaplains of a chapel; they likewise relied on the common law. William Clyff of London, a cleric himself, in 1451 hired Richard Chyld for £6.67 to celebrate divine services in the chapel of St. John the Baptist in the parish of St. Mary Aldermary, London, for one year.[29] People frequently hired priests to pray for the dead. Robert Curson, knight, hired Robert Courcy to celebrate divine services for Curson's soul in the church of St. Benet Fink, London, for one year for £10 in the 1380s.[30] John Spyne in the 1380s hired Henry Lowe, a chaplain, to say matins, mass, and vespers in Petherton, Somerset, for Spyne and his benefactors and all the dead for one year for £4.67.[31] Thomas Gousel, a member of the gentry, hired William Penyngton in 1466 to pray for his soul and his benefactors for six months in Norwich.[32] The widow of Richard Drake, a merchant of the Staple, hired John Dykke to celebrate masses for her husband's soul for twenty years: ten years at St. Bartholomew the Less, London, at £6.33 annually; then ten years at Hichin, Hertfordshire, at £6 annually.[33] Agnes Peyrs hired John Lysson to say mass for her soul for six months after her death for £3.[34] These clerics, serving as chaplains in a wide variety of capacities, found the common law, not their bishop, the effective tool for securing payment for their services.

Many chaplains, however, served either as auxiliary help in the parish or as the parish priest for an absentee rector or for the rector's lessees. Thomas Toly, a chaplain, hired William Goor for £1.33 to celebrate divine services in Sprowston,

27. CP40/521, m. 194d.
28. CP40/599, m. 132d.
29. CP40/825, m. 428. Thomson estimates that chantry priests in London averaged about £6.67/year but that such priests' pay varied widely and was generally less in the north of England. Thomson, *Early Tudor Church*, 179.
30. CP40/520, m. 142d.
31. CP40/505, m. 133d.
32. CP40/825, m. 230.
33. CP40/970, m. 443.
34. CP40/982, m. 662d.

Norfolk, for three months (an annual rate, then, of £5.33).[35] The parson of Allington hired John Auncel to be the parish chaplain for a year for only £3.[36] Robert Box (a cleric) and Thomas Wildemersh hired Walter Scot for £5.33 to serve as parish chaplain of Hatch Beauchamp, Somerset, for one year.[37] John Frankesh, a gentleman of London, hired William Penyngton to be the parish priest of Thurton, Norfolk, for a year in 1465 for £6, saying masses, matins, and vespers.[38] Thomas Inpeghe, rector of Redenhall, Norfolk, hired John Dykke to serve as the parish priest of Redenhall for three months for £2.[39] The parish priest of Barkby, Leceistershire, received only £5 for his year of service in 1522; the parish priest of Beccles, Suffolk, £6 in 1526; the parish priest of Crudwell, Wiltshire, a yearly rate of £6.67 in 1531; and the parish priest of Christow, Devon, £6 in 1521.[40] John Nunne, a husbandman, hired Richard Gybson to be the parish priest of Drinkstone, Suffolk, for £6.67.[41] The king's justices enforced the agreed-upon salaries for chaplains, even though a salary deviated from the statute.

That level of remuneration was not far different from the pay of an attorney. Around 1500, attorneys were paid fairly regularly £0.08 for each term they were actually prosecuting litigation for a client, a yearly rate of £0.33.[42] At that rate, an attorney would have to be working actively for about twenty clients to achieve a chaplain's income. The client reimbursed the attorney for the costs of litigation in addition to the fee, but such costs came from the money delivered over for the writs, seals, enrollments, serjeants' services, etc. In a similar way parish priests were usually not obliged to provide the bread and wine for religious services.[43] A parish priest, however, was more sedentary; attorneys had to travel constantly between the locality and Westminster, thus incurring further expenses, so equivalency might only be achieved by an attorney serving

35. CP40/933, m. 67.

36. CP40/521, m. 87.

37. CP40/509, m. 134; CP40/510, m. 348.

38. CP40/846, m. 258.

39. CP40/950, m. 410d.

40. CP40/1072, m. 477; KB27/1060, m. 14; CP40/1079, m. 419; CP40/1080, m. 331d.

41. CP40/1002, m. 500.

42. CP40/896, m. 284; CP40/1067, mm. 142d, 315; CP40/1070, m. 405d; CP40/1071, m. 307; CP40/1072, m. 558; CP40/1074, m. 507 (referred to as the ancient accustomed fee for attorneys); CP40/1083, m. 344. An attorney in a county court might claim rather less: 6d per session thus yielding £0.33 per year. CP40/1006, m. 311d.

43. CP40/844, m. 355d.

twenty-five or thirty clients, a fairly good caseload.[44] Chaplains and attorneys might have been on a par socially.

The king's court treated endowments for ecclesiastical services the same as it would any other grant under the writ *cessavit per biennium* to secure religious services in the locality. *Cessavit per biennium* allowed a donor to reclaim a grant when the services had lapsed for two years. The action was useful for enforcing the purposes of monastic endowments. St. Osyths Abbey had an endowment of sixty acres in Stowmarket, Suffolk, for finding a suitable priest for ecclesiastical services in that town on Mondays, Wednesdays, and Fridays; after about a century the abbey stopped providing the priest.[45] Similarly, the abbot of Woburn Abbey held an endowment to provide a chapel's chaplain on Wednesdays, Fridays, and Sundays, and, during Lent and Advent, also on Saturdays. The abbot was responsible for providing the appropriate books, chalice, bread, wine, wax, vestments, and other necessary ornaments. By 1503 the abbot had long since ceased finding either chaplain or supplies; four laymen alleged that their ecclesiastical services had been much diminished and claimed damages of £40.[46] The heir of Ralph Ridford sued Newsham Abbey to make it perform the ecclesiastical services for Ralph's soul, as it was obligated by a forty-acre endowment in Killingholme, Lincolnshire.[47] For about a century Lanthony Prime Priory had provided an annuity of £2 to a priest to pray for the soul of Roger de Kankeberge, but then defaulted after the Black Death for thirty years. Adam Feltewell, finally appointed to the position, was able to claim the arrears of £60.[48] Simply because the endowments were for the central ecclesiastical purpose of provision of religious services, whether for the living or the dead, did not exclude them from the purview of the king's government.

Annuities between ecclesiastics or payable from purely ecclesiastical sources, even though for ecclesiastical purposes, were matters for the king's court; and for annuities religious houses had exceedingly long memories. In 1340 Battle Abbey and the chancellor of Chichester had agreed in ecclesiastical court that the chancellor was to take the tithes from about seventy-three acres of land in

44. Palmer, *County Courts*, 98.
45. CP40/506, m. 456; CP40/507, m. 440. A different situation appears from 1516: the prior of Winchester St. Swithun had bound a yeoman under a £10 performance bond to find a sufficient priest to serve the parishioners of the chapel of Quidhampton, Hants, perhaps as part of a lease of the chapel.
46. CP40/966, m. 480d.
47. CP40/511, m. 248d.
48. CP40/503, m. 520.

return for an £0.80 annual rent to Battle Abbey to the use of its sacristan; they agreed also on a penalty of £5 for default. The bishop of Chichester ratified the agreement, which held for more than fifty years. In 1410 the king's court enforced that agreement after a default of sixteen years. Ninety-two years later, in 1502, the chancellor of Chichester tried to relieve himself of the annuity by claiming that the court had erred in enforcing an ecclesiastical composition for tithes. Fyneux confirmed the earlier judgment and preserved the jurisdiction of the king's court.[49]

The common law developed actions that proved important for church services and ecclesiastical possessions. The abbot and a monk of St. Benet of Hulme sued a husbandman for assaulting the monk in 1487 and claimed damages because the monk was unable to perform the church services in the abbey church for four days.[50] In 1499 William Newman, a cleric, sued a husbandman for assaults and threats that kept him from celebrating services and collecting tithes in the parish of Down Hatherley, Gloucestershire.[51] The dean of St. Pauls, London, sued a chaplain in 1504 for the return of a missal with two silver clasps, a gilded silver chalice, and two pairs of priest's vestments.[52] In the same year Robert Hone, a cleric, sued a gentleman, a cleric, and a chaplain for taking his goods and chattels in Southwark, Surrey; the goods included three books ("Prepared Sermons," another book containing fifteen sermons, and a book with the ceremonies for baptizing and burying) and various accounts for £8 from a term as parish priest of Southwark St. Margaret.[53]

Problems with funerals, both directly and indirectly affecting the church, insinuated themselves into king's court litigation. In 1499 Stephen Warde sued the abbess of Barking in Essex for detaining £12 worth of chattels: sixteen wax torches weighing three hundred pounds and four wax tapers weighing sixty pounds. The abbess alleged a custom that her monastery kept for its own use any torch or taper brought with a body to be buried at the monastery. The parties managed the process so that the case could have been determined by the justices on the legitimacy of the alleged custom, but was in fact determined in favor of Warde by jury verdict.[54] Such rights were not an inconsequential topic; St. German treated the question of church right to tapers burned at funerals as

49. KB27/964, m. 30.
50. CP40/911, m. 42.
51. CP40/950, m. 525.
52. KB27/971, m. 26d.
53. KB27/973, m. 105.
54. CP40/950, m. 340.

the first aspect of the law about mortuaries in his "New Additions."[55] A 1504 case likewise involved a funeral, but not an ecclesiastic. John Waren took a one-year periodic lease of a tenement in London from a wax chandler. Waren thereafter had discovered his father lying dead in the house; the body raised such a stench that no one dared go near to bury it, so Waren agreed to pay his landlord to wax the body and further purchased six candles and twelve torches weighing 366 pounds to burn during the funeral. They agreed that Waren would only pay for the use and wastage of the wax (1d for the use of each pound of wax and 5d per pound for the wax actually burned). The landlord/wax chandler eventually sued for a total of £12.29: £0.20 in rent, almost £2 worth of wax used in the funeral, and the rest for the cloths and waxing of the body.[56] The vicar of Carisbrooke, Hampshire, in the sixteenth century provided for the burial of corpses at Newport by a performance bond that allowed also for contingencies if the obliged chaplains encountered violent opposition from the parishioners.[57] Burying the dead was a part of life and fell within the purview of the king's court when it involved ordinary agreements and even at times when it involved church right or agreements among clerics.

The common law had elaborated rules and mechanisms covering the wide variety of disputes that occurred in society, and those rules and mechanisms applied to church property just as they applied to lay property. The king's justices considered bishops' sequestrations, wills, endowments to provide for religious services, priests' wages, funeral arrangements. The church was a part of the society that the common law structured, and churchmen actively used common law mechanisms.

Friction between Church Courts and Common Law Courts

While the church depended on the common law, relations between the institutional church and the common law courts were not uniformly collegial. The church, for instance, attempted to expand its ability to enforce tithe obligations under the rubric of suppressing heresy. In 1401 Parliament had passed a statute allowing bishops to imprison for up to three months anyone who spread false religious opinions; during that time a bishop could continue ecclesiastical legal process against them. The bishop of London attempted to use that statute to

---

55. *St. German's Doctor and Student*, ed. Plucknett and Barton, 317–18.

56. KB27/973, m. 79.

57. CP40/1073, m. 330.

help resolve one example of London's chronic problems with tithing.⁵⁸ In 1495 the bishop thus imprisoned Hilary Warner of London for maintaining that he did not have to pay tithes in the parish where he was resident: a false religious opinion. He escaped from the bishop's prison after one day and sued the three clerics and the yeoman who had imprisoned him. In 1497 the king's justices, after much delay, decided that such an allegation did not justify imprisonment; they awarded Hilary £18 in damages and more than £11 in costs. Hilary remitted more than £9 of his award, but the defendants brought a writ of error anyway: the legal determination was crucial for them in regard to tithes throughout England. Fyneux in king's bench simply affirmed the judgment.⁵⁹ The church wanted to repress any opposition to tithes vigorously, but Fyneux would have none of it.

Fyneux nevertheless did not directly attack church court jurisdiction over tithes. He only prevented the duty to pay tithes from becoming an issue of false religious opinions. Fyneux had assumed the power to issue premunire process directly from king's bench, so that he could authorize prosecutions that would protect king's court jurisdictions; defendants could be treated as enemies of the king. He did apply premunire process to the matter of tithing great trees,⁶⁰ for which there was a long tradition of prohibitions under statutory authority. He was willing to intervene in tithing matters by premunire when litigants resorted outside the realm to the papal court, as when William Fell, a cleric, went to the papal court to claim the fruits, lands, rents, proceeds, emoluments, oblations, and tithes that belonged to the royal chapel in the county of Durham. Even here the litigation was not limited just to tithes and concerned a royal chapel.⁶¹

58. Thomson, "Tithe Disputes," 1–17; Brigden, "Tithe Controversy," 285–301.

59. CP40/934, m. 327; KB27/945, m. 32.

60. KB27/969, m. 93 (1503); KB27/970, m. 64 (1504) (John Clerk of Brentwood v. George Rede vicar of Hornchurch, chaplain and Thomas Bodley of South Weald concerning an attempt to tithe trees allegedly more than a hundred years old); KB27/991, m. 9 Rex (1509) (Richard Girlyng v. John Smith of Fressingfield on indictment before James Hobart and other jp's on allegation of suit for tithes from great trees under cover of violation of church constitution prohibiting deprivation of rights of churches; Smith presented a pardon in king's bench); KB27/1006, m. 35 (1512) (Thomas Wryght v. James Brokeden rector of Rawmarsh); KB27/1031, m. 23 (James Trewynard v. George Trevilian rector of St. Mawgan et al. concerning an attempt to tithe trees allegedly more than a hundred years old). After Fyneux the court used prohibitions again for this matter: KB27/1068, m. 29 (1528) (Robert Locton v. Robert Thurkylde vicar of Papworth, for trees allegedly 30–60 years old).

61. KB27/1007, m. 32 (1513); KB147/2/5/1.

Fyneux also intervened when a layman sued a churchman in king's court for trespass at common law and the ecclesiastic resorted to a plea for tithes in church court to frustrate the common law litigation.[62] He could have gone further and conceptualized disputes about tithes either as claims of debts or as the taking of goods and chattels. As far as current research indicates, however, he did not interfere directly with the rector's everyday suit for tithes. Even St. German indicated that king's bench and common pleas (although not the exchequer of pleas) respected church court jurisdiction respecting ultimate determinations concerning tithes.[63] Tithing obligations presented a boundary of friction, but not startlingly so prior to the Reformation.

In other areas, such as defamation, the friction between common law and church courts was pronounced. The first evidence for a regular common law jurisdiction in defamation came only in 1507.[64] Well before that, in 1499, Fyneux had allowed a premunire to be brought on a church court defamation action that alleged that the defendant had said, "I sawe Robert Vincent huntyng in the kyngys game att kyngysthornys & his houndys with him." The premunire defendant, however, came into king's bench and challenged the basis of the suit; the court quashed the bill.[65] The second defamation premunire began as a presentment before justices of the peace in Norfolk. Since royal officers functioned also as justices of the peace, James Hobart, the king's attorney general, had been a member of that session. The accusation related to a prior session of the sheriff's turn in 1498, at which Robert Emondes had presented: "It is seid that Miles Wyf kepeth Sherewed rule and that your person [i.e., parson] kepeth her as his harlot." The presentment included the allegations that Nicholas Myles kept a house of prostitution at Swanton Abbot, that Geoffrey Cheteryng, cleric, often committed adultery with Nicholas's wife, and that Geoffrey continually entered Nicholas's house and slept with Margaret against Nicholas's will. Geoffrey, the cleric involved, proceeded then in ecclesiastical court against

62. KB27/1044, m. 78 (1522) (Thomas Wyberd v. William Richardson rector of High Ongar).

63. *St. German's Doctor and Student*, 323: ". . . in the kinges benche & comen place they wyll suffre no issue to be ioyned specially betwixte person & person, wherby the ryght of the tythes myghte be tried." One suspects that St. German was choosing his words very precisely here, not meaning simply that people could not use the common law to resolve disputes about tithes.

64. *Select Cases on Defamation*, ed. Helmholz, 42.

65. KB146/10/14/4; KB146/10/15/1 (both the allegation and the latitat, the latter tested 8 June); KB27/953, m. 76 (Buscher v. Hegyns).

Emondes, the juror who had brought up the accusation, and accused him of defamation. Three of the members of the sworn panel at the turn appeared in church court to testify against Emondes. Emondes resorted to the session of the justices of the peace and under oath informed the session of the situation. Hobart, the king's attorney general, thus delivered the information into king's bench in Easter term 1500. The parties demurred on the law; and king's bench, apparently including Fyneux, again quashed the premunire, declining to allow this kind of protection against church court attacks on presentments at a sheriff's turn.[66] The third defamation premunire came then in 1501, founded this time not straightforwardly with defamation cases as such but with the common law jurisdiction over trespasses and felonies: the defamation here was an allegation of homicide.[67] Apparently the rationale for the premunire was that church court adjudication of such language would actually result in church court jurisdiction over felonies, an area reserved to the king's court. Premunire suits attacking church court jurisdiction followed regularly thereafter.[68] With the

66. KB27/954, m. 3 Rex.

67. KB27/961, m. 75 (Calle v. Stubbys).

68. Baker provides a list of the cases he has in Introduction to *Spelman*, 2:67. I have not seen all his cases, and I have cases not in his list; neither of us has a comprehensive list as yet. The cases that follow are solely from Baker's list when the allegation is not included. KB27/961, m. 80d (1501, Penfold v. Facete); KB27/966, m. 5 Rex (1503, Rex [and Howet?] v. Sygrave) [accusation of theft]; KB27/972, m. 28, KB27/975, m. 32 (1504, Horwode v. Raynold) [theft by fishing]; KB27/973, m. 37, KB27/974, m. 61d (1505, Dudley v. Hatton) [defamation by testifying on behalf of king before jp's concerning felonies]; KB27/970, m. 61, KB27/974, m. 27d, KB27/975, m. 26 (1504, Reynolds v. Harward) [extortioner; countered by explanation that it was a prosecution for heresy]; KB27/980 (1506, Samford v. Walronde & Walronde) [allegation of felony]; KB27/983, m. 27d (1507, Warman v. Pyte) [felony alleged at peace session]; KB27/984, m. 84, KB27/986, m. 60 (1507, Graunte v. Wodward) [theft]; KB27/1002, m. 31 (1512, Fynes v. Benet) [theft]; KB27/1002, m. 33 (1512, Hutkell v. Cokkys et al.) [theft]; KB27/1004, m. 88, KB147/2/4/3, KB27/1006, mm. 36, 37 (1513, Hunne v. Marshall) ["Hunne, thou art accursed and thou standest accursed, and therefore go thou out of the church, for as long as thou are in this church I will say no evensong nor service"]; KB27/1011, m. 76d (1514, Newton v. Harward) ["Thou art a false horson"]; KB27/1020, m. 35 (1516, Dobbys v. Wrenne) [extortion]; KB27/1020, m. 23, KB27/1023, m. 78 (1516–17, Alee v. Markwik) [theft]; KB27/1024, m. 57 (1517, Lawes v. Blither) [breaking into house with intent to steal and murder]; KB27/1024, m. 81 (1517, Shudde v. Baylle) ["by the means of Sir Robert Baille a chalys longyng to the chyrche of Grene was conveyed & stolen"]; KB27/1024, m. 83 (1517, Newton v. Senacle) ["Thou art a false horson theffe"]; KB27/1032, m. 21 (1519, Ferrys v. Ryche) ["William Riche is a strong thef for he hath stolen a shepe of Adam Geffrey and more of other men & putt thereuppon his marke felonysly"]; KB27/1036, m. 80 (1520, Marlyn v. Manory

tools in place to enable church court defendants to frustrate the church court jurisdiction, king's bench began to handle defamation cases in 1507. The continuing stream of premunire suits in this area, however, indicates that the common law assumption of the jurisdiction was neither friendly nor considered final and that the church was far from being a passive victim.

The tension between common law and church court jurisdiction was even more pronounced in matters of debt, including not only minor debts but also matters touching on wills. The cases were brought both by and against executors and administrators,[69] and the court of common pleas had a lively jurisdiction involving testamentary and intestate assets.[70] When brought against executors and administrators, the case against the executor would be a preexisting debt fortified by the executors' own undertaking to pay the just debts. That

---

et al.) [theft]; KB27/1043, m. 79 (1522, Archer v. White) ["Thow art a false theffe for thou has stole my horse"]. Prohibitions on cases of defamation: KB27/1061, m. 78d, KB1064, m. 35 (1526, Awldwyn v. Aleyn) ["Margaret Alyn is a hore and a haude and it is nott yet iij wekys a goo sythens a man myght take prest betwene her legges"]; KB27/1061, m. 78 (1526, Crabbe v. Thomas) ["Thow art a bond chorle"].

69. KB27/934, m. 26 (1495) (Constable v. Holme: prohibition on debt of £40 from widow as executor on decedent's loan of £4.67 and 3 horses [justified *indebitatus, condidit testamentum*] guilty, damages of £2; costs of £6.67); KB146/10/16/4; KB27/960, m. 28d; KB27/963, m. 29 (1500) (Pere v. Sad; on a debt/breach of faith: Sad claiming £2 from executor [quashed]); KB27/978, m. 26, KB27/979, m. 23 (1506) (Sakvyll v. Boughton et al.; on a debt/detinue v. executors: debt/detinue by executors for £2.67); KB27/981, m. 6 Rex; KB27/984, m. 18; KB27/993, m. 13 Rex (1506) (Bradstrete v. Wode, executor; on a debt/detinue by executor against debtor for goods of value of £6.67: D pardoned); KB27/986, m. 8d Rex; KB27/989, mm. 4, 14; KB27/1006, m. 2 Rex (1508) (Smyth v. Oweden; on a debt/detinue by husband of dead administratrix against detainers: pardoned); KB27/987, m. 15 Rex (1508) (Rex [& Roberdes, executor?] v. Sandringham & Hare; on a debt/detinue (justification: by devisee's husband against executor for £3.33 which executor swore to pay (*indebitatus assumpsit*) wherefore perjury: pardoned); KB27/987, m. 9 before jp (1508) (Damport v. Spycer; on a debt/perjury by administrator on oath over performance bond for £0.67: quashed on lack of specificity of day); KB27/987, mm. 10, 20 Rex (1508) (Rex [& Bastard?] v. Thursby administrator & Churche; on a debt/detinue by administrator against joint tenant of wardship: pardoned). Cases directly on wills, not debts: KB27/1059, m. 20 (1526) (Clerk v. Stevyn & Parker; will forged in a clause with expenses of £7 enforced; found guilty, with damages of £1, costs £2); KB27/993, m. 33; KB27/995, mm. 26, 37 (1509) (Noreys feoffee/purchaser v. Portas executor; will impeding against executor who sued feoffee to uses of decedent alleged to have sold to feoffee while alive); KB146/10/14/4 (1499) (Constable v. Metham; will: impeding by executor hiding husband's widely varied goods; papal order).

70. See above, at notes 19–22.

sequence was probably one incentive for the common law actions that finally grew into *indebitatus assumpsit*[71] and mirrored the way in which premunire attacked defamation litigation in church courts well before the common law courts could themselves handle such cases. The premunire cases concerning debt, however, included not only cases involving executors and administrators, but also cases concerning small debts. Ordinarily, common law courts did not handle debts that were less than £2.[72] King's bench, however, could legitimately consider that its jurisdiction included lesser debts. King's bench allowed such cases for lesser debts against anyone imprisoned in its jail, and imprisoning people by a fictitious trespass suit precisely to make them vulnerable to such litigation was routine.[73] Thus Fyneux could rightly maintain that church court litigation regarding such lesser debts conflicted with its jurisdiction and use premunire process to undermine the activity of the church courts.[74] King's bench also attacked church court involvement with larger debts, often when there had been an oath or a promise or where the debt concerned tithes, detention of church goods, or the hiring of a priest, but in such matters the common law jurisdiction was even more clear.

The church court jurisdiction over sexual morality yielded not to the king's central courts, but to the justices of the peace. The rolls of king's bench provide some insight as to what justices of the peace were doing, but the insight is not

71. For that usage, see Constable v. Holme, KB27/934, m. 26 (1495), suggested also in KB27/987, m. 15 Rex. A different context that could also relate *indebitatus assumpsit* to the undermining of church court jurisdiction is Betson v. Brewode, KB27/977, m. 75. The analogue with defamation is tempting, but requires further work to prove it. *Indebitatus assumpsit* actions on this scenario are common later on: CP40/1212, mm. 647, 1185, 1270d.

72. Palmer, *County Courts*, 251–62.

73. Court personnel could also bring lesser debts by privilege, but that would not constitute a general jurisdiction. The Bill of Middlesex procedure open to anyone was different. Examples of such lesser debts: KB146/10/9/3, nos. 35 (£1.20), 38 (£1.07), 78 (£1.55); KB146/10/11/1, no. 16 (£1); KB146/10/11/2, no. 11 (£0.60); KB146/10/11/3, nos. 3 (£1), 17 (£1), 44 (£0.77); KB146/10/11/4, no. 56 (£1.65); KB146/10/12/1, nos. 26 (£1.25), 45 (£0.60), 101 (£0.59); KB146/10/12/2, no. 47 (£1); KB146/10/12/3, nos. 9 (£0.45), 43 (detinue of shield worth £0.25).

74. KB27/985, m. 14d Rex (1507) (Rex [Mathewe] v. Carpenter; on a debt of £0.59; jury says not guilty [law disputed as protest only]); KB27/985, m. 9d (1507) (Rex [Ap Richard] v. Vycars; on a debt of £0.45; jury says not guilty [law disputed as protest only]); KB27/987, m. 9 before jp (1508) (Damport v. Spycer; on a debt/perjury by administrator on oath over performance bond for £0.67: quashed on lack of specificity of day); KB27/994, m. 3 Rex (1510) (Bayne v. Marten [the judge]; on a debt of £0.65 owed as marriage fine for his serf daughter owed to abbess of Wilton).

very good. Most cases brought before the justices of the peace did not receive subsequent consideration in king's bench. John Gurney was indicted in 1486 for being a Lollard and meeting in heretical conventicles; in one of those meetings the prior of Latton supposedly baptized his own illegitimate child. King's bench quashed the indictment because it related to heresy.[75] In 1489, the 1480 indictment of a London housewife for maintaining a brothel that catered to both the laity and the clergy came before the king's court.[76] After 1495, activity before the justices of the peace might have increased because of the statute that empowered the justices of the peace to enforce old but unrepealed statutes simply by information presented to them; that statute, in any case, could be cited as support in premunire.[77] Further indictments followed, a few showing up finally in king's bench: Peter Tovet of Westminster indicted in 1500 and then outlawed for operating a brothel;[78] Margery Grene of Hendon indicted in 1500 for being a common prostitute along with Gilbert Androson, a cleric, for keeping her;[79] and John Myles and his wife Margaret indicted in 1501 for keeping a common brothel in Westminster.[80] The king's council led by Wolsey examined Thomas Leek for adultery with his nephew's wife and had him imprisoned in 1518 until he was pardoned finally in 1521.[81] The justices of the peace in Truro, Cornwall, in 1527 took an indictment of John Rychard, a rector, for having sex with a parishioner, citing church law: "whereas by divine law and ecclesiastical constitution it has been decreed and ordained that it is not allowed to any priest being curate of any parish to know carnally his spiritual daughter under penalty of

75. KB27/899, m. 5 Rex.

76. KB27/913, m. 4 Rex.

77. Statute 11 Henry VII, c. 3 (An Acte agaynst unlawfull Assemblyes and other offences contrary to former Statutes); KB27/975, m. 13 Rex: "henceforward both justices of assize in full session before themselves or any of them and justices of the peace in each county of the realm of England on information made for the lord king before them shall have full power and authority by their discretion to hear and determine all offences and contempts made and perpetrated by any person or persons against the form, order, and effect of any statute made and not repealed and that the same justices on the same information shall have full power and authority to award and make similar process against such trespassers and offenders and each of them as they should or might make against such person or persons who are presented or indicted before them concerning trespasses done against the lord king's peace. . . ." See also KB27/981, m. 6 Rex.

78. KB27/973, m. 2 Rex: outlawry quashed in king's bench for lack of certitude of place.

79. KB27/958, m. 4d Rex: quashed for lack of certitude of place.

80. KB27/976, m. 5 Rex: quashed for lack of certitude of place.

81. KB27/1029, m. 2d Rex.

privation both of his order and of his benefice."[82] How much sexual regulation was going on before the justices of the peace is unknown, but certainly some justices of the peace were becoming aggressive not only with prostitutes but also with lay and ecclesiastical males engaging in forbidden sexual conduct. At least in the earlier cases, however, king's bench seemed quite ready to quash the indictments as insufficiently precise.

King's bench probably preferred to see sexual regulation proceed not by indictment but by more expeditious process, although likewise before the justices of the peace. In 1507 Lawrence Corby sued John Alsoppe in the common pleas for assault and false imprisonment. Alsoppe justified his conduct by citing an immemorial custom, which, like some other "immemorial" customs,[83] might actually have been rather recent in origins:

If any priest or any other person within the liberty of the abovesaid city suspiciously frequent and use any house where women suspected of fornication or adultery reside, and if such priest or any other person thus frequenting any such suspect house is warned for the avoidance of fornication or adultery in that house by the constable of the parish in which such suspect house be sited or situated that he keep himself from that suspect house so as to avoid fornication or adultery and if, notwithstanding such a warning, he does not want to keep himself from that suspect house but afterwards frequents and uses thus that suspect house to the nuisance of the neighbors living there in enervation of the political regimen (*politice regiminis*) of that city, and if that material is notified by the constable of that parish in which the suspect house is situated to the mayor of the abovesaid city for the time being, the mayor of the same city for the time being according to the abovesaid custom used from the time abovesaid orally or by any precept in writing could legitimately and can and is used to order the said constable of such a parish in which such a suspect house is situated to arrest by his body such priest or any other person thus using such a house suspect of fornication or adultery to be conveyed to any prison within the liberty of the abovesaid city safely by the same constable and there to remain in prison according to the discretion of the mayor of the abovesaid city for the time being until he find sufficient security for bail for his good conduct.[84]

82. KB27/1067, m. 8d Rex.
83. Palmer, *ELABD*, 254–55, 277.
84. CP40/981, m. 316.

Such sexual regulation, summary process by oral order of the mayor followed by discretionary imprisonment, was much more rapid and effective than any church court process could possibly have been. Any resident who wanted to attack a brothel had here a much more efficient instrument. It is hard to see why people would have resorted to ecclesiastical court thereafter for sexual regulation. Indeed, the amount of church court litigation plummeted around 1500, at least in the Southeast.[85] The power of the mayor here was not likely related to London in particular, but to the mayor's standing as a justice of the peace. King's bench action that easily quashed indictments of adultery for lack of certitude of place probably showed a preference for such regulation.

In major categories of church court jurisdiction, then, king's bench after 1495 had set out to limit the kinds of cases that the church courts could handle. Nothing in this indicates doctrinal differences; the disputed matters were issues about legal power: whether the church courts should have any role in the mundane governance of the country, at least in any arena in which the common law could claim to have a similar jurisdiction. The one area in which Fyneux was less aggressive was that of tithes. Common law courts exercised significant power in regard to tithes, but declined to move aggressively against church court jurisdictions. Otherwise, the common law aggressively undermined the jurisdictions by which the church not only exerted but also continually reinforced its role in the world.

Church Wardens

In an even more focused way, the common law served the parish. Because the church wardens were lay people dealing with goods central to the maintenance of the parish church and parish life, they relied almost completely on common law for their dealings. Church wardens not only were lay in fact, but also used the common law precisely like other laymen in dealing with the goods in their charge. In this arena, absolutely central to the parish, the king through his courts was responsible for the mechanisms that ensured the well-being of the parish as a religious community.

Church wardens, in charge of parish ecclesiastical goods, relied on the king's criminal law to protect the various goods of the church. The church wardens of Launceston St. Stephens, Cornwall, thus kept six gilded silver chalices, a gilded

---

85. Haigh, *English Reformations*, 74–75.

silver pix to hold the eucharist, a large pix for carrying the eucharist, a gilded silver container for carrying saints' relics, a silver staff, two gilded silver candelabras, a silver belt, a silver pix, two gilded silver cruets, and two gilded silver censors, all of which was allegedly worth £200. A thief made off with the parish's treasure in 1487. While this was matter for the king's justices, the person indicted was acquitted.[86] The church wardens of Warfield, Berkshire, brought an appeal—a private prosecution of felony—against Richard Wattyngton, yeoman, in 1499 for theft of a gilded silver chalice worth £2.33 and £5 in money.[87] The criminal law protected sacred vessels and church property as well as land and money.

Similarly, church wardens used the common law to recover parish goods or recover for damages done to the parish. In 1469 the church warden of Leighton Buzzard All Saints sued a chaplain for taking a cloak, two blankets, a pair of altar cloths, a corporal, a tapestry, a canopy, three curtains of bolting cloth, six pairs of metal bells, two brass pots, two brass bowls, twelve tin dishes, six tin saucers, a breviary, two surplices, a monk's worsted cowl, and a kirtle, all of which belonged to the parishioners and had been in the warden's custody.[88] The church wardens of London St. Mary Bothaw sued the prioress of Bishopsgate in 1496 for taking and breaking the seal of a charter binding the priory to pay the parish an annual rent of £7.33.[89] Resort to the king's court seems to have been almost reflexive when the parish suffered an injury.

Church wardens could also serve a role in endowments; in that role, one way or another, they became involved in the king's court.[90] The founder of the chantry at the Blessed Mary's altar in the parish of St. Magnus, London, had relied on the church wardens. The rector of the parish had primary responsibility for naming the endowment chaplain, but if he defaulted for a fortnight, then the church wardens or two of the wealthier parishioners would name a chaplain to assume the chantry duties. The arrangement ended up in litigation in the king's court in 1486.[91] The church wardens of Waldron, Sussex, in 1513 claimed to have an endowment consisting of the proceeds of ten acres of meadow to be used for anniversary celebrations of the death of Richard Heggingworth. Each of the church wardens was to receive £0.05 for the work in

86. CP40/906, m. 482d; CP40/912, m. 323.
87. KB27/953, m. 70 (Richard Hawre and Robert Martyn).
88. CP40/833, m. 233d (church warden: John Billington).
89. KB27/939, m. 32 (church wardens: George Bulstrode and Henry Axstell).
90. For other endowment arrangements, see Thomson, *Early Tudor Church*, 183–84.
91. CP40/898, m. 155d.

performing the anniversary, with the residue put in the treasury of the church.[92] The legal capacity of the church wardens allowed the parish as such to receive gifts and manage property.

Church wardens became involved in building and repair projects of the parish. In 1410 the church wardens of Honiton, Devon, sued John Broun because Broun had negligently cast a bell for the parish; he maintained that he had only undertaken to repair, not to make the bell anew.[93] The church wardens of Tamworth, Staffordshire, contracted with Thomas Middelmore for the building of a chapel of the Blessed Mary. When Middelmore did not build the chapel within the time period, the four wardens sued him for damages of £20.[94] The church wardens of Norbury, Staffordshire, sued a Nottingham bellfounder on a performance bond that had been made on 1 May 1501 by one of them and another warden and the whole parish for the exchange of bells.[95] When the church wardens of Wittersham, Kent, sued three London bellfounders in 1530, they were most likely suing for the penalty amount of £40 on a performance bond for making bells for the parish.[96] Particularly for bells but also for building and the maintenance of the parish church beyond the chancel, the church wardens entered into arrangements based on the common law.

The money management of church wardens included taking an accounting from debtors to the parish. In 1511 the church wardens of an Exeter parish took the accounting of John Lympeney and thus were able to sue him for a debt of £12 owed to the parishioners.[97] The church wardens of Gunton, Suffolk, sued John Higham for an accounting for his time as farmer of the parish, a messuage and twenty acres in Oulton, Suffolk, during which time they thought he had received £20 belonging to the parish; he claimed that the £20 was his own.[98] The church wardens of Westwell, Kent, sued a yeoman in 1512 for £4.[99] In 1503 the church wardens of Mattishall, Norfolk, sued Simon Harliston of Mattishall, a wool trader, to account for various payments he had received for the

92. CP40/1004, m. 456.

93. CP40/599, m. 334d (church wardens: Walter Jambe, John Lyve, and John Tose).

94. CP40/970, m. 585 (church wardens: John Ferrers, knight; Richard Breton, Nicholas Bishop, and John Fraunces).

95. CP40/970, m. 157d (church wardens: Humphrey Jurden, gentleman, and Thomas Tayllour).

96. CP40/1067, m. 13 (William Hemmon and James Cook).

97. CP40/997, m. 138.

98. CP40/1006, m. 487.

99. CP40/1000, m. 27.

parish totaling about £10.[100] Church wardens used the common law to enforce parish claims.

Since church wardens handled the goods of the parish, they could also be sued. In 1508 the administrator of Richard Monyngton, a citizen of London, sued Richard Milard, who in 1488 had been a church warden of London St. Gregory's, for £2 by sealed bill and for a little more than £1.33 for a debt after an accounting.[101] In 1512 William Shalcros, a chaplain, sued two different sets of church wardens of Chelmorton, Derbyshire: one set for £3.67, the other for £3.33.[102] John Thursteyn, a citizen of London, sued John Clement of Leicester and John Chamberleyn of Leicester, the church wardens of Leicester St. Martin's, together with the bailiff of Leicester for £40 of a £45 debt in 1505.[103] Richard Marche, church warden of Tarring, Sussex, found himself defendant in a case of debt for £12, to which he had committed himself as church warden in 1500.[104] The legal capacity of the church wardens allowed the parish to borrow money to fulfil its obligations.

More complicated still, but thus also more relevant to the king's court, were the powers of an executor of a church warden. The church of London St. Mary Bothaw had two church wardens. One died, leaving George Bulstrode the sole church warden. In 1496 the prioress of Bishopsgate entered into a performance bond with the warden and the rector of the parish. The bond was for £333, the payment of which would be forgiven if the prioress stood to an arbitration to be made by two serjeants at law, with Fyneux, CJKB, as umpire. Then the warden died intestate. Two different people claimed to be administrator of his estate, each claiming to have been appointed by a different dean of the court of Arches. The first administrator had remitted the prioress's debts to the warden for pious uses and for his salvation; the second administrator sued for the penalty of £333. The first administrator's remission of the debt was binding, as the court determined, if he had actually been granted the administration of the estate.[105] In

---

100. CP40/966, m. 103d (church wardens: Robert Foster, Andrew Dean, and Geoffrey Dean, jr.).

101. CP40/986, m. 534d.

102. CP40/998, m. 267.

103. CP40/974, m. 411.

104. CP40/962, m. 349d.

105. CP40/998, m. 526 (the two administrators of George Bulstrode, the warden: John Tere, a citizen of London, appointed by Thomas Wodyngton, dean of the court of Arches, on 6 August 1509; James Ayskyrke, appointed earlier as administrator by Humfrey Hawardyn, a previous dean of the court of Arches, on 10 September 1506).

1507 the current church wardens of London St. Margaret Lothbury sued the abbot of Bury St. Edmunds, the executor of John Chetoke, who had been a warden from 1473 to 1476. As church warden along with John Water, Chetoke had been responsible for the care and administration of the goods and ornaments of the church, the payment and receipt of money, and the collection of rents from lands and tenements. In 1476 they were removed from their position and made to account before the new church wardens and two other men: the account ended with Water and Chetoke owing £3 to the parishioners. In 1507 the succeeding church wardens finally sued to collect that £3 from Chetoke's executor.[106] That the debts of the parish did not expire at the death of the church wardens was essential for the credit of the parish. That the executor of the church warden instead of the successor church wardens handled the affairs of deceased church wardens was necessary for liabilities incurred, but problematic for enforcement of parish rights under performance bonds.

Church wardens thus relied heavily on the common law for the performance of their parish duties and were also liable at common law for their dealings on behalf of the parish. The buying of bells, the collection of dues and debts, the recovery of detained property, contracting for repairs of the church nave, and holding people to their obligations were the day-to-day responsibilities of the church wardens. In these matters the wardens and their parish used the common law. Occasionally, every few years or perhaps less frequently, the church wardens would be called upon at a church visitation to report deficiencies in church discipline and the morals of the parish. That duty remained independent of the common law. That duty is the function of the church warden that appears best in church court records, but individual church wardens could easily serve their whole term without responding at a visitation. Seldom would a church warden serve without getting caught up in the mundane duties and contracts, debts, and private property management governed by the common law.

The late medieval English parish was genuinely a part of its society, completely involved in the common law and royal adjudication. At the highest level, of course, in the fifteenth century, the king assumed the responsibility of burning those adjudged by the church to be heretics and also took action to suppress heretical teachings. At the more important mundane level, however, parish matters as varied as tithes, mortuaries, and glebe lands, as well as annual rents, compromises, and parish customs, were regular matters for the king's

106. CP40/982, m. 547d (church wardens: William Wylford and Robert Wellys).

court. Ecclesiastical matters—protection of church property, church wardens and their doings, and the handling of tithes and parishes—appeared more often around 1500 than in the reign of Richard II and demonstrated not a proliferation of church goods, but a maturation of legal procedures in the king's court. Some of the legal procedures were already well developed in the late fourteenth century; a few were new in the late fifteenth century. In some ways that greater visibility under the Tudors is surprising, since rectors, vicars, and chaplains actually litigated proportionately somewhat less at common law than they had around 1400. Nevertheless, the degree of integration of ecclesiastical life into the commercial and legal life of England—already substantial by the reign of Richard II—had increased markedly during the fifteenth century. By the early sixteenth century, common law adjudication of disputes was integral to the functioning of ecclesiastical life, even at the parish level.

A wide variety of ecclesiastical matters thus could and did come before the king's court. The royal procedures were simply more expeditious and offered, even for ecclesiastics, a better likelihood of achieving their immediate needs. The crown certainly wanted—and particularly through its increasing recourse to premunire got—an increased role in church matters, but individual ecclesiastics, not "the church," advanced that agenda regularly, simply by making use of royal procedures. Clerics were, after all, people; and they lived in a world not neatly divided into secular and religious arenas. The church occasionally tried to limit the king's court, but the individuals who made up the English church found the royal government all too tempting as a means to achieve their own ends. Individual interests of clerics thus increased royal power over the church at the same time that the clerical order fought for its independent jurisdiction and governance. When Henry VIII became supreme head of the English church, he assumed the headship of a church that his predecessors had long managed thoroughly, but in a far less assertive fashion; his father's courts had already begun undermining the church court jurisdictions that had secured the church's claim to governance in the mundane world of the parish.

CHAPTER FOUR

Parish Leases: The Practice

From the late fourteenth century to the early sixteenth century, the English parish itself became a commodity. In retrospect the commercialization of the parish may seem inevitable, given its centrality in the collection and disposition of agrarian surplus and the increasing involvement of royal justice in parish matters. That result, however, was not a foregone conclusion. In the thirteenth century the church had taken steps to prevent parishes from being leased out to laymen: such lay control of the activities of the parish seemed inappropriate. Still, even then rectors were not required absolutely to be resident: rectors could appropriately attend university, be the abbot or prior of a monastery, the bishop, a diocesan or royal official, or merely a licensed pluralist. By the late fourteenth century, rectors and even perpetual vicars were often, perhaps normally, not resident. The typical rector increasingly leased the entire parish to tenants, without regard to whether the new tenants were lay or clerical. The rector or vicar thus received only the stipulated rent and retained no substantial contact with his parish. The severance of rector from involvement with the parish enabled rectors and perpetual vicars to become essentially a class of absentee landlords. For common people the result must have been greater difficulty in seeing the relationship between the heavy economic burdens put on them in the name of religion and the provision of their ecclesiastical services. The parish itself, along with all its religious duties and profits, became an item of commerce protected at common law, with its value the agricultural surplus extracted from the whole population, aristocracy to laborers.

Parish Management before the Black Death

Rectors needed people to manage the parish even before the Black Death, but they usually retained control of parish operations. Particularly when the rector was absentee or when the parish involved substantial holdings, the rector in person often could not manage the assets generated by the parish. The normal rector was not primarily skilled at agricultural management or fiscal arrangements; or, if the occasional rector was, he rapidly became absentee to work in the bishop's or king's administration. Rectors hired a bailiff as a specialized estate manager, as did lords of manors. The bailiff of a rectory had care of the physical properties of the parish pertaining to the rector. Bailiffs, unlike lessees, were simply agents. They received payment from the rector, while the rector received the benefits of good management or a good harvest, as well as the detriment of bad weather or poor management. Thus, with a bailiff, the rector retained direct responsibility for the provision of ecclesiastical services to the parish, although the rector himself need not have been and often was not in fact the ecclesiastic who performed those services. Before the Black Death, then, provision of services still retained some clear and direct relationship to the economic assets generated by the parish, although the rector was often not in a close, participatory relationship with the parishioners.

Rectors and vicars before the Black Death hired bailiffs to manage their parish much more frequently than they did in the late fourteenth century or thereafter. An indication of this difference is the different rates at which rectors and vicars sued bailiffs of their own parish to make them render an account of their management. In a normal Michaelmas term prior to the Black Death, more than thirty rectors or vicars would sue a bailiff to render account for his management of the rectory. In the Michaelmas terms of 1328, 1338, and 1345, for instance, there were respectively thirty-three, thirty-six, and thirty-six cases. The plague thereafter reduced the population of England by about 40 percent, and thus there were inevitably somewhat fewer parishes, although there was more litigation per person: government had become more comprehensive and worked through provision of legal remedies. Had management of the parish remained the same, litigation rates against parish bailiffs would have been approximately the same. The number of parishes was nearly the same, and there were no procedural or doctrinal changes that would have altered the rates. Nevertheless, such cases of account rapidly diminished. In the 1380s they dropped to about five cases a term, only about 15 percent of what would have been expected before 1350; by the fifteenth century they seldom appeared at all.[1] Although many rectors probably managed their parish themselves and the leasing of parishes was not unknown,[2] the pre–Black Death style of parish management

1. Figure 1.

2. CP40/344, m. 615: a covenant action in which Richard de la Poule tried to enforce his lease of the church of Hambury, Worcestershire, and all its fruits and revenues for a term of years. There was also some concern about lessees disguised as bailiffs.

thus seems to have been through a bailiff, an agent directly accountable to the parson.

A rector's bailiff had responsibility for the whole range of the rectory assets. The traditional duties of a bailiff would have indicated broad authority; fourteenth-century cases specify that expected range of responsibility. The vicar of Stoke was allegedly the bailiff of the rector of Chew, Somerset, from 1339 to 1343 and had the care and administration of the rectory; his responsibilities extended to the oxen, cows, horses, sheep, pigs, and grains (wheat, barley, hay, beans, and peas) and also to the oblations, revenues, mortuaries, and greater and lesser tithes. Those profits amounted to £600.[3] In 1345 the bailiff of the rectory of Wainfleet St. Mary, Lincolnshire, had care of all matters and goods in the rectory, both animals and crops, to the value of £66.67 annually, and during the four and a half years of service had taken a further £100 in offerings, dues, and small tithes.[4] In 1366 John Solers, the parson of Hildersham, Cambridgeshire, sued John de Abyton as his bailiff and receiver of money in the year 1365–66, having "the care and administration of all goods being in the said rectory, to wit, of horses, oxen, cows, sheep, carts, and plows, wheat, barley, and dredge." He also sued Abyton for a debt of £2 incurred by the purchase of six quarters of wheat.[5] In the same year Matthew de Ashton, the parson of Shillington, Bedfordshire, described John de Kirkeby, cleric, as his bailiff of that rectory in 1360–61. The bailiff had care of "horses, oxen, draft animals, cows, sheep, pigs, geese, capons, roosters, and hens, wheat, barley, rye, beans, peas, and oats, whether from large or small tithes, oblations, profits, mortuaries, heriets, and all other things looking to or proceeding from that rectory or church" as well as other goods worth £500 detailed in an indenture and various sums of money received totaling £13.50. Conceivably, the bailiff, as a cleric himself, also assisted in the church services. Kirkeby argued that he had already accounted in 1362, but the jury disagreed with him.[6] In a similar way John de Mere, parson of Limington, Somerset, sued Thomas "that-was-the-parish-priest of Limington" as bailiff and receiver in 1374.[7] When John de Benyngton sued Thomas de Evesham, a chaplain, as his receiver of money, however, Evesham replied that he served Benyngton in the office of chaplain of the parish of Kilsby, Northamptonshire,

3. CP40/351, m. 320.

4. CP40/344, m. 323.

5. CP40/425, m. 460d. See CP40/522, m. 365, for a similar rendition.

6. CP40/425, m. 258d. The plaintiff here was bachelor of canon law and a clerk of the privy seal from 1349 to 1361. Emden, *A Biographical Register*, 64.

7. CP40/456, m. 174.

FIGURE I. Parish Bailiffs in Account Cases

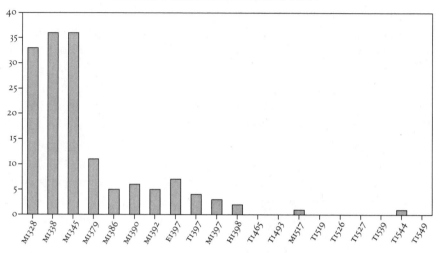

Note: This figure shows the number of cases of account in which a person described as *parson, rector,* or *vicar* of a particular parish sued a defendant in account for his time as bailiff of that same parish. Almost all of these cases were merely procedural entries. "M" indicates a Michaelmas term, the longest legal term in the year; "H," Hilary term; "E," Easter term; "T," Trinity term.

Sources: M1328: Public Record Office, *Index of Placita de Banco preserved in the Public Record Office, A.D. 1327–1328*, London, Lists and Indexes, no. xxxii, pp. 3, 4, 8, 176, 182, 186, 237, 246, 333 (2x), 338, 369, 407 (2x), 417, 425, 435 (2x), 457, 530, 545, 625 (2x), 634, 637 (831), 640, 697, 762, 767, 807 (2x), 816 (Litigation in the earlier terms of the first two years of the reign of Edward II were lower overall because of the political situation. The first three terms of 1328, nevertheless, contained 12, 20, and 15 such cases respectively. They are not included in the figure because they would provide a false reading that the practice was only beginning in the late 1320s, whereas they would really only reflect the typical course of litigation given the political situation and the recent change in government.) CP40/316, mm. 12, 35, 36, 43, 46d, 56d, 59, 59d, 79, 86, 98d (3x), 99d, 122, 139, 166d, 171, 177d, 181, 191, 219, 226, 262, 292d, 308d, 316d, 352, 354d, 357d, 367d, 384d, 387d, 394d, 461, 469. CP40/344, mm. 1d, 2d, 26 (2x), 70, 87, 97d, 101d, 106, 106d, 108 (502), 128, 139 (572), 152d, 155, 176, 230, 256, 261, 268d, 295, 323, 335, 349d, 443d, 449, 455d, 463d, 516, 571d, 579, 584, 617d, 621d, 628, 631d. CP40/476, mm. 14 (2x), 79, 211, 212d, 246d, 248, 334d, 413, 527d, 558d. CP40/503, mm. 9, 81d, 143, 181d, 293d. CP40/519, mm. 68d, 121d, 179, 200, 206d, 537. CP40/522, mm. 172, 173, 324, 365, 529. CP40/545, mm. 20, 65, 207, 333, 346d, 462, 491d. CP40/546, mm. 20d (34d), 77, 178d, 261d. CP40/547, mm. 65, 495, 540d. CP40/548, mm. 154, 262. CP40/816; CP40/925; CP40/1018, m. 144; CP40/1025; CP40/1051; CP40/1055; CP40/1102, m. 372; CP40/1122; CP40/1141.

and had received either directly from Benyngton or indirectly through Robert Moulton and William Boltesham a total of £2.33 as part of his salary as chaplain, not as a receiver of money.[8] Arrangements among rector, chaplain, bailiff, and financial agents might not always have been clearly defined, but generally the rectory bailiff managed the whole rectory.

8. CP40/456, m. 571.

The rector who hired a bailiff thus maintained some continuing relationship with his parish. Having a bailiff certainly left the rector or vicar capable of departing for lengthy periods of time. The bailiff cared for the business management of the parish; the rector or bailiff could hire a chaplain to provide the religious services. For some parsons, absence would have been normal and, in the context of the times, laudable. Still, the rector-bailiff relationship was such as to retain ongoing control in the hands of the rector: a bailiff had no security in his position and worked only as the agent for the rector, without secure rights to his position and certainly not as a representative of the parish community. Admittedly, at least a couple of the parish bailiffs discovered in the rolls might have been from the parish priest's own parish and a few more were from neighboring parishes. Such bailiffs would indeed have known local customs. Nevertheless, a reasonable number of bailiffs also were from different counties, and none of the rectors in this group received his own name from his parish. When both priest and bailiff did not derive from the locale, the potential of a clash of local custom was a real possibility. The bailiff accounted to the rector, not to the community. The rector could terminate or continue his employment or recommend him to others. Whether the rector was resident or absentee, he was as much (or as little) in control of the parish as the manorial lord was in control of the manor. Indeed, the situation and problems of both lord and rector would seem similar.

While some rectors leased out their parishes before the Black Death, the church seems to have retained control over the practice. Most rectors either hired a bailiff during an absence or were resident rectors with or without a bailiff. The frequency with which bailiffs of rectories appeared in common law records would indicate that it was relatively typical for a rector to hire a bailiff. Still, even in hiring a bailiff, an absentee rector retained a direct relationship to the parish. He still stood to gain or lose immediately by the efficiency of the management; and the benefits of good management accrued to the rector himself, not to the bailiff or to the community. As long as the rector retained real control over management of the rectory, parish resources and religious duties still could seem reasonably related to the provision of religious services.

Parish Management after the Black Death

After the Black Death and leading up to the English Reformation, leases became an increasingly prominent form of property management, and managing the parish by leasehold rapidly replaced management by bailiff. As already illustrated in the second chapter, some parsons even on the eve of the Reformation were quite content still merely to lease out various sources of revenue, prominently the tithes, perhaps the glebe. Nevertheless, in the late fourteenth century it was not unusual for a parson to find a lessee for the whole of the parish; by 1500 it was normal. Some part of the growth of this form of parish management merely adopted the general practice of society. The possibility of leasing parishes, however, had long been tempting, but had been limited by the church. The actual growth of the practice thus probably arose from the willingness of the common law to enforce the terms of the lease effectively despite the strictures of canon law. Such leases separated the rector from most real participation in the parish, could sever the obvious relationship between the parish's resources and well-being on the one hand and the parish rector on the other, could make it seem that certain lay persons instead of the rector actually controlled the parish. Certainly, the practice of letting out the parish at least gained credibility from the willingness of the king's court to enforce the terms of the lease. As a result of both legal and social developments, therefore, parishes in fact came to constitute the bulk of valuable leaseholds, were prime objects for entrepreneurial capital, and were precious opportunities for ambitious people to invest in prime business ventures and thereby to better themselves.

LEASING FORMS

The form in which rectors leased out their parish was typical for leasehold arrangements: some involved highly formal sets of documents; others were informal without any apparent documentation. The informal leases probably were relatively stereotyped: a grant of a parish and all the relevant rights. Formal instruments would have been particularly necessary for the implementation of specially tailored arrangements, although they would also have provided much greater security even for the uncomplicated lease.

The formal, documented leasehold transaction used typical common law instruments. The primary document was an obligatory deed in the form of a performance bond. That document could contain all the provisions in an endorsed condition or refer to a separate set of indentures that laid out the terms of the lease. The terms of the lease were formal and thus similar in different documents, but clearly adjusted to the individual situation. The terms in which lessors and lessees negotiated their own acceptable deal went far beyond the duration of the lease and the rent and into issues of responsibility for taxation and obits, repair of the church chancel and rectory buildings, reservation of accommodation rights in the rectory, the hiring of a chaplain to perform the services, the allocation of the rectory revenue deriving from tithes, mortuaries, church offerings, and glebe lands. The variations in form demonstrate that the leases represent actual negotiations of complete churches in a lively market for completely commercialized parishes. Three leasehold instruments will show the ordinary range of parish leasehold instruments.

The lease of Preston parish in Yorkshire in 1366 left a fairly complete record. The primary document was the lessee's bond that recognized a debt to the rector for £200. The endorsement on the bond provided that, if the debtor paid £100 annually for five years for the church of Preston as described in an accompanying indenture, the £200 indenture would be null and void. The accompanying indenture, in this case, found its way into the plea roll entry. The lessees were two laymen and a chaplain, so that in this situation as with many parish leases, the undertaking was one involving a partnership of some kind. The contribution of the partners was never specified. When a chaplain was a partner, he could have been contributing only his religious services (amounting thus to a £6 investment); in some situations, however, he was clearly simply an investor. A layman in the group could have been the business manager, but they all may have been absentee; the curate could have served as a receiver of money, and the lessees may only have supervised in person when the tithes were ready for collection. These indentures, like most historical documents, conceal as much as they reveal. The indenture for this lease began with the two major concerns: conveying the parish to the lessee and specifying the lessee's rent. It then detailed the particular concerns of the parties, here particular financial burdens, responsibilities for maintenance, and conditions for the surrender of the lease at the end of the term.

[Basic Lease:] This indenture made at York on 1 May [1366] attests that Sir William de Retford subdean of the cathedral church of blessed Peter of York delivered, granted, and demised at farm to Walter Frost of Kingston on Hull, Henry de Bristowe chaplain, and John de Wilflet of Preston in Holdernesse his church of Preston abovesaid with all its rights and all appurtenances to have and hold to the same Walter, Henry, and John from the day of the making of these presents until the end of the five years next following and fully completed,

[Rent:] rendering thereof each year to the said lord William £100 of legal money of England at two terms of the year in equal portions, to wit, at the feast of the Purification of Blessed Mary next following the date of these presents £50 and at the feast of Pentecost then next following £50 and thus in each year during the abovesaid term.

[Financial Burdens and Taxation:] And the abovesaid lord William will support at his own costs the burdens of the bedern of Beverley, of the obit of Roger Pepyn penitenciary of York archdeacon of the East Riding, and also the burdens of whatsoever tax of the lord pope and of the lord king that occurs in the meantime.

[Maintenance:] And the abovesaid Walter, Henry, and John at their own costs will support all other burdens and houses of the manor; and also they will support and guard the cloister of the same in laudable condition for the whole abovesaid time.

[Provisions for Concluding the Term:] Indeed the same Walter, Henry, and John at the end of the term abovesaid will surrender and leave as many acres of land sewn with whatsoever kind of grain and other demesne land pertaining to the abovesaid church as well manured or better with as much manure placed on it as they received and had at the beginning of the term of the same as more fully appears by other indentures made thereof. And if the abovesaid Walter, Henry, and John at the end of the term abovesaid leave more acres of land sewn than they received at the beginning, the abovesaid lord William wants and grants that of those costs thus spent in excess, they should be reasonably satisfied.

[Attestation:] In testimony of which matter the seals of the abovesaid parties are appended. Given on the year, day, and place abovesaid.

The dispute that arose from this lease, as was typical, concerned default in payment of the rent. The lessor maintained that there was a default in the amount of £43.33, whereas the lessee alleged proper payment made in money and in wine.[9] Although the lease undeniably concerned all manner of ecclesiastical matters, it was nonetheless a typical common law document and treated the elements of the church as ordinary property.

An equally specific set of documents recorded the terms of the lease of the church of Great Staughton in 1388. The performance bond was for £66.67, that debt to be made null and void by compliance with all the conditions contained in a separate set of indentures. The king's court enrolled the full document, this

9. CP40/505, m. 316.

time showing concerns about allocations of the revenue before the lease term began, the provision of religious services, security of the leasehold should the lessor change his position, and preservation of the timber on the holding:

[Basic Lease:] The abovesaid John Excestre granted, bailed, and demised at farm to the aforementioned John de Thorpe the parish church of Great Staughton in Huntingdonshire with the rectory of the same together with the lands, tenements, rents, services, suits of court, escheats, tithes, oblations, proceeds, income, and all its other profits and commodities and appurtenances whatsoever to have and to hold to the same Master John de Thorpe and his assigns from 24 December 1388 until the following 24 December,

[Savings of Revenue before Term:] saving that the same John Excestre would receive and have the rents and all profits proceeding from the said church pertaining to the same from the day of the date of the writing abovesaid [20 November 1388 at London in the parish of St. Gregory in the ward of Castle Baynard] until the said 24 December, on which day the same Master John Thorpe would enter his farm, and the same John Thorpe would receive and have the rents and profits proceeding from the same which ought to be paid on Christmas, to wit, at the end of his farm abovesaid,

[Rent:] for which certain farm of the same year the same John Thorpe would pay and make to be paid in part payment of the £80 to the aforementioned John Excestre or his certain attorney in advance £26.67; and on the Christmas following, £13.33; and on the feast of St. John before the Latin Gate [6 May] then next following, £20; and on Michaelmas then next following, £20, for the full payment of the abovesaid farm in the church of St. Martin Major in London.

[Provision of Religious Services:] And the abovesaid Master John Thorpe will make the aforementioned church and the parishioners of the same to be served in the divine offices, sacraments, and sacramentals well and praiseworthily during the abovesaid term and

[Taxes and Repair:] will undergo and support all other burdens both ordinary and extraordinary incumbent on or supervening to the same church with its appurtenances for the whole abovesaid time at his own cost and expense with the repairs of the chancel and houses of the same rectory only excepted;

[Change of Landlord:] and if it happen that the aforementioned John

Excestre within the abovesaid year exchange his aforementioned church with any other ecclesiastical benefice, or leave it simply or in any other way whatsoever, or retain it with himself, then the same John Excestre will warrant his farm of such kind to the aforementioned John Thorpe or his assigns for the abovesaid year wholly to be completed;

[Waste:] and that the abovesaid John Thorpe will neither sell nor alienate timber pertaining to the abovesaid church or rectory nor do waste in the same during the abovesaid term.[10]

In this case the lessee was a single ecclesiastic, not a group. The lease thus would have occasioned little problem even under traditional prescriptions as long as the rector obtained a license from the bishop. This lease was just as businesslike as the 1366 lease, although with varied allocations of benefits and burdens, and with an unusual payment at the beginning of the lease.

The instruments for leasing parishes had not changed significantly even by the early sixteenth century. A 1513 case recited not the separate indenture (although there was a separate indenture), but rather the terms of the transaction: the terms were somewhat more extensive, but basically similar to the late fourteenth-century indentures above. The record recited that Robert Norbourne had leased to William Marchall, a cleric, and Richard Upton

[Basic Lease:] his whole vicary of Appledore abovesaid with the manse of the same vicary with all lands, tithes, offerings, mortuaries, and all other dues and profits in any way looking to the same vicary to have and to hold to the same William and Richard, their executors and assigns from the feast of St. Michael the Archangel next following after the date of the same indenture until the end of a term of four years then next following and fully completed,

[Rent:] by rendering therefrom annually during the term of four years next following the feast of St. Andrew the Apostle next after the date of that indenture to the aforementioned Robert £10 of legal money of England at the feast of Easter and of St. Andrew the Apostle by equal portions, the first payment thereof beginning at the Easter next after the making of the abovesaid indenture,

[Provision of Religious Services:] and the abovesaid William and Richard by the same indenture covenanted and granted that they, their executors, and assigns would find an honest and able priest to guard the cure there

10. CP40/518, m. 101.

and similarly would find the bread, wine, and wax for the altar service there at their own cost and burden during the abovesaid term,

[Local Assessments:] and also the abovesaid William and Richard would pay all scots from all the marshlands looking to the abovesaid vicary which should accrue during the abovesaid term of four years;

[Visitations:] the abovesaid William and Richard as well would pay annually during the abovesaid term £0.10 for the meal of the official at visitation;

[Royal Taxes:] and if it should happen that any tenth or tenths be granted within the abovesaid term, the abovesaid William and Richard would pay for a one-tenth of the same tenths £0.33 at their own costs and burdens;

[Other Burdens:] and the abovesaid Robert by the same indenture covenanted and granted to pay all other burdens of the said rectory which should accrue or happen to be during the abovesaid term both ordinary and extraordinary burdens at their own burdens and expense;

[Warranty of Tithes:] the abovesaid Robert in particular by the same indenture covenanted and agreed to warrant to the abovesaid William and Richard all the tithes looking to the abovesaid vicary according to the custom of the Marshland and other places during the abovesaid term, providing always by the same indenture that if it should happen that the abovesaid William and Richard, their executors, or assigns be prosecuted in a suit with another person or some persons for the recovery of any tithes from lands lying and being within the parish of Appledore above-said, then the said Robert would justify and maintain at all times the action and suit toward whatsoever person or persons who retain or sub-tract any tithes or other dues pertaining to the said vicary and also pay half the expenses, costs, and reasonable burdens made on the same suit;

[Change of Landlord:] and also the abovesaid Robert by the same indenture covenanted and granted that if it should happen that the same Robert resign or exchange the abovesaid vicary within the abovesaid term of four years, then he in his resignation or exchange would reserve that the abovesaid William and Richard would hold, enjoy, and guard peacefully the said vicary in mode and form during the term of four years as is contained more fully in that indenture.

The lessees in the case based on this lease pleaded performance specially: payment of the £35 over three and a half years and offer of the remainder at the date due; the hiring of Richard Upton (one of the lessees) as the good and able priest, who served for three years but was prevented by the lessor in the fourth year; the finding of bread, wine, and wax; the payment of twenty-four scots for the twenty-four acres of marshland that amounted to almost £1.25 paid to the bailiff of Romney Marsh; payment of £0.10 to the official of the archbishop of Canterbury at visitation for his meals; and payment of the tenth granted at Convocation on 21 January 1512 that amounted to £0.33 paid to the collector. The lessor joined issue on whether the lessees had found a good and able priest for the fourth year of the lease, and thus sued to collect on a performance bond of £20.[11]

The extended lease forms tended to concern lessees at least partly ecclesiastical, as in the three retailed above; lay lessees, however, received the whole parish just as did the ecclesiastics. The nonmonastic rector of Nutfield, Surrey, leased to two laymen "his church of Nutfield in Surrey together with the rectory of the same, to have to the same Roger and Robert with all its rights and appurtenances."[12] The lay lessee of East Luccumbe, Somerset, hired the parish priest.[13] Similarly, the yeoman lessee of the nonappropriated parish of Clifton Campville, Staffordshire, received the rectory together with all and singular rights pertaining to the rectory or looking to it, together with the site of the rectory with houses, messuages, lands, tenements, tithes, fruits, oblations, mortuaries, and all other casual profits in any way looking to the rectory.[14] The gentleman lessee of Elm parish received the rectory with all and singular tithes, oblations, and other profits pertaining to the rectory.[15] The Bristol merchant who leased the vicary of St. Nicholas, Bristol, received the vicary with all profits, commodities, tithes, fruits, oblations, dues, and advantages that look to the church.[16] Most of the shorter descriptions are roughly that explicit, but when the rest merely refer to the demise at farm of the rectory or the vicary, they seem to refer to a demise of the parish as a whole.

A few explicit instances affirm that the briefer leases just of a rectory actually concerned at least most of the rectory complex. In 1410 one plea roll entry

---

11. CP40/1004, m. 521. The dispute about the adequacy of the priest could have been related to a visitation, which also cost the lessees. The visitation may have found Upton inadequate and put pressure thus on the lessor. This dynamic is somewhat more plausible than the absentee lessee retaining continuing supervision.

12. CP40/501, m. 303.

13. CP40/545, m. 114d.

14. CP40/1005b, m. 317.

15. CP40/982, m. 408d; CP40/986, m. 431d.

16. CP40/1093, m. 197.

specified that the rector leased out "his rectory of Linfield with all profits and commodities looking to the same rectory."[17] Later in the same plea roll, however, a companion case for the same transaction went on to fill out the description: "all houses, arable lands, and pastures pertaining to the said rectory [of Linfield] and also all manner tithes of grain, hay, and fruits pertaining to the same rectory as well as half of the mortuaries except and retaining to the same Henry the chapel, watermill, offerings, woods, and other emoluments looking to the same rectory."[18] Either "emoluments" had a very specific meaning, or else the generality of "rectory" was broad but imprecise, indicating that the particular case did not need that kind of precision. Later on, in 1493, a yearbook note indicates that "by a lease of a parsonage everything which constitutes the parsonage passes without a deed."[19] Perhaps the same case, but contained in the reports ascribed to 1506, has John Fyneux repeating that sentiment: when a "rectory" was leased without a deed, the word "rectory" carried with it the church, the cemetery, and the tithes.[20] The briefer descriptions in the leases thus might disguise exceptions and reservations, but included the vital matter of a parish lease.

The three longer leasehold documents related above accurately reflect a continuity in practice over about 150 years, certainly long enough for parish leasing to have become an integral part of the socioeconomic fabric of late medieval England. During that time rectors and perpetual vicars leased out parishes and treated them as an organized business endeavor that included the religious services and obligations. That practice was the mercenary conduct that Chaucer found objectionable.[21] When the parson thus received only a fixed return from the parish, he had essentially severed himself from involvement with the parish: the incumbent had become, in Chaucer's words, a mercenary instead of a shepherd who lived with and cared for his flock.

LEASE DURATION

While the duration of a lease depended both on individual conditions and on corporate status, it carried implications about responsibility and the maintenance of the parish complex. Fourteenth-century leases of any kind normally

17. CP40/599, m. 428.
18. CP40/599, m. 575.
19. *Reports of Cases by John Caryll*, ed. Baker, 1:196.
20. YB Easter 21 Henry VII, fo. 21, no. 11.
21. See Chapter 4 at n. 90.

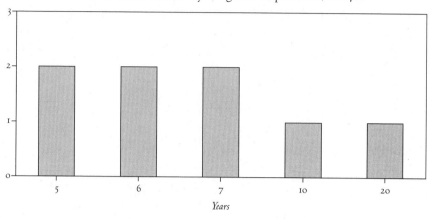

FIGURE 2. Leases Granted by Religious Corporations, ca. 1400

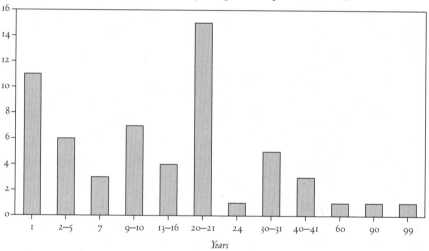

FIGURE 3. Leases Granted by Religious Corporations, ca. 1500

were for only a short term. Increasingly with religious houses, however, leases grew to last for decades. Repetitive short-term leases would not have helped much to relate dues to services in the view of the parishioners; but the rector who leased only at short terms would at least have a regular occasion to renegotiate terms, sue a negligent lessee for neglect of the premises, or upgrade the premises to attract a better lessee or a higher rent. A lease expected to endure for decades carried with it a strong potential for religious obligations to become severed completely from religious needs and thus to seem merely financial exactions.

FIGURE 4. Parish Leases Made by Noncorporate Clerics, ca. 1400

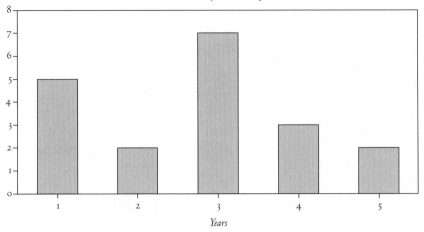

FIGURE 5. Parish Leases Made by Noncorporate Clerics, ca. 1500

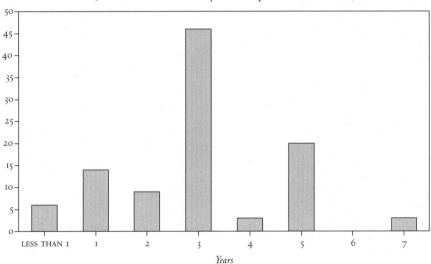

The duration of a parish lease depended primarily on the situation of the lessor. When the head of a religious house was the lessor of a parish, he or she could let the parish out at a longer term. A nonmonastic rector might die or exchange parishes, but a parish appropriated to a monastery was stable. Nevertheless, around 1400, based only on eight such leases that included the duration of the term, the terms ranged mainly from five to ten years.[22] The average

22. Figure 2.

term for such corporate rectors was more than twice as long as the ordinary parish lease. By the late fifteenth and early sixteenth century, however, monasteries had begun leasing out parishes for lengthy terms. Figure 4, based only on scattered terms, shows a concentration on both short and midterm leases, with the very long-term lease for forty years or more not being unusual.[23] The leasing practice of religious houses tended toward longer leases.

The ordinary lease by rector or vicar, however, was generally for a very limited term. From eighteen parish leases around 1400, it seems that 75 percent were for three years or less, with the remainder for not more than five years.[24] From 101 such parish leases around 1500, the pattern was only marginally different: slightly less than 75 percent were for terms of three years or less, and only three leases made for seven years exceeded a term of five years.[25] Rectors and vicars leased out their parishes for much shorter periods than did religious houses. A variety of factors contributed to that difference. Parsons of parishes could easily exchange benefices or be promoted, so that shorter-term leases might have given them more flexibility. Many parsons, new to the parish, would have found more beneficial a frequent chance to adjust the rental value to the real value of the parish than would a monastery with a long history with an appropriated parish. Lessees themselves, familiar with the habits of parsons, might have preferred shorter terms. Shorter terms likewise might have provided a parson with a set point at which to review the condition of a parish complex, an occasion that a monastery, with its large body of personnel and institutional routine, would not have needed. The terms for leases not concerning parishes that appeared in the plea rolls also showed a strong tendency toward terms under five years.[26] Still, most licenses for nonresidence in bishops' registers were limited to three years. Thus, market conditions as well as episcopal supervision, but not precisely canon law, were the primary determinant of the length of the lease.[27]

23. Figure 3.

24. Figure 4.

25. Figure 5; Appendix 3.

26. Appendix 2. For the leases in 1513–14, there were eighteen at one year, a total of twenty-five at five years and less, five between six and ten years, one each at twelve, twenty, and thirty years.

27. Canon law forbade leases for more than five years. See below, Chapter 4 at n. 104. Had canon law dictated the duration of the lease, the five-year lease would have been more common. Even under Richard II, normal, nonparish leases, to the extent that they appeared in the plea rolls, more often had been for terms longer than five years. If canon law had effectively restricted the terms, leases might have clustered as close to the lay norms as possible without violating the

During the fifteenth century, lessors began to use a periodic tenancy. A periodic lease was one not made for a specific term, such as for a set number of years or for life, but one that took a form such as "for one year, and thence from year to year as long as it please both parties." The history of the periodic tenancy is still not well known.[28] In 1473 the prior of Merton sued the administrator of William Barowe, a cleric, for £6 on the lease of the rectory of Somerford Keynes. The term had been for one year and thereafter at the will of the prior. The prior then sued for the £6 that was the rent due from three years of occupation at an annual rent of £2.[29] While that lease was not yet a periodic tenancy, it was close. The periodic tenancy nonetheless did predate 1500, but seems not to have become common until after that date,[30] probably as a result of the greater security of fixed terms of years given by the king's bench change in ejectment that allowed lessees to recover their term and not just damages.[31] Lessors could avoid that greater lessee security with a periodic tenancy, a form that left the lessor with the possibility of a continuing tenant, but with the ability regularly to renegotiate the lease to increase the rent. That alteration in leasing practices would have been available only for leases made anew; those tenants who had already taken parishes at long-term leases (thus, typically, lessees from monasteries) would have had the greatest benefit of the new security. That shift in leasehold practices likewise would indicate that the lessors of parishes had a sufficiently advantageous commodity for sale that they could alter traditional contractual expectations relatively rapidly.

LESSEES

Parish leases did not take much account of the propriety of leasing parishes to lay people. The most interesting figures about lessees concern the lessees of

---

limit under canon law. None of the ordinary parish leases under Richard II was for five years. Around 1500, while twenty-six leases were for three-year terms, only eight were for five-year terms. Many of these leases violated canon law anyway since they were made to the laity. If lessors ignored the canon law in regard to leasing and lessee status, most likely they were not rigid regarding canon law specifications about leasehold duration.

28. Baker's treatment of the periodic tenancy is only a couple sentences, without chronology, within the short section on the tenancy at will. Baker, *IELH*, 347. The subject is not one that has generated much interest yet.

29. CP40/846, m. 152d.

30. Appendix 2.

31. Baker, *IELH*, 340.

noncorporate rectors, vicars, and prebendaries. Corporate rectors could easily lease to lay people who would not be expected to have any direct managerial influence on the parishioners, because corporate rectors usually were accompanied by perpetual vicars. It is more significant, therefore, that around 1400, noncorporate rectors often already leased to lay people. The earliest lease found was made in 1370 concerning the parish of York St. George. Katherine de Barneby was the lessee.[32] Other sole lessees around 1400 were a chapman and four other people who seem to have been laymen. Six sole lessees were ecclesiastical people, but only two of them were chaplains, so only half the sole lessees were ecclesiastics, but from a relatively small sample. Noncorporate rectors around 1400 almost as often leased to groups. Three of such group lessees contained no clergy, and one of the groups included a citizen of London. Seven other group lessees included an ecclesiastic, five of them a chaplain.[33] The inclusion of a chaplain would make economic sense because the chaplain could participate as the parish priest. The lessee who served as a parish priest contributed his services so that the group did not have to spend perhaps £6 to hire a priest.[34] Lessors seemed more intent on finding a good lessee as such rather than putting a priority on securing a clerical lessee. The clerical proportion of lessees around 1400 might still indicate some real control by the church organizations; perhaps, however, it simply indicates the competitive advantage of clerics who did not have to hire another priest to serve the parish.

Around 1500 noncorporate lessors of parishes seemed even less inclined to give any priority to ecclesiastical lessees. Among single lessees, 65 percent were lay: a single woman, ten husbandmen, ten yeomen, four men of occupation, seventeen gentlemen, two squires, and fifteen people with status unspecified, a reasonable cross-section of society. Thirty-three ecclesiastics were sole lessees, and surprisingly only fifteen of them were chaplains. Chaplains, of course, were the ecclesiastics who could undertake a parish at a competitive advantage since they could serve as parish priest and avoid the major expense of hiring another chaplain; other clerics were supposed to be otherwise beneficed. Among group lessees, fourteen included ecclesiastics (only two of whom were chaplains), while twelve groups included no clergy. Parish leasing seems not to have been primarily a way for chaplains to secure their own parish to prove themselves

32. CP40/476, m. 254.
33. Appendix 3.
34. See Chapter 3 at n. 26.

acceptable for a benefice, but rather a fairly straightforward commercial relationship, not only around 1400 but even more so around 1500.

Clerical prohibitions of females in the priesthood did not govern parish
leases, although women were rare as lessees. In 1370 William de Ketilwell leased
the church of York St. George to Katherine de Barneby.[35] Anna, who later
became the wife of William Chapman, leased while she was unmarried the
chapel of St. Thomas the Apostle in Worcester on a one-year periodic lease in
1523.[36] John Passewater and Margaret, his wife, leased Waresley rectory in Huntingdonshire in 1525 for a term of twenty-one years. When her husband died she
became the only lessee and eventually left the term in her will.[37] In 1514 John
Daryngton and Agnes Daryngton, a widow, became joint lessees of the chapel
of St. Nicholas in the castle of Stafford.[38] At common law nothing prevented a
woman from leasing a rectory and hiring a priest: leasing a parish was simply an
ordinary transaction.

The practice of leasing the parish increased lay control, but not parishioner
control. Clearly, parish leasing could have been a simple mechanism whereby the
parish community effectively took control of the parish by becoming the lessees
of the rector and thus acquiring the right to hire their own priest. No example
of that kind of phenomenon has appeared, though, admittedly, locating the
residence of the lessee or lessees prior to the lease is difficult. Certainly some of
the lessees were local, but many seem not to have been. Nor are there even any
examples of known church wardens becoming the lessees of their own parish,
although that must have happened occasionally. The lessees were responsible
for the chancel—the church wardens and parish, for the remainder of the
church: that distinction remained very clear. From the evidence currently available, the lessees were simply investors, and not the whole parish or a group of
parishioners acting as agents for the parish community. Parish leasing thus
represented more lay control, although not more control by the parishioners
over their own church. Had the parish been the lessees, parish leasing would
have implied greater religious participation and local control. Quite the op-
posite occurred; parish leasing was a commercial phenomenon, and one that
disconnected the parishioners' duties from the provision of religious services.

35. CP40/476, m. 254.
36. CP40/1087, m. 514d.
37. CP40/1081, m. 453.
38. CP40/1084, m. 504.

THE LEASEHOLD MARKET

Parishes dominated the upper end of the leasehold market in late medieval England. Precision about the leasehold market is impossible to achieve at this point since the national market was far different from the local manorial market. I have taken the leases that appear with sufficient detail in the plea rolls for a full year in 1397–98 and again in 1513–14 as a basis for leasehold practice, with examples from other rolls. Because numbers are involved, the database might seem quantitative, but it is in fact somewhat more impressionistic. The leases that appear in the plea rolls might not be completely representative of social practice; longer studies of leasehold practices even from the plea rolls could alter the picture here. One part of the picture is clearly distorted. Even though the number of small leaseholds is larger than those at the upper end, small leaseholds were still even more frequent than large leaseholds: small leaseholds would simply be less likely to find their way into the king's court. These qualifications are significant, but conclusions made in reference to a database are better than ones based merely on anecdotes. The data thus far indicate that parishes ranked in the same range of economic properties as manors. Moreover, they increasingly dominated the high end of the leasehold market. Finally, even the poorer parishes and chapels worth relatively little could find a lessee.

The range of leaseholds in common pleas *not* concerning parishes seems to have included an increasing number of less valuable properties. The sample from 1397–98 contained sixteen nonparish leaseholds with rental details. The average rent overall was £9.70, of only those tenements renting out for £2 or more (12), £12.68.[39] The sample from 1513–14 contained almost double the number (31), but with an overall average in rent of £3.35, of only those tenements leasing out for £2 or more (17), £5.38.[40] These figures, moreover, are not inflation-adjusted. The appearance of manors in the rolls likewise declined. Manors varied greatly in value, but in 1397–98 eight tenements described as manors appeared in the rolls, but only five with rental values, which averaged £19.50 and ranged from £4.33 to £39.[41] In 1513–14, only two manors with rental values appeared in the sample, with rental values of £13 and £14.[42] A plea roll for

39. Appendix 2a. The average is somewhat more since part of one rent was to be paid in barley, which is not included in the average.

40. Appendix 2b.

41. Appendix 2a.

42. Appendix 2b.

one term in 1506, abnormally for that time, turned up as many as three healthy manorial leases: Mitton manor, Worcestershire, leased for twenty years at £20 annually; Mountnessing Hall manor, Essex, leased for seven years at £30 annually; and the manor of Milton-next-Gravesend, Kent, leased for one year at £13.33.[43] Other examples give a sense of rents around 1500. The occasional mill makes its appearance with highly variable yearly rates: a grain mill and a fulling mill in Meavy, Devon, at £1.33;[44] a watermill in Cawthorpe, Lincolnshire, at £2;[45] a watermill in Great Walsingham, Norfolk, at £2;[46] two windmills and nine selions of land in the city of York at £2.33;[47] a watermill in Thorp Arch, Yorkshire, at £10;[48] three watermills called "Castell Mylnes" by Nottingham castle at £11.50.[49] Clearly, anything renting for more than £8 in the late fourteenth century or around 1500 deserves to be considered a high-end rental tenement. Likewise, since historians consider leasehold to be a significant and growing phenomenon from the time of the Black Death forward, the numerical incidence of the leaseholds experienced in 1397–98 and certainly in 1513–14 is consonant with a significant social phenomenon.

Parish leases came to occupy the high end of the leasehold market. Regular high-end tenements, manors and such, appeared about twice as often in the plea rolls as did parishes in the late fourteenth century (ten regular tenements as against five parishes). In 1513–14, however, parishes appeared four times more frequently than did other significant tenements, even if the line for significant regular tenements is placed at a £6 rental value.[50] During 1513–14, the same period as that covered in Appendix 2, litigation in cases had proceeded far enough to reveal eighteen parish leases, fifteen of which contained the value of the rent. The average rent on those parishes was £21.95; the median was £11; the high value was £110; the low value was £4.17.[51] Parishes rented out at about the same value, with the same wide range, as did manors, but parishes at the same time seem to have constituted the overwhelming majority of the substantial

43. CP40/978, mm. 539, 456d, 428d.

44. CP40/966, m. 194d (lease made in 1499–1500).

45. CP40/974, m. 364 (lease made in 1499–1500).

46. CP40/848, m. 419d (lease made in 1466–67).

47. CP40/799, m. 155 (lease made in 1454–55).

48. CP40/799, m. 145d (lease made in 1457–58).

49. CP40/962, m. 505d (lease made in 1491–92).

50. Appendices 2, 3. I have ignored in this calculation the fact that one parish rented at £4.17; that low rental value was probably not related to the long-term value of the parish.

51. Appendix 3.

tenements on the market. Bowker calculated from tax assessments that priests in charge of parishes or dependent chapels averaged a stipend of nearly £10.50; segregating the rectors produced a figure in 1526 of more than £12.50, and a net income of a bit less than £9.50.[52] The parish leases in the plea rolls mirrored the whole range of parishes, not just the wealthier ones. Even poor rectories might attract lessees. In the early sixteenth century the free chapel of Bapchild, Kent, and the chapel of St. Nicholas in the castle of Stafford leased out respectively for £2 and £2.65.[53] A different duration of leases may have something to do with the frequent appearance of parishes, but by 1500 the court of common pleas, when it considered leases, had to think reflexively about parishes simply because of their remarkable frequency in litigation. There is thus little reason to consider the parishes that appear in court to be unusual. Dyer's assessment that put rectors economically somewhere among the lay knights, esquires, and gentlemen of late fifteenth-century England seems about right;[54] clerical claims about excessive impoverishment are difficult to accept in regard to beneficed clergy.[55] One way to relieve impoverishment, of course, would have been to reside on the benefice and perform the church services in person; a priest could thus recapture both the pay for the curate (about £6) and the lessees' profit margin.

Not all plea rolls showed the high incidence of parish leases in 1513–14. The plea roll for Trinity term 1526 revealed only one parish lease,[56] but few other leases also. A thorough survey of debt litigation in that term would serve for an estimate of how many parish lease agreements could have been under litigation that term, but not at a procedural stage that would reveal the significant details. Abbots, abbesses, priors, and prioresses brought sixty-five cases of debt. Forty of those cases claimed £8 or more, the value that would be typical of a parish

---

52. Bowker, *Secular Clergy*, 139.

53. CP40/1083, m. 435d; CP40/1084, m. 504.

54. Dyer, *Standards of Living*, 19–21.

55. Thomson seems to think that parishes yielded little surplus and that annuities and generally inadequate revenue sources produced a clerical estate that was economically in trouble. Thomson, *Early Tudor Church*, 173–87. Annuities, of course, hurt some rectors, but benefitted others; they were also usually the product of a mutually acceptable arrangement. Claims of clerical impoverishment are even less plausible because they consider only the ordinary parish revenue. From the range of economic activity apparent in prosecutions under the statutes of 1529, the parson had a range of activities that could increase his income substantially. The number of cases indicate that many parsons did so. It is not unusual for professional persons to claim impoverishment because professionals often have a very high estimate of the value of their own activity to society and the standard of living appropriate for themselves.

56. CP40/1051, m. 221.

lease, but also of several other things. None of those cases actually indicated a parish lease, and this was at a time when the *Valor Ecclesiasticus*, a survey of church wealth from 1535, indicates that religious houses typically leased out most of their parishes. At the same time, "clerics," parsons, rectors, and vicars brought 148 cases of debt, 91 of which claimed £8 or more, and only the one case actually indicated a parish lease.[57] The frequency of leasehold cases brought by ordinary rectors and vicars compares well with that of cases brought by the religious houses involved heavily in leasing out parishes; the number of debt cases that could have involved parish leases is large. Terms that showed few explicit instances of parish leasing thus do not indicate a low frequency of parish leasing.

The value of appropriated and normal parishes was similar, and both were roughly equivalent to the value of a manor: all varied within the same broad range. Although this study derives from common law records, the *Valor Ecclesiasticus* of 1535 provides an incomparable source for parish rental values and for the pervasiveness of the practice of religious houses leasing out their parishes. Although I have not analyzed that massive amount of data simply because the value of the parishes is not the focus of this study, a couple examples will suffice to give context to the common law material. The archbishop of Canterbury appears in the *Valor* with five rectories in Kent: all five were farmed out at rental values averaging a little over £30; the farm of the rectory of St. Nicholas in the Isle of Thanet was the same as the farm of the same manor: £40.[58] Fourteen rectories appropriated to the cathedral priory of Canterbury were held in diverse ways. Three the priory retained in its own hands; eleven were farmed out. Nine of the eleven averaged a rent of about £11.50, with a range from £4.33 to more than £30. The two other rectories were combined with the local manor; the two combined manors and rectories brought in rents respectively of £16 and almost £48.25. The three rectories the priory retained in its own hand were valued at more than £156; they cleared about £81 total after expenses.[59] These two examples seem fairly typical of the *Valor* data and coincide with both the values and the frequency of parish leasing suggested by the common law material for parishes not held by religious houses.

Comparing the value of a parish lease with the *Valor* data or other assessments is not helpful; "value" is a difficult concept and always has relation both to the condition of the parish itself and to other possible investments and prices. The parish of Brough under Stainmore, Cumberland, for instance, received an assessed value of £53.33 in 1344. That value had stayed stable for about a decade, but before that the parish had been worth about £100. A bit earlier, in 1318, an assessment valued the parish at only £6.67, in 1291, at £30.[60] The degree of fluctuation in the value of that parish over only half a century was not typical, but neither was it rare. The factors in the valuation of a parish would include the condition of the buildings, the kinds of agriculture practiced in the parish, the population of the parish, exercise of patronage in the granting, the kinds of burdens that went along with the lease, an annual rent burdening the parish revenue for a period, the tendency of the parishioners to tithe rigorously or not, the general level of prices; all these factors were significant variables. The obligation to provide a priest for the parish would itself be a £6 annual commitment on top of the rent or, if the rector wanted to stay and serve as priest, £6 additional that could be demanded in rent. Comparison of values over time would only be helpful in rare situations in which sufficient background detail survives.

Parishes were sufficiently attractive, whatever their value, that potential lessees might even hire others to solicit a lease. In November 1387 Thomas Holbrok retained Hugh Hikelyng, a cleric, to aid him in securing a lease of the parish of Clyst Honiton in Devon from the dean and chapter of Exeter Cathedral for ten years at a rent of £8. Holbrok offered Hikelyng a fee of £2 for the assistance, the fee due only after the lease had been secured.[61] In 1504 Henry Wode of Bradwell in Essex, a yeoman, hired Richard Bryand of Bristol, a chaplain, to ride to Windsor to convince John Esterfyld, the rector of Bradwell, to lease Wode the parish for seven years. Bryand's pay as agent to secure the transaction was to be £2. Bryand made the trip to Windsor, but then had to sue for his pay in 1513.[62] How specialized such agents were or how often they were used are questions impossible to answer. Clearly, not every lessee needed an agent. The most typical place to make the lease was on the parish in question; often the lessee was local, although lessees from outside the parish were very far from being unusual.[63] For residents of the parish, agents would have been unnecessary. Parish leaseholds,

60. *Register of John Kirkby*, 156–57.
61. CP40/519, m. 328.
62. CP40/1005a, m. 183.
63. Appendix 3.

however, were sufficiently desirable that they could induce a potential lessee to hire an agent.

FREQUENCY OF PARISH LEASING

Leasing the parish became about as typical for a parish as was incumbent residency, perhaps more typical. Estimating the frequency with which incumbents leased out their benefice, however, is fraught with difficulty, but is still a critical matter for determining not only the character of the late medieval English parish, but also the context within which the statutes of 1529 operated: parish leasing and clerical leaseholding were central concerns for those statutes. This section thus approaches the issue from as many different angles as possible: litigation frequency as such, litigation frequency compared to known social practices, visitation records both in regard to the problem of absenteeism (almost the obverse of parish leasing) and directly in relation to parish leasing, and social commentary. No precise percentage estimate is possible, but the conclusion is that parish leasing was a typical form of parish management, even for rectors or vicars who had only a single benefice.

A comparison of litigation frequency with known parish leasing practice suggests that rectors and vicars typically leased out their benefices. The *Valor Ecclesiasticus* in 1535 demonstrates that monasteries typically leased their parishes out to others.[64] Around 1500 religious houses held about 37 percent of English parishes. At the same time only about a third of the lessors in litigation concerning parish leases were institutions. The easiest conclusion would be that ordinary parishes were leased about as frequently as appropriated parishes, that is, much more frequently than not. That conclusion is perhaps correct for the early sixteenth century, but other factors make the argument less than certain. Monasteries leased their parishes for much longer terms than did ordinary rectors, and the length of the term might increase or decrease the amount of litigation for any number of reasons. Short-term lessees may have had less to lose by defaulting than long-term lessees, but long-term lessees may have defaulted on maintenance duties more frequently. Long-term lessors may have had more incentive to terminate the lease early because of inflation. Monasteries likewise may have been less willing to settle at an early stage of process than ordinary rectors, so more suits with monastic lessors would persevere to the

---

64. Knowles, *Religious Orders*, 3:248–49.

stage at which the records reveal that the suit concerned a parish lease. Monas-teries, of course, were leasing out a rectory that was designed to be disconnected from the parish, but the perpetual vicar who theoretically served the appropri-ated parish at the same time could lease out the vicary, so the parish might have two different sets of lessees for a single parish. Monasteries also might lease the rectory to the vicar and thus combine again the resources of the parish in a single person. Such dynamics might have dictated a different frequency in litigation for institutional lessors. Those or other factors undermine a com-pletely confident assessment of frequency simply from a comparison of litiga-tion rates between appropriated and nonappropriated parishes. Both around 1400 and around 1500 parish leases made by corporate rectors constituted about 35 percent of the litigation about parish leases in the king's court.[65] If the primary determinant of such litigation was the proportion of parishes actually possessed by such corporations, then one could conclude that somewhere between 80 percent and 90 percent of noninstitutional rectors leased their parishes also. That easy conclusion would probably be an overestimate. Still, the comparison of litigation frequency between institutional and noninstitutional lessors make it likely that leasing the parish out for a fixed rent was a typical manner of management for either a rector or a perpetual vicar.

Visitation records are tempting but deceptive sources for deriving statistical information about either absenteeism or the leasing of parishes; the evidence from those records nevertheless is congruent with a perception that parish leasing was typical in the early sixteenth century. The problems with visitation records, however, are numerous. The first problem is the meaning of "residence" and "nonresidence." After 1529, England had a clear, statutory definition of nonresidence: absence for a month at a time or two months total during one year.[66] Pre-Reformation England had no such definition.[67] A rector reported as nonresident might have been gone for three weeks, for two weeks each month, or for many years, might have lived in the next parish or a nearby town and tended well to the parish but not resided there, might have leased out the parish to a lessee who was either taking very good or very poor care of the parishioners, or might have simply abandoned the parish. In many situations, the visitation records do not indicate what the situation actually was. The assumption is that

---

65. Appendix 3.

66. Statute 21, Henry VIII, c. 13, section 15; below, Chapter 6 at n. 74.

67. Bowker, *Henrician Reformation*, 113: " 'non-residence' did not denote the same problem in all areas."

the church wardens would make that allegation not according to some fixed standard, but according to their assessment that there was a problem; the standard could at times be lower, at times higher than the statutes of 1529 would impose. Bowker, for instance, identified some rectors she was convinced from other data were absentee, even though the visitation reported them resident,[68] so the visitation did not always treat absence as nonresidence. On the other hand, the visitation records indicate that one lessee operated a tavern out of the rectory, so the rector probably was not resident, although that rector does not appear in Bowker's list of absentees.[69] The first problem with the visitation records prior to the statutes of 1529, thus, is the lack of a definition for the categories; we cannot even assume that there was a definition.

The second problem with evaluating absenteeism from visitation records is that the church warden responses were dictated by the changing concerns of the visitor. A. H. Thomson, who edited the earlier sixteenth-century visitation records for the very large diocese of Lincoln, concluded that the visitation process was fairly summary. The visitor would not actually visit each parish, but went to a regional center and there interacted with the church wardens summoned from the area parishes.[70] The visitor thus was not in the parish himself, talking to random people in the parish, but received partial information indirectly through church wardens. That input came according to standard questions, but the returns to the questions suggest strongly that what the church wardens concentrated on was greatly influenced by what the visitor was interested in on that particular day: sexual improprieties in one area, absenteeism or leasing in another, or physical defects in church buildings in a third.[71] Thus Thompson thought that the number of absentee rectors reported was significantly less than the number actually absent.[72] Because the visitor's varying concerns shaped the emphasis on the questions posed, the responses were highly inconsistent and the reports of absenteeism only partial.

The third problem is that the responses in the visitation records come from church wardens. It cannot be supposed that church wardens were automatons

---

68. Bowker, *Secular Clergy*, 87–88.

69. Ibid., 117, 211.

70. *Visitations in the Diocese of Lincoln*, xxiii.

71. Ibid., xxiv.

72. Thomson footnoted the number of recorded nonresident rectors and vicars for each deanery. Although he thus had the total number of reported absentees, he did not give the total in his introduction, but instead focused on the way in which the visitor's concerns shaped what the church wardens presented.

who rendered actual factual data to any question asked. One can assume that people who occupied the office of church warden by and large actually cared about the parish. (If they did not care, then the visitation records would be even more problematic than here argued.) People who actually cared about the parish, however, might be very reticent about reporting an absentee rector or vicar; they might thereby change the status quo when the parish lessee had hired a chaplain whom they liked better or at least as much as the absentee. In other contexts they might well worry about offending the absentee cleric or an influential lessee who had hired a less than sterling chaplain. What they would certainly report, whether the visitor pressed them or not, was the situation in which the absentee or absentee and lessee had left the parish without a priest at all. Those situations in which a lessee was performing according to the expectations of the lease and had hired a worthy chaplain to serve the parish, however, might reasonably not have moved the church wardens to complain; those situations should have outnumbered the situations in which the church wardens would have been outraged by neglect of the parish. Using the visitations records requires an understanding of the realistic concerns of both the church wardens and the visitor.

The problems that make the visitation records difficult in themselves combine with several initial problems in analysis that undermine the validity of current estimates about absenteeism. Historians who deal with numbers may, even after admitting the limitations of the sources, treat the numbers they derive as indicative of social reality: numbers are seductive. Thompson did not make that mistake, but the more recent historians of absenteeism seem to do so.[73] Clearly, the percentage of incumbents reported absent in the visitation is not the number of absentees, but only the lowest possible number of absentees, a figure that is a floor but not an estimate of the actual rate of absenteeism. Historians dealing with absenteeism have to describe reality not as a single percentage, but as a plausible range with a definite, but implausibly low floor. Moreover, historians occasionally equate absenteeism with pluralism, as if the only reason why an incumbent might be absent was that he had other benefices.[74] Because of the statutory changes in 1529, that assumption might well be

---

73. Bowker, *Secular Clergy*, 112–17; "Henrician Reformation," 90; *Henrician Reformation*, 112–21; Zell, "The Personnel of the Clergy," 514–15 (not Zell's major focus); Haigh, *Reformation and Resistance*, 27–28.

74. Haigh, *Reformation and Resistance*, 27–28: "Between 1490 and 1520 the rate of pluralism among county incumbents increased from 23 percent to 30 percent, and by 1550 exactly one-third

true for the social situation after 1529.[75] That assumption, however, is inconsistent with late medieval criticisms of the clergy and simply cannot be accurate.[76] Finally, the figures from the pre-Reformation visitations are compared with the post-1529 visitation figures as if they measured the same phenomenon.[77] After 1529, however, "nonresidence" had a statutory meaning: absence for one month at a time or for more than two months total in a year.[78] Moreover, illicit absenteeism after 1529 was a source of predatory profit from enforcers of the statute, so that a presentation of culpable absenteeism after 1529 would make an incumbent a target for a ruinous suit; at that point, then, one can expect that most reports of absenteeism by church wardens could be justified as falling within the bounds permitted by the statutes. What the post-1529 visitations measured was quite different and with different effects from the pre-1529 visitations. This complex of problems, however, does not diminish the need to quantify. The current estimates of absenteeism for the diocese of Lincoln around 1518 are something between 23 percent and 25 percent (but from subsidy rolls around 1526, 28.6 percent);[79] for the diocese of Rochester in 1523–24, 15 percent; in Lancashire, 30 percent. Absenteeism in these regions was not at those figures at all, but at something above those figures, probably significantly so.

Absenteeism was one of the major concerns of the 1529 statutes, and the rate of absenteeism was related to the frequency of parish leasing, the precise concern of this chapter. Visitation records do contain occasional reports about leaseholding. Bowker, although covering the other aspects of her visitation records, fails to discuss or to take into consideration the phenomenon of parish

---

of rectors and vicars were pluralists. . . . Despite the extent of pluralism, and presumably, therefore, of non-residence, the ecclesiastical authorities only rarely proceeded against the guilty." Haigh was working from prosecutions, not from visitation records, but similarly treats the figures derived from visitation records by others. His figures are thus treated in Bowker, *Henrician Reformation*, 26: "In Lancashire, Dr. Haigh has shown that before 1520 the absenteeism of the clergy was lower than that prevalent in the Lincoln diocese, but he shows also that it was increasing and that by 1520 it had reached 30 percent and by 1550 33 percent." Haigh in *English Reformation Revised*, 224, in his index seemed to equate pluralism with nonresidence. Bowker does the same thing with Zell's figures for Kent: "In Kent the incidence of non-residence is considerably lower: the see of Rochester had only 22 per cent pluralist incumbents and that of Canterbury 15 per cent." Bowker, *Henrician Reformation*, 43.

75. See Chapter 6.
76. See below at nn. 90–110.
77. Bowker, "Henrician Reformation," 90–91; *Henrician Reformation*, 112–17.
78. Statute 21, Henry VIII, c. 13, section 15.
79. Bowker, *Secular Clergy*, 90–91; *Henrician Reformation*, 43.

leasing, except in regard to prebends after 1529 and appropriated rectories.[80] Seemingly, that omission results from the assumption that the leases only concerned lands and not whole parishes. Nonetheless, the Lincoln diocese visitation from around 1518 reveals that at least 10 percent of the parishes were leased. Even more than with nonresidence, however, this figure was a floor, an unrealistically low figure. In each of the seven archdeaconries, the percentage of parishes in which a lessee was mentioned, even tangentially, was substantially lower than the figure of reported absentees: Bedford, 14.8 percent nonresident, 2 percent leased; Buckingham, 25 percent nonresident, 15 percent leased; Lincoln, 19.6 percent nonresident, 9 percent leased; Huntingdon, 22 percent nonresident, 9 percent leased; Oxford, 35 percent nonresident, 19 percent leased; Stowe, 35 percent nonresident, 21 percent leased.[81] Management by bailiff was rare by the sixteenth century,[82] so the difference between reported nonresidence and leases could not be the result of incumbents using bailiffs. Similarly, an absentee rector could have hired a parish priest during his absence, but left the financial side of the parish unmanaged. That scenario, however, is implausible; few incumbents were likely to endanger their revenue but still provide for the parish when they could just as easily lease the whole parish to the priest. The only reasonable conclusion accords with the impression from the visitation records: the visitors were much more concerned with absenteeism than with parish leasing. The rate of parish leasing must have been far higher than reported in the visitations.

The contexts and content of the reports of parish leasing in the Lincoln visitation indicate indeed that the rate of parish leasing was higher than that minimum of 10 percent; indeed, the rate of leasing was probably well above the rate of reported absenteeism. The normal occasion for mention of a lease was a report of an unlicensed leasing to a layman (always singular for this purpose).[83]

80. Bowker, *Henrician Reformation*, 42, 46–57, 96–100, 111. In calculating absenteeism from subsidy returns, she did not take into account parish leasing in assessing when a rector would hire a curate. She assumed that a rector might hire a curate when absent but occasionally when present and that the parish might hire a curate. Lessees simply did not appear in this analysis, although they would have normally been the person to hire the curate; an absentee rector was actually less likely to hire a curate than was a resident rector or a lessee.

81. I have accepted Bowker's figures for absenteeism reports where available at Bowker, *Henrician Reformation*, 114; for the rest and the lease figure, *Visitations in the Diocese of Lincoln*.

82. Figure 1.

83. *Visitations in the Diocese of Lincoln*, 41, 44, 46–47, 49–42, 68, 73–75, 78, 82, 83, 88, 92–97, 105, 107–12, 115, 119–27, 127–35, 138–39.

Single lessees who were chaplains or clerics might be mentioned, but not often. Single laymen who had received the lease after a license, while occasionally mentioned, were not a concern; and the wardens might present a lay lessee not knowing whether there had been a license or not. Lessees of any description who performed their duties well might go unremarked when the visitor did not press the subject, just as did absentees. Groups of lessees usually included an ecclesiastic who would serve as the parish priest; in such a situation the church wardens might not even realize that laymen were involved in the lease; if they did, the presence of a cleric among the lessees might have been sufficient for them to overlook the lease.[84] Lessees occasionally, even though lay, invited attention only because they were running animals in the cemetery[85] or because parishioners were concerned about women, even the wife of the lay lessee, living in the rectory:[86] they apparently had received the ordinary's license, but were abusing the lease. The mentions of leases in the visitations, in other words, barely scratch the surface of the phenomenon. The plausible rate of parish leasing is somewhat above the plausible rate of absenteeism since some incumbents leased their parish out but continued to reside.[87]

A reasonable calculation of absenteeism is thus essential for an estimate of parish leasing. In the Lincoln diocese about 23 percent of the parishes reported an incumbent absent; 2 percent affirmatively mentioned a resident incumbent. Thus 75 percent of the parishes did not mention residency at all. To the 2 percent clearly resident, one can add a further 10 percent in which the rector or vicar kept a woman in the rectory, whether the woman was a suspect woman, a relative, or a servant (note that many of these situations were not sinful, and many by twentieth-century standards would be laudable care for elderly family members).[88] Conceivably the incumbent in these situations might also have been absent, but that is unlikely. Arbitrarily, it would seem reasonable to assume that for every rector who was reported with a woman in the rectory there were two others that obeyed the rules and had a unisex household. If those assumptions are reasonable then the least possible figure for absenteeism would be 23 percent and the highest plausible figure would be 68 percent. A midrange estimate would be between 40 percent and 50 percent, probably closer to 40

---

84. For the status of lessees, see above at nn. 32–35.

85. *Visitations in the Diocese of Lincoln*, 44, 50, 77, 91, 123, 132.

86. Ibid., 74, 76, 86–87.

87. See below, Chapter 5 at nn. 72–75.

88. *Visitations in the Diocese of Lincoln*, 82, 126, etc.

percent. The figure for parish leasing would be a bit higher than that, somewhere around 45 percent. All one can really conclude, however, is a range, but a range that would support the statement that parish leasing was a typical way of parish management. That statement accurately describes likewise the judgment derived from the plea rolls, both from the degree of litigation and from comparing the institutional and noninstitutional leases against the background of the *Valor Ecclesiasticus*.[89]

Those two estimates from different sources are congruent with Chaucer's well-known criticism of clerical practices. Chaucer's comments indicate that parish leasing was common even in the late fourteenth century, although the practice was then probably not as prevalent as it would become by 1500. In "The General Prologue" of *The Canterbury Tales*, Chaucer describes his idealized parson: poor, learned, dedicated to preaching the gospel and teaching his parishioners, reluctant to excommunicate for nonpayment of tithes, a model for his flock. Chaucer then took eight lines to lionize his parson for not doing what that acute observer of fourteenth-century life clearly considered a typical flaw in parsons: leasing out his parish.

> He sette nought his benefice to hire
> And leet his sheep encombred in the mire
> And ran to London, unto Sainte Poules,
> To seeken him a chaunterye for soules,
> Or with a bretherhede to been withholde,
> But dwelte at hoom and kepte wel his folde,
> So that the wolf ne made it nought miscarye:
> He was a shepherde and nought a mercenarye.[90]

The vice Chaucer saw had nothing to do with absenteeism deriving from licit pluralism (with an official license for taking more than one benefice requiring care of souls), for administrative work for pope, king, or bishop, or for study at Oxford, Cambridge, or abroad: situations in which leasing, at least to ecclesiastical lessees and pursuant to a license from the bishop, would have conformed to canon law. This parson had but one parish, and the vice he refrained from was leasing out that single, his only, parish and going to London for

---

89. Thompson's assessment about absenteeism was similarly qualitative, but in the same direction: "non-resident rectors were common." Ibid., xxv, xxix.

90. Chaucer, "The General Prologue," *The Canterbury Tales*, ll. 509–16.

additional easy employment with a chantry or fraternity. For this passage to have struck a chord with fourteenth-century readers, that conduct must have been familiar.[91]

Bishops clearly encountered the problems of leased parishes and found them very persistent. Robert Reade, bishop of Chichester, thus lamented several different problems in 1399 in a way that reinforces Chaucer's criticism: that priests licensed to be absent from their benefice for one reason did something else; that priests licensed for absence for a certain time did not return at the end of the period; that ecclesiastics leased out their benefices against church constitutions; that beneficed clergy took stipends to pray for the dead instead of caring for the souls in their charge; and that priests would celebrate mass twice a day for pay in violation of church law. He ordered an archdeacon to inquire and remedy that situation.[92] Several years later, in 1404 when a tax was granted on the church for the king, the bishop ordered collection of the tax by having "the possessors, occupiers, or farmers" to appear before the collectors; the presumption was thus that the lessees were just as typically in possession of parishes as rectors or vicars.[93] Then, also in 1404, he ordered his archdeacons to notify all absent rectors, vicars, and chaplains to be warned to return to their benefices within twenty days and to undertake to maintain residence and hospitality.[94] Any success Reade had early in his episcopacy seems to have been temporary. John Chandler, the dean of Salisbury in the early fifteenth century, seems to have treated with farmers as often as with the beneficed clergy, taking procurations from lessees and ordering them to make repairs.[95] Absenteeism was again the subject of church legislation in 1486 and in 1518.[96] Finally, the statutes of 1529, with which the second part of this book is concerned, sought to remedy

---

91. Cooper, *Oxford Guides to Chaucer*, 52: "The portrait is a double one, of the good parson, and of the bad. Contemporary criticism of bad priests can be reconstructed from the description simply by omitting the negatives: they readily excommunicate for non-payment of tithes, they expect a high standard of living, they leave their pastoral duties undone, they rent out their benefices in exchange for the easy life of a chantry priest in London. . . ."

92. Register of Robert Reade, bishop of Chichester (1396–1415), f. 6r: a mandate to inquire concerning the names of those not resident on their benefices, noting his interest in those who had leased out their churches against the ecclesiastical constitutions. By this time, however, the bishop could probably do little to subvert such leaseholds as a general practice.

93. Ibid., f. 10v.

94. Ibid., ff. 11v–12r.

95. *Register of John Chandler*, ed. Timmins, 1–116.

96. Heath, *English Parish Clergy*, 58–59.

precisely such mercenary conduct by parsons. Leasing the parish simply was a well-known management tool for rectors and vicars in the late fourteenth century and a typical tool by 1500, so typical in fact that the statutes of 1529 that attacked absenteeism permitted the leasing of parishes to continue, although in a transformed context, as a major mechanism for handling agrarian surplus.

Such leasing was also decidedly against church law, since Chaucer accurately mirrored the official position of the church on this issue. The church had repeatedly voiced the ideal of a noncommercial clergy and prohibited clergy from seeking filthy lucre, from participating in commercial transactions, from buying cheap to sell high,[97] and thus also even from serving as bailiff or steward for a lay person.[98] Church law opposed the leasing of parishes by both rectors and vicars without specific approval by the ordinary,[99] but particularly opposed any such leasing to lay people.[100] Such prohibitions could apply even to leasing tithes to laymen.[101] Leasing out a rectory and then serving as a stipendiary priest was specifically forbidden,[102] and the leasing of churches could be seen as simony for a lessee priest.[103] Even with that comparison, canon law would allow, with the ordinary's permission, the leasing of a church to clerics, but not for more than five years.[104] Overall, however, rectors and vicars were supposed to refrain from involvement in commerce and to reside on their benefice.[105] The ideal and the actual, however, diverged.

Although that legislation came before the fourteenth century, the church ideals remained the same in the fourteenth, fifteenth, and early sixteenth centuries. Archbishop Bourgchier in 1455 upbraided absentee clerics who spent their time in dissolute living while their benefices deteriorated and lay lessees took the wealth of the parish.[106] Visitations might inquire into absenteeism and

---

97. *Councils and Synods*, ed. Powicke and Cheney, 151, 187, 270, 519, 565, 605, 711, 769, 1022, 1023.

98. Ibid., 270–71, 310, 406, 476, 1023–24; Heath, *English Parish Clergy*, 53.

99. *Councils and Synods*, 29, 83, 119, 130, 186, 384, 1023.

100. Ibid., 130–31, 149, 176–77, 270–71, 347, 352, 406–7, 412, 426, 459, 491, 605, 658, 666, 709, 769, 910.

101. Ibid., 352, 412, 436, 459, 491.

102. Ibid., 406, 709.

103. Ibid., 658.

104. Ibid., 248–49, 249, 310, 459, 769.

105. Ibid., 249, 362, 519, 564, 1024.

106. *Registrum Thome Bourgchier*, 20–23. Heath, *English Parish Clergy*, 58. Heath regards Bourgchier's comments as "rhetoric," but Bourgchier was simply trying to apply canon law at the

leasing, but action concentrated either on compelling absentees to purchase a license to legitimate a lease already made or to return to the parish or on disciplining clerics who had simply abandoned their parish, that is, leaving it without any care for the ecclesiastical services.[107] During the vacancy of the see of Coventry and Lichfield in 1490–91, the guardians of the spirituality were empowered, optimistically, with the power to punish those illicitly leasing or receiving benefices at lease and to compel rectors and vicars to reside in person.[108] The York Convocation of 1518 repeated under the authority of the Statutes of Chichester of 1289 the threat of sequestering the proceeds of the parish for unlicensed absenteeism.[109] Nothing would indicate any change in church law; the church was still struggling, perhaps more hopelessly, with the leasing of churches and the accompanying absenteeism. Indeed, the practice seems to have been so regular that the inquiries about licensing a lease and absenteeism might have been more about exacting money for the license than about insisting on residence and complying with the expectations of the law, although on occasions ecclesiastical process elicited from absentees the promise to reside on the benefice.[110]

What had changed was the common law involvement in enforcing leases. Clearly, the church had had a problem with such leases even in the thirteenth century; otherwise the proliferation of church law on the subject in that century is inexplicable. Still, the common law was not much involved in enforcing leases in the thirteenth century, so the church had a relatively unrestricted ability to regulate the practice. Enforcement then depended solely on the vigor of the bishop. Common law enforcement of parish leases, however, complicated matters considerably. The church might still compel the rector or vicar to reside or get a license, but it would have to fight a surely losing battle with the common law to void the lease. Under church law bishops could license absenteeism, and the fee for such a license ran from about £0.12 to £0.50.[111] Exercising such

---

beginning of his episcopate; moreover, his complaint was not that rectors and vicars leased out their benefices to laymen, but that they did so without his license.

107. Heath, *English Parish Clergy*, 66.

108. *Register of John Morton*, ed. Harper-Bill, 2:2. See also 12, 23, 62, 105, 124, 127. When the vicar-general visited the archdeaconry of Coventry, he ordered the archdeacon to cite all who did not properly reside or who let their benefices at farm to show their dispensations or license, 113.

109. *Councils and Synods*, 1089; Heath, *English Parish Clergy*, 59.

110. *Episcopal Court Book*, ed. Bowker, 18, 21, 68–69, 71, 104, 130, 132.

111. Heath, *English Parish Clergy*, 58.

discretion yielded revenue, while it also avoided a confrontation with the common law. All but vigorous reformers avoided the confrontation and often seemed to avoid even the supervision; they understandably reserved their attention for truly abandoned parishes. Occasionally one can find an admonition that the rector or vicar return to his benefice or else secure the provision of ecclesiastical services for the parish.[112] That alternative went to the substance of pastoral care, while it overlooked what the church found to be an insoluble problem: absenteeism and parish leasing. A well-run parish lease, of course, included the hiring of an honest and worthy priest to perform the services. One might well see how a parish with even an unlicensed absentee rector might still report that all was well at a visitation: *omnia bene*. The parishioners might even prefer the hired priest of a lessee or a clerical lessee to the rector himself, particularly since hired priests made their living precisely by attending to the care of the parishioners, whereas the rector was in a different stratum of society and could have different concerns.

Investing in parishes was a major opportunity for entrepreneurial activity. The church imposed and enforced the obligations such as tithing that yielded the revenue, equivalent to more than a tenth of the agricultural produce of England and a much larger percentage of the actual agricultural surplus. The parishes that collected that surplus constituted by 1500 the most frequent substantial leaseholds available on the market. The bishops who were vigilant enough exacted a minor fee for a license to lease the parish or to be absent, and, in visitations, could correct abuse by the leaseholders or lax conduct on the part of the hired curate. After an initial optimistic estimate about Bishop Longland's deputies' capacity for correcting wrongs in the diocese of Lincoln, however, Bowker concludes that section with more pessimistic assessments: ". . . he did little to see that these things were done unless the delinquent was a man of stature" and "The only time when the bishop could be guaranteed to interfere in the affairs of the parish was if there was a suspicion of heresy among the parishioners or in the person of their priest."[113] The bishop's control of the parish had become more tenuous; the parish had been assimilated into the secular marketplace. The common law through ordinary actions of debt and through performance bonds provided the reinforcement of commercial transactions that allowed the parish lease to be secure, so that the parish became a

112. Ibid., 65.
113. Bowker, *Henrician Reformation*, 37–38, 46.

liquid asset. Parishes were thus at the heart of both the economic life of the country and the common law regarding leases.

Conclusion

From the late fourteenth through into the sixteenth century, rectors and vicars as well as the heads of religious houses leased out entire parishes. Some parsons simply rented out tithes or various subsidiary rights for a period of years, but by 1500 the norm was otherwise. In leasing out a parish, the parson treated the parish as a complex whole that included not only the sources of direct profit (tithes, mortuary, offerings, and glebe land), but also the infrastructure (rectory building, barns, and dovecotes) and the responsibilities that went along with the parish: repair of the chancel and payment of royal and ecclesiastical taxation. In most, but not all, cases of parish leases, the parson's only remaining right during the term was the right to the rent. After the Black Death in the fourteenth century, it seems, an increasing number of rectors and vicars thus changed their relationship to the parish, abandoning direct contact and responsibility for the running of the parish in favor of making the parish simply their method for generating income. At the same time and in a closely related development, the parish became increasingly both a community through the actions of the church wardens and (from the rector's point of view) simply an economic complex that generated income. The practice of leasing parishes continued to be regarded as an abuse, one which bishops occasionally tried to remedy, although whether in any instance solely to compel the rector to purchase the license or actually to compel residence is difficult to ascertain. Nonetheless, when Henry VIII and the Reformation Parliament undertook to legislate on clerical commercialism and absenteeism, they were providing a remedy for problems that the bishops of late medieval England had recognized as an abuse, had been willing to regulate, but had been either unable or unwilling to resolve.

CHAPTER FIVE

Parish Leases: Conflicts and Consequences

The practice of leasing parishes brought with it both normal lease-hold problems and the changes in power relationships that are inevitable when new economic practices are introduced. The normal problems included controversies over both lessors' rights (payment of rent, repair of premises, and payment of taxes) and the lessees' rights to possession and to quiet enjoyment of the premises. Leasing the parish, however, severed the rector from the parish community. In leased parishes the rector would interact intermittently with the lessees. The lessees or their designee interfaced directly and regularly with the parish community, but the lessees operated outside the traditional interactions among bishop, patron, and rector. Real control of parish life now increasingly resided at a level almost concealed by the official ecclesiastical records; control rested rather in the hands of individuals empowered not by ordination and installation but by virtue of a contractual economic investment that ignored clerical or lay status. While many lessees probably provided either well or adequately for the spiritual needs of the parish, parish leasing produced for the clergy an involvement in litigation and commerce that conflicted with the stated ideals of the church. When Henry VIII found he could no longer tolerate the independence of the church, the commercialized absentee clergy would become a natural object for reform.

This chapter, much like Chapters 2 and 3, has very diverse purposes. Its overt purpose is to flesh out the practice of parish leasing through an examination of the various concerns highlighted in litigation. In that straightforward examination, however, the very detail reveals a different aspect of clerical and parish life. Historical research on the clergy often centers on areas that seem directly related to their religious duties: whether they were literate, how they performed their liturgical duties, how they were supposed to aid their parishioners, and how they fulfilled their administrative tasks within the church and sought benefices and positions. The litigation about parish leases shows them completely mired down in the real world of commercial relationships and the conflict of mundane common law suits. The litigation is also important for revealing the ways in which legal remedies allocated power to be used by people to secure parish resources and to attain personal ends. Each case, while litigated at Westminster, was a local confrontation shaped by legal rules; each one thus demonstrates parish relationships that were far more typical than idiosyncratic. Only immersion in the mundane, typical world of the rectors and lessees can give some sense of the way in which rectors regarded their parishes and the way in which parishes had become items of commerce.

Possession

The strong position of the lessor dictated that the lessee's possession of the tenement be protected not only by the litigation process but also by the ordinary dynamics of self-interested relationships. Litigation was the most powerful mechanism then available to the English government for the management and shaping of society. The mere provision of an ordinary legal remedy, however, was not effective protection of the lease. Both the crown and individuals thus structured legally enforceable arrangements in ways that, given ordinary perspectives of self-interest, would increase the lessee's security without litigation. To reinforce those social arrangements and those ordinary legal remedies, the courts then developed mechanisms that were so punitive that a lessee who had been cautious at the beginning of the lease could feel extraordinarily secure.

The normal assurance of possession rested in customs for the payment of the rent. Lessees did not usually pay in advance, but paid rent for a period of possession already completed. Thus, in a term of one year with the rent due at the end of the year, the tenant owed nothing at all if the lessor ejected him after only eleven months, because the courts did not engage in proportional allocations of the rent. That custom of payment only after enjoyment provided a substantial incentive for the lessor to allow the lessee to remain on the premises, even if their agreement was not embodied in written instruments. Nevertheless, after a default in payment, the lessor did not need to delay. The parson of Bradford Peverell thus simply removed his lessees, and the subsequent litigation in 1388 was about payment of the rent for the immediately preceding full term.[1] When a neighbor tore down his own tenement, a lessee around 1396 demanded that the lessor enclose the tenement, because it was open to the elements. When the lessor refused, the lessee quit the tenement before any payment had come

1. CP40/508, m. 110.

due: he thus would not owe.[2] The abbot of Selby was also parson of Snaith and Cowick in Yorkshire. He leased the tithes of the parish to a husbandman for twelve years at £16 annually. In 1507, after almost a full year of the lease but before the first due date, the abbot expelled the lessee. In 1508 the justices considered this an acceptable defense against the abbot's claim for £13.33.[3] Payment only after a time of possession was completed increased the lessor's incentive to respect and protect the lease.

Keeping the times designated for payment at less than a year, normally three or four times a year, provided the reciprocal benefit for the lessor. Michaelmas and Easter were typical payment times; the feasts of St. John the Baptist and the Purification often completed the payment cycle. The payments on the specified feasts were ordinarily the same, even though the revenue for the period would have been decidedly unequal. Michaelmas was almost always one of the payment times precisely because Michaelmas marked the end of the harvest, so the lessees at that feast would have just taken in the tithes. Leases nevertheless began at any point in the year. Lessees who began their terms in August would have found their first payment easy to meet. Lessees who began their term in October and thus after the harvest and payment of tithes had to plan carefully. Default patterns, however, indicate that lessors and lessees worked around the problems predictable at the beginning of a term. Short terms for payment still meant that the lessor would lose less on a default. These customs about times of payment regulated the leasehold according to self-interest, so that completely external to litigation lessees could have reasonable security in their possession, while lessors would not lose excessively by a default.

Legal protection of leaseholds remained somewhat tenuous, however, because a leasehold was not a "free tenement." A free tenement was a property interest held for life or longer (that is, heritably) for specific and nonservile services. The ordinary remedies protecting such tenements were the remedies for property: the assizes of novel disseisin and mort d'ancestor, the writs of entry, dower, formedon. A term of years, no matter the specified duration, was at law always considered less than the duration of a life so that leaseholds fell outside the protection of the normal legal actions for real property. The legal remedies available for normal leasehold protection were thus a patchwork of remedies that even together were not comprehensive: covenant, performance bonds, and trespass (*quare ejecit* and ejectment).

---

2. CP40/547, m. 332. See also CP40/547, m. 430.
3. CP40/986, m. 317d.

Protection of a parish leasehold was even more problematic. The least complicated ordinary leasehold was the lease of an agricultural tenement for personal occupation and farming.[4] Manors were somewhat more complicated because a good portion of the value of a manor came in the form of customary payments from tenants, and simple occupation of a manor leasehold could not ensure the willing cooperation of the tenants.[5] A parish leasehold, however, must occasionally have been exceedingly difficult to manage. The lessee had to rely heavily on the tithing habits of the parishioners, even when those parishioners knew that their tithes did not go directly to the rector, vicar, or curate, but rather only increased the profit margin of the lessees, who were most often simply investor managers. The lessee could fall back on the rector/lessor's willingness to prosecute the parishioners for the tithes in ecclesiastical court, but a rector who had to be sued to protect the possession was unlikely to be vigorous in supporting the profits of the lessee. John Slaghterman found that the parishioners so interfered with his lease of Skerne parish that he simply surrendered the parish lease back into the hands of the prior of Watton.[6] The lessees of Biggleswade parish found themselves evicted by a papal provisor.[7] The lessee of Woodford and Widford had to cope with a situation in which the parson exchanged his rectory for another and gave the bishop of Salisbury the right to the first fruits for a year: the bishop took the lessee's twenty-seven acres of barley and the carts, plows, and other utensils of the rectory.[8] Lessees of a parish worked in between the lay and ecclesiastical worlds and had to cope with both.

Even with the arrangement of payment schedules that provided an incentive for compliance, lessees needed the protection of legal actions developed in the thirteenth and fourteenth centuries. Covenant, dating from around 1200, was the most obvious remedy for protection of the leasehold from the lessor. The protection of leasehold possession from the lessor was in fact the prime pur-

---

4. Baker is correct in asserting that the typical leaseholder was the tenant who wanted to cultivate the land. Baker, *IELH*, 339–40. The question is whether it was the typical leasehold situation or the more visible and costly situations that shaped the law. As with the centrality of the military fee in the development of property law (instead of the more common socage tenancy), it seems that parish leases and monastic manor leases were more important than the typical husbandry lease in the development of leasehold protections.

5. Palmer, *Whilton Dispute*, 124–51.

6. CP40/503, m. 629.

7. CP40/510, m. 410.

8. CP40/511, m. 115.

pose of the writ of covenant, and it allowed the evicted lessee to recover the remainder of the term.[9] Since the early fourteenth century, however, covenant had only protected those leasehold agreements evidenced by a deed under seal. While that limitation obviously excluded many informal, agrarian agreements, it also excluded many and perhaps most parish leases.[10] Still, a reasonable number of parish lessees would conceivably have found the action of covenant useful: recovery of the unexpired term was possible; damages were available if the term had expired before judgment could be rendered.[11] William and John Abbot used the action of covenant in 1486 after they had been ejected from their leasehold parish only one year into their three-year term.[12] At times, both lessee and lessor sued each other. Henry Winchester thus demised his rectory of Lindfield, Sussex, to Thomas Dyer for a year and a half for £10.67 annually in 1405 and had to sue him in 1410 for the whole of the £16 in rent.[13] At the same time Dyer sued the rector in covenant to make the rector abide by the lease of all the houses, arable lands, and pastures pertaining to the rectory as well as half of the mortuary fees; the rector had reserved for himself the chapel, water mill, church offerings, woods, and other emoluments.[14] Use of the action of covenant, however, required formality at the beginning of the arrangement.

The performance bond, developed in the fourteenth century, was a far superior protection of leasehold available to those willing to initiate the leasehold with formal documentation. Performance bonds were acknowledgments of a debt that the creditor stipulated would be void if the debtor did certain things. For a leasehold the lessor thus acknowledged gratuitously a debt that the lessee stipulated would be void if he enjoyed the leasehold peaceably during the term. The lessee thus simply sued the lessor on the debt acknowledgment if the lessor disturbed him. The resulting suit of debt on an obligation would be

9. Palmer, *County Courts*, 203–9.

10. The standard view seems to be that medieval people routinely made formal documents for any covenant concerning land. Baker, *IELH*, 362; Ibbetson, "Words and Deeds," 72. I have disputed that view before. Palmer, "Covenant," 97–117. This material, along with the material in Chapter 4 at note 21, fortifies the view that leases concerning land were often made without formal documents. In debt litigation not involving performance bonds, creditors did not cite written evidence at least as often as they did cite such evidence. Ibbetson continues to disregard that evidence, largely because he is interested in doctrine and disregards the interplay between jurisdictions: Ibbetson, *Historical Introduction*, 24–25.

11. Baker, *IELH*, 362.

12. CP40/898, m. 338.

13. CP40/599, m. 428.

14. CP40/599, m. 428.

expeditious, and the debt recovered on the bond would often have been far in excess of the actual damages sustained by the lessee. The whole point of the performance bond was to define damages as a debt and to set the debt sufficiently high to coerce the parties to abide by their agreements. The bonds were so punitive that the court frightened people into compliance with their duties without resort to actual litigation. The protection of leaseholds, including leases of parishes, was one of the major functions of the performance bond.[15]

These performance bonds could be quite specific about quiet enjoyment. Robert West, a cleric, obtained such a performance bond of £26.67 for his sublease to protect his possession against William Alston the main lessor and apparently also against the first sublessor, both of whom had entered into the performance bond: "The condition of this obligation is such that if Robert West, cleric, farmer (lessee) of the parsonage of Ragdale and Willou(ghby?) in the county of Leicester peaceably have, possess and enjoy to him and to his assigns the said parsonage with all manner of lands, tenements, issues, profits, emoluments, tithes, oblations, and altarages to the said Robert West without paying anything for the said parsonage to the said William Alston and to his successors during the said term comprised in the said indentures, then this obligation be void, else to stand in his full strength and virtue." The main lessor's successor finally demanded £3.70 under the threat of removing West from the parsonage. West paid, but then sued the sublessor who had also acknowledged the debt for the whole £26.67.[16] Another condition, similar in form, protected the lessee of the parish of Yeovil, Somerset:

> The condition of this obligation is such that if one John Busshe chaplain have, hold, and occupy the farm (lease) of the vicarage of Yeovil in the county of Somerset and peaceably have, take, and receive all manner of rents, tithes, offerings, fruits, and all other profits pertaining to the said vicarage from the day of the date within-written until the feast of the nativity of St. John the Baptist then next ensuing after the form and effect of a pair of indentures between the within-named Richard and the said John Busshe thereof made without any let or interruption of the within-bound John Trensham or any other for him or in his name, that then this present obligation shall be void and had for no strength, else it shall abide in all his strength and virtue.

15. Palmer, *ELABD*, 79–87.
16. CP40/1067, m. 528.

The value of this bond was £40 and likewise resulted in litigation in 1499 when the lessor ejected the lessee in the last period of the lease.[17]

Performance bonds for quiet enjoyment covered a wide range of situations. The two bonds already cited concerned the straightforward ejection of the lessee by the lessor and a much more complicated situation involving sublessees and a problem with a successor main lessor. Other examples expand the possibilities. The parson of Great Staughton intruded on his lessees and cut down forty oak trees and various cherry, apple, and pear trees in the rectory; that action precipitated the lessees' suit in 1390 for the £100 the parson had recognized as a debt in the performance bond for quiet enjoyment.[18] Two lay lessees leased the church of Nutfield, but the parson continued to take the tithes. The lessees subleased to a citizen of London, who found the situation intolerable and surrendered the parish back to the parson. The original lessees then sued the parson in 1386 for the £100 recognized in the performance bond.[19] The parson of Writtle had reserved the use of a solar, two storerooms, three gardens, a choir stall, and the vicary houses and appurtenances when he leased out his church. Thereafter he simply seized in addition two granges and the "house of clerics" in the rectory and ejected the lessees from thirty-five acres of land and twenty acres of meadow. The lessees, however, had a performance bond and sued him in 1388 for the £100 recognized in the bond.[20] Subleases, reservations of use, ordinary desires of the rector to use the premises, pressure by the bishop in visitations, all could result in the disturbance of the lessees. The performance bond was more than adequate compensation for the aggrieved lessee.

Lessees who did not formalize their leasehold in documents could utilize trespassory litigation increasingly from around 1300. The lessees of Choseley rectory in Norfolk in 1495 thus sued John Wylle of Docking, a gentleman, for expelling them from their leasehold. The defendant was claiming the tenement as his own free tenement. Still the parties took issue not on the bare intrusion, but rather on whether the defendant had thereby disseised the lessor monastery.[21] Richard Gryffyn had let the parish of Chipping Warden to Edmund Haselwode. Since the lessor reoccupied the parish, the lessee in 1511 sued him for impeding the taking of his profits.[22] John Hore was the lessee of Battle Abbey in

17. CP40/950, m. 423.
18. CP40/518, m. 101.
19. CP40/501, m. 303.
20. CP40/510, m. 407.
21. KB27/937, m. 62.
22. CP40/997, m. 264.

the rectory of Exning, Suffolk, and sued the rector of Newmarket for taking the tithes from twenty acres of land. The jury decided that the twenty acres were indeed in the parish of Exning and not in the parish of Newmarket, awarding £0.50 in damages and £5 in costs. Since the successful lessee/plaintiff then remitted the damages, this suit was probably a collusive trespassory action brought to resolve the boundary between the two parishes without involving the lessor.[23] Such trespassory litigation provided a lessee with various options useful for preserving his rights in the parish against a whole variety of plausible opponents.

The trespassory remedies for lessees, however, might not have been equal to the real value of the lease. Little information survives on what the monetary damages would be for deprivation of a leasehold. In one case of *quare ejecit*, however, the fee holder was the master of the house of St. Thomas of Acon, London. The master had leased the tenement, which was not a parish, to a tenant for eighty years; the lessee after about four years leased to a sublessee for twenty-four years. On the allegation that rent of £0.67 (the rent for one year) had not been paid, the master ejected the sublessee. The case determined that the rent had been paid, so the plaintiff would receive the damages for loss of the leasehold. A jury assessed the damages for the lessee's loss of a messuage in London on a sublease with twenty-one years remaining at almost £3.33: the equivalent of five years' rent.[24] If this award was typical, as it seems, the damages for loss of a leasehold were clearly inferior to a remedy that would restore possession.[25]

The trespassory remedy that would eventually become central to leasehold protection was the action of ejectment, a thirteenth-century action seldom used in medieval England. Ejectment before 1500 was available for lessees to sue for damages from eviction by people not closely connected to the lessor. Lessors, however, seemed adept at managing evictions in ways that would prevent lessees from using covenant to recover the term; lessees thus had to resort to ejectment

23. CP40/935, m. 330.

24. KB146/10/11/4, KB146/10/12/1, KB27/941, m. 35 (Thomas Derker citizen of London v. John Harding master of house of St. Thomas of Acon, London).

25. What the measure of damages was, was unclear. It could have been the profit the lessee might have expected on the lease, that is, the difference between what he was paying under his lease and what he would have to pay for an equivalent new lease. It could also have been the immediate costs the lessee would incur in losing the current lease and securing another. Measures of damages are not discussed, so historians are left to make educated guesses; for leaseholds we do not have sufficient information even for that.

to recover damages. The legal significance of ejectment, however, changed dramatically in 1500: it became a remedy by which the lessee could recover possession of the leasehold, not just damages. Ejectment thus provided for all leaseholders the protection that covenant provided for lessees of documented leases. Changes in law, however, have a differential impact depending on social situations. The possibility of restoring possession to lessees by ejectment hurt religious houses the most. Manors were not on the market frequently, and ordinary parishes and agricultural tenements for personal occupation usually leased for a very limited term of years. Monasteries rented out their parishes and manors for long terms and thus had greater incentives to have lessees ejected when inflation over the course of decades made their original agreement less desirable. They could adapt by using periodic tenures for leases made after the change so that they could adjust the terms each year. For the long-term leases already granted by 1500, however, they were powerless. The justices of the king's court must have known that their change of the remedy for ejectment was particularly damaging to religious houses: the ordinary handling of litigation would have informed them, even had they not been active members of their own society familiar with the ordinary patterns of commercial relationships.

Ultimate responsibility for the change in ejectment probably rests with John Fyneux, CJKB. In 1499–1500 Fyneux made clear how he felt about arbitrary termination of leases, and it was in the context of a parish lease. The four lessees of a London parish had sued William Nuttyng, a new lessee of the rector who had evicted the four prior lessees, now plaintiffs,

> of this that, whereas Adrian Castellum rector of the parish church of St. Dunstans in the East in the Ward of the Tower of London on 8 June 1497 at London in the same parish and ward had demised to the aforementioned John Arnold, Robert Rydon, Benjamin Dygby, and Thomas Elderton the rectory of the abovesaid church together with all and singular tithes, offerings, profits, fruits, and emoluments whatsoever pertaining or looking to the same rectory to have and to hold to them and their assigns from Easter then next following until the end of a term of five years then next following, which term has not yet expired, by rendering therefrom to the same Adrian during the term £50 of legal English money to be paid at Easter annually, by virtue of which demise the abovesaid John Arnold, Robert Rydon, Benjamin, and Thomas Elderton were thereof possessed, the abovesaid William Nuttyng on 21 June 1498 with force and arms, to wit, with clubs and knives, entered the abovesaid rectory of the

church and ejected the same John Arnold, Robert Rydon, Benjamin, and Thomas Elderton from his abovesaid farm and took and carried away their goods and chattels, to wit, 100 chrisms, 120 pounds of wax worth £8 and £120 of legal English money in numbered coins of the same John Arnold, Robert Rydon, Benjamin, and Thomas Elderton found there then, against the king's peace etc., to the damage of the same John Arnold, Robert Rydon, Benjamin, and Thomas Elderton of £200 etc.

This case went rapidly to a jury, which met under the supervision of Fyneux himself. The jury returned a verdict that the rector had indeed demised as alleged to the first lessees. Fyneux awarded damages of £120 in this case concerning the lease of a rectory to laymen, but the lessees remitted £40 to the new lessee. Plausibly, the remission was in response to the return of the chattels.[26] An award of this size, however, indicated the seriousness with which the court of king's bench and its chief justice had decided to consider leasehold rights. The same year the court of common pleas changed the remedy in ejectment, and that judgment was upheld on error in the court of king's bench.[27] Long-term lessors could no longer simply lease to a third party to evict their sitting lessees, so as to limit their own liability.

Subsequent improvement in the lessee's position seemed to be linked chronologically to erosion of ecclesiastical power. The action of ejectment lay against others than the lessor, so the lessee's position was only moderately improved. Leases not protected by formal documents remained vulnerable to the lessor's actions. Even formal leases, however, were vulnerable as to the lessor's lord if the lessor's heir went into wardship. That vulnerability was eliminated in 1514 and for the duration of Fyneux's tenure, and then finally in 1540.[28] The two dates may be significant indicators of a relationship between church prestige and the remedies of lessees as a whole. The year 1514 was in the middle of the Richard

26. KB146/10/15/1; KB27/954, m. 29. The jury verdict was on the eviction, not on the chattels. That the damage award was in the same amount as the money allegedly taken raises interesting questions, such as whether the allegation of money taken was actually a more precise statement of damages than the traditional statement at the end of the count. More examples would be necessary for any such conclusion.

27. Baker, *IELH*, 341–43; note the similarity in the process with the change of remedy in detinue of charters after the Black Death: Palmer, *ELABD*, 99–102. There was even a prior case in which restitution was requested: Goodyer v. Frowyk, KB27/933, m. 92 (MI494). None of these cases involved the lease of a parish, but parish leases were so frequent the consequences were clear.

28. Baker, *IELH*, 340–41.

Hunne premunire controversy in London.[29] And then by 1540 the crown had dissolved the last of the religious houses. Reductions in the political standing of the church removed the barriers to better protections for lessees. A different ruse for lessors who faced their own formal document was closed off by statute in 1529, an act of the Reformation Parliament.[30] Such remedies for the lessees now protected and made more beneficial the leases of confiscated lands made to the laity; the remedies also stabilized the commercial mechanism that governed the collection of foodstuffs in a society undergoing a social transformation and a major inflation. Parish leases and leases by religious houses were central to any legal alteration in leasehold protections.

Parish leaseholds could be as complex as any other financial transaction, and legal records routinely obscured that complexity. *Fyncheley v. Creswall et al.* in 1512 would have passed as a mundane trespass case had only the original writ and mesne process survived. The writ retailed a complaint of a layman against three yeomen and three husbandmen for the taking and carrying away of four cartloads of hay, two cartloads of peas, two cartloads of wheat, two cartloads of oats, and two cartloads of barley in Staffordshire. From all appearances, it would seem to have been a routine agrarian dispute. When the defendants appeared in court, however, the context broadened somewhat to reveal a problem with a parish lease. One of the prebendaries of the collegiate church of Penkridge had met problems in managing his parish. He had established a bailiff there with a proxy. The bailiff had leased the parish to the now plaintiff in the suit, purportedly for three years at £2 annually. Two weeks later, the prebendary himself had leased the parish to the brother of the now main defendant, who had then expelled the first lessee. That was a more interesting situation, and the question sent to the jury was whether the bailiff had had the power to grant a lease.

The context expanded further at trial level, a level that only rarely appears in the legal records. The bailiff apparently had a proxy to manage and an oral authorization to lease. The lease he had granted to the now plaintiff was not a three-year lease but a one-year lease with periodic renewals until a debt that the prebendary owed to the plaintiff was satisfied—a predicted three years. The first lessee had apparently loaned money to the prebendary to help him acquire the prebend. The prebendary allegedly held himself satisfied with this arrangement,

29. Milsom, "Richard Hunne's 'Praemunire,'" 145–47; Haigh, *English Reformations*, 77–80; Brigden, *London and the Reformation*, 98–103.

30. Baker, *IELH*, 341.

but then leased the parish to the brother of the main defendant nonetheless. The defendant's lawyer, the formidable Anthony Fitzherbert, demurred to the evidence and thus tried to settle the matter on an issue of law: whether an oral authorization to lease was sufficient to have empowered the prebendary's bailiff to grant a lease of the parish. The jury rendered its verdict just in case, saying that if the law was for the plaintiff, he sustained damages of £2 and costs of £0.67. After more than a year the court decided not to determine the matter on the issue of law, but rather to send the original question back to a jury: had the bailiff had the power to grant the lease in the first place. The jury replied that the bailiff had had the power; with the jury assessment and court additions to the verdict, the plaintiff recovered in the end a total of £5.[31] The plaintiff would have had a difficult time recovering the lease, since he had a periodic lease instead of a lease for three years. The first lessee, however, had an independent claim against the prebendary for repayment of the loan that had enabled the prebendary to acquire his prebend. The whole matter then was complicated by two people thinking they had the right to grant the lease. Such a complexity could easily lurk beneath many of the seemingly simple agrarian disputes that populate the legal records.

Protection of the lessee's possession varied according to the formality of the lease and the particular problem the lessee encountered. Even at the end of the period, leaseholds were not as well protected as were free tenements, but protections improved substantially between 1500 and 1540. At least the chronology of the changes would suggest that the situation of parish leases and leases of the lands of religious houses formed a critical part of the decisions to improve the situation of the leaseholder. Still, the combination of covenant, performance bonds, and the varieties of trespassory protections only reinforced the allocations of responsibilities and payment schedules that allowed self-interest to provide the major incentive to both lessor and lessee to abide by the terms of the lease.

Rent

If the central concern of the lessee was quiet enjoyment and possession, the central concern of the lessor was payment of the rent. Default in rental payments constituted the most frequent cause for litigation concerning leaseholds.

---

31. CP40/1001, m. 604.

Nevertheless, since the leasing of parishes was an established, continuing, and successful phenomenon, lessors must have found the complex of remedies to receive their rent at least adequate.

The specifications about payment of the rent were highly varied; the terms of payment, however, always appeared in the agreements. Occasionally the rent was due only annually; more usually the lessee paid in specified, but not always equal amounts two, three, or four times a year. Leases began at any time of the year, not at some particular season. Lessees must have had a certain amount of capital to handle their responsibilities in the parish until the revenues began to accrue, because the lessee might have had to hire a chaplain, provide bread, wine, and wax, and perform other duties. By the time the first payment was due, however, sufficient revenue should have accumulated to permit the rental payment.

Defaults in rental payment occurred at any point in the rental term, without any indication that lessees found a particular difficulty either at the beginning or at the end of the lease. In some cases the lessee had paid no rent at all. Thomas Pigot was not abnormal in failing to meet any of his payments for his two-year leasehold in Wistow parish, Yorkshire: the rector sued him for the entire £28 of the £14 yearly rent.[32] More frequently, however, lessees defaulted only near the end of the term. In 1483 Master Walter Hert leased his rectory of Wheathamstead, Hertfordshire, to Richard Lawdy for a term of three years at £20 annually. Probably during the lease Hert died, so that finally in 1489 his executor sued the lessee, claiming that £40 of the rent was arrear.[33] John Lynce, a clothier and the lessee of Westbury parish, Wiltshire, defaulted in 1486 on the rent for the last third of the fifth year of his five-year lease: £21 of a £63 rent. He found himself in court finally in 1492.[34] Defaulting at the final term was predictably more frequent than at other times, because at that point the lease was completed and the lessee had no particular reason to keep the lessor contented. Overall, however, default occurred at various times, coinciding with all the economic and personal situations a lessee might encounter. Nothing in the record of defaults for parish leases would indicate that those leases were any different from other leases.

Performance bonds increased the incentive for lessees to pay on time, because the bonds established a specific and severe penalty for default. Without a

32. CP40/1002, m. 261.

33. CP40/910, m. 358.

34. CP40/922, m. 355d.

performance bond, the lessor could only demand the rent that was actually owed. Performance bonds were much more severe. The prior of Merton had leased to two lessees for seven years at £8 annually, with payments to be rendered once a year on 1 November. He alleged that the lessees had defaulted in the second year, but only sued midway through the fifth year. Instead of the £8 due for the actual rent, however, he claimed the £10 that had been established as the penalty in the performance bond.[35] John Couper, parson of half of Muggington parish, Derbyshire, leased for nine years the other half of the parish from the prior of Breadsall for £5.33 yearly, to be rendered half at the feast of St. James, half at the feast of the Purification. In the seventh year he missed a payment of £2.67, so that the prior sued him in 1480 for the amount specified in the performance bond: £13.33.[36] When the parties agreed at the beginning of the lease on the sum that would be forfeited on default, they considered the whole range of the obligations of the lease. The whole forfeiture, however, would come due on a default of only a minor part of those duties. In Couper's case, the lessee stood to lose five times the amount of rent he had failed to pay. Performance bonds were the strongest mechanism available for protecting the lessor's right to the rent.

Default in payment of the rent was the major cause of lessor litigation, whether or not the lease used a performance bond. Nevertheless, lessors seem to have been patient. The prior of Merton, in the case above, could have sued immediately after the default in the second year, but chose to wait until toward the end of the five-year lease. That patience was not atypical, and other lessors waited until well after the term had expired completely. The delay had nothing to do with the religious character of the parish, because lawyers demonstrated the same patience with their own clients.[37] More likely the delay was a calculation about their reputation as lessors, their ability to secure a desirable different and new tenant after the expiration of the current lease, the desire to keep an otherwise good tenant who had had difficulties with a parish that was simply not returning a proper yield in a given year or who had been burdened by unexpected taxation, the exercise of patronage and beneficence toward a given lessee because of family or political connections.

Whatever the dynamics of the individual situation, however, the law seems to have provided adequately for the enforcement of the rental payment. While

35. CP40/874, m. 143.
36. CP40/874, m. 401.
37. Palmer, *County Courts*, 95–97.

there was some tendency for defaults to occur at the final payment, that tendency was not so pronounced as to indicate that most lessees would default then or that lessors basically wrote off the final payment. Indeed, the practice of leasing out parishes was a typical way of handling that form of property in late medieval England. That the practice could become so frequent for about a century and a half must indicate that the legal remedies for both lessor and lessee were at least adequate.

Repair

Repair obligations were subsidiary to rental payments in the lessor's mind, but certainly not insignificant; the leasing of parishes generated a whole new dynamic to the chronic problem of church maintenance. The rector was responsible for the repair of the church chancel[38] as well as the rectory and other auxiliary buildings of the parish. The parish itself was responsible for the upkeep of the remainder of the church. The rector's obligation of repair was one of the subjects of the bishop's visitation of the parish.[39] With medieval leaseholds of all kinds, the lessee was normally responsible for everything but an act of God. In some ways the leasehold dynamic could have generated a better situation for repair of church buildings, but whether churches on the whole benefitted in fact is unclear. Repair problems did arise disproportionately in parishes with a corporate rector (appropriated churches and the like).[40] Since corporate rectors, particularly monasteries, leased out rectories for much longer periods, long-term leaseholds were probably not conducive to keeping a church in good repair. With the relatively short leases for ordinary parishes, however, leasehold practice might have been somewhat more favorable for good upkeep.

The leasing of parishes provided a mechanism by which rectors could ensure repair without continual attentiveness. A resident rector necessarily balanced the attraction of self-interested spending with the needs of the church chancel and buildings. The visitation might protect against the resident rector's negligence. A lessor rector encountered a different dynamic. He had to upgrade his parish initially to receive a good rent or else settle for a lower rent in return for a lessee's undertaking to improve the premises. Once that investment was made,

38. Bowker, *Secular Clergy*, 129.

39. Thomson, *Early Tudor Church*, 165.

40. Bowker, *Secular Clergy*, 130. Corporate rectors seem to have accounted for about half the complaints about lack of repair.

the rector could lease and at the end of the term sue the lessees to ensure repair, even the costly repairs that could come with failure to maintain adequate roofing. Aggressive rectors could thus have seen to church building maintenance quite nicely; aggressive maintenance, however, could discourage subsequent lessees. Rectors also had a personal reason to demand upkeep of the buildings: if they wanted to exchange benefices with a colleague, the other side would often require repairs to be completed before the exchange.[41] Still, the dynamics were not always as beneficial in fact as it might seem to have been in theory. Introduction of parish leases created new potential for neglect as well as new incentives for rectors and vicars to ensure that the physical parish was properly maintained.

Religious houses with appropriated parishes used the common law to en-force repair obligations; they responded rapidly to the new leasehold dynamics. In 1386 the prior of Launde sued his lessee in covenant for leaving uncovered the church chancel of Ashby St. Ledgers, the hall, two rooms, a kitchen, a brew house, two granges, a cattle shed, a sheepfold, a malt kiln, a dovecote, and a cart house so that the buildings rotted; the negligent lessee had also allowed the fallow land to go unplowed.[42] The prior of Thetford alleged in the same year that his three lessees had not only defaulted on the rent, but had also neglected to repair the chancel and a grange and had not paid the taxes.[43] In those two instances, the prior of the religious house had apparently retained the repair obligations and then contracted them down to the lessees. In 1505 the abbot of Kenilworth sued his lay lessee for lack of repair ten years into a twenty-one-year lease: the lessor could intervene within a longer term. The jury, however, found that the buildings' roofs had been kept in repair.[44] The repair obligations of an

41. William Kyngesley sued Thomas Crundale cleric in account for payments of £20 from Robert Douceamour. Thomas replied that in London he and Robert Douceamour had con-corded, such that Thomas would exchange with Robert his church of Sutton in Surrey and that Robert would exchange with Thomas his chapel of "Henthill" in Gowersland, Wales. Robert would pay Thomas £20 for repair of the chapel that was then ruinous. Robert had paid Thomas £10 in William's presence. For the other £10 he prosecuted Robert before the mayor in Guildhall by bill until he recovered by judgment. Thus Thomas thought he should not have to render account. CP40/503, m. 373d.

42. CP40/501, m. 234; CP40/503, m. 132; CP40/504, m. 119d.

43. CP40/507, m. 627d.

44. CP40/974, m. 354. See CP40/1080, m. 521, for the lease of the rectory of Napton on the Hill in Warwickshire on 16 May 1520 for thirteen years at £20 annually; the duty of repair was carefully divided between lessor and lessee. CP40/1081, m. 548, has another elaborate division of

appropriated parish might also be, at least in part, within the purview of the
vicar, who could likewise pass them along to the lessees of the vicary. Thus, the
lessee of the church of Shilton, evicted by the vicar for lack of repair, in 1388
claimed that he had not been permitted sufficient wood for the necessary
repairs: the vicar was thus at fault.[45] When Roger Darley resigned the vicary of
East Rigton, Yorkshire, in favor of John Atkynson in 1509, the new vicar
formally assumed all duties of repair to the vicary.[46] The duration of the lease
for an appropriated parish increased dramatically between 1390 and 1500, but
both early and later on religious houses resorted to common law mechanisms to
ensure the performance of repair obligations.

Leases also provided direct mechanisms to secure the improvement of appropriated parishes. Instead of improving the parish prior to leasing, a religious
house could reduce the rent temporarily or long-term in return if the lessee
assumed the burden of substantial necessary repairs. In 1480 the abbot of
Gloucester sued his lessees (a husbandman and his wife) on a covenant to repair
the rectory of Coln during a twenty-one-year lease.[47] Richard Ode, a spicer of
Thorpe Market, Norfolk, had covenanted in 1480 to repair the church barn in
Bradfield; the prior of Coxford eventually had to sue him to secure performance.[48] In 1471 the abbot of Thornton leased to Thomas Gylby the parish of
Kelstern, Lincolnshire, for sixty years at an annual rent of only £3. Part of
Gylby's obligations, however, was to construct the church chancel from the
ground up, as well as to repair the other rectory buildings and then maintain
both chancel and rectory buildings. The abbot as late as 1496 sued Gylby's
executor to secure performance, since Gylby had chosen to repair the existing
chancel rather than to rebuild. The justices thought that that repair would be
sufficient if the repair matched the original building specifications.[49] John
Archer, the lessee of the parish of Rousham, Oxfordshire, subjected himself to a
performance bond for £20 in 1511; part of his leasehold obligation thus secured
was to repair the parsonage. Judgment of the satisfactory completion of the task
was left to neutral third parties: two named gentlemen of the parish. The

---

repair responsibilities; this one involved the vicar of Lowdham, Notthinghamshire, who was the
lessee of the rectories of Matlock and Bonsall in Derbyshire for three years at £40 annually.

45. CP40/511, m. 523d.
46. CP40/1003, m. 317.
47. CP40/874, m. 400.
48. CP40/899, m. 117.
49. CP40/935, m. 312.

creditor under the bond, however, was the bishop of Lincoln, who sued him in 1514 for the penalty amount.[50] Bishops as well as religious houses adapted successfully to the new regime and used leasehold conditions and mechanisms to upgrade the physical parish.

Performance bonds and actions of covenant sufficed to enforce repair with formal leases; for informal leases lessors resorted to the old action of waste. Waste was a traditional remedy against a tenant with restricted rights who seriously diminished the value of a tenement. The doweress, who had only a lifetime interest in her dower, was a typical defendant in waste. Landlords could utilize that same remedy against lessees. The abbot of Notley on 1 April 1502 had leased the rectory of Stoke Lyne, Oxfordshire, to the rector of the neighboring parish of Fringford and a gentleman. In 1514 the abbot sued them because they had not taken care of the roofing of the buildings, and the large beams had rotted. The abbot complained specifically about a hall worth £3.33, a chamber worth £4, a bake house worth £2, and a barn worth £5.[51] The abbot of Missenden in 1484 had leased the rectory of Chalfont, Buckinghamshire, for twenty-one years to William Wycle and Eleanor, his wife. William died, and Eleanor subleased the rectory to Edward Brudenell. In 1503, toward the expiration of the term, the abbot sued Brudenell for waste. He had allowed the roofing of a barn worth £5 and a kitchen worth £2.67 to deteriorate so that the beams rotted. He had cut down forty acres of wood, including eight hundred oak trees, two hundred beech trees, and one hundred ash trees, as well as four apple trees and a pear tree. The damage, by the abbot's estimate, was £20.[52] Whether by planning in advance with performance bonds or by using the action of waste, the lessor could protect the parish from damage done by the lessees.

While institutional rectors were more prominent in cases regarding repair obligations, ordinary rectors were no less concerned about the failure of lessees to maintain the parish buildings. The parson of Todenham complained that his lessees had not repaired the roofing of the cattle shed and sheepfold and had allowed twenty perches of earthen wall to become ruinous.[53] In 1514 the rector of Knapwell, Cambridgeshire, sued one of his three lessees for the parish for the

---

50. CP40/1002, m. 224d.

51. CP40/1006, m. 276d; CP40/1007, m. 335.

52. CP40/962, m. 363. See m. 340 for the abbot's claim of rent arrear from the rectory in the amount of £40, which the abbot actually recovered.

53. CP40/499, m. 193.

penal sum of £29.50: the lessees had allowed the roofs of the church buildings and the chancel to fall into disrepair, with consequent structural damage.[54] In 1411 the parson of Clayton, Sussex, sued Richard Eyer of Lewes, a draper, on a performance bond of £5. The defeasance provided that the debt would be void if Eyer repaired the hall, kitchen, barn, and stable of the rectory of Clayton at his own expense in those things that had happened by his negligence or default.[55] Such matters predictably might find their way to arbitration. A panel of arbitrators had thus rendered an award in 1535 that gave the lessee security in his third year of the lease of Baginton rectory, but also required him to execute a performance bond. The £20 performance bond ensured payment of the rent, sufficient repair, and construction of an enclosure, as well as satisfaction for a dispute about some wood. The eventual dispute on the performance bond was whether the repair of a barn had been sufficient.[56] Parish buildings in good repair were central to the rector's ability to secure an appropriately high rent, so rectors had a strong incentive to enforce repair obligations on their lessees.

The continuing difficulties with ill repair finally resulted not in a better remedy enforced by ecclesiastical officials, but in a direct remedy at common law. The new remedy alleged a custom that rectors and prebendaries were obliged to maintain rectory buildings; if a rector or prebendary left the buildings in disrepair, whether by death, exchange, or mere resignation, the succeeding rector could recover sufficient damages from the departing rector or his estate to repair the premises.[57] This remedy even applied against bishops:

Devon. John, bishop of Exeter, by his attorney presents himself on the fourth day against Richard, bishop of Ely late bishop of Exeter concerning a plea why, whereas according to the custom of the realm of the king of England hitherto used and approved all and singular bishops of the same realm for the time being are held to repair and sustain all and singular houses, edifices, and mills of their dioceses and to leave them to their successors sufficiently repaired and sustained, and if they do not leave such manner houses, edifices, and mills to such their successors repaired and sustained as already set forth but at the time at which they are translated from such bishopric they leave them unrepaired and dilapi-

54. CP40/1006, m. 491.

55. CP40/845, m. 198.

56. CP40/1093, m. 330 (1537).

57. Thomson mentions the liability of executors for repairs, but seems to assume that only the bishops enforced it. Thomson, *Early Tudor Church*, 165–66.

dated, they are held to satisfy their successor bishops of the bishoprics from their own goods and chattels after their translation according to the true value of such lack of repair and dilapidation, and although the abovesaid Richard now bishop of Ely was lately bishop of Exeter and from that same bishopric of Exeter was translated to the bishopric of Ely recently and the abovesaid John now bishop of Exeter afterwards was lawfully translated from the bishopric of Coventry and Lichfield to the bishopric of Exeter, nevertheless the said Richard now bishop of Ely left the houses, edifices, and mills of the said bishopric of Exeter in Clyst, Bishop's Crediton, Nymet, Bishop's Tawton, Bishop's Chudleigh, Ashburton, Paignton, Radway, Taynton Bishop's, and Exeter in the abovesaid county unrepaired and dilapidated, which same dilapidations reach the value of £1,000 as we are given to understand and that the houses, edifices and mills abovesaid cannot be repaired for a smaller sum than £1,000, for which certain repairs of dilapidations the abovesaid John often asked the aforementioned Richard now bishop of Ely to satisfy after he was translated from the said bishopric of Coventry and Lichfield into the bishopric of Exeter as has been related, nevertheless the same Richard now bishop of Ely wholly did not want and still refuses to satisfy the aforementioned John now bishop of Exeter for those repairs and dilapidations, to the damage of the same John, bishop of Exeter of £1,200.[58]

The new writ was available at least as early as 1497 and was brought by rectors and prebendaries against living predecessors or their executors and for repairs valued from £40 to £1,000.[59] In 1513 the new rector of Kettering sued the executor of his predecessor for damages of £20 to the church chancel, £20 to the hall, £20 to six chambers, £40 to two barns, £20 to a stable, £10 to a dovecote,

58. CP40/962, m. 173.

59. Other examples of the writ, whose effect continued after 1529: CP40/942, m. 72 (prebend of Leighton Buzzard); CP40/966, m. 299 (prebend of Langford); CP40/1067, m. 564d (rectory of Glatton, Huntingdonshire); CP40/1078 (parish of Warkworth, Northumberland); CP40/1077, m. 15d, CP40/1078, mm. 381, 587 (parish of Clyst Hydon, Devon); CP40/1074, m. 595, CP40/1075, m. 171d (parish of Stanway, Essex). The writ survived the 1530s. In 1544 the rector of Upwell sued the executors of Leson, the late rector, for repair: CP40/1122, m. 384d. In 1546 Augustine Dudley, the rector of Castor, sued the executor of John Bayton claiming for repair £2 for the church chancel, £1 for the hall, £6.67 for four rooms, £5 for the eight-foot long barn, £10 for the malthouse, £5 for another barn, £2 for the dovecote, and £1 for the surrounding stone wall: KB27/1139, m. 130.

and £20 to four stone walls.[60] No longer did repair obligations rest solely on ecclesiastical process, performance bonds, or waste. Despite the common law action, however, St. German wanted to go somewhat further and make that action statutory, but without increasing its scope.[61] Nevertheless, after 1497 rectors could have been in no doubt about the need to keep parish buildings in repair, particularly if they had any aspiration to exchange or change benefices.

In these areas the executors of a deceased priest who had not repaired might avoid litigation by submitting to arbitration. The vicar of Kenton, Devon, died leaving his vicarage in disrepair. His two executors committed themselves to a performance bond of £20 to stand to the arbitration of four arbitrators concerning the repair "whereof strife and debate now hang between the said parties." The arbitrators awarded that the executors pay £3.30 for all the repairs on the chancel of the church and for all burdens in the vicarage of Kenton. When the executors failed to pay, the successor vicar sued them for the £20 provided in the performance bond.[62] John Soham, gentleman and apparent lessee of Great Massingham parish, similarly entered into an arbitration agreement with the rector concerning the repair of the church chancel. He gave to Robert Borowe, citizen and alderman of York, his bond of £20 to stand to the arbitration award of three men, with the stipulation that the bond was only to be considered his bond if the rector submitted a similar bond. Since the rector had not submitted such a bond, Soham claimed that the bond was not his. The jury disagreed with him on the facts.[63] The lease of the parish of Burneston, Yorkshire, included specifications for the repair of the manse and associated buildings: two barns, a brew house, a malt kiln, a granary, a dovecote, and a residence outside the gate of the hall. Adequate maintenance on this leasehold, fairly typical as a lease for three years at £29 annually, was to be adjudged by the supervision of four or six men chosen by the lessor and lessee, and was ensured by a £100 security bond subscribed by four sureties.[64] The availability of performance bonds made arbitration an acceptable alternative to straightforward litigation, and lessors and lessees resorted to arbitration thus reinforced with the same ease as did the parties of any other dispute.

60. KB147/2/5/1, Thomas Lark rector of Kettering, Northamptonshire v. William Harryngton executor of James Whitscaus late rector of Kettering, by bill of Middlesex.

61. "St. German's Parliamentary Draft of 1531," ed. Guy, 128.

62. CP40/978, m. 334d.

63. CP40/986, m. 509d.

64. CP40/1004, m. 532.

Performance bonds were just as useful for shielding rectors from repair obligations as they were for binding lessees to sufficient repair. The new rector of Compton, Sussex, thus committed himself to a performance bond of £100 on 28 February 1531. He was supposed to deliver within twelve days of his induction an acquittance of all dilapidation and repairs of his church to the outgoing rector, the new rector of Rattlesden, Suffolk, as well as a decree giving the old rector a pension.[65] Apparently the rector failed to deliver the required documents; the ensuing suit would have more than compensated the outgoing rector for any damages. The vicar of Effingham, Surrey, similarly entered into a performance bond on 23 January 1533; it recited his intention to resign his benefice to the use of another. The new vicar was to secure a pension for him and to deliver an acquittance of all dilapidation, as well as to ensure the old vicar's ability to continue to collect and store tithes for the following two months. The bond, again, was worth £100; it likewise came to litigation.[66] A bond for £66.67, made on 14 March 1531, enforced similar provisions for the vicary of Croydon, Northamptonshire.[67] This kind of performance bond between rectors functioned to facilitate exchanges of rectories rather than to regulate the relationship between lessors and lessees.

Although the common law remedies played a prominent role in church repair, they did not positively exclude bishops from being involved in the repair of churches. The bishop of Norwich got himself into trouble precisely because of his aggressive stance on an issue of repair of a church chancel in a dispute between the abbot of Bury St. Edmunds (who was also the rector of Mildenhall, Suffolk) and the vicar of Mildenhall. Litigation before the bishop raised some questions about the disposition of the tithes, so neither the abbot nor the vicar could collect the 3,600 sheaves already left in the field. The bishop ordered the parishioners to guard those sheaves at their own expense; the parishioners refused to accept this additional burden. The bishop then excommunicated the parishioners until they repented and paid a fine: nine parishioners paid £1.50 each; eighty-two parishioners, £0.50; one parishioner, a bit over £2. The fines from the parish totaled almost £57. The bishop's actions were then presented to the justices of the peace, of whom James Hobart, the king's attorney general, was one. Those indicted in the process were the bishop, the vicar, the sum-

65. CP40/1076, m. 343.
66. CP40/1077, m. 510.
67. CP40/1073, m. 348d.

moners, and a scrivener. When the case arrived in the king's bench, the bishop had already arranged a pardon.[68] The bishop of Norwich had also supervised a settlement of a dispute between a cleric and several laymen that had the laymen in 1505 agreeing to pay the cleric an annual rent and to exonerate him concerning the dilapidation of the church of Great Melton. The bishop's settlement took the form of having the laymen put themselves under a performance bond of £20.[69] Bishops could participate best using common law forms, but they could also use their own courts within the bounds prescribed by the king's law.

The new leasehold regime dictated changing methods for ensuring repair of churches. Once a church was in appropriate repair, rectors had every reason to make sure that lessees kept them maintained: the rector's ability to exchange his current position for a better one and the right to repair the buildings without additional cost to himself were great incentives. Bishops, moreover, could intervene to insist on repair, and subsequent rectors came to be able to reach their predecessor's estate. Parishioner activity would seem to have been the natural outcome of the situation in which rectors themselves were often not personally involved in the parish. By determining that the leasing of a parish was an ordinary leasehold transaction, the common law changed the dynamics of ensuring the upkeep of church buildings. The treatment of parishes as leaseholds could in itself have led to less rigorous repair; the auxiliary remedies available under the common law might have counterbalanced the ordinary expectations attendant on leaseholds.

Taxes and Expenditures

While some instruments specified in great detail the obligations of the lessee and included responsibility for taxes, even the informal lease of the parish probably carried that obligation as well. The lessee's assumption of both taxes and ordinary expenses emphasized the degree to which the rector was no longer involved with the parish for the duration of the lease. As long as the rector received his rent, he had no reason to bother with the parish during the term of the lease.

The miscellaneous responsibilities assumed with the lease at times substantially increased the burdens of the lessee. Cuthbert Tunstall, the vicar of Kirkby in Kendal, in 1514 sued the archdeacon of Richmond on a performance bond for £300 made 14 March 1511 for a one-year lease of Kirkby in Kendal. The arch-

68. KB27/977, m. 17 rex; KB27/1008, m. 11d Rex; KB27/1013, m. 15 Rex.
69. CP40/997, m. 282.

deacon recounted that he had paid almost £10 for having divine services performed for that year in the parish and had paid £1.33 to the pope, more than £3.50 to the procurator of the abbot of York for tithes, £1 to the procurator at the time of visitation, more than £7.70 for bread, wine, and other ordinary expenses in the parish. In that parish the expenses added about £23 to the burdens of the lessee, about a fifth of what was paid in rent.[70] The ordinary and extraordinary expenses of the parish were a significant part of the cost of running a parish.

Some of those expenses were fixed; others were as unpredictable for expenses as mortuary fees were for income. The lease of Colwich parish, Staffordshire, had specified that the lessees would bear the burden of any taxation. The lessees held the parish for half of the five-year term at £21 annually and then surrendered the parish back into the hands of the prebendary lessor. Before the surrender, however, Convocation had granted the king a levy of two-tenths on ecclesiastical property. For the Colwich prebend, that grant amounted to £8.67. The lessees maintained that they had paid; the lessor would not admit that payment, but alleged a default on the following rental payment of £10.50. The taxation seems to have put the lessees into a position that was no longer profitable.[71] An unexpected levy equal to more than a third of the rent due could easily consume the whole profit margin on a lease.

The unpredictable character of extraordinary expenses should have made taxation a frequent cause of litigation. Seemingly, it did not. Had the responsibility remained with the rector, default would have had an impact on the lessees. Since the basic responsibility seemed to reside with the lessees, more cases should appear in which the imposition of taxation provoked the surrender of the leasehold. Perhaps the offer of surrender itself would produce a compromise between lessor and lessee, with the lessor not wanting to drive off a good tenant. Perhaps lessees paid the taxation in accord with the agreement, but then were unable to make the rental payment, so that the consequences of extraordinary burdens appeared in a failure to pay the rent.

Reservations

Not all rectors who leased out their parish actually lost touch with the parish; a lease could provide a retirement option for an older or infirm rector. Retirement

70. CP40/1007, m. 346.
71. CP40/950, m. 520.

may have been behind the lease from William Throkmorton, rector of Great Houghton, Northamptonshire, to William Crawne, a papal notary, in 1507. The lease was for a term of three years at a rent of £20, secured by a performance bond for £40. The terms provided that the lessee would assume the stipend for the chaplain, repair obligations, and ordinary and extraordinary burdens and receive all profits whatsoever from the parish. The rector, however, explicitly reserved two chambers in the rectory tower and a stable for his horses, as well as the right to choose who the chaplain for the parish would be. He had chosen Hugh Aspnall to be the parish priest at a stipend of £5.67. Within the first year, however, the rector intervened for default of payment of the rent and expelled the lessee. The situation resulted in two different suits: the lessee sued the lessor in covenant to regain the leasehold; the lessor sued the lessee in debt to obtain the £40 under the performance bond.[72] This rector had retained a continuing relationship with the parish and was perhaps in residence but retired.

A few lessors chose to retain some hold on the parish for other reasons. Richard Nele was the rector of North Pickenham, but also the rector of South Pickenham, Norfolk. In 1510 he leased South Pickenham parish to Thomas Sylesden, a gentleman of London, but reserved for his own use a room in the rectory with free entry and exit for the whole three years, as well as the use of a barn. Since the rector continued to carry the burden of finding a priest to serve this parish and his other parish was close by, he was still in contact with the parish, even though he had leased it out.[73] In 1410 Mr. John Wodham, parson of Milton, leased out the fruits and profits of his parish to John Knapton, a chapman of Cambridge, but the parson retained the advowson of the vicary, the houses of the manse with the kitchen and other buildings, and the adjacent garden and wood and all the profits of wood of whatever kind. The annual rent was £20 for the duration of the three-year term. At Easter of 1411, however, Richard Lord Strange, with the assent of the parson, proceeded to occupy the rectory with his family and horses, with the intent of expelling the lessee from his leasehold. The lessee responded, he now alleged, simply by surrendering his leasehold to the parson.[74] John Denham, rector of Great Brickhill, leased out his parish in 1498, but retained the chief chamber in the manse and stable and pasture for two horses. He retained as well the obligations for taxes and for the

72. CP40/982, mm. 414, 512.
73. CP40/1005b, m. 558; CP40/1006, m. 305.
74. CP40/623, m. 307.

initial upgrade of the buildings. The clerical lessee had the responsibility of finding a priest to care for the parish—probably himself.[75] In these three leases, the lessor had retained a physical presence on the parish, so leasing clearly did not inevitably entail insulation from the parish.

The reasons for making a reservation within the lease, however, could be idiosyncratic. John Elton, rector of Stanton, Nottinghamshire, reserved accommodations in his rectory when he leased it. He wanted to reside in Collingham, but was worried that there might be an outbreak of the pestilence there and wanted to retain the right to live on the rectory during such a dangerous period.[76] This reservation had no relationship to duty or attachment to the parish. The varieties of human motivations could inevitably find matching documentation elsewhere in the records.

Most leases did not contain reservations of accommodations in the parish; only a few lessors seemed to retain that kind of close attachment to the parish. The fact that some did make such reservations, however, indicates that leasing the parish was very much like any other lease. Leases were flexible instruments, capable of being used for both beneficent and self-interested reasons, purely for economic gain, or for adjustment for illness and old age, or from disinterest in financial management.

Parish Relationships

The presence of lessees changed relationships within the parish. Treatment of the parish normally has assumed a dynamic between the ecclesiastics (rector, vicar, curate/chaplain) and the parishioners internally, and then between the parish ecclesiastics and the external officials.[77] Such a treatment of the parish assumed the rector or perpetual vicar actually retained control. The insertion of lessees, however, complicated the allocations of power within the parish. The lessees had common law rights against the rector, before, but particularly after, 1500. The lessees, not the rector, normally appointed the priest who served the parish. The lessees would often have been the force that compelled the rector to sue in church court to enforce the parish's fiscal dues. And, finally, the bishop's actions to remedy problems in the parish would often have burdened the rector, who, instead of performing himself, would have had to take action, with conse-

75. CP40/962, m. 554.
76. CP40/1084, m. 522.
77. See Haigh, *English Reformations*, 46–47.

quent liabilities, against the lessees. A commercialized parish presented a much more complex web of relationships that made for less expeditious episcopal supervision.

The rector's lease of the parish actually reduced the effective supervision of the bishop over pastoral care in the parish. The bishop, of course, was ultimately responsible for the spiritual welfare of those in his diocese. Prior to the Black Death archdeacons seem regularly to have visited parishes to inquire into defects; bishops often fulfilled their obligation to visit parishes every third year. After the Black Death archdeacons could treat the visitation right solely as a right to levy fees even when they did not actually visit. Bishops only occasionally performed systematic visitations.[78] If actual visitations did decline in frequency, the decline occurred at the time that rectors regularly began to lease out their parishes.

Leasing a parish would not protect it from a visitation, but enforcement of ecclesiastical expectations would have been more difficult. With a rector who retained control over a parish, whether in person or through a chaplain or bailiff, responsibility was clear. When the common law was available to enforce a rector's leasing obligations to a lessee or even a sublessee, the scope of action for the visitation was less clear. The visitor could still correct problems within the parish, such as local morality concerns raised by the church wardens, the upkeep of the nave, the provision of religious services, the morality of the de facto parish priest. The visitor, moreover, could sequester the profits of the rectory for maintenance of the chancel.[79] If the lessee hired a chaplain for a year, however, the chaplain could well be gone before any effective action could take place because of mandates from a visitation. Swanson indicates that bishops may have been more intent on pursuing problems that appeared with individual parishes rather than making visitations of every parish;[80] with the leasing of parishes becoming the norm, that might have been a very reasonable adaptation. Certainly, vigorous action on parish problems was still possible. Haigh cites twenty-three sequestrations for lack of cure from 1507 to 1515 in the Norwich diocese and five for lack of repair.[81] Bowker at times viewed the visitation

---

78. Swanson, *Church and Society*, 163–65. Thomson, however, concludes that visitation practice was maintained and that it remained an important means of episcopal control. Thomson, *Early Tudor Church*, 120–21. This assessment may be a bit optimistic about the institutional competence of church organization. Haigh, *English Reformations*, 40–44.

79. Thomson, *Early Tudor Church*, 12, 122.

80. Swanson, *Church and Society*, 164.

81. Haigh, *English Reformations*, 43.

process in the Lincoln diocese in the early sixteenth century positively.[82] The practice of leasing parishes complicated regulation of local church practice, whether or not the visitation process remained an effective device for regular supervision of the late medieval parish.

A bishop's control over selection of parish personnel had always been limited because of advowson rights, but with the leasing of parishes, the bishop's ability to ensure the quality of parish priests could become nominal. The bishop continued to have the right to examine the nominee made by a patron for a rectory: that examination was the bishop's traditional limitation on the right of advowson. Prior to the Black Death, that ability at least put the bishop in control over the person with direct responsibility for the parish. That rector could then hire a chaplain, and every diocese ordained many chaplains to serve auxiliary to rectors. The bishop at least had a chance to approve the person who hired the chaplain and who retained direct responsibility and control. After the Black Death the bishop still examined the candidate for the position of rector, although the examination may not have been as searching as after the Reformation.[83] After the examination, however, the rector often took on a lessee, perhaps a layman, who then hired the chaplain. The lessee could even sublease the parish, so that the bishop's examination and the rector were even further removed from determining who provided parish services. Any chaplain, of course, had to be licensed to practice within the diocese: the bishop still retained that form of minimal control, but he was now at a much further remove from parish activity.

Bishops apparently did not supervise the leasing process effectively. Lander thinks that few rectors were nonresident without official permission and provision of a substitute, at least in the 1520s; a lease, however, would have provided for the hiring of that substitute.[84] Thomson is somewhat more circumspect: "When parish clergy served their cure by deputy, this could have been officially authorized."[85] Certainly, many such licenses survive, and unlicensed absence was considered an offense.[86] The real question, however, is whether unlicensed nonresidence was considered any offense when the lessees had appointed a sufficient chaplain who was fulfilling the duties: when the parish was in fact

82. Bowker, *Secular Clergy*, 17–18, but see Bowker, *Henrician Reformation*, 37–38, 46.
83. Bowker, *Henrician Reformation*, 129–31.
84. Lander, "Church Courts and the Reformation," 42.
85. Thomson, *Early Tudor Church*, 171–72.
86. Ibid., 172.

working well. None of the writers considers the effect of leases of entire parish operations. Any action to void a lease rather than simply to compel the purchase of a license, however, might have made the bishop vulnerable to an accusation that he was overturning an arrangement protected by the common law. A rector could, of course, stipulate the necessity of the bishop's license for the lease, as happened once in 1407. John Colley, parson of Kelshall, Hertfordshire, had leased his parish to Thomas Shene, a chaplain, in 1407 for three years at £17.33 annually. The parson stipulated that the lessee would find security for the payment of the rent and would also obtain a license from the bishop for the lease. When the lessee had neither found security nor obtained the license within three months, John entered and ejected him. In 1410 Thomas sued the rector for ejecting him within the term. The lessee was willing to admit the condition about finding security for the rent (and he maintained that he had found such security), but expressly denied the stipulation about a license from the bishop. Whether that stipulation had been made or not was the question that would be put to the jury to determine the case.[87] That the parties took issue on that point indicates that such a stipulation about obtaining the bishop's license was a special provision, not one assumed in all parish leases. That the alleged stipulation about the license required a license to be obtained only after the lease began would likewise indicate that the bishop's license was not a precondition for the validity of the lease, but only a formality required by the rector. Leases in 1497, 1516, and 1523 similarly had provisions about securing the bishop's license.[88] All four of these leases indicate that the lease arrangements were worked out prior to the license from the bishop; the rector wanted to avoid the problem of being cited, but was confident enough of the lease to proceed in the negotiations before obtaining the license. The arrangements that determined who in fact received the tithes and mortuaries, lived in the rectory, and hired the chaplain to serve the people of the parish took place out of sight of the bishop and without his supervision. The bishop might compel the rector or vicar to obtain the license, but only after the fact.

Had the church courts been able to retain jurisdiction over litigation involving church leases, the bishop might have been in a better position to enforce church rules. Fyneux, however, made leases more secure by allowing plaintiffs in ejectment to regain possession of the term; he thus imperilled the position of religious houses that had made long-term parish leases. Shortly thereafter, he

87. CP40/599, m. 375.
88. CP40/962, m. 437; CP40/1067, m. 528; CP40/1052, m. 534.

also made premunire process available against church courts that tried to handle parish leases. Such premunire cases appeared in 1502, three times in 1504, then thereafter at least in 1508 and 1522.[89] The availability of premunire did not mean that church courts in fact did not handle cases concerning church leases, but the difficulties for church jurisdiction were greater than would have been the case with only prohibition procedure. Under prohibition procedure, the court could at least have proceeded safely if neither party objected. With premunire process a disappointed and losing defendant could prosecute after the case had concluded. Only dedicated church court judges would take such risks.

The lease of parishes circumvented the bishop's reasonably direct control over who served the parish. The ability of the rector or vicar to lease his parish out to any lay or clerical person removed the rector himself from direct involvement with the parish: it severed the direct relationship between the religious dues of the parishioners and the provision of religious services. At the same time, however, the insulation of the rector from the parish accomplished a similar reduction of the bishop's involvement with the parish. The relationship of the bishop with parishes had changed drastically between the thirteenth and the fifteenth century, even though the relationship between the bishop and the rector had remained the same.

Conclusion

English common law considered parish leases as no different from leases of commercial or agrarian properties, but that judicial stance altered the allocations of power surrounding the English parish. The parish was in fact the fundamental unit of religious organization; the rules governing the parish assumed that the bishop could exercise regulatory power to encourage religion and derive revenue. In the late fourteenth century, however, the common law regularly enforced parish leases and then also developed the performance bond to secure the legal relationship, seemingly even when the bishop had not been consulted in advance. After 1500 lessees could reclaim possession of the lease itself in ejectment. Those legal developments dictated new legal rights and thus new patterns of relationships. Those new relationships, structured along the lines of leasehold—rental payments, possession of leasehold, reservation of rights to reside, allocation of the duty to hire a priest and of the right to collect

89. KB27/963, m. 34; KB27/970, m. 29d; KB27/971, m. 69; KB27/973, m. 35d; KB27/988, m. 61d; KB27/1044, m. 77.

various tithes, mortuary fees, and offerings—marginalized bishops and transformed the rector primarily into a landlord/lessor who was often only interested in the fixed return received from the lessees. Few parishioners would have been gracious enough to consider the indirect benefit of their tithes to the rector or the abstract way in which paying tithes to a lay lessee satisfied a religious duty. For many parishioners the accurate and rigorous payment of tithes would have seemed simply a contribution to the lessee's profit margin. Even the chaplain who served the parish only received a set stipend, and church offerings and mortuary fees likewise went to the lessees. The late medieval English parish was, put simply, an item of commerce regulated by the common law. While parish leasing made the aggregation of agricultural surplus more efficient, commercializing the parish encouraged complaints like that of Chaucer and drew the clergy even more from their pastoral duties. In 1529, when Henry VIII and Parliament began the reformation of the parish by statute, they were reforming a parish whose operations had become integral to commercial society. The king's court had subverted the traditional operations of the parish; the king's court would be Henry VIII's instrument for reforming the parish back into some reasonable congruence with the traditional expectations.

CHAPTER SIX

Reforming the Parish by Statute

n 1529 Henry VIII through Thomas Cromwell began the reformation of
the English parish by statute. These statutes transformed church management immediately, and the effect only increased over the succeeding
decade. In their range, aim, and insight into human behavior, they were extraordinary. They reformed the lifestyle of priests by dictating that priests were to be
dedicated to properly spiritual tasks and not involved in commerce. They
empowered the laity to compel rectors and vicars to reside on the parish and to
avoid commerce, although the rector could still use leases as a management tool.
They limited the revenue available to the church. No legislation can make
individuals, even priests, into spiritual persons in fact, but these statutes coerced
priests into channeling their overt actions in that direction. The statutes took
special notice of the leasehold and thus of a central phenomenon of parish life
in late medieval England. Clerical involvement in holding a lease and the
attendant entanglements in the commercial sphere were to end. Had Henry
VIII and Cromwell, like Luther or Calvin, been focused primarily on religion
and spirituality, they would have abolished the leasing of parishes altogether.
They were not and did not. Parish leaseholds were integral to the economy and
the collection and distribution of food. The parish therefore continued to be
for sale, but only to the laity.

The statutes struck a deep chord in English minds because so much of the
content was traditional. The English church, particularly in the thirteenth
century, had been quite straightforward about prohibiting clerics from engaging
in commercial enterprises. English canon law had explicitly prohibited clerics
from secular commercial activity and at times prohibited the clergy from seeking profit by buying cheap and selling at a higher price merely by lapse of time.
Church statutes likewise forbade clerics from becoming bailiffs to laymen in any
relationship that would require them to give an accounting. In the same manner,
the church had prohibited the leasing of tithes and of churches to ecclesiastics,

but particularly to laymen.[1] Chaucer lionized the godly parson who as a shepherd stayed in his parish and did not become the commercial entrepreneur who leased out his rectory and went to London to increase his wealth.[2] Those sentiments were still alive in England. Cardinal Wolsey, backed by the king, had begun in 1518 to punish those who fled from the rural parishes, who chose to absent themselves from their benefice and to live in London with a revenue augmented by serving as assistants in the London parishes.[3] The statutes continued Wolsey's initiative; they implemented after Wolsey fell a reform agenda that was traditional in content. The agenda, however, was revolutionary in its assumption of the right of the crown to regulate the church directly, in its imposition of substantial penalties, and in its use of the laity to implement royal policy. Using the laity to implement royal policy effectively empowered them to regulate their priests. The statutes implemented a local reformation by dramatically reallocating power within the parish from priests to the laity. By implementing traditional ideas about keeping the clergy out of commercial endeavor, the statutes left the commercial arena decisively to the laity.

The Historiography of the Statutes of 1529

The statutes of 1529 restructured a central element of the religious and socio-economic fabric of Tudor England. The intent was to compel the clergy to direct their activities to a spiritual, noncommercial realm; the statutes thus remedied as much as possible the abuses of clerical commercialism and absenteeism that the church had not resolved effectively. The clerical society of towns, the absence of rectors from their parishes without accountability, and pluralism were to become exceptional. Moreover, as of 1529, the leasehold market became lay; lay investors acquired a much greater range of opportunity before, but particularly after, 1536 when the lands of the religious houses became available. As of 1529, however, the statutes tightly regulated the upper sector of leaseholds. No longer could the clergy lease land or parishes; the number of parishes leased would decline. Clerical lessors now had to rely mostly on lay lessees; changing the market put those lay lessees in a much more favorable bargaining position. By intervening in the utilization of landed wealth, the statutes set up a spiritual, that is, noncommercial, side of society that was in its own way as distinctive as

---

1. See above, Chapter 4.
2. Chaucer, *The Canterbury Tales*, General Prologue, ll. 505–18.
3. Brigden, *London and the Reformation*, 56; Haigh, *English Reformations*, 84–86.

the medieval clerical order. Clerics would still be able to own land outright; they likewise could be lessors; they could sell the produce paid in to the rectory. What they could not do was invest for speculative profit: holding a lease or buying produce for resale. Succeeding statutes completed the reformation of the parish clergy and the erection of the new divisions in society.

The statutory agenda of 1529, nonetheless, has received little attention from historians; even those who treat the statutes seriously concentrate on the less important, more "religious" provisions. General works largely ignore the statutes or mention them only briefly, because the subject matter seemed traditionally Catholic. David Keir considered that the 1529 statutes did not "invade any really new ground." He only mentioned the content of the statutes in passing.[4] Loades only mentioned the regulation of probate, mortuary fees, and clerical pluralism; and that mention came only in one clause leading into a consideration of premunire actions. The concerns, he thought, were "traditional grievances."[5] Geoffrey Elton ignored them completely in both his survey and his collection of Tudor documents, barely mentioned them in *Policy and Police*, and showed interest in them otherwise only insofar as Cromwell was involved or as they could be ascribed to official governmental policy.[6] John Guy, concerned mainly with setting out the alliances and dynamics of the Reformation Parliament, simply left out the statutes in his survey; in his treatment of Sir Thomas More he was dubious about how important the statutes were for the laity, but emphasized, correctly, the radical intrusion into spheres that had traditionally been subject only to ecclesiastical regulation.[7] Leo Solt had at least a sentence on the statutes, but only as a probable precedent to later matters.[8] Susan Brigden thought that the statutes "contained so many loopholes that the clergy found endless ways of evasion."[9] For these historians, there was no parish reformation in 1529.

The historians who do treat the statutes treat them only partially. Margaret Bowker analyzes the pluralism prohibition sensibly together with the tax on newly acquired benefices as part of a dynamic that encouraged longer-term tenure in benefices and made more benefices available to the clergy. She thinks the same dynamic concentrated pluralism within the wealthier benefices by

4. Keir, *Constitutional History*, 59.

5. Loades, *Politics and the Nation*, 154.

6. Elton, *England under the Tudors, Tudor Constitution, Policy and Police*.

7. Guy, *Tudor England*, 118–26, *Public Career of Sir Thomas More*, 120–21.

8. Solt, *Church and State*, 19.

9. Brigden, *London and the Reformation*, 178.

reducing the possibility and/or incentive to retain a poorer benefice upon promotion. Nonetheless, she ignores both the enforcement possibilities of the statutes and the whole set of provisions about leaseholds; indeed, originally she systematically avoided the practice of leasing parishes.[10] More recently, she deals with the statutes at length, but concentrates on absenteeism and education; leaseholding is mentioned only in passing.[11] Bowker's work, nonetheless, is exceptional in that it successfully identifies at least part of the dynamic that made the 1529 statutes important. R. W. Hoyle also treats the statutes seriously, but never their provisions or dynamic. His concern is in assessing the beginnings of the movement to dissolve the monasteries and thus the process that resulted in the statutes, rather than in what the statutes actually did. As for the effect of the statutes, Hoyle is completely dismissive: "The omnibus bill against pluralism and the economic activities of the clergy was wrecked by the insertion of amendments which greatly diminished the force of the original bill."[12]

Absorption with proving that Catholics were basically contented with the church when the English Reformation began has actually diverted attention away from the statutes. Christopher Haigh, for instance, focuses on the provisions concerning mortuary, probate, and pluralism. He completely ignores the leasehold provisions in his attempt to demonstrate that the statutes were not the product of an anticlerical movement, but rather part of the attack on Cardinal Wolsey (with those two scenarios apparently exhausting the possibilities).[13] As for the provisions about pluralism, his comments are revealing: ". . . it was so hedged about with provisos that any priest influential enough to secure two benefices would surely qualify to hold them. While a fifth or a quarter of parishes had pluralist incumbents, it seems that adequate curates almost always substituted for non-residents and neglect only rarely resulted."[14] As for the

---

10. Bowker, "Henrician Reformation," 85–93.

11. Bowker, *Henrician Reformation*, 113–23.

12. Hoyle, "Origins of the Dissolution," 286–89.

13. Haigh, *English Reformations*, 95–99.

14. Haigh, "Anticlericalism," 60–61. The method for determining curates' adequacy is not specified, unless it is merely that they are seldom accused by church wardens. Haigh's comment, 62, that probate discriminated against merchants and favored landholders because it levied fees based on moveable goods and not on land is somewhat perplexing. Most land was not involved in probate, because one could not devise land ordinarily before 1540, and uses were not technically wills and thus did not run through probate. Land became directly devisable in 1540 and would thereafter go through probate, but that later change would not have had any effect on the earlier statutes. Borough land was devisable, but merchants were hardly the only holders of

whole statutory scheme, it was but "the dampest of squibs, dramatic only in comparison with the claims made by their proponents and minor changes in comparison with ecclesiastical practice"[15] or "three petty acts."[16] He dates his first reformation period, the Henrician political reformation, as only beginning in 1530.[17] His focus on the issue of anticlericalism emphasizes where the statutes came from rather than what they did. In his survey, he dismissed 210 prosecutions of violations of the 1529 statutes in exchequer court from 1530 to 1535 as only brought by troublemakers; the pluralities bill had been "emasculated by amendments."[18] He ignores the leasehold provisions completely. He concentrates solely on issues of plurality, probate, and mortuary: the seemingly "religious" issues. In questioning whether the statutes resulted from an anticlerical movement, historians have focused on the red herring of anticlericalism and failed to assess what the statutes actually did.

The one exception to this trend was J. J. Scarisbrick. In his doctoral dissertation in 1955 Scarisbrick dealt briefly with 210 prosecutions under the statutes in the exchequer of pleas. Because there were few convictions, however, it seemed to him that those prosecutions were mostly ineffective.[19] After his dissertation, therefore, Scarisbrick set that material aside as not likely to produce substantive insight into the Reformation. The enforcement actions only merited a few sentences in his treatment of Henry VIII.[20] That reaction was not surprising; even most legal historians still see little importance to cases if they do not proceed to judgment. Since social-historical insights to legal history were not then available, the fourteen convictions seemed weak evidence for the effectiveness of the statutes.

The historiography surrounding the statutes of 1529 is thus completely defective and open to an examination based on the actual litigation and practice under the statutes. The issue of whether or not there was an anticlerical movement will not go away. Indeed, the analysis that follows could reinforce either position quite well. The significance of a statute, however, cannot rest wholly in

---

borough lands. His comment does not seem to account for the dissatisfaction that resulted in the probate statute. A better explanation is that high and late medieval statutes were often not based on general movements but on the surfacing of individual instances of problems.

15. Ibid., 62.

16. Ibid., 57.

17. Haigh, *English Reformations*, 14, 21.

18. Ibid., 98.

19. Scarisbrick, "Conservative Episcopate," 87–96.

20. Scarisbrick, *Henry VIII*, 252.

the motivations that prompted it. More important are the insight its drafters had into social interactions, the inducements it provided for compliance, and the degree of social change it produced in fact. By these measures the statutes of 1529, far from being damp squibs, must rank among the more important of England's legislative acts.

The Legislative History of the Statutes of 1529

The statutes of 1529 were in nature reformist and royalist, but not anticlerical. Nothing in the statutes sought to abolish the clerical order; the intent was only to bring the clerical order more, but not completely, into line with its traditionally stated ideals. The motivation for the important parts of the statutes did not derive from a social movement: the limited measure available for assessing any general level of anticlericalism would not indicate anything sufficient to give rise to such a major change in governance. The king, rather than any social movement, initiated the critical parts of the statutes. Henry VIII at that point was hostile to elements of the established church and the papacy, but not to the continuance of the clerical order. Likewise, the king's agenda must have been, in part, to put the church on the defensive so that he could get his divorce, but the tactical need to frighten the clergy does not equate to anticlericalism, regardless of how the defenders of the status quo portrayed it. The fall of Wolsey certainly made the church seem vulnerable; but the motives of Parliament, considered in its lay aspect and apart from the king, were much more related to self-interest and reform than to anticlerical convictions. The statutes constituted a reformation in the parish and transformed the power relationships between priest and parish. The effects of the statutes certainly formed a major foundation for the separation from Rome, for royal power over the church, and even for lay power within the church. Inferring intent from effect, however, is very dangerous. The statutes, instead of being anticlerical, were quite simply reformist, royalist, and beneficial to the laity.

Assessing anticlerical sentiments, at least as has been done so far, is a fairly useless endeavor. The term properly should indicate attitudes hostile to a clerical order as such or to a clerical order whose superiority was ensured by control over the sacraments. People who would have been content with the Catholic clerical arrangements if the clerics were merely more spiritual were reformers, not anticlericals. Lollards would be a good example of people with anticlerical sentiments, as would later Congregationalists or Quakers. Defenders of the status quo would, of course, label critics as anticlerical as a rhetorical tactic, but such tactics are not analysis. Reform-minded bishops and clergy were not anticlerical, nor would be their lay counterparts who were equally critical. John Fyneux, CJKB, would be the typical anticlerical lawyer for some, simply because he was attacking church governance: he much preferred royal governance. Yet Fyneux was a traditional Catholic in most ways, with children in the church and lands left to various religious houses and for alms at his death.[21] Fyneux was hardly a likely proponent of radical Protestantism, and his convictions about royalist right should not be confused with hostility to the clergy as such. As long as assessments of anticlerical feeling include people who, like Fyneux, were traditional Catholics in most ways but were annoyed at church pretensions or simply advocates of the king without being hostile to the clerical order, analysis will suffer. Description of the statutes in terms of anticlerical attitudes makes discussion so imprecise and subjective as to be useless: the statutes of 1529 accorded in many ways with medieval canon law and clerical ideals, although not with medieval practice.

A better measure of hostility to the clergy would be something objective, such as the level of assaults against clergy in the years right before the Reformation Parliament. Although an assault on an ecclesiastic might not relate to anticlericalism in the individual instance, general anticlericalism, hostility to clerics as such, would probably result in more assaults against clerics. In Trinity term 1526, however, the court of common pleas reveals no such hostility. The term contained allegations of fifty different assaults. Forty-one of the cases did not contain the status of the plaintiff; those plaintiffs thus can be presumed not to have been ecclesiastics. Six of the plaintiffs were gentry, and two were nobility (a duchess and a countess).[22] Only one of the fifty assaults (thus 2 percent) complained of an assault on an ecclesiastic: a chaplain.[23] In Trinity term 1386 (with a much higher volume of litigation overall) twenty cases were lodged by ecclesiastics, but out of a total of 341 assault cases: 6 percent.[24] In Trinity term 1465 ecclesiastics brought six out of 101 assault actions: again 6 percent.[25] The relative frequency of personal assaults might be an objective indicator of an

21. Jernigan, "Law and Policy," 48.

22. CP40/1051, mm. 62, 67, 116, 147d, 215, 218d, 388d, 390.

23. CP40/1051, m. 368d.

24. Two abbots (CP40/502, mm. 12, 119d); three priors (CP40/502, mm. 36d, 38, 116d); two parsons (CP40/502, mm. 176, 205d); seven clerics (CP40/502, mm. 127, 198d, 199, 264, 279d, 282, 393d); six chaplains (CP40/502, mm. 75d, 79, 86d, 253d, 281d, 360).

25. Two abbots (CP40/816, mm. 287d, 450); four clerics (CP40/816, mm. 26d, 113, 420d, 492).

increase in genuine anticlerical feeling as distinct from reforming or royalist feeling, but the level ascertainable from 1526 falls well under the range of previous years. Hostility to the clerical order would not seem to have increased so much that it could form a plausible foundation for the extraordinary events of the Reformation. The English Reformation arose not from a social movement but from Henry VIII.

The statutes of 1529, deriving from parliamentary action over about five weeks beginning on 3 November 1529, were indeed highly offensive to the church, backed strongly by the king, and almost certainly engineered by Thomas Cromwell to enable his transition from servant of Wolsey to minister of the king. Cromwell had become known as Cardinal Wolsey's "chefe doer for him in the suppression of abbeis."[26] With Wolsey's fall, Cromwell determined to become serviceable to the king, whether to save Wolsey or to avoid being dragged down with the cardinal. He arranged at the last moment to get into Parliament, almost as a probationary king's servant. He had no official standing with the king, but had sought and obtained royal support for entry into Parliament.[27] He then had to make himself obviously useful for the royal interest. He was an unusually able man, desperate to prove himself valuable to the king.

Henry VIII was clearly not in such need as was Cromwell, but always required able servants, even more so after events proved that Wolsey would neither become pope nor be able to secure the king's divorce.[28] The earls of Norfolk and Suffolk were to succeed Wolsey in influence, and they had encouraged Thomas Lord Darcy, even before Wolsey's fall, to prepare an agenda. The resulting memorandum was dated 1 July 1529. That agenda was too ambitious in part for 1529: it suggested, for instance, that all the abbeys might be suppressed. Parts of the agenda, however, would clearly be implemented in 1529. The chapters that indicate a purpose similar to what later appeared in the 1529 statutes deserve repeating:

> "Item to view what of all temporal lands the spiritual men hath, and by what titles, and for what purposes and whether it be followed or no.
> "Item better and much more merit honour and virtue is it for the king's grace to proceed and determine all reformations of spiritual and temporal [matters] within this realm, so that . . .

. . . .

26. Hall, *Henry VIII*, 174.

27. Elton, *Tudor Revolution*, 76–80.

28. *Letters and Papers Foreign and Domestic*, ed. Brewer, Gairdner, and Brodie, nos. 5320, 5417, 5725.

"Item exactions and such used by spiritual men.

"Item for probations of testaments after the old rate.

"Item against letters of administration, and what great injuries and wrongs daily grows [*sic*] of these besides, death is well broken thereby."[29]

The memorandum thus proposed royal power to reform clerical abuses directly and not through the bishops or Convocation, expressed concern about clerical landholding, probate and the administration of estates, and clerical exactions: the time seemed ripe for direct royal reform of the church. Norfolk and Suffolk came to control the king's government by September; their attitudes seem consistent with the direction proposed by Darcy. The conveyance of the king's approval for Cromwell's entry into Parliament had arrived with notice that he should conduct himself according to directives from Norfolk.[30] Darcy's memorandum, indeed, was part of the attack on Wolsey, but not directly: the proposals suggested would only damage Wolsey if the king found those proposals so attractive that their propounders gained influence.

Henry VIII had made it clear that such ideas would be well received. In April he had discussed, without overtly adopting, ideas about confiscating church property "to reduce the ecclesiastical state to the condition of the primitive Church, taking from it all its temporalities."[31] Henry VIII himself, according to Guy, began to shape attitudes in preparation for the Parliament: in September he showed diminished worry about heresy by ordering Wolsey to release a prior who had become Lutheran. His public posture on clerics continued through the first session of Parliament.[32] The king's attitudes and the ideas that Norfolk and Suffolk played with set the stage for the way in which the Mercers Com-

---

29. SP 1:54, fo. 240v, printed in Guy, *Public Career of Sir Thomas More*, 206–7; also in *Letters and Papers Foreign and Domestic*, vol. 4, pt. 3, no. 5749.

30. Elton, *Tudor Revolution*, 78: "Whereuppon my saide lorde of Norffolk answered . . . that he had spoken with the king his highnes and that his highnes was veray well contented ye should be a Burges, So that ye wolde order yourself in the saide Rowme according to suche instructions as the saide Duke of Norffolk shall gyve you from the king."

31. *Letters and Papers Foreign and Domestic*, vol. 4, pt. 3, no. 2379.

32. Guy, *Public Career of Sir Thomas More*, 110–11. Bowker seems to presume an anti-Lutheran sentiment in the Commons, so that the bills would spring neither from royal initiative nor from a Protestant groundswell, but from a Commons sentiment to fortify the English church against heresy. Bowker, *Henrician Reformation*, 112. The presentation here presumes that the initiative comes much more from the king and that the Commons were receptive to that influence, probably from a mixture of traditional morals, greed, and deference to royal preferences.

pany, the Commons as a whole, and Cromwell in particular would shape the workings of the Parliament, even when the Lords grew more cautious.

The Commons in Parliament were more than willing to cooperate with the king in forwarding reforming bills. When Parliament opened, the Commons voiced six major complaints against the clergy. Two of those six complaints came out of London and particularly out of the Mercers Company:[33] complaints about probate fees and mortuaries. Four other complaints, destined to be the most important of these statutes, were of more rural concern: complaints about clerical leaseholding, commercial activity, absenteeism, and pluralism. The origin of these four complaints is unknown. Since Cromwell got a seat in Parliament so late and the complaints surfaced at the very beginning of the session, he likely was not the proponent, but that is only a guess. The parliamentary proponents presented these complaints as being in accord with royal will; they were certainly in accord with the king's actions and comments. Before that time, they indicated, no one had dared speak against these practices because the clergy were so powerful in protecting their economic interests: "no man durst once presume to attempt any thyng contrary to their proffit, or commoditie."[34] The king himself, however, now perceived the evils, so they felt they could bring forward complaints advocating reform. The king's comments in the preceding month would have been sufficient for such a presumption, but the fact that Henry Guilford, the comptroller of the king's house, had begun the complaint about probate fees would likewise have justified their perceptions. The Commons thus set up a committee of members learned in the law to draw up three bills: "one bill of the probates of Testamentes, another for Mortuaries, and the thirde for none residence, pluralities, and taking of Fermes by spiritual men."[35] The six complaints would find remedy in three bills. Both Elton and Lehmberg were confident that Cromwell found his way onto the committee that would draft those three bills, although there is no way to know for sure.[36] Cromwell would certainly have wanted to be central to what was happening; he would likewise have been one of the most able and competent candidates: he

33. Miller, "London and Parliament," 143–49; Guy, *Public Career of Sir Thomas More*, 117; Lehmberg, *Reformation Parliament*, 81–82.

34. Hall, *Henry VIII*, 166.

35. Ibid., 166–67.

36. Elton, *Tudor Revolution*, 81, *Studies in Tudor and Stuart Politics*, 2:83; Lehmberg, *Reformation Parliament*, 83.

was trained in the law and knowledgeable about the workings of the clergy, government, and commerce.

The Commons sent forward the two bills on probate fees and mortuaries first, so that the initial battle was fought without at least explicit reference to the bill on nonresidence, pluralities, and leaseholding. Both the bills forwarded at first concerned church revenue from the estates of the dead. The clerical lords were willing to accept the bill on mortuaries. Hall explained that willingness as the result of their calculation that it would not affect their own economic interests since mortuaries were sources of revenue for rectors and vicars but not for the clerical lords. That explanation is not completely satisfactory because bishops and abbots were also rectors and received some income from mortuaries; but a reduction in mortuaries would not have been as threatening to them as to ordinary rectors and vicars. The bishops, particularly Fisher, the bishop of Rochester, objected vehemently to the bill on probate fees. Not only would that bill have directly implicated episcopal revenues, it went directly to the handling of wills. The handling of wills had increasingly become a matter of concern of the secular law because of the statute about counterfeiting wills, the melding of the duties of feoffees to uses and executors, and the trimming of ecclesiastical court jurisdictions over the immediately preceding decades.[37] Hall recorded Fisher as saying, ". . . now with the Commons is nothing but doune with the Church, and all this me semeth is for lacke of faith only."[38] This statement, made in the context of references to what had been happening in Germany, was effectively a threat to the Commons, who appealed for assistance to the king. The passage of these bills would not go smoothly or without substantial opposition from the clergy.

Henry VIII's response, although not as strong as desired by the Commons, was nicely calculated to move the process along without terminally alienating the clergy or discouraging the Commons. The Commons had sent the speaker, Thomas Audeley, together with thirty members of the Commons to Henry to protest Fisher's speech. In such a large delegation, it would be surprising if Cromwell was not present: he wanted all the royal attention he could garner. Hall thought the king was not pleased with Fisher's comments, but that the royal response to the Commons delegation was mild: the king would check the

37. See below, Chapter 8.

38. Hall, *Henry VIII*, 167. For the matter about counterfeiting wills and the alterations of church court jurisdictions, see Chapter 3, and for the mixing of uses and wills, see Chapter 8.

matter out with the bishops. Fisher and some brother bishops thereafter appeared and explained that the comments about lack of faith had applied to the Bohemians and not to the members of the Commons at all.[39] Since the bishops were willing to back down, Henry accepted that excuse and sent it to the Commons. The Commons clearly would have preferred the king to have rebuked Fisher. What they got was less than that, and they were not pleased; but the king's support had delivered what they needed. The bishops had granted that the Commons were at least not stepping over the line into heresy. The Commons could thus continue without facing that threat.[40] Moreover, Henry's inquiry left the bishops in no doubt about where he stood on the matter. These first two bills, anyway, were not as important as the one still to come. The king could well afford to give the bishops some room to save face at this point.

The probate fees and mortuary bills then went to conferences, still matters of heated debate, but with the Commons now clearly confident that the king did not regard them as overstepping proper bounds. The temporal lords seem to have been on the sidelines during the discussion, while the Commons and the spiritual lords were very engaged. The Commons supported the measures concerning probate fees and mortuaries on the basis of canon law. The bishops were not able to deny the arguments based on formal law, but countered on the basis of long practice to the contrary. The heat of the debate appeared in a comment analogizing these fees to robbery recorded by Hall as coming from "a gentleman of Greyes Inn": "the usage hath ever ben of theves to robbe on shoters hill, ergo is it lawfull?" Precisely who made that comment is unclear; but Cromwell was a member of Gray's Inn,[41] and at this point in Cromwell's career Hall might not have seen fit to mention him by name. Hall, however, was also a member of Gray's Inn and might thus have been referring to himself.[42] The bishops were almost as offended by that remark, of course, as the Commons had been by Fisher's attack. The matter remained contentious, even though the temporal lords now inclined to the Commons.[43]

During that time of controversy, the Lords assented to a bill that forgave the king loans he had borrowed during his reign from individuals and groups. The

39. A different account has Fisher defending his words forthrightly. Lehmberg, *Reformation Parliament*, 88–89. Guy interprets Henry's intervention here as a reproof of Fisher: Guy, *Public Career of Sir Thomas More*, 118.

40. Hall, *Henry VIII*, 168.

41. Elton, *Studies in Tudor and Stuart Politics*, 2:223.

42. Lehmberg, *Reformation Parliament*; Guy, *Public Career of Sir Thomas More*, 118.

43. Hall, *Henry VIII*, 169.

debate on that bill in the Commons is a good indication of the way in which the Commons in 1529 was in tune with the royal interest. Hall mentioned that "the moste part of the commons were the kynges servauntes, and the other were so labored to by other, that the bill was assented to." Many people outside Parliament were of course much opposed to the bill: both the creditors who thus lost repayment of significant amounts of money and others who might foresee themselves in a similar position. All this had happened already by 20 November, since a London burgess was defending that bill before the Mercers Company by that date.[44] Only two and a half weeks had passed since the opening of Parliament, and the passage of the bill remitting royal debts was decidedly unpopular.[45]

The king once again intervened at this point to take pressure off the Commons, to break the deadlock on the bill about probate fees, and to emphasize that he had adopted these bills as royal initiatives. He ascribed the bill remitting royal debts to Parliament. He publicly responded to that bill by issuing a general pardon, but also by putting the clergy on the defensive. The general pardon did not apply to clergy who violated provisors and premunire. Lehmberg interpreted that sufficiently on its own as a threat to the clergy. But Henry also took credit for the drawing up of revised bills on probate fees and mortuaries.[46] Henry's intent was thus very clear to all concerned; and the spiritual lords consented, reluctantly, to the two bills. Both measures had been sufficiently qualified as to mute their immediate effect; indeed, they were to be less important in the next few years than the third bill. These first two bills, however, had started as complaints pushed in large part at the beginnings of Parliament by London, with the expectation of favorable royal support; they had emerged as a part of royal policy with Henry's express support. The king himself took credit for the bills, not unfairly but surely supportively.

44. Lehmberg, *Reformation Parliament*, 90–91.

45. Hall, *Henry VIII*, 169. For the necessity and politics of the debt remission, see Guy, *Public Career of Sir Thomas More*, 114–15; Lehmberg, *Reformation Parliament*, 189–91.

46. Hall, *Henry VIII*, 169–70: "The Kynge lyke a good and a discrete Prince, seynge that hys commons in the Parliament house had released the loane, entendyng some what to requite the same, graunted to them a general Pardon, of all offences, certayne greate offences and debtes only xcept: also he aided them for the redresse of there greves against the spiritualtie, and caused twoo newe bylles to be made indifferently, both for the probate of Testamentes and mortuaries, which billes were so resonable that the spyrituall Lordes assented to them all though thei were sore againste there myndes, and in especial the probate of Testamentes sore displeased the Byshopes, and the mortuaries sore displeased the persones and Vicars."

The third bill, the one concerning pluralism, nonresidence, commercial activity, and leasing, thus assumed a position as presumptively espoused by the king, but the spirituality was nonetheless even more opposed to this bill than to the two previous ones. Perhaps they merely felt that enough had been conceded already; more likely they recognized that more was now at stake. When the commons passed the bill, "the priestes railed on the commons of the common house, and called them heretikes and scismatikes, for the whych diverse priestes wer ponished." The spiritual lords "woulde in nowise consent" to this bill.[47]

The king intervened a third time to move this next bill for church reform through Parliament. He summoned eight members each from the Lords and from the Commons to meet in star chamber. Right about this time, the king independently revealed his mind on the matter. On 28 November Henry remarked that he agreed with Luther on the necessity of getting rid of clerical abuses. Then he drew a direct link between the matter of this statute and the question of his divorce: "Now, I ask you, how can the Pope grant a dispensation for a priest to hold two bishoprics or two curacies at once, if he will not allow two women to one man? For here is the point . . . all doctors say that a dispensation in the former case is as necessary as in the other."[48] The spiritual lords were clearly outnumbered; the temporal lords sided with the Commons: the bill was accepted in committee with a little qualifying and then passed the Lords, "to the great rejoysynge of the lay people, and to the greate displeasor of the spirituall persones."[49] This third bill, now passed to become a statute, would accomplish the parish reformation.

Cromwell's role in all this is circumstantial, but nonetheless highly likely. His documented activities in this first session of the Reformation Parliament were not such as would have proven himself all that useful to the king. He procured the dropping of the attainder against Wolsey. He headed a committee investigating problems of "protections" and thus became directly involved with Edward Hall. He began work on what would become the "Supplication against the Ordinaries," a work that would see the light of day only in a later session.[50] These matters might have made Cromwell look interesting to the king, but would not have shown his usefulness. Elton and Lehmberg both suppose Cromwell to have been on the committee working with these three church reform

47. Ibid.
48. Guy, *Public Career of Sir Thomas More*, 110–11.
49. Hall, *Henry VIII*, 170.
50. Elton, *Tudor Revolution*, 81.

bills. The statutes, particularly the third, were masterful in their understanding of how to effect social change by statutory action; one supposes at least that a person of some ability was behind the drafting. Moreover, Cromwell's handwriting appears on several documents concerned with reforming the clergy;[51] his work on the "Supplication against the Ordinaries" demonstrates where his interests were directed that session. His rapid rise to influence after the Parliament would indicate that he had achieved something in Parliament that had proven his utility, probably something whose effect was becoming increasingly recognized in the months after the statute. It is no great speculation, even though it cannot be proven, to suppose that Henry's interest and Cromwell's ability together produced the statutes that arose out of the Commons' complaints and the agenda drafted by Darcy for Norfolk and Suffolk only months earlier.

Cromwell had almost certainly been on the committee that drafted the bill and thus on the various delegations before the king and with the Lords. In only a few months after the Parliament, he would be sworn as an official king's servant.[52] He now not only had his skills acquired under Wolsey in confiscating the goods of religious houses, he also had shown similar skills in Parliament in being central to the three bills, one of which would segregate the clergy from the commercial world. The third bill in particular, in laying down statutory rules for pluralism, nonresidence, and clerical lifestyle, eliminated a vital area of the bishops' power of dispensation over normal canon law rules.[53] The power

---

51. Lehmberg, *Reformation Parliament*, 83–85.

52. The most likely date for Cromwell's formal entry into royal service, as distinct from his showing himself useful to the royal purposes in the Parliament, is late January 1530. Elton, *Tudor Revolution*, 79–84. ("Perhaps we shall not go far wrong if we suggest that it was the fruit of Cromwell's activities in parliament which he had entered with the king's approval and pledged to support the royal cause.") Guy would place that date a little later: Guy, *Public Career of Sir Thomas More*, 130. The heat in discussing formal entry into royal service seems to be related to the unstated but anachronistic assumption that one can separate the king from policy, that the king formally chose ministers, but was then somehow insulated from policy.

53. Guy emphasizes the way in which this bill attacked the power of Convocation, clearly an issue at that time. Guy, *Public Career of Sir Thomas More*, 119. Henry's perspective, however, seems to have been directed much more to the exercise of the power of dispensation. If he was maintaining that the papal dispensation did not legitimate his marriage, then it was not inconsistent to think that bishops should not be able to dispense clerics from abiding by canonical regulations. The statutes set down rules for these matters and prohibited a royal dispensing power over them. Despite the implications for Convocation's power—implications that were both real and important—the more important point is probably the power of the ecclesiastical hierarchy to dispense.

of the ecclesiastical hierarchy to dispense individuals from obeying ordinary church rules, as the king had pointed out, was at the very center of the problem of the king's divorce. The king had good reason to be interested in these bills: not only would they threaten the clergy and keep them on the defensive, but they also pursued the same principle he was advocating with his divorce case. Thomas More, the earl of Norfolk, and the earl of Suffolk, indeed, the temporal lords as a whole, had shown no leadership on this issue at all during the parliamentary session, despite Henry's clear interest. Certainly More would never have engineered such legislation. Cromwell had chosen his issues well and had proven himself useful to the king.

The Statutes of 1529

The statutes of 1529 forbade the participation of ecclesiastics in the commercial life of England. In regard to the most important socioeconomic feature of the rectory, the statutes so punished clerical absenteeism that parish leaseholds might have become an unusual phenomenon. The statutes nevertheless punished absenteeism, but did not prohibit the leasing of parishes. The statutes reduced pluralism, but for those clerics who could still hold more than one parish or had a legal reason for absence, leasing the parish remained a legal management strategy. Reduction of pluralism and absenteeism in fact diminished the number of parishes leased, but the statutes also protected a class of pluralist clerical lessors now radically dependent on lay lessees. While the leasing of parishes thus survived, that practice now functioned in a fundamentally different context. Overall, ecclesiastics were to be dedicated to God's service. Rectors were supposed to serve God's people on the parish without striving after filthy lucre; if rectors were not resident on their parish, they should only be absent in service to the aristocracy or to education.

Priests and other ecclesiastics could no longer participate in the leasehold market as lessees, particularly of parishes but also of other lands. The stated reasons for the prohibition of clerical leaseholding were religious: the increase of virtue; the maintenance of religious services, preaching, teaching and good example; better care of the parish; provision of alms; and the better reputation of the clergy. Regardless of the personal and conflicting motivations resulting in the statutes, the provisions certainly accorded with a strain of late medieval English religion that sought to ensure that "spiritual persons" were indeed spiritual. Prohibiting them from being lessees kept them from investing for profit in the commercial land market. Leasing out land was only a management tool and was permissible; holding land for a term of years was a speculative investment for profit. The most prominent change under the statutes was the ending of the leasing of parishes and other property to ecclesiastics, although not to the laity.[54] Moreover, spiritual persons who currently held leaseholds of any kind had to divest within a year, and divest in such a way that they would not receive annual profit from the leasehold: they could not simply sublease to a layman and receive rent annually.[55] While clerics could still be lessors of lands they held in fee and even of parishes,[56] they could retain neither the status of lessee nor the profits of a leasehold. All leases made directly or indirectly to spiritual persons were void.[57] The statutes specifically prohibited spiritual persons from holding leased benefices.[58] Thus, spiritual persons could not participate in the commercial profits deriving from leases as such, but particularly when the leasehold was a parish. Lay persons could still lease parishes from rectors legally absent, and those lay persons would still hire the parish priest to serve the parishioners as they had in late medieval England. The clerical order was to be an order insulated from commerce, even when a lease to a cleric might have been a more appropriate result for the parishioners. The parish reform thus concentrated on the clergy and the allocations of power within the parish, but left the vital economic mechanisms intact.

The statutes isolated spiritual persons not only from the leasehold market, but also from all overt commercial enterprise. Commercial activity by ecclesiastics had always seemed inappropriate, but until the statutes it had been tolerated.[59] Now, neither normal clerics nor members of religious houses could lawfully buy to sell for profit. They could not participate in markets or fairs or

54. Statute 21 Henry VIII, c. 13, section 1.

55. Ibid., section 2.

56. Milo Wyllen, rector of Willingham, Lincolnshire, leased his rectory to two gentlemen for £13.50 in 1531, and the lessees, as had been customary before the statute, were obliged to find the priest: CP40/1080, m. 426.

57. Statute 21 Henry VIII, c. 13, section 3. The only exceptions were for the leasing out of institutional temporalities during a vacancy (such as the vacancy of a bishopric) and with certain situations in regard to freehold property (property held for life or longer, specifically not terms even of many years) spiritual people held.

58. Ibid., section 19.

59. Thomson, *Early Tudor Church*, 168, 181.

deal in any part of the foodstuff or wool market or, indeed, in any item of victual or merchandise. All such transactions were void.[60] Priests could indeed sell the agricultural produce that derived from the parish, such as tithes, mortuary fees, and the produce from the glebe; such transactions were only sales, whereas the statute forbade buying for resale for profit. The statutes did make certain exceptions, but the exceptions only emphasized the rigor of the main provisions. Spiritual persons could buy for their own use and the upkeep of their establishments; they could resell excess purchases or items they found useless as long as they were not trying to circumvent the statutory intent.[61] Religious houses with income of less than £533.33 could still occupy their leaseholds, but only for the support of the establishment and for good works, not for commercial enterprise and not to exceed their traditional extent of leaseholding.[62] Typical agricultural business activity, such as breweries and tanneries, the statutes likewise prohibited for spiritual persons.[63] Breweries, at least, had shown up in medieval parish leases when the rectory buildings were listed.[64] In parishes with glebe or demesne lands insufficient to support the rector, the rector could lease further lands to remedy the shortfall and could buy to provide for the agricultural needs of the land and sell the produce. The income from such permissible leasehold activity could be applied only to his household and hospitality (good works, alms, etc.), not for personal enrichment.[65] Only impoverished parsons could hold leases, and even they could not do so for personal profit. "Spiritual persons" were supposed to be spiritual, segregated from the profit-oriented side of society.

The statutes, however, did not prohibit additional income as such, and that loophole could conceivably have provided an incentive to provide basic education at the parish level; an increase in teaching was actually one of the expressed motivations for the statutes. The statutes otherwise favored education: if rectors were university students, they were allowed to be absent from the parish. The statutes certainly did not prohibit running a local school; and rectors, while not all educated to the level the humanists would have demanded, had both the time and often the capacity to run schools. Moreover, Convocation in March 1530, after passage of the statutes of 1529, ordered rectors and vicars to expend their

60. Statute 21 Henry VIII, c. 13, section 5.
61. Ibid., section 6.
62. Ibid., sections 7, 23.
63. Ibid., section 21.
64. CP40/501, m. 234; CP40/503, m. 132; CP40/504, m. 119d; CP40/1004, m. 532.
65. Statute 21 Henry VIII, c. 13, section 8.

time outside of ecclesiastical services and exercises in, among other things, instruction of children in reading and grammar.[66] If they complied and ran local schools, either in the 1530s or thereafter as the new regime shaped the expectations of new rectors, the results of a more educated populace would have become apparent in Elizabethan England. Whether parish priests in fact turned to such activities to increase their revenue, to fill the days, or to carry out God's work remains at this point unknown; most parish work of that kind would not have been institutionalized. Moreover, the educational services provided by religious houses were not, as it happened, going to be available beyond the 1530s.[67] The new restrictions on clerical activity certainly made dangerous most clerical activities besides prayer, reading, contemplation, and helping and educating people.

The statutes also regulated the traditionally condemned but widely tolerated practice of pluralism. The medieval church had prohibited clerics from holding more than one ecclesiastical post that entailed care of souls, but then had licensed individuals to violate that prohibition. Very successful clerics held a great many benefices. The statutes prohibited that practice and provided that the acquisition of a second benefice automatically vacated the first, as long as that first benefice was worth at least £8 annually.[68] They prohibited attempts to obtain dispensations from this rule.[69] The final form of the statutes avoided the draconian effect this would have had on the wealthiest ecclesiastics: current pluralists could keep up to four benefices.[70] Only the privileged few would have been holding more than four benefices. This amelioration of statutory rigor would have had a modest and temporary effect. The greatest pluralists would likely have been older, so the effect of this leveling provision would increase dramatically over about a decade as older, wealthier clerics died. Pluralism on a large scale, if the provisions were rigorously and continuously enforced, was going to be a practice only of the past.

As with the medieval church, the legislation bowed to economic necessity with pluralism, but now in a way that tightly bound the clergy. Medieval pluralists had increased their independence with the acquisition of more benefices and thus an increased annual income. This provision allowed pluralism,

66. Orme, *English Schools*, 254.
67. Ibid., 252–71.
68. Statute 21 Henry VIII, c. 13, section 9.
69. Ibid.
70. Ibid., section 10.

but only for those people who were dependent chaplains of important people, scholars, or the sons and brothers of aristocrats. The greatest pluralists would henceforth be the spiritual persons on the king's council: they could hold three parishes each. Otherwise, personal chaplains could hold no more than two parishes, and they could be absent from both. The chaplains so privileged were designated. Royalty could have pluralist chaplains. Archbishops could have eight chaplains; dukes, six chaplains, each of whom held two parishes. The provision then stipulated in descending order the number of chaplains other magnates could have. Bishops, for instance, could have six such chaplains; the chief justice of king's bench, one chaplain who could hold two benefices.[71] The number of pluralists was thus significant, but the occupants had to be dependent to be pluralist: personal chaplains to magnates were powerful but not in their own right. The only exceptions to that restriction came in deference to education and the aristocracy. Doctors and bachelors of divinity or canon law who received their degrees from English universities could hold two parishes without being a personal chaplain, although they had to purchase a license.[72] In a similar way, the children and siblings of the aristocracy who entered the church could likewise be pluralists.[73] The legislation implemented dramatic changes in pluralism. Very few clerics would hold more than two benefices; but, had the aristocracy regularly hired personal chaplains and had the clergy at the same time become much better educated, the number of pluralists could have actually increased. Immediately, however, the route to wealth as a cleric, as far as it lay within an individual's capacity to effect, had changed: advancement lay with service to magnates or advanced education in spiritual matters. Hopeful medieval pluralists had purchased their privilege, because licensing pluralists was a revenue-producing device. The new rules that allowed certain ecclesiastics to hold two (or for the clerics on the king's council, three) benefices were an overt matter of statute, the result of the legislation even though the pluralist still

71. Ibid., sections 11, 13.

72. Ibid., section 12.

73. Ibid., section 11: "And that the bretherne and sones of all Temporall Lordes which are borne in wedlocke may every of them purchase lycence or dispensacion and receyve have and kepe as many parsonages or benefices with cure as the chapleyns of a Duke or an Archbysshop: And lyke wyse the bretherne and sones borne in wedlock of every knyght may every of them purchase licence or dispensacion, and receyve take and kepe two personages or benefyces with cure of soule." The enforcement suits do not yield any evidence of this exception. The exception might have come up in allegations of absenteeism, but need not have; the more likely source for evidence of implementation would be in *quare impedit* suits.

had to purchase the license. Tudor pluralism served the aristocracy and scholarship, but it also faced a low ceiling on the number of possible benefices. The clergy of Henry VIII had a different route to prosperity and to access to the wider national world; that route led through service or learning instead of commercial endeavor.

The prohibitions against clerical leaseholding and pluralism received their significance from the mandate for spiritual persons to reside on their benefice. No longer were rectors normally capable of simply being absentee. Those who lawfully were pluralists had to reside on one of the benefices or, more likely, at university or with the magnate they served. The prohibited absence for normal rectors and vicars was quite precise: they could not be absent for more than one month at a time or for a total of more than two months in a year.[74] The legislation prohibited any dispensation from its provisions, except for royal service abroad, scholars studying at university, those attending the king or magnates, or those required to be present at the king's council or chancery.[75] Spiritual persons could still lease residences in towns, but such houses could only have orchards or gardens and they could not reside there in violation of the absentee provisions.[76] Late medieval rectors had often held multiple benefices and been able to be absent for their own purposes; that principal characteristic of late medieval rectors vanished. The most educated clergy would probably reside at university or become personal chaplains and remain absent: service to the aristocracy trumped service to the parishes. Dependency on magnates, however, dictated a rather different, less independent way of life: the Reformation was both a national and a very personal experience. Other rectors found themselves exiled from their chosen environment and confined to their rural parish, like prisoners with much reduced horizons.[77]

Under the legislation spiritual persons could no longer take a second spiritual income. In medieval England, as noted by Chaucer, absentee rectors could augment their income by taking a stipend to pray for the soul of a dead person.

74. Ibid., section 15.
75. Ibid., section 17.
76. Ibid., section 24.
77. Bowker, in tallying the reported reasons for reported nonresidence in the diocese of Lincoln, tracked 185 nonresidents in 1518, 81 in 1530–33, and 102 in 1540. Bowker, *Henrician Reformation*, 116–17. Those figures still assume that the definition of "nonresidence" remained the same, a questionable assumption. Even though the reports were probably not measuring the same thing, nevertheless, they still reveal something about absenteeism, probably a greater change than the mere numbers would suggest.

Statute now prohibited that practice, even by members of religious houses who had care of souls.[78] The prohibition here did not extend to spiritual persons beneficed without care of souls: deans, archdeacons, prebendaries, or rectors in parishes that had an endowed vicary to care for souls.[79] Those who by office had care of souls in theory were now required by and large to care for the souls in fact.

By negative implication these statutes contained a new view of the laity. A negative implication, of course, need not indicate the intent behind a statute or even a foreseen effect. Negative implications, without additional proof, only indicate the effect of a statute once implemented. For Cromwell, however, foreseeing the benefit for the laity is not implausible. Implementation of the statutes limited the clergy and reproduced a bifurcation between the lay and ecclesiastical spheres that had been central to medieval life, but now more in the socioeconomic arena than in governance or jurisdiction. The laity, already the predominant actors in the commercial sphere of lessees and traders, would now occupy those realms exclusively. The socioeconomic division, moreover, came just before the crown united in itself both secular and ecclesiastical jurisdictions and governance. Medieval society had achieved a certain separation between clergy and laity in governance and jurisdiction and had even idealized geographical separation, particularly with monasteries but also even in rectories. Henry VIII preserved the subordinate distinction between clerical and secular governance by retaining separate church courts and episcopal powers, but constructed a separation between clergy and laity that the medieval church had failed to achieve.

The 1529 statutes thus embodied a different vision both of the parish and of the world. Rectors typically were either to be present on their parish or involved in spiritual service to an individual or to learning. Clerical activities were to be sharply different from those of their parishioners: spiritual persons were apart from the commercial world, their endeavors dedicated to teaching, preaching, religious service, and hospitality. The typical rector would likewise not be as wealthy as in the past since the rector could not accumulate many benefices with care of souls or take additional stipends. Those who were particularly dependent on magnates could get a second benefice, but that wealth was possible only for those who were personal chaplains, scholars, or brothers and sons of the aristocracy; and the second benefice was not automatically bestowed. Spiritual

78. Statute 21 Henry VIII, c. 13, section 19.
79. Ibid., section 20.

people were now dedicated to spiritual endeavors and service, and the laity were left in sole possession of the commercial arena.

Enforcement Provisions

Prohibiting is one thing; prohibiting effectively is completely another. The 1529 statutes operated in the context of a government that had no broad regulatory bureaucracy to identify, investigate, and prosecute offenders. The statutes thus relied on personal interest and private prosecution to marshal private effort, individual reforming zeal, and personal greed to implement a parish revolution. With a keen insight on human motivation, the statutes relied on an effective combination of traditional morality and economic self-interest to generate help in enforcement.

The statutes provided cumulative penalties to ensure the vigorous prosecution of offenders. The imposition of a penalty of a set sum for each period of time of violation, half of which would go to any person who chose to prosecute, basically set an escalating bounty on prosecutions.[80] A spiritual person who took a leasehold, for instance, was subject to a £10 forfeiture for every month of violation plus ten times the profit derived from the lease. Even a £10 forfeiture for a single month of infraction was the return many rectors would have received from their rectory for a whole year. A private person would find the £5 return on such a prosecution (half the £10 forfeiture) tempting, but not overwhelming. After six months, however, the forfeiture would have risen to £60, with the return to the private prosecutor worth £30. For every spiritual person who chose to lease land, there was at least one other person who knew about the lease: the lessor. The lessor himself or someone the lessor informed could sue the lessee, as could anyone else, whether local resident or regional self-appointed enforcer. The escalating forfeiture also set a premium on suing early: delay might result in someone else suing first. Cumulative penalties, available to any person who chose to sue, were an effective stimulus for enforcement, even without an administrative bureaucracy.

Clerical parish lessees received particular attention. Although rectors and perpetual vicars normally had to reside on their benefices, legitimate pluralists could still let out a parish, but not to fellow clergymen. Clerics who became lessees were involved in a public, observable, continuing act; their forfeiture was

80. For *qui tam* suits as an enforcement mechanism in a different context, see Elton, "Informing for Profit," 149–50.

particularly severe. Instead of the £10 forfeiture for each month of an ordinary leasehold, the clerical lessee of a parish lost £2 each week. The forfeiture thus escalated every week. Subsequent practice indicates that prosecutors could choose which forfeiture rate to claim for a parish lease, either the weekly or monthly calculation. The clerical lessee likewise could not offset any of the forfeiture with the profit from the lease because a multiple of the profit was also subject to forfeiture. Indeed, any substantial time spent as a clerical parish lessee would have resulted in an economic disaster.

The fines were not only severe in being cumulative; they were also severe for the initial infraction (see Table 1). Although the person prosecuting received only half the value of the forfeiture, the penalties were so high that any violation presented an immediate temptation for those who would put private interest ahead of loyalty to the parson. The rector in the 1530s was probably often newly resident on the parish and disgruntled at his required relocation and the closing off of economic opportunity. How much loyalty such a rector could claim from parishioners would vary widely, but speculatively might normally have been minimal. The accumulating forfeitures were seductive. Anyone might calculate the weeks or months of clerical absence or leasehold, wonder what that forfeiture would do for his family, or worry whether someone else might sue first: all these were being won over to the new regime of royal ecclesiastical power. Those who decided to sue had already crossed the threshold. The penalties were also severe by comparison. In 1534 Parliament provided a *qui tam* action to deter farming land from being diverted to sheep pasturage. Anyone guilty of holding more than two husbandry tenements at leasehold was subject to a forfeiture by *qui tam* action of £0.17 per week, about one-twelfth the punishment for a cleric leasing a parish. That forfeiture was trivial beside the forfeitures set for clerics, but prosecutors stepped forward by the dozens to claim even those lesser penalties.[81] The 1529 statutory scheme was well conceived to provide the crown with a cadre of active people who had effectively bought into the reformation of parishes and the new royal power; they realized from personal experience the increased power of the laity to regulate their own clergy.

The statutes, moreover, cleverly diminished the number of offenders. The provisions requiring severe life adjustment applied only after an appropriate lapse of time: up to a year. Immediate application would have seemed unfair, and many ecclesiastics and supporters would have been enraged at the unavoid-

81. I did not count the number of cases, but they constitute a substantial body of litigation in E159/324 (1346–47).

TABLE 1. Statutory Penalties

OFFENSE	PENALTY	EFFECTIVE DATE
Taking lands at lease	£10/month	29 September 1530
Not divesting leasehold already held	£10/month + 10x profit of leasehold	29 September 1530
Buying and selling for profit	3x the value	immediate
Prohibited pluralism	loss of earlier benefice	1 April 1530
Obtaining dispensation for plurality	£20	1 April 1530
Prohibited absence from benefice	£10/month	29 September 1530
Obtaining dispensation for absence	£20	1 April 1530
Taking stipend for prayers for dead	£2/week	29 September 1530
Occupying leased parish	£2/week + 10x profit	29 September 1530
Keeping tan house or brew house	£10/month	1 April 1530

able loss. A reasonable delay in the application of the statutes deflected criticism that they were an arbitrary and unfair attack on the clergy: the clergy had the time to divest. In addition, however, the clergy had time to think. For a year they had the opportunity to learn about the legislation, talk to each other, assess the potential reaction of their parishioners: to realize, in short, the gravity of the situation and the dynamics that would inevitably result in financial ruin if they did not comply. Then they had adequate time to get rid of their leaseholds. The delay of a year for the leasehold provisions meant that most clerics had a reasonable chance as well as a great incentive to submit instead of resist. Those who chose to ignore the mandate were those who simply would not manage their affairs, who thought they could hide, who insisted on taking a stand, or who thought that they could slip into a narrow lawful exception. Likewise, the rules that allowed certain ecclesiastics to hold two benefices were an overt matter of statute; the licenses were indeed purchased but allowable by statutory standards, not by mere discretion. The vast majority of clergy would have seen the necessity and thus complied with the very traditional standards of conduct now imposed by a king with new authority over the church and enforced by the newly empowered laity.

Prosecution was intentionally easy. Litigants had the whole range of the courts open to them. Such suits could begin by original writ, bill, or plaint of debt in any of the king's courts. The potential litigant could thus choose whichever court he personally preferred. Moreover, trial would only be by jury, not by compurgation. Compurgation was an easy method of trial for defendants, and plaintiffs preferred to be able to force a defendant to a jury trial. Even the right of the defendants to delay was curtailed. Thus plaintiffs could use king's bench, common pleas, or the exchequer of pleas; in appropriate situations they could also use king's council, chancery, or star chamber. The statutes thus opened up the full array of the king's court system to enforce the prohibitions and made the choice of the potential plaintiff as easy as possible.

The enforcement provisions ensured that the statutes would be more than damp squibs. They were very severe. They accurately perceived the social dynamics that could develop when royal power joined traditional moral prescriptions to economic self-interest. Even many who finally did not sue would have thought seriously about clerical deficiencies and thus revalued royal authority. The repercussions of enforcement as well as the carefully circumscribed possibilities for personal gain probably made the priesthood less attractive or at least attractive to a different kind of person. While there were occasional signs in the 1520s of problems recruiting priests, the situation grew very serious after 1532,[82] that is, once those who had already become subdeacons or deacons by 1529 had been ordained. Probably unnoticed in the turmoil of the passage of the statutes but rapidly realized by the lay plaintiffs, however, was the revolutionary nature of the means to enforce the traditional standards: the empowerment of the laity. While lay regulation of the clergy was almost certainly not the objective intended, it was a clear consequence of the statutes.

Profits from Death

At the same time that these statutes revolutionized the economic context of the parish, other provisions transformed the dues the church exacted from the estates of the dead. With regard to the practice of mortuary, the statutes reduced the value of the fees exacted by the church at the time of death. With respect to wills, the statutes limited the fees charged for probate. The church

---

82. Bowker, *Henrician Reformation*, 40. Bowker attributes the decline possibly to the effect of more rigorous examinations. Higher selectivity may have accounted for some of the problem, but the enforcement of the statutes of 1529 could not but have presented a very real career disincentive for those concerned about their standard of living.

was to tread more lightly at times of death. In this kinder and gentler church, the economic opportunities available to the clergy rapidly diminished. The regulation of mortuary and probate also eliminated the ability of the clergy to substitute increased death duties for the loss of commercial profit.

Historians have insisted that the alteration of probate and mortuary fees could have been detrimental. The scale of probate fees was higher than some dioceses used; the statutory mortuary payments exceeded the level of mortuary payments that was traditional in some places.[83] Those comparisons, however, are misleading. Both the mortuary and the probate provisions were very explicit that they were never to be implemented to increase existing rates. The intent and direct effect of the legislation was to reduce clerical exactions and compel the priesthood into a spiritual realm of service. They were particularly necessary after the statutes of 1529: when the clerics found their normal, alternative sources of revenue diminishing, they would likely have become more rigorous in exacting their remaining revenues.

Mortuary practices, once variable across England at times from parish to parish, now largely followed a statutory rate. The mortuary statute sought basically to regularize and minimize mortuary dues. Certain categories of people were now statutorily exempt from mortuary: those who lived in areas where previously no mortuary had been due at all; those decedents whose moveable goods, after their debts were paid, amounted to less than £6.67; married women, children, or persons not householders. The statute eliminated payment of more than one mortuary in situations where mortuaries had been due from a decedent according to his tenures or place of dying. Mortuary was due to the parish in which the person primarily resided.

If mortuary was due at all, the act set up a scale for a monetary mortuary, instead of a mortuary in kind. When a decedent's estate after payment of debts amounted to between £6.67 and £30 in moveable goods, the proper mortuary was £0.17: thus from 2.5 percent to 0.6 percent of the estate of moveable goods instead of the best animal. When a decedent left £30 to £40, the mortuary was £0.33: from 1.2 percent to 0.8 percent. For decedents who left more than £40 in moveable goods after payment of debts, the mortuary was to be no higher than £0.50: starting then at 2.5 percent and decreasing in percentage as the estate increased in value. The statute thus mandated uniform exemptions and a statutory rate, both of which would reduce the value of mortuary fees to the rector. If a parson violated the statute, he lost both the amount of the excess charge and a

83. Haigh, "Anticlericalism," 61–62; Bowker, *Henrician Reformation*, 51–53.

penalty of £2. Mortuary became a charge that the decedent's survivors could live with, instead of a crushing exaction at a time of great need and insecurity.

Statute also reduced the amount the church could take for the probate of wills or administration of estates. For small estates, those that did not exceed £5, there was no fee. For estates from £5 to £40, the fee was no more than £0.18 (3.5 percent of £5; 1.75 percent of £10; 0.9 percent of £20; 0.4 percent of £39.99): £0.13 to the bishop and £0.05 to the registering scribe. For estates above £40, the fee was only £0.25 (0.6 percent at £40, then decreasing): half to the bishop and half to the scribe, with the scribe able to substitute a charge of one pence for every ten lines at ten inches a line. The statute prescribed that intestate administrators were to be the wife or the next of kin, and that lands, profits from lands, and money from the sale of lands were not included in the estate for the calculation of fees. Violation of this statute would result in a forfeiture of the excess and a £10 penalty, half of which would go to any person who would prosecute the case. The aim of Parliament was to lighten the burden of ecclesiastical exactions; the effect was largely in accord with that aim.

The statutory probate fee rates have been considered inconsequential. Historical discussion has centered on whether the statute arose from anticlericalism among the populace at large and a resentment against the church that led into the Reformation, as if resentment by the husbandmen and yeomen of the country were probable sources of such legislation. Many people even before the statute, however, were exempt from payments, except plausibly payments for the scribe and for the commission.[84] But the statute gave relief to more than just the very wealthy. Bowker found that in the archdeaconry of Lincoln half of those who paid anything for probate had paid less than £0.25; half, £0.25 or more.[85] Under the statute, £0.25 was the maximum anyone would pay, unless the will exceeded three hundred lines of writing. That maximum rate applied to only 9 percent of the wills probated, whereas according to the old schedule, a fee of £1 had applied to 36.2 percent of wills.[86] Moreover, not only did the schedule seemingly relieve many people and make wills a more plausible option, it also prevented clerics from enlarging their revenue in the future to make up for the economic opportunities taken away from them by the statutes of 1529. While implementation (not the statutory language or intent) may have resulted in probate fees that were actually higher by a maximum of £0.03 for those devising

84. Lander, "Church Courts and the Reformation," 45; Bowker, *Secular Clergy*, 150.
85. Bowker, *Henrician Reformation*, 53.
86. Ibid.

goods worth £5–8.50, inflation made even that level of higher fee for a few people actually a decrease in fees in real terms in comparison to fifteenth- and early sixteenth-century levels. The purpose of the probate statute, thus, was to limit the exactions of the church at the time of death, both as those exactions had been and as they might have become after other sources of clerical income were terminated in 1529.

Finally, in 1532 Parliament prohibited any further permanent endowments of parishes. Prior to the 1532 statute, people could grant land to trustees to hold for the benefit of a parish, chapel, church wardens, or guilds and thus provide a permanent endowment without giving complete ownership to the parish. Limitations on giving landed wealth to the church were traditional. The 1532 limitation on the channeling of wealth to the church or church-related entities was dramatically new. The statute voided any future such grant or similar transaction unless the effect was limited to no more than twenty years. Parish endowments thus could last no longer than about a single generation.[87] Once again, statute limited strictly the economic resources that could be dedicated to religious purposes.

King and Parliament continued to be concerned about this complex of matters. In 1536, at the same time that the dissolution of the religious houses began, lay lessees of parishes obtained greater security. Up until that year, a resignation of the parish by the lessor worked to terminate even a written lease. Now, by the statute of 1536, the lessees would be able to continue their lease during the life of the lessor up to six further years, although they had to pay the rent to the new appointee.[88] That six-year term would have protected the complete duration of almost all the leases of the nonappropriated parishes.[89] Parliament likewise found the statute that prohibited absenteeism somewhat too loose. The primary class of those allowed to be absent was that of depen-

---

87. Statute 23 Henry VIII, c. 10. I have seen no evidence to indicate whether or not this statute had any effect on endowments that had already been made to parishes.

88. Statute 28 Henry VIII, c. 11. Statute 21 Henry VIII, c. 15, likewise increased the security of lessees, by preventing common recoveries from voiding a preexisting lease. Guy, *Public Career of Sir Thomas More*, 123. That provision in 1529 probably had no effect on parish lessees, unless parishes were subject to common recoveries (a phenomenon I have not seen). It is conceivable that after the dissolution of the religious houses, the statute became an important protection for parish lessees. That eventual possible effect would be an implausible background for the statutes themselves, unless the drafters of the statutes in 1529 intended the dissolution already (a possibility I consider conceivable but not provable).

89. See above, Chapter 4, Figure 5.

dent personal chaplains, but participation in higher education was also favored. In 1536 Parliament tightened the regulations so that scholars over forty years old received particular attention along with scholars who did not attend lectures or other exercises.[90] The fine-tuning of the earlier statutes indicates that those statutes were not merely symbolic and that Parliament's interest was not ephemeral. The age limitation provided a focus for scholarship: it was not for self-improvement or for the enjoyment of the scholar who found parish life too rigorous or insular, but was available when there was a probability that the scholarship could thereafter be put to use.

The complex of statutes that reformed the clergy and parish life covered a broad range of clerical revenue-producing activities and imposed on ecclesiastics a particular lifestyle. The mentality behind the reforms was completely in accord with traditional ideals that the medieval church had been unable or unwilling to enforce. The clergy would actually be separate from the laity and not immersed in commercial life; they would be resident on their benefices; they would not be able simply to maximize their income. The legislation, hopeful in those aspirations, was also pragmatic in that it melded self-interest with traditional ideals about the clergy to enlist ordinary people to investigate, accuse, and prosecute violating clerics. The means to achieve those completely traditional ends were revolutionary. Royal authority regulated the parish directly by Parliament and through the king's court, not only by the bishops and through the church courts. Moreover, the statutes empowered the laity to enforce those traditional aspirations. This power produced a new variety of parishioner: one with the ability, duty, and incentive to inflict punishment on priests who did not adhere to the standards imposed. These statutes predicted a less wealthy clergy, as well as a clergy whose special advancement was predicated either on education or on service to or membership in the aristocracy. The king in Parliament acting through the laity in the parishes now imposed on the church those matters that the church had been unwilling or unable to impose on its own personnel. The statutes were remarkably traditional in intent and content, but startlingly revolutionary in execution, means, rigor, and effect. Although the leasing of parishes would continue, the practice would be less frequent and would function in a different context and thus with a different meaning. The church was as always in service to God, but served God now by serving the laity, not itself.

90. Statute 28 Henry VIII, c. 13.

CHAPTER SEVEN

Enforcing the Statutes of 1529

The statutes of 1529 put both the burden and the benefit of enforcement on private individuals; the incentives were sufficient to regulate the clergy and thus reform the parish. Private individuals stepped forward, whether from personal conviction in accord with the reforms, malice toward individual clerics, personal greed, or, most likely, a variable but powerful combination of those motives. Litigation appears for most of the provisions, although the prohibition of clerics from holding leases received the most attention by far. Since the penalties were continuing parts of the remedy structure, the effect of the statutes stayed constant, not altered by the shifting factions around the king. Legal remedies, particularly with the plaintiff incentives provided by *qui tam* actions, functioned as consistent governmental policy. These statutes and remedies stayed on the books and worked a fundamental reformation of the English parish. The litigation in itself is the direct evidence of the effect in local parishes throughout England.

Litigation under the statutes was frequent and provided a popular foundation for the reformation. J. J. Scarisbrick located 210 suits in the exchequer under the statutes in the years 1530–35.[1] Haigh dismissed that level of litigation, noting that there were "only" 210 suits.[2] Nevertheless, given the opportunity provided the clergy to divest and reform before the penalties applied and thereafter to take advantage of two pardons, 210 suits seems rather a substantial number. Most clergy would already have been in compliance; the vast majority would have calculated the coming dangers over the course of the year before the penalties applied and would have made appropriate adjustments. The defendants in these suits, thus, were the clergy who were negligent, naive, or intransigent. Even had the enforcement litigation really only amounted to 210 cases

1. Scarisbrick, "Conservative Episcopate," 87–96. Professor Scarisbrick generously was still able to share with me sufficient information on 190 of those cases to aid me in this analysis until I could examine the documents myself.

2. Haigh, *English Reformations*, 98.

between 1530 and 1535, the enforcement would have been significant, certainly in comparison to any *qui tam* category other than Statute of Laborers violations.

The enforcement, however, was actually much more vigorous. Because of the delayed effect of the statutes, only one case came in 1530; real enforcement began in 1531. Between the beginning of 1531 and the end of Hilary term, 1536, thus in a period of about five and a quarter years, litigation brought under the statutes of 1529 came to 552 cases in the exchequer of pleas, the court of common pleas, and the court of king's bench.[3] Even the total of 552 cases underestimates the vigor of private willingness to sue, not least because we know so little about prosecutions before justices of the peace and nothing about cases in the various prerogative courts. Many of the provisions delayed the imposition of forfeitures until late September of 1530. Then the king pardoned the ecclesiastics of the Canterbury province for all offenses committed up to 10 March 1531, thus forgiving about the first six months of transgressions for most clerics.[4] Suits already initiated, since initiation of the suit turned the infraction into a debt owed, could go forward on an offense committed before that date, but potential prosecutors who were waiting for the forfeiture to accumulate or who discovered the offense too late lost their opportunity. The pardoned ecclesiastics could observe that their colleagues were in fact being sued: they thus had a further opportunity and incentive to divest, reside, or otherwise comply; they had a month to act before forfeitures once again began to accumulate. The low figure of sixty-eight prosecutions in 1535 was the result of another royal pardon, this time for acts committed prior to 3 November 1534. This pardon the king granted for the whole realm when he was recognized as the supreme head of the church.[5] Undetected ecclesiastical offenders thus had a third chance to comply without penalty, and private prosecutors lost further opportunities. The pardons were in traditional form and not designed for the 1529 statutory offenses. The 1531 pardon was the result of a grant of £100,000 from Convocation, from a clergy fearful of a general indictment in premunire;[6] the 1534 pardon was part of the management necessary for the king's assumption of direct control over the church. Still, the pardons could not have worked better had they been par-

3. Appendix 4.

4. Statute of 22, Henry VIII, c. 15. For the application of the pardons to the statutory enforcement suits, see Appendix 4 with the number of cases in which the infraction alleged began immediately after 10 March 1531 and 4 November 1534.

5. Statute of 26 Henry VIII, c. 18; E159/313, m. 19 (Hilary); Figure 6; Appendix 4.

6. Guy, *Public Career of Sir Thomas More*, 149–51.

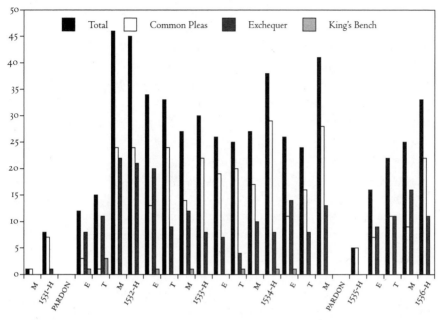

FIGURE 6. Enforcement Litigation, 1530-M to 1536-H

ticularly designed to induce compliance with the 1529 statutes. Indeed, the king probably recognized the tangential benefits to his pardons. The occurrence of the pardons encouraged prompt litigation and better enforcement; the pardons also gave ecclesiastics occasions to divest their leaseholds or change residence without fear of precipitating a suit. The whole process, from the king's point of view, was not one of revenue collection, but of enforcement of royal policy and of securing compliance. The vigor of the private response was even in excess of that indicated by the substantial figure of actual cases.

The vigor of the prosecutions continued after Hilary term 1536. Exchequer cases are relatively easy to extract because the scribes gathered cases of a similar kind together in the memoranda rolls, and all the later process was entered with the original enrollment; the entries are essentially a series of case files and provide a nice history for each case. In common pleas, by contrast, the litigation is scattered through more than a thousand sides of densely written legal records each term; and each successive stage in the process often appears in a different, unindexed roll. The easier exchequer records, however, indicate continuing enforcement. Cases declined in number while the exchequer was involved in the confiscation of the religious houses, but thereafter picked up again to the level prior to 1536.[7] Litigation in the court of common pleas continued, but perhaps at a somewhat lower rate. In Easter term 1537, seven suits were in process; in Easter term 1542, six suits appeared in common pleas. Since Figures 6 and 7 include only cases *initiated* in the individual term, the level of litigation in common pleas seems to have been lower. The statutes clearly continued to have effect through the reign of Henry VIII. Even as late as Michaelmas term 1550, plaintiffs initiated eleven new exchequer suits;[8] in Hilary term of 1565, ten.[9] The statutes of 1529 were certainly an important factor in shaping clerical activity and the structure of the parish right through the reign of Henry VIII and seemingly well beyond. They became part of the cultural environment within which the clergy structured both their lives and their expectations, dictating the kind of person who chose the clerical life.

The prosecutions followed different patterns in the different courts. The court of king's bench took only ten prosecutions and probably discouraged other cases because king's bench would be the venue for writs of error: king's bench was not to be a major forum for original suits. Most prosecutions came in the exchequer of pleas and the court of common pleas. The profiles of litigation in those courts, however, had two major differences. The average claim in the exchequer of pleas was double the average claim in the court of common pleas (about £113 as compared to £56). A statute from 1519, although at first ignored in these prosecutions, insisted that private parties had to sue their *qui tam* actions within a year of the infraction. Regardless of how long an offense had continued, therefore, when that statutory limitation was applied, the maximum award that a plaintiff could receive with a penalty of £10 for each month of infraction was £120 (plus, of course, the multiple of the profits). While plaintiffs in the early years tried for a higher forfeiture occasionally, most claims moderated finally to conform to the statute.[10] While it seems to have been

7. Figure 7.

8. E159/329, mm. 58d, 82, 82d, 83d, 84, 101, 102, 103, 104, 105, 105d.

9. E159/350, mm. 39, 154, 154d, 155, 156, 156d, 157, 157d, 158, 158d.

10. The problem first arose in the judgment on Marmaduke Darrell v. Alexander Shaa, a suit alleging the holding of the lease of a rectory for sixty-nine weeks yielding a forfeiture of £138. Like most such suits, the plaintiff did not take advantage of the additional forfeiture of ten times the profit derived, probably because the profit was not known to the plaintiff. The judgment in Trinity term of 1534 forgave the forfeiture for the seventeen weeks of infraction that exceeded a year. E159/311, m. 23 (Easter) (but see also E159/313, m. 25 [Easter]). In another suit between the same parties claiming a different leasehold and a forfeiture of £170, in which the jury returned not only that forfeiture but also ten times the value, Shaa brought a writ of error challenging whether

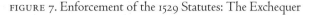

FIGURE 7. Enforcement of the 1529 Statutes: The Exchequer

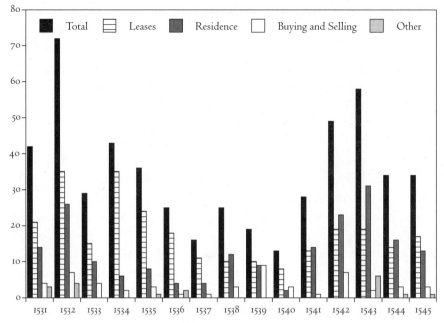

possible to claim a separate infraction for each lease,[11] most plaintiffs treated leaseholding from even multiple lessors as a single offense. Claiming more than the cleric could conceivably pay, of course, was useless, except, perhaps, to terrify. The difference between the courts in the amount of claim was thus between the approximate maximum that could be claimed and half that. The other major, and related, difference was the role of the plaintiff. In the court of common pleas, the plaintiff hired his own lawyer and prosecuted his own plea.

---

the jury could award a forfeiture that had not been requested and whether the award could be made, since the jury did not specify how much of the profit had arisen during the time exceeding the period of twelve months. These two challenges and others Shaa made in this case seem convincing. Instead of going to judgment on the allegation of errors as the court did in a different case of error on these statutes (KB27/1094, m. 39), the justices simply adjourned the case for judgment repeatedly until Henry VIII died. KB27/1092, m. 33. The courts adjusted pleading and enrollment forms in other cases to handle the problems that Shaa raised. KB27/1092, m. 33.

Plaintiffs at times still claimed more even though it would be limited by the statute, perhaps *in terrorem*: E159/313, m. 15 (Easter) (claim of £460). It was still possible to seek more than £120 if the cleric had, for instance, been leaseholder of several distinct leases, by separating them out as distinct offenses: E159/314, m. 27 (Michaelmas).

11. E159/314, m. 27 (Michaelmas 1535); Appendix 4.

In the exchequer of pleas, the king's attorney general supplanted the plaintiff.[12] That practice was normal in the exchequer of pleas, but was the basis for one error allegation. The court of king's bench rejected that claim,[13] and the attorney general's aggressive role in the exchequer of pleas continued. Plaintiffs in exchequer claimed forfeitures twice as high as plaintiffs in common pleas and also avoided much of the legal cost of prosecution; plaintiffs in common pleas claimed less but bore their own legal costs until judgment.

The dynamics of the prosecutions in the court of common pleas served not to swell the king's coffers, but to empower plaintiffs to compel compliance and maximize their own gain by settling the suit out of court. Most enforcement actions in the court of common pleas, as with all litigation there, disappeared during the procedural stages. Litigants had experience with this kind of *qui tam* action already: in 1511 Henry VIII had used *qui tam* actions with cumulative penalties of £5 for each month that physicians or surgeons practiced their occupation within seven miles of London without having been examined.[14] Even earlier, enforcement of statutes providing *qui tam* actions against those who tried to bribe jurors gave prosecutors half the forfeiture.[15] The crown in such cases had neither the interest nor the mechanism to track the suits or to claim a portion of any pretrial settlement. The litigation dynamics in the court of common pleas thus brought powerful incentives for private settlement. In the enforcement of the 1529 statutes, once a defendant cleric realized that he was probably going to lose, he could easily have struck a deal with the plaintiff. From a claim of £40, the plaintiff would get only £20 from a full judgment since the remaining £20 went to the crown. If the defendant cleric offered the plaintiff £30, both were better off, and the crown never inquired. Thus the half of any judgment award that would go to the king, the litigation costs the defendant would spend in his own defense, and the plaintiff's costs that an adverse judgment would award to the plaintiff provided the margin for negotiation and the incentive to settle. The king only profited when the cleric held out to the very end. The incentives for out-of-court compromise explain the lower average claim in the court of common pleas: the expected actual recovery was about the

12. Scarisbrick rejected the idea that the prosecutions in the exchequer were "in any way the government's work." Scarisbrick, "Conservative Episcopate," 89. He is of course correct in pointing out that few cases began by crown prosecution. Appendix 4. The role of the attorney general in the exchequer, however, means that the government adopted these suits.

13. KB27/1096, m. 21 (Trinity 1535); Appendix 4.

14. KB27/1020, m. 33; KB27/1039, m. 64d.

15. CP40/479, m. 93.

same. Moreover, an enrollment of even the first stage of process in a prosecution seemed to bar any subsequent prosecution of the same defendant by a different plaintiff on the same offense. The reasoning for the protection seems to have been that the first case was not concluded: it was still pending.[16] The cleric was also protected from the current plaintiff: had the plaintiff attempted to resume the suit, the cleric could claim a discontinuance and quash the suit. With an unenrolled compromise, both plaintiff and defendant were better off. The whole structure put great incentives on compliance, rather than on raising revenue for the king. Not surprisingly, most cases in the court of common pleas disappeared prior to judgment and were all the more effective for doing so. The court of common pleas was a good venue for prosecuting a cleric who was probably guilty and would at some point be willing to reduce his liability by compromise.

Effective enforcement, however, required prosecution of the innocent who came close to infraction: the exchequer of pleas was the better site for these prosecutions. That venue was more appealing for prosecutions of clerics who stoutly and plausibly maintained innocence and were thus unlikely to compromise. Such defendants were also less likely to be convicted. In the exchequer the attorney general took over the prosecution, so that the plaintiff avoided legal expenses. Informal compromise in the exchequer was impossible, of course, because the king's attorney general did not compromise, although occasionally he withdrew the suit because he became convinced that the cleric was innocent in fact.[17] A few clerics could prove that they were innocent by submission of proof that they were personal chaplains and thus fell into one of the statutory exceptions.[18] Of the 222 cases in the exchequer through Hilary term 1536, eighty-one (40 percent) recorded a final outcome. Seventy-one of those (80 percent of the 40 percent) were acquitted. These cases were failures only if the crown's interest was pecuniary. The crown, however, was much more interested in securing compliance and submission. The prosecutions in the exchequer, seemingly mostly against clerics who could justify their actions, were critical in that endeavor. The laity were quite willing to take a chance on the prosecution and make innocent clerics justify their acts; the cleric in the process faced the

16. E159/314, m. 17 (T1535).

17. E159/310, m. 34 (E1531); E159/310, m. 20 (M1531); E159/310, m. 21 (M1531); E159/310, m. 22 (M1531); E159/310, m. 23 (M1531); E159/310, m. 17 (H1532); E159/311, m. 21 (T1532); E159/311, m. 23 (T1532); E159/311, m. 30 (M1532); E159/311, m. 31 (M1532); E159/311, m. 40 (M1532); E159/311, m. 27 (H1533); E159/312, m. 21 (H1534); E159/313, m. 23 (E1534).

18. E159/311, m. 39 (M1532); E159/313, m. 25; E159/314, m. 11 (E1535); E159/314, m. 19.

FIGURE 8. Attorney General Management of 1529 Statutory Enforcement Cases

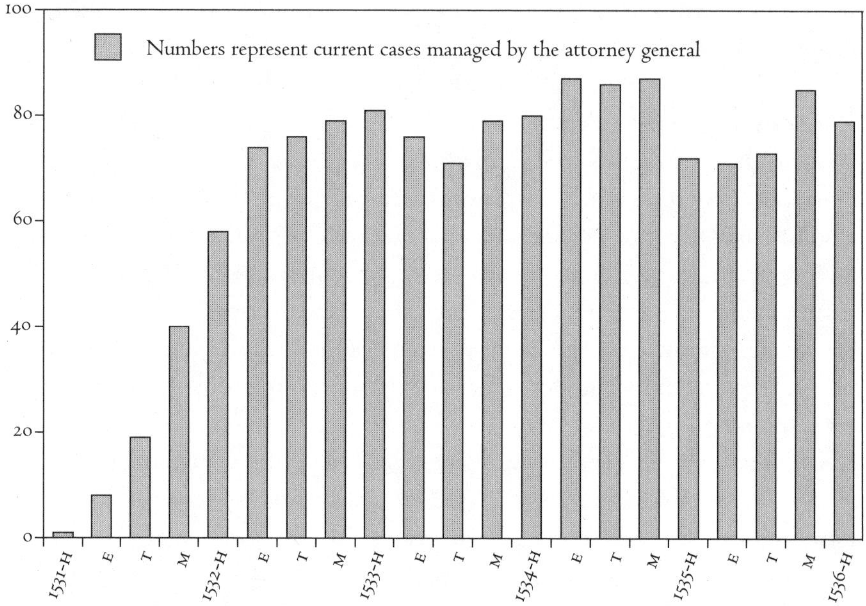

reality of royal control both in the possibility of losing a huge forfeiture and in the unrecompensed burdens of legal costs. Even for the innocent this structure intended to frighten. The statutes, for instance, allowed clerics to hold leases if they had insufficient glebe as long as they applied the profits of the leasehold not for their own profit but solely for hospitality and the maintenance of their household. Exchequer prosecutions made certain that clerics who considered taking advantage of that loophole did so very cautiously, because even though innocent, they might have to expend their own resources defending themselves. Even the innocent might rightly have felt insecure in submitting their fate to a jury because jurors could have strong perceptions about the clergy, particularly in the 1530s. Moreover, the innocent who were confident or desperate enough to brave the possibility of a jury might still hesitate because legal expenses for a defense might consume whatever revenue they derived from a lease.[19] Prosecution of the innocent ensured the effectiveness of the statutes.

19. The profit from the lease was supposed to be used solely for household and hospitality. I have not seen it discussed, but it would seem that legal expenses might have to come out of regular revenue, not out of the money derived from the lease. If so, the cleric would have to continue to apply the proceeds of the lease to hospitality but pay the expenses incident to the litigation from his own resources.

The burden both on innocent defendants and on the attorney general was substantial. In the 222 cases in the exchequer through Hilary term 1536, the average duration was more than ten terms or two and a half years. From a different perspective, 38 percent of the 222 cases concluded within four terms or one year; 65 percent, within two years; and 76 percent, within three years. Nevertheless, 15 percent exceeded five years, of which six lasted ten years[20] and one lasted an extraordinary fourteen years.[21] The fifty-one cases that went to a jury that acquitted the accused averaged a duration of over thirteen terms, or more than three years: the innocent thus bore the burdens of long worry and legal costs. Even with the fourteen cases in which the king withdrew prosecution because the attorney general was satisfied that the allegation was not true, the accused was under threat for over two years. While they were under prosecution, clerics would not have wanted to attract attention. Most clerics appeared very rapidly; under subpoena they showed up in court, sometimes at the submission of the original information, but regularly in the term thereafter. The delay thus came mostly after pleading, while waiting for a jury. The attorney general between Easter term 1532 and Hilary term 1536 had to track consistently between seventy-one and eighty-seven of these cases, and these cases constituted only a small portion of his responsibilities.[22] An innocent party could not force the attorney general to request the *nisi prius* order that would actually summon a jury to determine the case;[23] a guilty party would prefer to avoid attracting the attention that would provoke the attorney general. The exchequer prosecutions were threats to the clergy as a whole. Those who thought about taking advantage of the loopholes in the statutes had to contemplate the grim reality that even innocent they might have to hire legal assistance for years to fend off the attorney general's actions. Prosecutors, moreover, may only have been malicious enemies, overzealous reformers, or local rivals in the sale of agricultural produce. Local agrarian tensions were still inevitable, of course, because the rector or vicar still sold agricultural produce; the statute prohibited not the sale of

20. E159/310, m. 9 (Hilary); E159/310, m. 10 (Hilary); E159/313, m. 8 (Trinity); E159/313, m. 10 (Trinity); E159/314, m. 12d (Easter); E159/314, m. 19 (Trinity); E159/314, m. 21 (Trinity); E159/314, m. 26 (Michaelmas); E159/314, m. 27 (Michaelmas); E159/314, m. 20 (Michaelmas); E159/314, m. 16d (Michaelmas).

21. E159/310, m. 20 (Trinity).

22. Figure 8.

23. Technically, a *venire facias* writ summoned the jury, but that writ was usually ignored unless it was accompanied by the *nisi prius* order. It seems the plaintiff or prosecutor had the initiative in deciding when he was ready to proceed after reaching an issue to be submitted to a jury.

agricultural goods derived from the glebe and tithes, but only the purchase of goods for the purpose of resale. If the statute was to be effective, many innocent people had to be prosecuted; otherwise, statutory exceptions would in practice expand to permit almost all activity. The cases against the innocent were critical for coercing the clergy into submission in fact. The long duration of the cases, plausibly the simple result of the oppressive caseload of the attorney general, helped nevertheless to control those clerics for the years the case was pending.

The difference between the exchequer of pleas and the court of common pleas was not rigid. Clearly, innocent as well as guilty clerics were sued in the court of common pleas; guilty clerics sued in the exchequer of pleas occasionally found sympathetic juries. Cautious plaintiffs might choose the exchequer of pleas solely to avoid the initial outlay for legal costs. Some plaintiffs would simply be more familiar with one court rather than another, and repeat plaintiffs might sue in the court in which they had already litigated. In general, however, because of the difference in the amounts claimed, the plaintiffs must have tended to use the court of common pleas when compromise seemed likely, but otherwise went to the exchequer of pleas. In either case, however, the overriding fact is that the crown was much more interested in compliance than in revenue. The attorney general did not intervene to continue the many suits in the court of common pleas that simply disappeared; there was no tracking system to prevent compromise so that the king could get his share of a forfeiture. The litigation in the exchequer of pleas simply did not yield great dividends for the effort of the attorney general: few cases yielded revenue for the crown. The forfeitures that went to the crown totaled under £600. Most of that sum was tied up in challenges by writs of error,[24] and a large part of the final forfeitures was probably not recoverable.[25] After the expenses involved in the time and trouble of the justices and the attorney general, the king probably did little better than to break even.

The enforcement prosecutions were a critical part of the Reformation in even a different way. Haigh detailed how the monarchy might enlist help in the Reformation: royal prestige, pageantry and propaganda, power, patronage. His

---

24. See particularly KB27/1094, m. 39 (forfeiture to the crown of £85, judgment in error delayed through into H1549); KB27/1094, m. 65 (forfeiture to the crown of £64.33, judgment in error delayed through into H1549); KB27/1096, m. 21 (forfeiture to the crown for £64.33, judgment in error delayed into E1537).

25. Appendix 4.

comment in that context is compelling: "The Reformation required reformers."[26] *Qui tam* suits provided different and more compelling methods of enlistment: self-interest and greed reinforced by traditional morals. Not only those who actually brought suit, but also those who thought about prosecuting, counted the number of days their parson was absent, began to pay attention to who leased land, questioned what their parson was doing with his income, envied those who sued, even those clergy who surrendered their leases, moved back to their parishes, or sought appropriate service with a magnate: all were crossing the threshold into the new order, not a new order of doctrine or piety, but a new order of governance and a new role for both the laity and the clergy in the life of the parish.

As interesting and important as are the origins, intent, and politics of the passage of the statutes, the essential message of these statutes was their effect. Haigh's focus with the statutes is consistently on intent and politics, because those questions relate directly to whether there was a social movement from below that resulted in the policies of Henry VIII toward the church. That issue continues to predetermine the questions asked and eclipses questions equally important. Regardless of the impetus for the statutes, the forfeitures were in fact enacted; and litigants were induced to bring enforcement actions. Those enforcement actions recruited reformers, but also must have polarized parishes. Anne Boleyn and the issue of Henry's marriage served as both icon and lightning rod for feelings rooted in local parish dynamics generated by the central government and finally pitting king against pope.

Enforcers for the statutes were many and widely dispersed. From all the data currently available, there were at least 411 different plaintiffs through the first quarter of 1536. That diversity of plaintiffs need not have been. The sixteenth century knew well *qui tam* suits basically monopolized by officialdom. Under Henry VII, Henry Toft worked for the attorney general,[27] but almost monopolized *qui tam* litigation against local officials for taking bribes.[28] The *qui tam*

26. Haigh, *English Reformation Revised*, 210.

27. KB27/969, m. 32 (Toft was clerk to James Hobart); KB27/973, m. 26.

28. In 1503 he sued John Payne late itinerant bailiff in Essex for £160 (KB27/969, m. 32); Robert Newport late sheriff of Essex for £120 (KB27/969, m. 92; recovers £40); John Nycolas a bailiff of Essex for £80 (KB27/969, m. 36d). In 1505 he sued William Crowmer late sheriff of Kent for £80 (KB27/973, mm. 26, 78; KB27/976, m. 25; KB27/976, m. 83d [recovers £40]); William Tey late subsheriff of Essex for £440 (KB27/973, mm. 61, 103; KB27/976, m. 40; jury for defendant, attaint process thereafter, pardoned 1506); William Pirton late sheriff of Essex for £200

litigation authorized in 1529 did not follow that pattern. Of the 411 different plaintiffs who sued under the 1529 statutes, only a few were very active: William Barton (ten suits in Yorkshire);[29] Richard Brandeley (nine suits in Norfolk and Yorkshire);[30] Humfrey Walrond (six suits, mostly in Somerset);[31] William Cowper (who sued together with William Skynner, Robert Gilmyn, and John Cokeyn) (six suits in Suffolk);[32] Thomas Milner (seven suits in Nottingham-shire);[33] Roger Bexwell (seven suits in London and Kent);[34] Gerard Chauncey (five suits in various counties);[35] and John Stokedale (five suits in Worces-tershire).[36] Only a few of the plaintiffs were enrolled as clerics.[37] There were also at least 468 different clerical defendants in the suits. The enforcement of the statutes was broad-based both in plaintiffs (but only among the laity) and defendants.

The enforcement of the statutes was similarly national. The geographical distribution of the enforcement litigation was similar to the ordinary distribu-tion of litigation except in two instances. The enforcement litigation from Yorkshire was triple what would have been expected from the distribution of ordinary common law litigation in the early sixteenth century. The ordinary litigation from Yorkshire had in fact been declining consistently through the

---

(KB27/973, m. 102, pardoned 1506); Thomas Prestwych subsheriff of London for £80 (KB27/973, m. 104); William Capell late mayor of London for £300 (KB27/973, m. 78); William Pulter of Hitchin late sheriff of Hertfordshire (KB27/973, m. 101); and also for £240 (KB27/976, m. 104). He brought many other suits under the same statute in other terms. He also brought *qui tam* suits to enforce other statutes (importing prohibited goods; usury): CP40/970, m. 117; KB146/10/14, 3, no. 24; KB27/973, mm. 29, 71d.

29. CP40/1071, m. 671 (all ten suits). For succeeding process, see CP40/1072, mm. 194d, 196.

30. CP40/1073, m. 39d; CP40/1074, mm. 278d, 280d, 691d (3x); CP40/1075, mm. 265d, 665d, 726.

31. E159/311, m. 27 (Easter) (Som); CP40/1076, mm. 198 (Hants), 542d (Som); CP40/1077, m. 223 (Som), 223d (with John Hannam) (Som); CP40/1078, m. 598d (Som).

32. E159/310, mm. 12, 14, 17, 18, 23, 24 (Hilary).

33. E159/310, m. 8 (Hilary); E159/310, m. 9 (Hilary); E159/310, m. 10 (Hilary); E159/313, m. 31 (Michaelmas); E159/314, m. 12 (Easter); E159/314, m. 17 (Easter); E159/314, m. 12d (Easter).

34. CP40/1081, m. 37 (London); CP40/1082, m. 434 (Kent); CP40/1085, m. 93d (London); CP40/1086, mm. 460, 639 (3x) (all London).

35. E159/310, m. 24 (Michaelmas) (Staffordshire); E159/310, m. 53 (Hilary) (London); E159/314, m. 19 (Trinity); E159/314, m. 23 (Trinity) (Essex); E159/314, m. 14d (Trinity) (Essex).

36. CP40/1072, m. 514d (2x); CP40/1074, m. 464d; CP40/1079, m. 551; CP40/1080, m. 793.

37. William Boleyn, CP40/1088, mm. 574d, 577d; Robert Gurnell, CP40/1079, m. 78d; John Hoskyns, CP40/1072, m. 565.

fourteenth and fifteenth centuries until it accounted for only 4 percent of litigation in the court of common pleas; Yorkshire enforcement suits, however, accounted for 13.8 percent of the total (or, eliminating all litigation before 1532 to equalize for the Canterbury Province pardon, 12.3 percent).[38] At the same time, litigation from London and the Southeast accounted for only 14.5 percent of the enforcement suits. That figure was less than half of what might have been expected since the Southeast in the early sixteenth century accounted for close to a third of ordinary litigation. The far north might at first seem to have been extraordinarily active, but was not. Enforcement suits came not only from Northumberland, Cumberland, and Westmorland, but also from Durham, Cheshire, and Lancashire: counties that did not generate litigation in the court of common pleas at this time.[39] The Yorkshire figures are thus truly exceptional and establish that county early on as a region of particular vigor either in enforcement or in resistance. The statutes of 1529 were not the target of the Pilgrimage of Grace, but the enforcement process must constitute part of the background for the uprising. Overall, however, the litigation came up from a large number of plaintiffs, attacking many clerics spread across the whole country. The statutes were of truly national significance. Moreover, had clerics doubted the power of statutes that melded traditional ideals with possibilities for personal advantage, the reaction of the populace dispelled that confusion rapidly. (See Tables 2 and 3.)

Holding Property at Term

The main effect of the statutes, judging by the prosecutions, was the removal of the clergy from the commercial profits arising from leases.[40] Two-thirds of the

38. The final column in Table 2 if only litigation in and after H1532 is considered would be, respectively, 2.6 percent, 12.3 percent, 6 percent, 11.9 percent, 22.8 percent, 8.1 percent, 20.2 percent, 15.5 percent, 0.6 percent. While the pardon had some effect, the effect was not sufficient to alter any conclusions or to justify a separate table.

39. Table 2.

40. Many prosecutions under the statute did not differentiate the manner of holding, only the period for which the cleric had actually held the tenement in violation of the statute. Almost all prosecutions under this provision concerned leases for terms of years. The prohibition of life estates is peculiar because it would apply also to life estates acquired before a person became a cleric or by operation of a conveyance to a cleric as a member of a family (that is, as to a younger

prosecutions concerned the holding of leases, either the holding of arable, meadows, and pastures or the holding of a parish by lease. While the clergy could still hold heritable estates,[41] the statute intended to exclude clerics from anything that looked like commercial interests in land.[42] Litigants brought 370 such prosecutions by the end of Hilary term 1536, averaging more than seventy cases a year. Although the provisions concerning absenteeism and pluralism may have had the prominence in the minds of the drafters that they have had in the minds of historians, the vigor of prosecutions about leaseholds established the segregation of the clergy from commercial activity as the major social effect of the statutes and thus the statutes' essential social message. The clergy would have their separate order, but not the separate order of hierarchy, governance, and jurisdiction that was the medieval clerical goal, but a "spiritual" order segregated from the commercial sphere of the laity.

As with the prosecutions in general, the litigation underestimates the effect of the statutes. Since the clergy had a year in which to divest before the forfeitures could begin and since the penalties were so severe, most clergy would have divested. Ten defendants in the exchequer of pleas pleaded that they had in fact divested; often they had waited until the last month before the forfeitures took effect.[43] Further divestments must have occurred when the king granted the various pardons. The geographical distribution of the prosecutions likewise ensured that the defendants' colleagues out in the counties were very familiar with the problems suffered even by the innocent who confronted an enthusiastic prosecutor. The four-county band of Yorkshire, Lincolnshire, Norfolk, and Suffolk accounted for 44 percent of the leasehold cases, only slightly more than

---

son). A prohibition of life estates granted by nonfamily members to persons who were already clerics could have conformed to the broader aims of the statute. Such a grant to a person already well into adulthood might have seemed more like a term of years. I have not seen a prosecution of an ecclesiastic for a life estate that did not seem suspect for some other reason.

41. E159/310, m. 16 (Hilary).

42. A subsidiary effect that may not have been intended was a diminishment of clerical dependence. Except only personal chaplains, clerics could not benefit from those mechanisms normally used to secure dependents in Tudor England, such as annual retaining fees.

43. E159/310, mm. 22 (Easter), 28 (Easter), 19 (Michaelmas), 28 (Michaelmas), 19 (Hilary), 53 (Hilary); E159/311, mm. 23 (Easter), 29 (Easter), 29 (Michaelmas); E159/314, m. 36 (Michaelmas). One case elaborated the leasehold offense, saying that the cleric had not bargained, sold, given, or granted the term, interest, and profit to some lay person or persons. CP40/1073, m. 131. Roger Walcott of Graveney resolved his problem by resigning his benefice of Graveney, Kent, to Thomas Thornham, a cleric, on 12 May 1530.

TABLE 2. Geographical Distribution: Enforcement of the Statutes Compared to Ordinary Litigation in the Court of Common Pleas

COUNTIES	T1305	1327–28	T1386	T1465	T1526	1529 STATUTE ENFORCEMENT
Northumberland, Cumberland, Durham, Westmorland, Lancashire, Cheshire	3.6%	2 .9%	1.5%	0.4%	1%	2.7% (15)
Yorkshire	12.7%	11.8%	7.5%	5.7%	4%	13.9% (77)
Lincolnshire	8.1%	9.3%	7.8%	6.4%	4.3%	5.6% (31)
Derbyshire, Nottinghamshire, Shropshire, Staffordshire, Warwickshire, Leicestershire, Rutland, Herefordshire	16%	12.3%	12.1%	11.9%	13%	13 .2% (73)
Norfolk, Suffolk	15.9%	17.4%	12%	16.9%	17.6%	21% (116)
Northamptonshire, Huntingdonshire, Cambridgeshire, Bedfordshire, Buckinghamshire, Oxfordshire, Berkshire, Worcestershire	14.2%	14.7%	14.5%	11%	10.7%	9.4% (52)
Cornwall, Devon, Somerset, Dorset, Gloucestershire, Wiltshire, Hampshire	13.5%	15.6%	21.6%	18.1%	17.9%	19% (105)
Hertfordshire, Essex, Middlesex, London, Surrey, Sussex, Kent	16%	14.9%	22.1%	29.1%	31.4%	14.3% (79)
Other (South Wales, Calais)						0.7% (4)

the 40 percent of all prosecutions that they produced. The seven southeastern counties yielded 11.5 percent of the leasehold cases—the six western counties, 16 percent. Statutory enforcement thrust clerics out of the commercial sphere the length and breadth of England.

Clerics, while excluded from the commercial sphere of society, were still and

TABLE 3. Distribution of Enforcement Suit Subject Matter

LEASES	RESIDENCE	BUYING AND SELLING	STIPENDS	MORTUARY
370 (67%)	117 (21%)	43 (8%)	8 (1%)	4 (0.7%)

legitimately immersed in agriculture and in the handling of agrarian surplus, perhaps more involved after being required to be resident in their parish. The clergy collected tithes and properly and legally sold that produce on the market. They managed their glebe. They could legally lease out both tithes and glebe, or the whole of the parish, although the statute required most priests to remain on the parish. It also prohibited them from buying produce to sell for profit. The statutes did not prohibit them from engaging in agriculture, selling their own produce, or buying produce for consumption, but only from entering into the commercial world. The commercial utility of tithing remained untouched: towns and the merchants could still rely on a parish collection system to accumulate the agrarian surplus.

The enticement to sue had to be substantial to overcome the social detriment of suing the clergy: only the accumulation of the potential forfeiture to £40 normally precipitated the prosecution for a plaintiff in the court of common pleas. Only nineteen of the suits in common pleas were for less than £40; more than 130 were for £40. The significance has nothing to do with the ability to pay the costs of a successful suit; courts awarded costs in addition to the debt claimed, usually in the range of £0.67 to £2. Conceivably, the £40 threshold figure reflected a balance of the possibility of winning against the detriment of paying the costs while losing. More likely, the £20 that was the litigant's share of a £40 recovery was the point at which temptation overcame not only thoughts about costs if unsuccessful, but also the worry about alienating the cleric, detriment that would be experienced at the parish level socially, and the assessment about how much the relevant cleric could actually pay. Part of the calculation also had to be the plaintiff's assessment about what level of potential forfeiture would tempt someone else to sue. The frequency of claims for £40, for whatever reason, indicates that the incentives at that point significantly outweighed the detriments. Because of the different dynamics in the court of the exchequer of pleas, the higher claims there would indicate the same level of incentive to sue.

The statute did allow poorly endowed clerics to lease land if the proceeds

PROBATE	CITING OUTSIDE DIOCESE	TANNERY	UNKNOWN	TOTAL
2 (0.4%)	2 (0.4%)	1 (0.2%)	5 (0.9%)	552

were used solely for the support of the household and for hospitality. The least visible and easiest lease for a vicar to hold would be the rectory of his own parish. Many vicars did lease the rectory of their own parish, some from poverty, some thinking that that would be the easiest illegal lease to hide.[44] The vicar of Upton, considering himself insufficiently supported by the glebe and demesne land, leased the rectory of his own parish from the prior of Butley. He lost £40 by jury verdict because he had sold six quarters of wheat, twenty quarters of malt, and three quarters of barley, and did not apply the proceeds solely for hospitality at the vicary.[45] The rector of Nidd, Yorkshire, similarly leased the chapel of Nidd, claiming that his rectory was not worth £8 annually; he was sued for continuing his leasehold for twenty weeks beyond the deadline, for a total of £40.[46] The priest who held a chantry in the church of Arlington, Devon, apparently leased half of the same church, claiming again that there was insufficient glebe attached to his chantry. The jury had to consider how he had used the proceeds.[47] While the same cleric could plausibly handle both rectory and vicary or rectory and chapel, the statutes clearly prohibited clerics from holding leasehold lands. Only if they fell within the exception of having too little glebe or demesne lands could they avoid the forfeitures, and then only if they used the proceeds precisely as the statutes specified and not for personal enrichment. The ability to perform the duties of both rector and vicar without absenteeism did not legitimate such a lease: the holding of a parish lease by an ecclesiastic was specifically forbidden. The statutory provisions intended to restrict leaseholding by clerics as such.

Some religious establishments took advantage of the statutory exception for religious houses without revenues exceeding £533.33. Such houses could lease

---

44. E159/310, mm. 26 (Hilary), 22 (Easter), 13d (Trinity), 26 (Michaelmas), 39 (Michaelmas); E159/311, m. 24 (Hilary); E159/312, mm. 21 (Hilary), 16d (Easter), 13 (Trinity), 15 (Trinity), 4 (Michaelmas); E159/313, mm. 21 (Michaelmas), 27d (Michaelmas).

45. CP40/1073, m. 408. The verdict: "circa expensa hospicii sui solomodo non apposuit nec applicavit."

46. CP40/1075, m. 450.

47. CP40/1078, m. 396d; CP40/1079.

additional lands to the level that the house had had within the previous century, as long as the proceeds were used for the sustenance and maintenance of the house and for hospitality. The prior of Mount Grace, Yorkshire, leased the nearby parish of Ingleby from the prior of Guisborough.[48] The prior of Ixworth leased thirty-eight acres of pasture, five acres of meadow, eight acres of woods in nearby Ashfield Magna and Ashfield Parva, Suffolk.[49] The abbot of Roche leased four messuages, one hundred acres of land, and forty acres of meadow in nearby Maltby by demise of the prioress of Arthington.[50] The dean of the college of Holy Trinity at Westbury-on-Trym leased a nearby park called Pene Park and one farm called Stoke Bishop in Gloucestershire from the bishop of Worcestershire for twenty-one years.[51] The prior of Malton leased a pasture right in Malton for twenty-one years. He used the statutory defense that his lands did not exceed £533.33 annually.[52] They all had to defend themselves in litigation. Conceivably, the religious houses thought their activity would go unnoticed. More likely, the majority of the religious houses that did not in fact exceed the £533.33 limitation felt free to lease land to subsidize the maintenance of household and hospitality. In closing off the commercial opportunities of leaseholding for ordinary parish clergy, however, the statutes had not opened the door to unrestricted enrichment of the religious houses through leases.

Other clerics leased at a farther remove and in more obviously dangerous conditions. A manor was probably a difficult lease to hide. Nonetheless, the prior of St. Olave's held William Paston's manor in Fritton, Norfolk, for four months after the deadline;[53] the prior of Mount Grace held a quarter of the manor of Greenhow Bottom in Yorkshire for the same period.[54] Clerics who leased rectories were in a particularly hazardous position. A Herefordshire rector leased the rectory of Longhope, Gloucestershire, from the prior of Monmouth, far enough from his own parish that he could not have been present on both.[55] John Alye, a cleric, leased the rectory of Aikton, Suffolk, from the prior of Hatfield Peverel.[56] John Stayner, cleric, leased the rectory of

48. CP40/1071, m. 267d.
49. CP40/1077, m. 605.
50. CP40/1082, m. 211.
51. CP40/1078, m. 434.
52. CP40/1074, m. 350.
53. CP40/1078, m. 319d.
54. CP40/1071, m. 267.
55. CP40/1085, m. 404 (2nd); CP40/1085, m. 406 (2nd).
56. CP40/1082, m. 105.

Puriton, Somerset, from the dean and chapter of the College of St. George of Windsor.[57] Richard Croweler took from the president and scholars of Magdalene College, Oxford, the leasehold of the rectory of West Tisted in Hampshire, hardly near his own vicary of Alfriston, Sussex.[58] Some clerics could not even trust their clerical lessor. John Hoskyns, the vicar of Colaton Raleigh, Devon, leased forty acres belonging of right to his vicary to Richard Alyn, a cleric, on 29 September 1529, before the statute, for three years. Regardless of propriety, he then sued his own lessee for holding over the deadline of 29 September 1530 for four months: he should have alienated the leasehold, said Hoskyns, to some layman.[59] Clerics who leased lands were vulnerable, but some clerics recklessly put themselves in danger.

For many clerics, even smaller leaseholds were difficult to hide. William Curson of Garboldisham, a cleric, leased forty acres of land, six acres of meadow, twenty acres of pasture, four acres of marsh, and a hundred acres of gorse and heath with a sheepfold in Garboldisham.[60] Henry Hunt of Shenstone, a cleric, leased a variety of tenements in Shenstone, Staffordshire: a messuage, a croft, half a virgate of land, and a meadow from three different people.[61] William Hull of Waresley, a cleric, leased a messuage, forty acres of land, twenty acres of pasture, and sixteen acres of meadow in Waresley.[62] Other leaseholds would similarly have been known to at least a few people. Certainly, harvest times and the death of a trusted lessor would have been obvious times of vulnerability. Some clerics must simply have thought that the statute would be a dead letter.

Clerics often leased truly small holdings in violation of the statute; in regard to them, the statute was particularly vicious. For those ecclesiastics holding leases after the statutes, the penalty depended primarily on length of time, not the value of the leasehold. Thomas Wolaston, a chaplain, thus faced a penalty of £40 for taking the issues and profits of two acres of pasture in Pershore, Worcestershire, for four months.[63] John Sponer was an ecclesiastic who likewise faced a £40 forfeiture for holding a half acre of land in Souch Cove, Suffolk, for

---

57. CP40/1078, m. 431. T 25 Hviii.

58. CP40/1075, m. 360.

59. CP40/1072, m. 565; CP40/1073, m. 131.

60. CP40/1077, m. 517.

61. CP40/1077, m. 628.

62. CP40/1075, m. 558d; CP40/1077, m. 452.

63. CP40/1079, m. 551.

four months.[64] John Wynter of Tattersett, a cleric of Norfolk, held only four acres of arable; Robert Thompson of Copdock, a Suffolk cleric, only six acres; and Thomas Rydley of Sutton, a Gloucestershire cleric, only common of pasture for thirty sheep: they all faced the same penalty as those who had leased a rectory, manor, or a hundred acres of arable.[65] The vicar of Beighton, Derbyshire, leased only three acres of pasture in Yorkshire and found himself sued for £460.[66] The vicar of Bulbridge, Wiltshire, leased three acres of land for £0.70.[67] The rector of East Bilney, Norfolk, leased only two acres of pasture but thus precipitated a suit for £50; he was finally acquitted, but still had had to pay his legal expenses and face the possibility of financial ruin. Since the statute focused on the act of an ecclesiastical person holding property for a term, clerics who leased relatively little land faced immense forfeitures. Even those who could legitimately lease might have found all their profit and more consumed in legal fees.

Since the initiation of this kind of suit only required the ordinary writ of debt, a person could start the suit knowing only that the ecclesiastic was holding a lease. Substantial detail, however, might have been the reason for successful suits. The person most likely to know such details was the lessor, but the lessor seldom sued in person. Roger Pole, however, did exactly that.[68] In another case the attorney for the plaintiff was the lessor.[69] In a couple others the plaintiff was apparently a relative of the lessor.[70] If lessors at times felt it unseemly to prosecute in person, cooperation with another person would have been an acceptable way simply of making a profit or of removing an unsatisfactory lessee. Certainly the lessor would have been in possession of all the necessary information. Since the penalty did not depend on the precision of the detail, however, nothing depended on accuracy. Moreover, the lessor faced no penalty at all for having made the lease. The layman or cleric who leased to a cleric had done nothing illegal: the whole burden and liability was on the clerical lessee.

---

64. CP40/1078, m. 77.

65. CP40/1078, m. 502; CP40/1079, m. 649; CP40/1093, m. 515d.

66. E159/313, m. 15 (Easter).

67. E159/313, m. 32 (Michaelmas).

68. E159/311, m. 12d (Easter).

69. CP40/1079, m. 160: John Manser v. Adam Elward of Dersingham, cleric, for £80 for a leasehold in Shernborne. Arthur Hewar was both the lessor and the plaintiff's named attorney.

70. E159/312, m. 18 (Easter); E159/314, m. 16d (Michaelmas).

Lessees could make use of the exceptions provided by the 1529 statutes, but the exceptions were narrow. Thomas Bramford, a chantry priest in Arlington, Devon, discovered the difficulties when Robert Fyrebaron sued him. Fyrebaron originally accused him of leasing half the rectory of Arlington, the rectory in which his chantry was. Bramford was willing to admit holding three acres and pleaded that there was insufficient glebe attached to the chantry. Fyrebaron did not have to prove the lease of the rectory, but focused on the use of the three acres: he alleged that Bramford had not applied the proceeds to the establishment and hospitality.[71] If any infraction of the statute was found, the plaintiff recovered. In the exchequer of pleas, defendants normally pleaded insufficiency of glebe; the issue put to the jury then was whether the proceeds of the lease had been used solely for household and hospitality. In the court of common pleas, most defendants denied the leasehold.[72] When George Waryng, vicar of Upton and lessee of the rectory of Upton, Norfolk, tried the insufficient glebe defense, the plaintiff asserted that he had used the proceeds for his own use and detailed further the amount of grain sold and the names of the purchasers. The jury found for the plaintiff, so that Waryng forfeited £40, half to the king, half to the plaintiff.[73] While the statute had provided some reasonable exceptions, the exception had to be proven to the letter: neither individual ecclesiastics nor religious houses were to prosper personally by holding leaseholds. And both innocent and guilty faced litigation.

More than 200 cases included enough detail to ascertain the identity of the lessors, and religious houses might well have seemed to be an aggravating factor. In that set of cases, 142 (69 percent) involved only ordinary land, and almost two-thirds of those allegations concerned leases granted only by lay people. Thirty-one cases (22 percent of the subset) involved leases from religious institutions. Sixty-five cases (31 percent) involved grants of parishes, tithes, or glebe land. Thirty-six of those leases (55 percent of this subset) derived from religious institutions, as against twenty leases from noninstitutional vicars or

71. CP40/1078, m. 396d; CP40/1079, m. 659.

72. CP40/1079, m. 660 (Nicholas Page, vicar of Buckfastleigh, Devon); CP40/1079, m. 160 (Adam Elward of Dersingham); CP40/1093, m. 506 (John Makyn, rector of Clippesby and Billockby, Norfolk); CP40/1093, m. 432 (Thomas Draper, rector of Witton, Norfolk); CP40/1085, m. 101 (Richard More, vicar of Inkberrow, Worcestershire); CP40/1085, m. 112 (Richard Benett, rector of St. Veep, Cornwall); CP40/1075, m. 450 (William Assheton, rector of Nidd, Yorkshire: not beneficed at £8/yr.); CP40/1074, m. 350 (Prior of Malton, not worth £800).

73. CP40/1073, m. 408.

rectors. Overall, about a third of the leasehold cases that left details involved leases made by religious institutions to ecclesiastics.[74] The laity could easily be excused for leasing land to clerics because of the insufficient glebe exception. Religious institutions that leased parish rectories to ecclesiastics, however, would seem complicit in the offense but immune from punishment. Moreover, religious houses had been put into a bind of their own. They used leases as a primary management mechanism. Having clergy as potential lessees prior to 1529 had increased the value they could ask for their appropriated parishes because the clerical lessee could perform as the parish priest, cutting his expenses by £6. Clerical lessees could thus have offered higher rents. The statutes of 1529 both eliminated those desirable lessees and substantially lessened the number of potential lessees as such. The religious houses necessarily faced a much less advantageous market for their appropriated parishes and their other lands, so they might well not have hesitated to deal with a cleric who was himself in an awkward position by attempting to lease after the statutes. Putting an end to a commercial clergy could make the religious houses seem a source of trouble, and enforcement might well turn from concentrating on demand to attending to supply, and thus, in particular, to the religious houses.

The pleading and details of the amount of land leased focus attention incorrectly on the cases that went to pleading and even more on the few that received a jury verdict. The more important figure is the much larger number of ecclesiastics who were sued, but whose cases disappeared after only the barest notation in the legal record. In almost all forms of litigation concerning any subject matter, most of the suits brought disappeared with only such formal entries: people compromised; parties died; plaintiffs reconsidered. In suits like those authorized by the 1529 statutes, however, any ecclesiastic, once his leasehold had been discovered, had a great incentive to compromise with the plaintiff. He could buy off the plaintiff for less than the amount of the possible judgment. Other defendants would not compromise because they were innocent. Even though innocent, they had had to acknowledge royal regulatory power and the supervision of the laity. Even those ecclesiastics who dared to lease land legitimately under the statutory exceptions had to refrain from commercial profit for themselves. Ecclesiastics were now isolated from the world of commercial lessees, constituting a more "spiritual," noncommercial side of society.

74. Appendix 4.

Buying and Selling for Profit

The prohibition on buying and selling for profit most directly captures the central idea of the 1529 statutes, that clerics were to be taken from the commercial arena. While this prohibition was relatively difficult to enforce, there were forty-three suits by the end of the Hilary term 1536. Buying and selling involved discrete actions, whereas absenteeism and leaseholding were continuing activities. An accumulating penalty was plausible for leaseholding and absenteeism, but not for buying and selling for profit. Parliament opted instead for a forfeiture of three times the value of the goods purchased. The result was a prohibition that was more difficult to prosecute and that carried a lesser incentive for potential plaintiffs.

Since the forfeiture depended on the value, plaintiffs had at least to try to specify the goods and their worth. James Rokesby alleged that Robert Blessyng of Kirkby Ravensworth, a chaplain, had, on 2 December 1530, bought oxen, sheep, and chicken meat, pepper, saffron, and primrose worth £5, together with thirty quarters of wheat (£10), ten quarters of rye (£3), and sixty quarters of malt (£5) for resale.[75] Fulk Raddoun detailed how Thomas Baker, rector of Minton, Shropshire, purchased 140 sheep for £9 and twenty stones of wool for £2.67 and sold them for a profit of £0.82 on the sheep and £0.02 on the wool.[76] Still other allegations detailed the buying of barley and the selling of malt from the barley.[77] Still, the accuracy of the detail was not critical. When John Day sued Nicholas Marche of East Bilney, Norfolk, a cleric, he sought a forfeiture of £40 based on detailed allegations. Marche allegedly had made two purchasing forays. On 28 November 1533 he bought from James Aleyn seven half-quarters of barley (£0.62), from William Burdon eleven half-quarters of barley (£1.01), from William Haryson twelve stones of hemp (£0.30), and from William Smyth twelve stones of hemp (£0.30). Then, on 10 December 1533 at Ingoldisthorpe, he bought from William Marche sixty half-quarters of barley (£8) and from Simon Alrede 1,200 pounds of lead (£3.22). He sold those goods for a profit. A jury found that he had indeed bought a total of seventy-four half-quarters of barley worth £9.40 and twenty-four stones of hemp worth £0.40 for profit by resale, but not the 1,200 pounds of lead. The justices in Bench then

---

75. CP40/1077, m. 571.

76. E159/311, m. 30 (Easter).

77. E159/312, m. 15 (Trinity) (with profits of 24 percent and 50 percent, but totaling less than £3).

realized that the case had been mispleaded because issue had been taken on the whole, without the necessary specification by the defendant that he had not done all *or any part* of the alleged violations: the jury found that he had done only part. They thus corrected the pleading and sent it back out to the countryside for another verdict.[78] Sellers, neighbors, or laborers could have acquired the requisite detail, but the damages were based only on that portion of the sale that the jury in the end found had been made.

Other neighboring residents may well have known about and pursued completely on their own for the forfeiture. Richard Wychehalse alleged that Richard Wykys of South Tawton had purchased £13.33 worth of white tin; they went to a jury on Wykys's defense that he had bought it not for resale, but for his executors to use in performing his last will after his death.[79] When George Denton sued Richard Bainton, cleric, for leaving various animals with other people for them to use for Bainton's profit, Denton was able to specify 180 sheep and a profit of £13.33, but the court left blanks for the number of horses and cows to be filled in later.[80] John Hacon, a gentleman, sued George Washington of Burgh, Suffolk, a cleric, for a purchase for resale on 12 August 1532 of twenty-one acres of barley and four acres of oats from John Frances, but was unable to specify the price.[81] These cases seem like prosecutions without insider information.

While the suits themselves might have been sufficiently difficult to prosecute that litigation was not frequent, social dynamics would have added a different kind of penalty. Every cleric who bought and sold for profit had to buy and sell from someone else, and those other parties might know that they could turn around and sue the cleric. Many clerics would not thus have tempted fate. Others who did violate the statute would not have been in a good bargaining position with either sellers or purchasers. An annoyed party was much more likely to sue. Only parties who thought they were getting a very good deal would shelter the cleric's misdeeds. Since rectors and vicars would have had to sell their tithes and the produce of their glebe, they might have been able to hide illicit sales of goods bought for resale along with legitimate sales. Still, the actual profit for clerics in illicit transactions must have been much lower than before the statute and undertaken with very much less confidence. Clerics may

78. CP40/1083, m. 418; CP40/1085, m. 311.
79. CP40/1077, m. 412d.
80. CP40/1073, m. 638.
81. CP40/1076, m. 432.

not even have had a bargaining position in legitimate sales that was as good as they had had before the statutes.

Absenteeism

Not only were ecclesiastics to be isolated from participation in commercial endeavor, but they were also supposed to be on their parishes. If parishioners were watching priestly leaseholding practices, they must have been even more vigilant about absenteeism, which now had a precise definition. Plaintiffs brought 118 of the suits in the database to punish absenteeism. That the number of suits concerning absenteeism is less than that for leaseholding probably indicates that ecclesiastics were aware that it would be more difficult to hide absenteeism. If so, during the grace period provided by the statute, rectors must have, even though unwillingly, moved to their parishes in substantial numbers or sought out a qualifying personal chaplaincy. Bowker, indeed, compared nonresidence— whatever that meant in the visitation records—in 1530 with nonresidence in 1518: reported absenteeism had declined dramatically in 1530, although absenteeism seems to have begun to increase somewhat again by 1540,[82] perhaps an unintended consequence of the dissolution of the religious houses, perhaps a growth in the number of clerics taking service as personal chaplain or attending university. The statutes had a clear impact on clerical behavior.

Potential prosecutors kept careful track of a parish priest's whereabouts. When William Gedney sued William Hewton, vicar of Welton, Lincolnshire, he claimed £20 based on absences totaling two months: the sixteen days beginning with 12 June 1533, then fourteen days after 27 June, then fourteen days after 29 September, and the whole month after 25 February 1534. At those times, Hewton apparently was resident neither at Welton nor at another of his benefices.[83] Anthony Woode sued Richard Morys, rector of Salford, Oxfordshire, for £80 and alleged that for eight whole months Morys had lived at Warwick away from his parish. In court Morys's attorney had no proper defense, so Woode recovered his share of the £80 as well as damages of £1.[84] William More, even as prior of the Worcester cathedral priory, also found himself in court

82. Bowker, "Henrician Reformation," 89–91.
83. CP40/1082, m. 509d.
84. CP40/1071, m. 780d; CP40/1075, m. 715; CP40/1076, m. 434.

explaining his absence from his post over an eight-month period.[85] More pointedly, a yearbook report preserved the judicial comment that the residence statute applied also to abbots and priors.[86] Most suits were like More's in that they concerned long, continuous absences. Rectorial absence was likely much resented anyway and would have been very public. Parishioners could not but have noticed absence.

Most rectors simply denied the allegation of absenteeism. Confusion about the status of domestic chaplains and of legitimate pluralists seems to have been a problem only occasionally. William Kempe was sued for £70; he was the rector of Ditton, Kent, but had resided continually in the London parish of St. Nicholas Acons for seven months. He admitted the absence, but claimed that he was a domestic chaplain of John Zouche, a baron and thus a person entitled to have domestic chaplains who could be absent from their benefice. The justification went to the jury on a question about precisely when Kempe became the baron's domestic chaplain.[87] William Burbank tried to justify his six-month absence from his prebend by alleging attendance at the university at Oxford. The plaintiff, however, maintained that he had been living at a monastery near Lincoln.[88] The few cases arising from legitimate pluralism and from the legitimate absences of personal chaplains and scholars might indicate that such cases were often weeded out prior to litigation, perhaps even by the initial confrontation between the cleric and the potential prosecutor out in the parish.

The court did appear willing to allow an interesting exception for absenteeism: unavoidable absence by reason of illness. John Willoughby was parson of Kemble; Humfrey Walrond claimed from him £20 for being absent from 1 November 1532 until 1 January 1533: he had been at Wood in Devon, 44 miles from Kemble. Willoughby explained that he had left his parish of Kemble on 29 October with the firm intention of returning within twenty-six days. On 11 November, however, he fell victim to "le Splene" and was so weakened that he could not travel for fear of death. The case went to the jury precisely on whether he had been so weakened that he could not travel back. The court would not

---

85. CP40/1082, m. 403d.

86. YB P 27 Henry VIII, fo. 10, no. 24: "Nota auxi, qe ilz parlent secretement entre eux, qe un abbe ou prior doit estre resident in nul autre lieu, come sun grange, ou autres lieux, et s'il fait, il forfetera come appert in meme le statute."

87. CP40/1082, m. 434.

88. CP40/1083, m. 514.

accept the mere allegation of any sickness: the rector had to convince a jury that he was not only sick, but too sick to travel without danger of death.[89]

The prohibition of absenteeism was the issue most likely to come under close scrutiny by parishioners. Buying and selling of goods for profit and the holding of leaseholds could not be completely concealed, but absence of the rector from the parish would have been a matter of common knowledge. When the rector mounted his horse, some parishioners would have begun to mark the days. Such close personal supervision probably was not conducive to inculcating in the rectors a great deal of solicitude for the parishioners. Most suits, however, were for long, continuous absences. Rectors and vicars went rapidly from being participants in the wider world of the cities to being prisoners on rural parishes. Any gain in good relations within the parish had to await the reorientation of the rector or the appointment of a new rector with far different expectations.

Mortuary Fees

Confined to his parish and his domestic and religious activities, the rector faced a restriction on economic advancement that the limitation on mortuary fees only exacerbated. The mortuary statute set a ceiling on such fees, but stipulated that it would not serve to increase those fees in areas in which the customary fees had been less. Since mortuary fees came at a time of family stress anyway, rectors would have expected parishioners to enforce the statute; on the other hand, the forfeiture entailed was not as drastic as with the greater prohibitions concerning leaseholds, absenteeism, and pluralism. While mortuary fees beyond the statutory rate would thus have produced great resentment, the incentive to sue was not as strong. Nevertheless, when John Webster of Hinxton, Cambridgeshire, took a dead woman's gown as mortuary, her husband took him

---

89. CP40/1077, m. 433. This was Redgate's second chance. He had sued earlier in the exchequer of pleas claiming an absence of nine months. The rector admitted the absence from October 29 to January 21, but with the same defense. The attorney general abnormally did not take over this case; Redgate demurred, but there was no judgment. E159/311, m. 26 (Hilary). He then brought his case to the court of common pleas, modifying the allegation. This is the only case in which a plaintiff sued the same defendant in both courts on the same offense.

to court. Heads of households owed mortuary, not married women. The husband sued to recover the value of the gown (£1) and the £2 forfeiture.[90]

The interruption of mortuary fee custom produced some perplexity, perhaps an inevitable result no matter how clearly that statute was written. Thomas Judwyn, a resident of Washington, Sussex, on 20 December 1530 made out his will and appointed his wife, Joan, as his sole executor; he then died. On 24 July Joan proceeded to marry Philip Benett, and Joan had still not paid the mortuary at that time. The claim of mortuary made so late raised problems about the liability of the succeeding husband for the mortuary due from his wife's first husband. Robert Wylsun, citing canon law, decided to avoid that problem by citing Joan herself as sole executor, although married, to appear alone at the court of arches in London to answer for the mortuary fee; her husband had left moveable goods worth between £6.67 and £30, so the proper mortuary fee would have been £0.17. The dispute then revolved around a series of allegations. Philip and Joan made two claims. They charged that the rector was demanding an additional £1.17 in damages for detention of the mortuary fee. Then, when Philip had offered only the original £0.17 on 4 December (after a delay in the court of arches on 1 December), the rector had refused to accept it, thus giving them their claim for £2 under the statute. The rector denied all of that, explaining that it was a misunderstanding occasioned by different offers from Joan's attorney and Joan herself. The jury returned that the rector had declined Philip's offer on 4 December; they assessed damages of £1.33 with costs of £2.67. The court declined to render judgment immediately in the case, and it was continued on in the court of common pleas for at least another half year, although it may have had a more general effect.[91] Apparently, survivors could delay payment of the mortuary fee until the rector had actually begun litigation, and then could still make an offer of the mortuary fee itself without compensating the rector for his own costs in initiating litigation. Such a rule would have been an extreme hardship on rectors and greatly diminished the collection of mortuary fees once the rule became widely known.

---

90. CP40/1067, m. 573.

91. CP40/1073, m. 553. In timing and content, this case is a plausible source for the complaint in "The Common Supplication against the Ordinaries" of 1532: "And where any mortuary is due after the rate of the statute sometimes curates before they will demand it, will bring citations for it and then will not receive the mortuary till he may have such costs as he says he hath laid out for suit of the same . . ." (text in Elton, *Tudor Constitution*, 326).

Stipends

Stipends for rectors presented two very different issues, both of which harmed the parish. Rectors had been able to rent out their parish and thus receive the rent, while at the same time they were absent receiving a stipend for praying for the dead. This stipend was an inducement for rectors to abandon the management of the parish. Such a stipend increased the current rector's income; other stipends decreased the current rector's income. Rectors often agreed to relinquish a rectory only on receipt of an annual stipend from parish revenue; that practice reduced the income of their successors. Some rectors arranged such stipends for themselves so that they could retire—others, so that they could exchange their first benefice for a better one. The statute prohibited rectors from taking a stipend for praying for souls. Recognizing the other interests served by stipends from parish revenues, however, the statute only limited stipends paid from parish proceeds to no more than a third of the value of the benefice.

Beneficed clergy thus could no longer augment the revenue from their benefice by taking a stipend to pray for souls. William Kempe, the parson of Ditton in Kent, otherwise sued for absence from his rectory, also faced prosecution for taking an additional stipend. The executors of John Bruges had apparently hired him for forty weeks to say mass for Bruges's soul in the London parish of Nicholas Acons, beginning on 22 June 1533. For that service he was to receive £3 on 29 September 1533 and £3 on 25 March 1534. Roger Bexwell thus sued him for £80. Kempe argued that, as to £10 of the claim, he had not been rector of Ditton for the first four weeks and three days; as to the remaining £70, he denied that he had taken any money during that period for the prayers. He admitted having done the services. He could have simply forgone the payment in deference to the statute, or conceivably the executors had accelerated the payment, or he was simply throwing the matter to a jury in an attempt to escape lawful but severe punishment.[92] This restriction on stipends, together with the other economic

---

92. CP40/1082, m. 429. Another stipend suit is unclear. Robert Hill sued John Alger for £178 citing that provision, but retailed that Alger, already beneficed in Bagborough, Somerset, received a seven-year term in the rectory of Bishop's Lydeard from the dean and chapter of Welles. The alleged time of double payment is about eighty weeks, making the return from the rectory (the forfeiture is £2/wk. plus ten times the value of the stipend) implied by the sum very small. A suit for forfeiture by the rector as a lessee for a little less than eighteen months, however, would have yielded a similar sum. It is possible that the plaintiff was simply citing the wrong provision. CP40/1074, m. 353d.

limitations in the statutes and the enthusiastic supervision by the laity over so much of the cleric's life, must have contributed to the decline in the popularity of the priesthood as a profession in the early years of the English Reformation.

Moreover, this statute limited the burdens that could be put on a rectory. A frequent burden was a pension used for retirement, although the cases never specify the reason for the pension.[93] John Thuxton was sued by a mercer in Easter 1538 for £26.67. The debt derived from a penal bond, obligating the mercer and another person in that sum if they did not pay the rector annually £2.67 from the rectory of Higham by Norwich for the remainder of the rector's life. The mercer defended himself by claiming that he had been paid up into 1534, but that the statute of 1529 prohibited ordinaries from assigning more than a third of the worth of the benefice to a rector on promotion or resignation of a benefice: any excess was not to be paid. The mercer explained that the benefice was worth only £6.67 and that he had been willing to continue paying the reduced sum, but that Thuxton had not found that acceptable. The parties here came to issue on the value of the rectory.[94] The statutory limitation put a priority on connecting the wealth derived from a parish into the hands of the current parish priest, and emphasized the current spiritual needs over the seeming property rights of the priest that had made retirement and exchange of benefices easier.

Implementation

The statutes did not put an abrupt or total end to absenteeism or parish leasing, but reduced those practices to such a degree and by such means that the parish experienced a revolution. Absenteeism continued, but only for those who were personal chaplains of magnates, real scholars, or brothers or sons of the aristocracy. Major pluralists at a certain level were grandfathered in under the statutes, but their numbers would decline fairly rapidly by mortality. Mortuary fees

93. For pensions to support retirements, see Thomson, *Early Tudor Church*, 158–62. In 1531 an incoming rector was obliged under a penal bond of £100 to the outgoing rector to give an acquittance for repairs and to obtain a decree about the annual rent encumbering both the parish tithes. CP40/1076, m. 343. Another performance bond, this one in 1516, burdened the rectory of Barnham, Norf., at the resignation of John Long. CP40/1026, m. 404. In 1533 the vicar of Effingham, Surrey, put his successor under a £100 performance bond to secure an annual pension to be assigned by the ordinary, an acquittance of repairs, and the harvest of grain already sewn on the glebe without tithes. CP40/1077, m. 510.

94. CP40/1093, m. 308.

continued, but with a ceiling now dictated by statute. The leasing of parishes continued, but priests would no longer be the lessees; and a declining number of priests would be able to be lessors as those pluralists who had been grand-fathered in progressively died. The consistent thread in the legislation was that priests would not be involved in the commercial arena and that parish priests would most often actually tend to the parish, but with lessened economic incentives and opportunities. At the level of individual practice, however, much that was traditional about parish and clergy survived, even though the laity now supervised the clergy.

Some traditional elements survived for a time at law because the justices would not apply the statute retroactively. They continued to apply previous legal practice in regard to mortuary fees to situations arising before the statute. Thomas Mawre of Sunningwell, Berkshire, had taken an ox as mortuary due from Richard Clerk on 10 June 1529. When the lord of the manor sued, the traditional dispute about the priority between heriot and mortuary arose. The court sent the matter to a jury to determine the local custom, just as it would have done at any time in the century and a half before the statutes.[95]

In a similar fashion, leases made to lay people prior to the statutes continued to be enforced; they were still legal. The lease of Dame Alice Belknapp on the rectory of Wolfhamcote for twenty-one years at £31 annually had been made on 25 January 1529, before the statutes, but the dean of the collegiate church of Warwick could enforce its provisions even in 1542: Alice had agreed to build a competent rectory there within five years and to provide honest and sufficient hospitality. She had failed to build the rectory; the chancel was in such disrepair that priests had been unable to say mass there for five years; the grain in the barns was ruined. The jury returned a verdict against Alice on all counts, with damages of £17.[96] William Cordall, a gentleman, had received the lease of the rectory of Burham on 7 March 1529 from the prior of St. John of Jerusalem for a term of forty years; he felt quite competent to proceed to sublease the rectory to John Fowle of Halling, another gentleman, on 6 December 1529 and then later on to sue for half a year's rent due in 1534.[97] Henry Carbott, a doctor of law and archdeacon of Richmond (so that he certainly had a valid reason for absentee-ism), leased his vicarage of Heversham to James Bolkescale of Kirkby Lonsdale, a yeoman, on 25 April 1529 for five years at £33.33 annually; he did not have to

95. CP40/1069, m. 541.
96. CP40/1113, m. 691.
97. CP40/1085, m. 170.

alter his arrangements because of the statute. He sued Bolkescale in 1535 for the unpaid rent from 1530.[98] Thomas Thornton, an Essex vicar, leased his vicary to John Longman, a yeoman, on 6 May 1529 for three years at £15.17 annually. He enforced his claims for rent from 1531–32 in the court of common pleas in 1533.[99] Master Thomas Webster, vicar of Tetford and Baston, Lincolnshire, had leased his vicary to Thomas Cope, a husbandman, and Alice his wife on 17 September 1529 for £40 per year. In 1533 he sued for £2.50 due on Michaelmas 1532.[100] Robert Brudenell, Chief Justice of Common Pleas (CJCP), and his wife, Philippa, had demised the rectory of Chesham Leicester, Buckhamshire, to William Barton in 1516. Robert died, then Philippa died, and finally, in 1532 Philippa's executors sued for rent due on 25 March 1531.[101] Leases of parishes made prior to the statute continued to be enforceable, when they had been made to lay people.

Pluralist rectors and vicars continued to lease out parishes after the statute was passed and before the deadline of 29 September 1530. Thomas Fowler, a gentleman, leased the rectory of Bugbrooke, Northamptonshire, from William Vaughan, a cleric, for £2 each year, on a one-year periodic lease beginning 23 April 1530.[102] Robert Otys and Gilbert Otys, his brother, entered into a performance bond of £20 on 21 January 1530 for the lease of his Yorkshire vicarage.[103] On 4 July 1530 John Prestall, rector of Ash by Kingsdown, Kent, leased his parish to William Wode of Gravesend, yeoman, and John Baylle of Wrotham, a cleric, for five years. Baylle was miscalculating about the statute, because he would be in danger as of 29 September 1530. Nevertheless, the lessees had made sure that the first rent would not be due until 25 March 1531: well after they would be able to ascertain the effect of the statute. When Prestall sued them in 1531 for the first rental payment, they simply answered that they did not owe: under the statute, of course, at least Baylle should have abandoned the lease shortly after taking up the parish.[104] Perhaps they had simply abandoned the leasehold instead of surrendering it to the lessor.

Rectors continued to lease out their parishes even after the statute when they could be legally absent, as when they were a personal chaplain to a magnate. When John Roberts, rector of Fovant, on 4 July 1540 leased his rectory to

98. CP40/1085, m. 321.
99. CP40/1077, m. 402d.
100. CP40/1077, m. 630.
101. CP40/1074, m. 454d.
102. CP40/1078, m. 422.
103. CP40/1070, m. 205.
104. CP40/1070, m. 406.

Thomas Rendall, a Wiltshire husbandman, he had Rendall make out a performance bond for £40 to guard against waste in the parsonage, houses, or glebe lands.[105] John Williams, the vicar of Bristol St. Nicholas, leased his vicarage to Thomas Wynsmore of Bristol, a mercer, for three years at £18 annually on 28 May 1535.[106] John Whelter of Droitwich, a gentleman, was the lessee of Grafton Flyford rectory, Worcestershire, from 24 October 1530. His five-year lease from George Byllyngton, the rector, was protected by a performance bond for quiet enjoyment for £26.67. The rector may have wanted to terminate the lease to facilitate compliance with the statutory mandate for residency, because the lessee sued in 1532.[107] William Bulleyn, archdeacon of Winchester and vicar of Aylsham, Norfolk, demised the vicarage to James Hawe of Cromer for three years on a periodic tenancy from 14 January 1533. Bulleyn committed himself to a severe performance bond: he would pay Hawe £20 annually for the remainder of his life if Bulleyn resigned the vicarage or was dispossessed; if Bulleyn failed in that, Hawe could sue on a £300 bond.[108] Rectors would still be leasing their parishes out in the reign of Mary.[109] The practice of leasing parishes continued, but with a much reduced frequency and in a very different context. The parish church continued at times to be for sale.

That lay people could still take leases of parishes did not mean that they were not concerned about the consequences of the statutes. George Malory, provost of Cotterstock, leased his manor place and provostship, in reality the parsonage attached to the provostship, to Robert Hyrkham, squire, for three years on 20 April 1532. Hyrkham was to receive the tithes and oblations of the parish for a rent of £18. The agreement was to stand, however, only with the license of the ordinary "and also if the law will suffer it without danger."[110]

Some clerics tried to evade the statute by manipulating rental payments. A lessor and lessee, both clerics, made a performance bond and indenture on 18 June 1529, well before the statutes, but probably in the expectation that Parliament would act on clerical absenteeism. The lessee finally sued in 1532 for £200 on a performance bond, revealing a lease of the rectory of Ilfracombe, Devon, for five years. The lessor retained responsibility for all repairs and agreed to sue

105. CP40/1113, m. 343.
106. CP40/1093, m. 197.
107. CP40/1075, m. 444.
108. CP40/1093, m. 521d.
109. CP40/1173, m. 432: the lease of Stickney, Lincolnshire, for three years at £19.25 in very traditional form.
110. CP40/1075, m. 522.

any parishioner who detained dues owed to the church. The clerical lessee was to provide the priest to perform the services and pay the ordinary and extraordinary taxes unless they exceeded the payable tithes. The other rental provisions were unique. The lessee paid £60 in advance for the first two years' rent, rendering only a peppercorn at 25 March for the first two years if he was asked for anything at all. For the final three years the lessee owed £40 each 25 March. The rental provisions avoided having the lessee pass any money to the lessor for a few years, hopefully until the urge to reform had passed. The plaintiff in the case, however, was the clerical lessee: the enrollment of the case terminated immediately after the enrollment of the indenture, probably because the court realized at that point that the plaintiff had admitted being a clerical lessee and thus had confessed a violation of the statutes.[111] This cleric had arranged his lease to hide what he thought might become a statutory violation, but then imprudently revealed an actual violation by suing his lessor.

The 1529 statutes sought to remedy the problem of clerics with more than one benefice with care of souls; they had an expanding application. Current pluralists could retain up to four benefices; as those major pluralists died increasingly over the next decade or two, the major pluralists would be those who could hold two benefices. The immediate effect was not a sudden end to pluralism as such, although absenteeism declined. Not all the effect of this reform appeared in *qui tam* litigation: patrons of the first benefice of a pluralist were entitled simply to present a new candidate to the bishop. Possibly *quare impedit* cases would reveal the extent of the effect on the problem of pluralism. The two major effects of the statute against pluralism were the restricted economic opportunities of new pluralists and the different role of dependency to the wealth that pluralism offered. Even in the long term, the statute only eliminated excessive pluralism and changed the particular ends that pluralism would advance. Pluralism now supported personal chaplains of the aristocracy, scholarship, and aristocratic family members.

Conclusion

The statutes of 1529 and their successors were revolutionary, not because they eliminated particular activities immediately, but because they changed the char-

---

111. CP40/1075, m. 509.

acter of the parish and the life of the clerical establishment. Clerics were now to be isolated from the commercial sphere, resident on their parish or with a magnate as chaplain, limited in their economic ambitions, coerced from activities not considered spiritual, and regulated by their parishioners. Many priests in 1531, thrust from a more clerical society in the towns, must have felt imprisoned on the parish. The immediate result would perhaps have been hostility or, at least, real discontent. In the midterm, however, they may well have begun putting their education and wealth to work by teaching and preaching at the parish level; possibly those activities served as the foundation for the reformation of piety that would take place later in the century if only by contributing to literacy and interest in religion. When William Brandesby of Nafferton, a yeoman, arranged before the Reformation to have his daughter marry the heir apparent of Thomas Wandsford of York, a gentleman, he had obliged himself to take over the raising of Wandsford's son: to send him first to school to learn grammar and then to London to study the common law for three years as was appropriate for one of the gentry. He also bound himself to put his daughter with a convent to learn the reading of matins, hours, and vespers and gentry manners.[112] Those educational needs did not disappear in 1529 or by 1540, but the institutions providing those needs would be altered. These priests were not the humanists, nor would their level of education have been impressive to humanists. But they were among the better educated people in their society, and the statutes now scattered this precious resource of educated people out into the country parishes. Patient research may yet reveal an intriguing educational benefit to the localities.

Parish life likewise had a different dynamic under the statutes. In more parishes the economic assets of the parish commanded the presence of the rector, and the power to command that residence was in the hands of the individual lay person. One might suspect a greater sense of participation would result. Similarly unquantifiable, and thus far unexamined, was the economic functioning of the post-1529 parish. Before the statutes the beneficiary of the parish religious dues spent his wealth away from the parish. After the statutes the rector much more frequently was resident and would be spending rather

112. CP40/922, m. 265. Even by 1516 the court of king's bench had begun regulating church court jurisdiction in educational matters, issuing a premunire on an ecclesiastical court in a suit that sought to prevent Richard Catersale from teaching grammar at St. Albans. KB27/1019, m. 61d.

more of his wealth locally. This local spending would not have been a startling increase in the flow of economic resources, but for many communities it would have been significant.

The most significant element of change in parish dynamics, however, was the empowerment of the laity, the element least likely to have been intended. The amount of litigation is dramatic testimony of the way in which the statutes, not as a matter of doctrine but only as a strategy to introduce a reformation of parish life and of the clergy in line with traditional ideals, empowered the laity to supervise the clergy. The late medieval parish had lessees, often lay, who basically controlled the parish. After 1529, however, parishioners, or anyone else, were fully capable of regulating the clergy in accord with both their own self-interest and the traditional ideals of residence and a spiritually oriented, non-commercial clergy. The combination of traditional morality and economic self-interest worked wonderfully well. The practice of lay regulation of the clergy quite plausibly influenced English attitudes about the appropriate involvement of the laity in the parish and local religion. The result could look like a triumph of Lollardy or an introduction of radical Protestantism, but its successful roots rested rather in a king's reliance on the laity to enforce his policy.

CHAPTER EIGHT

The Dissolution of the Religious Houses

etween 1536 and 1540 Henry VIII dissolved the religious houses of England; he thus not only changed the religious landscape of England but also expanded the impact of the statutes of 1529. Those religious houses had grown up over the course of centuries and worked themselves in various and changing ways into the social fabric of medieval England. At the time of the dissolution, something under 9,000 clerics lived dispersed in about 837 religious houses, rather less than 1 percent of the English population.[1] Economically they were important for their control of much of the landed wealth of England as well as for their alms giving. In the religious arena they were the archetypical embodiment of what the Catholic Church regarded as the "perfect" life and of a works-oriented theology: celibate and, at the level of institutional aspiration, given over to prayer and the search for personal sanctity. They also controlled more than a third of the English parishes. In the governmental arena, the religious houses were, with the bishops, the last major holders of governmental franchises, administering the government at the local level in numerous areas throughout England; they also participated in Parliament through the House of Lords. In just five years Henry VIII seized that wealth, that religious influence, and those governmental powers. Reformation England, from the central and national level down to the local parish, would simply look very different from medieval England. At the local level, the heads of the religious houses had been legitimate absentee rectors. Those positions now

---

1. Knowles, *Religious Orders*, 3:247, n. 2; Swanson, *Church and Society*, 83. Knowles figures 650 religious houses but with an additional 187 friaries and hospitals, for a total of about 837. Mackie estimated 563 religious houses with 9,000 members housing 35,000 laymen of various kinds. Mackie, *The Earlier Tudors*, 247–48. That estimate seems to have been based on those houses with significant lands and thus excluded friaries and similar establishments; figures from 553 to 563 usually appear for estimating the average wealth of religious houses. Inclusion of the friaries would distort that analysis. For estimating the effect on the religious context, however, the figure 837 is necessary. Guy accepts 7,000 as an approximate number of monks, nuns, and friars. Guy, *Tudor England*, 148.

became fully subject to the statutes of 1529. For about 3,300 more parishes, the absentee rector would no longer be clerical. An absentee rector who was lay (a lay impropriator) diverted resources away from the parish, but did not violate the new model of the clergy. While those rectories would continue to be leased, neither the lessor nor the lessee would be a cleric. And the greater landed resources that had been controlled by the religious houses would no longer be part of a leasing market dominated by clerics. Tithes to a lay impropriator lost all vestiges of a relationship to the provision of religious services: they were in fact overtly just a mechanism for extracting and accumulating the agrarian surplus for no religious or economic return to the parishioner. The clergy were supposed to be spiritual; the laity increasingly had exclusive possession of the commercial sphere.

The dissolution, however, took place within the context of a decade of extraordinary events. In 1529 the king proceeded against Cardinal Wolsey by premunire, although his objective of obtaining effective governance over the church remained unaltered. Henry VIII thus abandoned his strategy of governing the church through the medium of a very powerful archbishop. Henry followed the attack on Wolsey with premunire prosecutions of other prominent clergy in 1530.[2] By then, king and Parliament had aggressively violated the traditional jurisdictional isolation of the clergy, mandated increased royal regulation of the clergy exercised by the populace at large, and banished the clergy from the commercial sphere of English life. The same statutes regulated probate fees and the issuance of process by ecclesiastical courts; they intruded into the heart of what had been acknowledged ecclesiastical rights.[3] In 1532 Henry obtained the submission of the English clergy, a submission that was confirmed by statute in 1534.[4] Likewise in 1532 and 1534 the crown cut the flow of revenue from England to the papacy.[5] In 1532 Thomas More resigned as chancellor. In 1533 Henry VIII married Anne Boleyn secretly, and thereafter severed the appellate structure that linked English ecclesiastical courts to the pope[6] and received a formal annulment of his marriage to Catharine of Aragon. In 1534 the king assumed the headship of the church and the power to appoint bishops,[7] but

2. Guy, *Tudor England*, 127.
3. See above, Chapter 6.
4. Statute 25, Henry VIII, c. 19; Guy, *Tudor England*, 131, 133–34.
5. Statutes 23, Henry VIII, c. 20; 24, Henry VIII, c. 20.
6. Statute 24, Henry VIII, c. 12.
7. Statute 26, Henry VIII, c. 1.

waited until 1536 to abolish the authority of the pope in England.[8] After a 1531 statute that limited parish endowments made by use (roughly equivalent to a trust),[9] the statute of uses, which took effect in 1536, sought either to eliminate or to limit the use, and thus make it more difficult for churches to conceal wealth and easier for the crown to confiscate monastic properties.[10] Likewise in 1536 the crown by statute seized from religious houses and most bishops their governmental franchises, privileges that had recognized ecclesiastics as properly and intimately involved in a wide range of direct governmental activity.[11] In this context, between 1536 and 1540 the crown dissolved or accepted the surrender of all the religious houses and seized their lands, eliminating from the landscape 837 institutions that had represented in a striking manner the separate clerical order in every corner of England.[12] These institutions also held about 3,300 parish positions with absentee rectors. The dissolution left the personal chaplains, scholars, and aristocratic relatives as the only legitimate clerical absentees. Crown and Parliament progressively dismantled the institutional forms and jurisdictional rules that had become traditional after the Investiture Contest of the eleventh century and substituted a model of a clergy that was insulated from both governmental and commercial endeavor and involved only in spiritual service and education.

Marginalization of the Dissolution

The general trend of historical argument on the English Reformation has marginalized the dissolution of the religious houses. Discourse has concentrated on the forces that initiated the Reformation in England: was the reformation of the 1530s the result of a social movement to which the crown merely responded, or was it rather an imposition by the crown on a population that was content with traditional Catholicism?[13] Whether the reform was "bottom-up" or "top-down," of course, some religious roots for the dissolution of the religious houses might be plausible. Spiritual motivations would be more plausible if there was a socially significant anticlerical movement, and particularly so

8. Statute 28, Henry VIII, c. 10.
9. Statute 23, Henry VIII, c. 10.
10. Statute 27, Henry VIII, c. 10.
11. Statute 27, Henry VIII, c. 24.
12. Statutes 27, Henry VIII, c. 28; 31, Henry VIII, c. 13.
13. Haigh, "Recent Historiography," 19–33.

if the religious houses were lax and licentious. Within the last few decades, however, a consensus has grown that popular piety only changed much later in the century.[14] The dissolution of the religious houses could not thus have arisen from a social movement. Historians have therefore come to a new appreciation of traditional Catholic culture in the early sixteenth century and have also been able to dismiss the more vehement criticisms of monastic life. Thompson's appraisal seems to strike a nice balance: "The monasteries may often have lacked burning zeal and failed to produce classics of spiritual writing, but they still contained men whose devotion to their way of life evoked a fair measure of respect."[15] If the Reformation was not a social movement, however, it seemed more difficult to ascribe the dissolution of the religious houses to Henry VIII's spiritual convictions than to his greed. From that perception the dissolution did not relate to religious reform, but only to fiscal concerns. Moreover, the fact that the monasteries could be dissolved so successfully and rapidly might have indicated that the religious houses had become less central to popular spiritual needs. Historiographically, thus, the dissolution of the religious houses has come to appear as a major event in the finances of the realm, but, perplexingly, almost irrelevant to the reformation of religion.

The importance of the dissolution is now open for reexamination. The current literature supposes only two elements to the English Reformation: the changes in the central government best symbolized by Henry VIII becoming supreme head of the Church of England in 1534 and the general change in personal piety that happened finally in the late sixteenth century. This study, however, has identified a third facet of the English Reformation: the reformation of the parish and clergy that occurred with the implementation of the statutes of 1529. That third facet was local and not related to doctrinal change, personal piety, or any extraordinary anticlerical movement. The dissolution of the religious houses was also local: England knew about 837 religious houses in a territory approximately the size of Iowa today and of the population of modern Houston. Those religious houses, whose members constituted a bit less than half of 1 percent of the population, controlled more than a third of English

---

14. Haigh, "Anticlericalism," 56–74; Haigh, *English Reformations*, 269–95; Guy, *Tudor England*, 24. See also above, Introduction.

15. Thomson, *Early Tudor Church*, 225. See Haigh, *English Reformation Revised*, 3. Elton's evaluation was rather lower: "Monasticism was, then, in such a decline that its end might have come spontaneously . . ." Elton, *England under the Tudors*, 142.

parishes and much more than a tenth of the landed wealth.[16] Whether or not the dissolution of the religious houses was related in intent to the parish reformation, it was certainly part of the same overall change in society. So many local institutions embodying a theological ideal could not simply disappear from the landscape without also changing the religious context of life. The options available for religious expression changed, particularly for women; the institutions that best embodied a works-oriented theology vanished; the monks and nuns would no longer reinforce the economic, political, and cultural importance of the priestly orders in society. English society would inevitably be more lay, and the rest of the clerical order more restricted.

Because historians have been so concerned with anticlericalism or the intrigues around the king, the historiography concentrates to an extraordinary degree on the motivations and intentions behind governmental action. Eamon Duffy has more realistically evaluated the role that the religious houses played in English religious life.[17] Duffy carefully integrates the monasteries with traditional religious practices. Otherwise, historians only comment on the fiscal importance of the dissolution and maintain vigorously that the scope of the dissolution was not planned in advance. The first seizure of religious houses in 1536 was not part of any larger plan, so runs the argument, because a portion of the assets of the first houses suppressed were used to establish a few new monasteries.[18] Henry VIII and Cromwell, however, have fairly good reputations for being masterful in politics; they could easily have disguised their general intentions in ways that would mislead not only their contemporaries but thus

16. Mackie gives a range of estimates. Contemporary estimates went as high as a third of all land; some modern estimates place the minimum at a sixth of all land. Mackie, *The Earlier Tudors*, 372, n. 3. Midmer apparently finds the figure of a quarter believable. Midmer, *English Medieval Monasteries*, 26. Swanson finds that an estimate of a fifth to a quarter of agricultural land is believable for the wealth of the church as a whole, including bishops and land attached to parishes: religious houses would be a rather smaller subset of that figure. Swanson, *Church and Society*, 196. Guy recites that 20 percent of the manors in England had belonged to the church as a whole in 1535, but only 6.5 percent remained in ecclesiastical hands by 1558. Guy, *Tudor England*, 149. This would allow a rough estimate of the manors of the religious houses as something like 13 percent of the total. That figure for manors, however, would not include other holdings. And all these figures might be defective for not including lands leased for a term or held to the use of religious houses but for which the title rested in lay hands until after the *Valor Ecclesiasticus*. The range of estimates for the holdings is thus extremely broad.

17. Duffy, *Stripping of the Altars*, 383–87, 454.

18. Guy, *Tudor England*, 143–45; Youings, *Dissolution of the Monasteries*, 40.

also later historians. Knowles, in a more judicious evaluation, found a general intent quite plausible, but not provable.[19] Knowles's willingness to entertain probabilities is still refreshing and probably the best approach.

The dissolution of the religious houses also appeared until now to be isolated from legal changes that occurred at the same time. Here the history profession has basically followed the lead of legal historians, who have adopted analytically correct but clearly artificial categories that separate public law and private law matters. The dissolution of the religious houses and the statutes of 1529 that reformed parish life thus fall within the public law category. Such matters might seem more to be in the range of political history.[20] The dissolution itself seems not a topic for legal historians. At the same time, the statute of uses appears only as one of the most important statutes in the development of Anglo-American property law, within the category of private law and thus an appropriate matter for legal historical attention. For a legal historian, the statute of uses and the dissolution of the monasteries occur almost in different universes, although they were approved by the same Parliament, at the same time, and in the same social context. The reluctance to consider the interaction between public law and private law distorts the field. At some level, the dissolution was certainly relevant to property law. Religious houses in 1536 still controlled an immense amount of real estate, so alterations in property law must have been relevant to the religious houses in their final years. The dissolution also had a corresponding impact on sixteenth-century land use. Keeping the public and private law categories separate ignores such interactions and emphasizes the doctrinal elements of private law. Neither Henry VIII nor Cromwell much cared about keeping the categories of public law and private law distinct. In the parish reformation between 1529 and 1535, public and private law interacted by handling leaseholds within the context of a governmental religious policy. In a similar way, this chapter suggests relationships between various major legal events that occurred after 1535 that have hitherto been segregated from each other because some were private law matters and others were public law matters.

The only area in which historical investigation has not marginalized the

19. Knowles, *Religious Orders*, 3:198–204.

20. John Baker's scholarly history of English law, for instance, refers to the dissolution only twice: once in treating of feudal incidents, the other time in treating of the law of personal status—the elimination of the special legal status for monks and nuns. Baker, *IELH*, 276, 531.

dissolution is the impact on the crown's power and wealth. The wealth of the religious houses as a whole was immense, even if some houses were poor and even though the combination of long-term leases, the security of leases since 1500, the increased bargaining power of lay lessees since 1529, and inflation had eaten into the economic resources of the wealthier houses. The church as a whole, considering religious houses, bishops, and parishes, directly controlled between 20 percent and 25 percent of the landed wealth of late medieval England, without counting its leasehold investments.[21] The religious houses accounted for about half of the landed holdings of the church, or something significantly over 10 percent of the real property of England, as well as about a third of England's rectories.[22] The religious houses considered as a whole thus wielded great economic power and controlled a substantial proportion of the agricultural surplus of the country. That power, however, was not focused: it fell into the hands of about 837 monasteries, friaries, and hospitals, each of which had somewhat different objectives, each of which was led by an abbot, prior, or master who often had personal and familial ties with different magnates or the crown. About a fifth of the religious houses (excluding the friaries) could be accounted wealthy.[23] Once confiscated and concentrated into the hands of the monarch, that economic power was astounding: the annual income from the confiscated estates was triple the annual income from the king's traditional estates.[24] Confiscation, moreover, was not limited to the income from land: the crown confiscated likewise the substantial accumulations of jewels and gold and silver items in the monasteries and felt free to sell off the monastic lands that had been confiscated. To the significant extent that revenue is the basis of governmental power, the dissolution of the monasteries with the consequent confisca-

21. Swanson, *Church and Society*, 196. Youings, *Dissolution of the Monasteries*, 15: "The Dissolution of the Monasteries has taken its place in historical studies primarily as a revolution in land-ownership, second only to that which followed the Norman Conquest." For other estimates, see above, note 18.

22. Swanson suggests that around 1500 there were about 8,800 parishes in England. Swanson, *Church and Society*, 4–5, 30, 44. The number of appropriated parishes rose from about 2,000 in 1291 to about 3,300 in 1535.

23. Knowles, *Religious Orders*, 3:248. Knowles figures that about 650 religious houses and 187 friaries and hospitals were involved in the dissolution. "Reasonably wealthy" would indicate an annual income exceeding £300. Youings indicates that there were nearly 900 communities. Youings, "Dissolution of the Monasteries," in *Historical Dictionary*, 143.

24. Solt, *Church and State*, 32.

tion of wealth would translate into vastly increased central governmental power. The crown had unprecedented reserves to draw upon, and felt free to do so.[25]

The dissolution of the religious houses thus currently plays various, but limited historiographical roles. The confiscation of the landed wealth, it is widely agreed, increased royal revenue and thus royal power. Likewise, the sale of those lands broadly in society provided substantial vested interests that would obstruct any attempt to return to a late medieval religious organization. Historians seem to agree also that the dissolution was not the result either of an anticlerical movement or of a reaction to extraordinary deficiencies in monastic discipline. However, because the statutes of 1529 have until now been largely dismissed, the relationship between these statutes and the dissolution of the religious houses has not been examined. Nor have historians related the dissolution to the statute resuming liberties or to the statute of uses, two major initiatives contemporaneous with the dissolution. Simply put, the dissolution has been as marginalized as the statutes of 1529.

The Process of Dissolution

Henry VIII and Thomas Cromwell dismantled the centuries-old medieval monastic establishment in just five years. Whether or not they planned from the beginning for a complete extirpation of the religious houses, they proceeded in a piecemeal fashion. With the reform of the parishes well under way and the church already surveyed to provide for royal taxation, they proceeded first against the lesser monasteries. Many of those smaller houses gained a reprieve; some of the proceeds of the first seizure went toward establishing even a few new houses. Thereafter, forfeitures and surrenders accomplished much of the rest of the dissolution, ending finally with the great monasteries, the friaries, and miscellaneous orders like the Knights Hospitallers. The members of the houses first dissolved were allowed to move to other religious houses. In the end, the members were pensioned off instead of being simply cast adrift in society, even though they were not without the capacity to fend for themselves.

The dissolution of 1536–40 was not unprecedented. Suppression of religious houses was always permissible under canon law for cause, although such suppressions came from the church, not the crown. The crown nevertheless had

25. Guy, *Tudor England*, 144–46. Guy recites that Henry VIII realized almost £800,000 from land sales, normally more than £50,000 more each year in income from land, and a net of over £1.3 million from the dissolution.

seized priories dependent on foreign religious houses during the Hundred Years War and used the proceeds in part for educational purposes.[26] Relying on papal authorizations, Cardinal Wolsey suppressed twenty-one religious houses in 1524 to establish what would become Christ Church College at Oxford and then, with papal authorizations in 1528–29, suppressed a further seven monasteries.[27] Current historiography disparages any thought of a continuing crown policy, in part because historians prefer to link policy to ministers instead of to the king. Neither the agenda laid out by Thomas Lord Darcy for the earls of Norfolk and Suffolk in 1529[28] nor the suppressions by Wolsey, implemented by Thomas Cromwell, are thus still considered indicative of any long-term goal because those ministers did not continue.[29] In terms of policy, the survival of the religious houses was not completely inconsistent with the initiatives of 1529. Still, abbots and priors certainly were absentee rectors and often excessive pluralists; they controlled too much wealth not to be involved in the commercial sector of society even though they were clerics; and they continued to lease parishes and lands to clerics. The statutes of 1529 had tried to emphasize that the clergy should serve God through service to the laity, particularly the magnates, and to scholarship, whereas the religious houses were often oriented to their own spirituality and salvation and almost always valued clerical communities. Even if they could have survived the initiatives of 1529, the mentality of the religious houses was often discordant with the new order. Wolsey under Henry VIII set Cromwell on the track of dissolution. Norfolk, Suffolk, and Darcy, trying to appeal to Henry VIII, pushed in the same direction in 1529. Henry VIII himself occasionally voiced such sentiments. Historians' steadfast denial of an overall policy thus seems strange, particularly in the context of all the prosecutions under the statutes of 1529. Conceptualization of governmental policy about the church requires consideration of a reigning king. Regardless of whether there was a "policy," however, the Wolsey suppressions laid the groundwork for the complete dissolution of the religious houses.

Cromwell gained the expertise of suppressing monasteries under Wolsey; in implementing the dissolution he acquired his data from the *Valor Ecclesiasticus*. In 1534 the crown had succeeded in getting a statute that transferred two lucrative

26. Knowles, *Religious Orders*, 2:157–66; Youings, *Dissolution of the Monasteries*, 26.

27. Knowles, *Religious Orders*, 3:157–64; Youings, *Dissolution of the Monasteries*, 27–28.

28. See above, Chapter 6.

29. Midmer, *English Medieval Monasteries*, 27; Guy, *Tudor England*, 112–13, 143; Haigh, *English Reformations*, 84–85.

forms of papal taxation to the king. The king thus was to receive the first year's income from any spiritual benefice (any position such as bishop, rector, abbot, etc.) but also thereafter a tenth of each year's income. Parish priests, already confined to their parish, regulated by the laity and precluded from commercial activity, now owed taxes to a much more rigorous master and were thus discouraged from exchanging benefices and thus incurring the tax. Ascertaining the wealth of the church in its various forms thus became a pressing matter for Henry VIII, and commissioners were sent out to collect the data. That data, assembled, constituted the *Valor Ecclesiasticus,* so that overtly the survey was a document designed to enable taxation, not seizure; Cromwell's motivations, however, were often complex and might well have included seizure in the future as well as taxation in the present. Whatever Cromwell's motivations were, however, the commissioners for the *Valor* did their work in 1535; the seizure of the monasteries began with a statute passed in March 1536.[30] The *Valor* in fact became the database for the dissolution. Conceivably, the *Valor* might also have been projected as a check on clergy who claimed the right to continue holding leases because they had insufficient glebe. The attorney general had not actually joined issue on that assertion, but rather had regularly continued to challenge the use of leasehold profits; he may, however, have seen an advantage to a proof of that issue by record, although I have not seen it so used. Simply put, the church and its wealth were matters of considerable governmental interest, and the motivation behind the *Valor* was probably not myopically tied to taxation.

In 1536 Henry VIII and Cromwell by parliamentary statute closed those monasteries with annual revenues of less than £200. That decision, momentous as it was, was fairly cautious. It suppressed potentially more than three hundred monasteries (more than half the total of monasteries, less than half of all religious houses), but of those more than seventy escaped immediate suppression by fines paid to the crown. Cromwell took pains to reassure the greater monasteries, whether because he thought those monasteries were secure in fact or, more likely, because he sought to avoid political problems. The monasteries did not believe Cromwell, and neither should historians. The government had to face a revolt in Lincolnshire and the Pilgrimage of Grace, a significant revolt centered in Yorkshire.[31] In both instances, the suppression of the monasteries was a central concern, although by that date isolating a cause is difficult; the context was one in which members of the laity had been prosecuting their

---

30. Statute 27, Henry VIII, c. 28.
31. Haigh, *English Reformations,* 143–49; Guy, *Tudor England,* 149–53.

rectors, vicars, and religious houses under the 1529 statutes, property law had been severely dislocated, and the king's power had been remarkably expanded by the declaration that Henry VIII was supreme head of the English church. Those matters would feed into people's worries, frustrations, and convictions in important ways that still might not find explicit voice in complaints. The revolts, successfully suppressed, resulted in the death of the abbots and religious who had supported the uprisings and also in the suppression of their houses. The rate of prosecution of allegations under the statutes of 1529 fell off while the religious houses were being dissolved; the reason for the decline was probably a combination of exchequer burdens, the uncertainty of prosecutions in which religious houses had been implicated either as defendants or lessors, and the distraction of prosecutors who might have found better opportunities for their energies in this upheaval. The suppression of the lesser monasteries generated its own bureaucracy and commissions to handle the details and then to manage the acquired lands; the burdens of that bureaucracy grew as more religious houses fell into the king's hands.[32]

The seizure of the lesser monasteries proceeded by sanction of parliamentary statute; the greater monasteries and other religious houses fell largely without such a mandate. Cromwell used various means at his disposal to secure their capitulation. In some instances, abbots or other heads of religious houses were appointed who could be relied upon to surrender their house to the crown on request. In other instances, Cromwell's agents bullied and threatened houses to capitulate and surrender themselves to the crown. Finally, in 1539 Parliament validated such transfers of religious properties to the crown,[33] but by then almost all of the religious houses had ceased to exist.[34] The work was rapidly completed, and the crown now faced the substantial but welcome burden of managing vastly increased landed holdings and moveable goods. What had taken the church literally centuries to build up, the crown dismantled completely in about five years.

The success of the dissolution depended on the reduction of the social impact of the suppression of the monasteries. Removal of that many institutions was dangerous anyway: most religious had some family connections; most houses had worked themselves into the social fabric; each religious house represented a particular aspect of the religious culture of the country. Moreover,

32. Youings, *Dissolution of the Monasteries*, 91–116.
33. Statute 31, Henry VIII, c. 13.
34. Knowles, *Religious Orders*, 3:336–66; Youings, *Dissolution of the Monasteries*, 56–90.

seizure of the landed holdings held by the religious houses constituted a major transformation of the distribution of property and, given the prominence of leaseholds, implicated many of the commercially active people in the country. The crown acted to ameliorate the situation in three ways. It bought off the members of religious houses, giving generous pensions to the heads of the religious houses, but also relatively generous pensions to the members; the much larger number of servants employed by the institutions, on the other hand, received nothing.[35] The crown could afford such generosity with its new wealth, and the obligation to the members of the houses would diminish over time by mortality, the effects of inflation, and pensioners who found better but incompatible livings. More importantly, however, the dissolution left relatively intact the leasehold arrangements that it found: leaseholds contracted except in contemplation of the dissolution were allowed to stand, paying the rent now to the crown instead of to the church.[36] Lessees had no particular reason to feel that their interests were in jeopardy, although they might be dealing in the future with a more rigorous landlord. Finally, a good portion of the lands was recycled back into society: sold to bring in revenue to the crown.[37] Probably some of the purchasers were in fact the lessees, simply securing and completing their interests. Possibly the rate of liquidation depended in part on the need to allow the lease terms to expire before true value could be recouped on a sale. But every purchaser, like every prosecutor under the statutes of 1529, had acquired also a reason to support the new order, and, particularly for them, the dissolution. Not even Mary was so brave as to restore the monasteries with their traditional lands: that would have been as large a displacement as Henry's dissolution, but would have struck a chord that no monarch dared touch. The religious context of life in England had irrevocably changed.

The Dissolution and the Parishes

The dissolution of the religious houses extended the parish reformation. After 1529 the heads of religious houses remained as the most frequent absentee rectors and pluralists. Even when a monastery had not appropriated a parish, it might well have acquired an advowson right. For those parishes the dissolution brought with it an increase in lay control of the parish. While the dissolution

35. Knowles, *Religious Orders*, 3:402–17.
36. Statute 27, Henry VIII, c. 28, section 4.
37. Knowles, *Religious Orders*, 3:393–401; Guy, *Tudor England*, 146–49.

cannot be proven to have been a conscious continuation of the 1529 initiative (that is, there is no document that states it expressly), its effects both with the appropriated parishes and with advowson rights were congruent with what had been happening in the parishes since 1529.

The dissolution of the religious houses was the de facto completion of the reform of the parishes begun by the statutes in 1529 in regard to pluralism and absenteeism. The statutes of 1529 had grandfathered pluralists up to a limit of four benefices and provided exceptions for academics, personal chaplains, and aristocratic relatives. Those exceptions allowed and, for personal chaplains, encouraged a certain continuance of absentee rectors, but the most significant exceptions were for religious houses. Religious houses had appropriated around 3,300 parishes; the advantage for a religious house in having such an appropriated parish was that the head of the house could be an absentee, pluralist rector and derive the profit for the religious house. Abbots, priors, and masters were thus notorious but legal absentee rectors. The perpetual vicars had theoretically been in charge of the appropriated parishes, but they had likewise often leased out their interest in the parish. The statutes of 1529 had remedied to some extent the absentee perpetual vicar, and the heads of religious houses remained as the greatest offenders to the ideas underlying the reformed parish. They also leased lands, subject to the ceilings imposed by the statutes of 1529. The dissolution resolved that offense for the 3,300 parishes controlled by religious houses.

The dissolution did not stop the commercial treatment of the rectory; it did ensure that specifically clerical rectors would be absentee much less frequently. Likewise, fewer rectors would be pluralists since the heads of religious houses had usually been pluralists. The 1529 statutes, after all, had objected to excessive pluralism, absenteeism not related to service as personal chaplains or to scholarship, and clerical leaseholding, but not to the leasing of parishes by the laity. The manors and parishes appropriated to monasteries were often already let out on long-term leases. While such leases entered into immediately before the dissolution were annulled by statute, older leases continued without a problem.[38] At the local level, that provision would often mean that the same lay individuals who had occupied monastic lands and parishes before 1536 would have remained in possession, paying the rent now to a nonclerical landlord. The crown had shown no aversion to the laity holding parish leases. The abbey of Cockersand, for instance, had held, among others, the appropriated rectories of

38. Statute 27, Henry VIII, c. 28, section 4.

Garstang and Mitton. The crown, after the dissolution, leased the rectory of
Garstang out to John Burnell and Robert Gardiner, but found that the abbey
had leased out Mitton on a lease for eighty-one years.[39] That confusion would
have been typical throughout England, but resulted either way in rectories
leased to lay people. Since the 1529 statutes set out to remedy clerical leaseholding and limit and change the conditions for clerical absenteeism and pluralism,
the dissolution eliminated the major exceptions for absenteeism and pluralism
not provided for in the statutes and went even further by also eliminating the
ecclesiastical organizations that were both lessees and lessors. The dissolution
cast the church even further out of the commercial arena.

In an indirect way, the dissolution may have actually increased pluralism in
one area. The religious houses had sent a substantial number of scholars to the
universities. Those monks who thus attended university would not have been
absentee rectors since the members of religious houses that were not themselves
abbots, priors, or masters were not rectors. That population of monks and
friars disappeared rapidly after 1536. For clergymen, however, the academic life
was one of the few occupations that justified absenteeism and pluralism. The
different population of scholars at the university may account for at least part
of the increase in pluralism and absenteeism discovered in the 1540s, at least if
the clergy followed the career paths defined by statute for clerical success.[40]

With the dissolution the crown seized not only appropriated rectories, but
also the advowson rights held by religious houses. Advowson rights enabled the
holder to nominate clerics to ecclesiastical posts, including the posts of rector
and perpetual vicar. In appropriated parishes the rector (head of the religious
house) often had the right of advowson for the perpetual vicar of the parish. In
instances in which a religious house held a manor but had not appropriated the
parish, the head of the religious house could easily have held the right of
advowson to the position of the rector. In either case, dissolution would result
in crown seizure of the advowson. In a case study Margaret Bowker found that
religious houses controlled 40.6 percent of such patronage rights for rectories
and vicaries before 1536 and that other clerics, including bishops, held a further
12.4 percent. At the same time and in the same area, the crown exercised
patronage over only 5 percent. After the dissolution, the crown, despite the sale
of confiscated lands and rights, emerged with 21.4 percent: at least in the diocese
of Lincoln, the king's share of patronage rights to ecclesiastical benefices more

39. Youings, *Dissolution of the Monasteries*, 206–8.
40. Bowker, "Henrician Reformation," 89–91.

than quadrupled.[41] The religious houses had not been irrelevant to society in the aggregate. Their property rights and control over religious positions, as well as their religious functions, made their dissolution a major transfer of power.

The effect of the transfer, beyond the financial benefits that accrued to the crown, concerned the laity as a whole. With the statutes of 1529 the crown had empowered the general populace to regulate the clergy, and that regulation put clerical wealth at risk for transfer to the laity, who took advantage of it rapidly. The dissolution took the larger sector of clerical wealth into the king's hands, but the crown then alienated those lands back into society, although the process took decades. The crown could have retained the lands, the advowson rights, and the rectories in its own hands and thus could have had both a permanent endowment for government and permanent direct power over ecclesiastical appointments. It did not. Clearly the government's near-term fiscal priorities motivated this policy, and thus it was to some extent shortsighted. But likewise regulation of the church by the laity did not seem dangerous. The crown found it acceptable to disperse the advowson rights broadly but unevenly among the laity. Whether the control by the laity was an assumed part of religious policy, an acceptable by-product of fiscal policies, an attempt to enlist the gentry into the new religious order, or a plausible mix of those motives is a matter of conjecture. The result was so consistent with the statutes of 1529 in making the clergy serve the aristocracy, however, that it is difficult not to conjecture that it was at least in part religious policy, even though well subordinated to the need for revenue generation.

The Dissolution and Governmental Powers

The government reformed the exercise of governmental powers at the same time that it initiated the dissolution, and the two acts were probably related. The major religious houses were involved in governance at all levels, from Parliament down through the hundreds into the manors. Their governance power was important, but since it was dispersed into so many hands, it was not coherent. The same powers, gathered into the crown's hands, unified governmental authority. The king not only assumed the headship of the church in England, he also assumed the governmental powers traditionally exercised by other powerful people.

41. Ibid., 85; Bowker, *Henrician Reformation*, 123.

England from the thirteenth through to the sixteenth century characteristically had magnates and institutions exercise what later generations considered public governmental rights. In 1316 more than 60 percent of English hundreds (subdivisions of counties) were private in one degree or another.[42] The distribution of governmental powers into private hands partly derived from genuinely ancient practice, partly from modeling on those ancient practices as new governmental powers emerged in the thirteenth and fourteenth centuries.[43] Edward I had established, in his *quo warranto* prosecutions, the principle that governmental powers derived from crown grant. The political price for that significant recognition of royal authority had been acceptance, by and large, of the status quo. In return for acquiescence to the principle of delegation, the government presumed that the formal, written governmental grant had been lost if the claimant of the privileges could demonstrate the exercise of the privilege from time beyond memory: basically the fiction of the lost grant. That fiction legitimized royal supervision at the same time that it perpetuated the distribution of public power in private hands.[44] Edward I had established that in theory the crown had delegated in centuries past all the governmental franchises in fact exercised in England.

The private hands that had held those jurisdictional liberties were in large part ecclesiastical. The most significant ecclesiastical jurisdiction, of course, was held by a bishop: the county of Durham. Durham was outside the common law; cases from Durham simply do not normally appear in the court of common pleas: such cases came before the bishop's court located in Durham.[45] What was true for Durham, however, was also true for the six and a half hundreds of the abbot of Bury St. Edmunds and for the franchises of the abbots of Glastonbury, Battle, Ramsey. Beaulieu as late as 1533 still claimed to have sanctuary rights even for those treasons touching the king, as well as the typical run of lesser liberties: view of frankpledge; assize both of bread and ale and of weights and measures; appointment of the coroner; goods deriving from deodand, felons, waif and stray; return of writs.[46] Lesser institutions had lesser franchises, perhaps only the ability to name the bailiff of a hundred or to take the profits of court. Even with the high liberties, royal personnel were often used to adjudicate the cases,

42. Cam, *Law-Finders and Law-Makers*, 59.
43. For the example of the franchise of return of writs, see Palmer, *County Courts*, 263–81.
44. Sutherland, *Quo Warranto Proceedings*, 91–97.
45. Palmer, *County Courts*, 312; Jewell, *English Local Administration*, 70–72.
46. KB27/1087, m. 5 (rex).

and the law applied tended to be the same. In some sense, then, the liberties were symbolic, but symbols are not irrelevant to the exercise of power. While the law may have been the same as or at least similar to the common law, justice, no less than the local economy and the local society, could be in the control of a monastery. King's bench would, even under Henry VII, entertain an indictment against royal officers who had infringed the liberty of the abbot of St. Albans to handle the justice concerning all felonies in his liberty in Hertfordshire.[47] Under Henry VIII the intervention of the abbot of Bury St. Edmund's bailiff in the arrest of Thomas Skynner provoked eight local people (smiths, cloth-makers, laborers, and a shoemaker) to rescue Skynner, saying, "Thowe shalt arrest noo man in this towne, for we hold no thyng of my lord of Burys fraunches, and also thou shalt swere uppon the crosse of thy swerd or thou goo hence that thou shalt not trouble noone of us nor cause no suytt to be made ayenst any of us for our demeanour ayenst the in this behalff."[48] Who administered the law was a matter local people cared about. The medium was in fact the message, and the message concerned the role of the church in government. When Henry VIII began using *quo warranto* procedures to challenge the liberties, the defendants were mostly ecclesiastical holders of franchises.[49] The defense of their liberties was not the defense of mere empty privileges or abstract symbols, but of rights to mediate governance and thus to secure a position in society.

In 1536 the crown took back the powers that it had thus "delegated" into private hands in earlier centuries. The statute took back the authority from any holder to pardon treasons, felonies, and outlawries, as well as the power to constitute justices for eyres, assizes, or jail delivery or justices of the peace. It then mandated that all process at law, whether criminal or civil, would be in the king's name only. These provisions eliminated the great liberties; other provisions unified the ordinary administration of justice inside and outside liberties. This "sweeping" statute "in effect destroyed the difference between liberties and ordinary shire ground."[50] Nevertheless, the great lay liberties had mostly lapsed

47. KB27/940, m. 10 (rex). The justices of the peace of Hertfordshire had assembled more than a hundred armed men to enforce their ability to handle their pleas within the abbot's liberty against the abbot's will and to the detriment of the individuals the abbot had appointed (who included royal officials).

48. CP40/1001, m. 10 (1512).

49. Garrett-Goodyear, "The Tudor Revival," 259.

50. Elton, *Tudor Constitution*, 32.

already to the crown.[51] The statute furthermore contained several exceptions, exceptions that narrowed the impact of the legislation in ways that focused its effect. The archbishop of York and the bishop of Durham both had their liberties limited: they were reduced to acting as justices of the peace instead of handling criminal justice on their own authority. Nonetheless, their authority survived in some measure. Cities, corporate towns, and boroughs were likewise protected in their franchises. The great lay franchises—the duchies of Lancaster and Cornwall and the palatinates of Chester and Lancaster—had lapsed into Crown authority more than a century before. The great monasteries like Bury St. Edmunds or Glastonbury Abbey, however, received no such protection. The effect of the 1536 statute resuming liberties disproportionately disadvantaged the religious houses: they were targeted.

When Parliament dissolved the lesser monasteries, it thus also disarmed the greater monasteries. Although the dissolution of 1536 did not touch the greater monasteries, the seizure by separate legislation of the liberties of the great monasteries meant that they no longer controlled governmental process in their own locality: it limited their economic resources a little, but eliminated any practical ability to control the populace or to be seen as a rightful participant in governance. The resumption of the liberties was in fact aimed directly at the church. Thomas Cromwell indicated as much by writing in his memorandum on this statute, "For the dissolution of all franchises and liberties throughout this realm, and specially the franchises of spirituality."[52] The statute diminished the bishops' great liberties, while the monasteries found their liberties completely abolished. To the significant extent that attitudes about appropriate participation in governance develop from actual participation in governance, the monasteries here became defenseless. They no longer exercised governance. After the statutes of 1529 had targeted the parish clergy, that deprivation of the governance rights of the major monasteries would have been sufficient to mark even the major monasteries as vulnerable. The transfer of wealth from clergy to laity that had begun in 1529 was clearly going to proceed.

Monasteries also held some of the larger areas of sanctuary and managed jails: both were particularly troublesome for Henry VII and Henry VIII. Sanctuary provided felons with zones of safety as small as a church or as large as the county of Durham: if a felon fled successfully into the geographically defined

---

51. Ibid.
52. Guy, *Tudor England*, 176.

zone, he was safe from arrest.[53] Henry VII from early in his reign attacked abuses in sanctuary right.[54] Henry VIII continued that attack off and on, culminating in statutes in 1529, 1531, 1536, and 1540 that eliminated abusive sanctuary anomalies.[55] Churches often also kept jails. At least under Henry VII the crown attempted to compel ecclesiastics to make the jails secure.[56] Benefit of clergy, ecclesiastical jails, extraordinary or normal governmental franchises all involved the church in governance of the realm in ways proving increasingly unacceptable to the Tudors. The dissolution of the religious houses finally resolved several long-standing governmental problems.

At the national level, the heads of major religious houses had attended Parliament as lords. Forty-eight senior ecclesiastics sat in Parliament under Henry VII: as many as twenty-one bishops and archbishops and twenty-seven abbots and priors. At most there were forty-three secular lords.[57] Numbers, of course, did not translate directly into power; nor did Parliament have a really determinate political role. Indeed, when dissolution came before Parliament under Henry VIII, most monastic lords simply elected not to attend: they could not stop the inevitable and thus chose not to participate.[58] Their role in Parliament, ended by 1540, had nonetheless asserted their status in society and their rightful participation in government. They had been an important component of the process for the granting of taxes, the passing of statutes, the politics of the realm. The dissolution ended that role and thus inevitably also altered Parliament.

The statutes in and after 1536 were clearly consistent with the main tenor of the statutes of 1529. The statutes of 1529 had indicated quite clearly that clerics should be involved in spiritual matters related to lay service instead of commercial enterprise, and the ambit of the 1529 statutes had included monasteries and

53. Baker, *IELH*, 585–86.

54. Chrimes, *Henry VII*, 161, 244; Haigh, *English Reformations*, 75, 79.

55. Thomson, *Early Tudor Church*, 97–104.

56. The most intriguing case was that concerning the great jailbreak very early in the morning of 23 November 1494, when twenty prisoners, some having been in prison since 1487, escaped from the bishop of London's prison in Stortford, Hertfordshire. Five of them made so much noise dragging their chains and irons that they were recaptured within a quarter hour and only 300 feet from the castle; the rest apparently vanished. The prisoners were listed as two chaplains, a scholar, a gentleman, nine yeomen, two tailors, a haberdasher, a chapman, an ironmonger, a baker, and a laborer. KB27/984, m. 4 (rex).

57. Chrimes, *Henry VII*, 140.

58. Haigh, *English Reformations*, 131.

limited the extent of their acquisitions and the use of their resources. The complex of statutes in and after 1536 indicated likewise that clerics should be involved in spiritual things, not in governance. The church courts, of course, continued on, but their purview was supposed to be spiritual. The bishops continued to play a substantial role, both in Parliament and in their now-reduced liberties. The Crown proceeded against first the poorer monasteries, while seizing the governmental franchises of the major monasteries. By 1540 all the religious houses had disappeared. While bishops remained as magnates and important councillors, monks, friars, and other members of religious houses vanished completely from government. "Secular" government as much as commerce was for the laity; the clergy should be devoted to the spiritual realm.

The Dissolution and Uses and Wills

In between the crown assertion of supreme headship of the English church and the abolition of papal authority in England, in between the reformation of the parish and the complete dissolution of the religious houses, the crown chose to transform property law. Early in 1536, along with the statute beginning the dissolution, Parliament passed the statute of uses.[59] In the Pilgrimage of Grace, the rebels complained primarily about the dissolution, but also about the statute of uses.[60] In 1540, immediately after the completion of the dissolution, Parliament passed the statute of wills,[61] ameliorating greatly the social effects of the statute of uses. The statute of uses and the statute of wills are still fundamentally important for understanding modern property law. Just as with the statute for seizure of the liberties, however, these statutes seem to modern historians isolated from the other major initiatives in the 1530s. Nonetheless, monasteries were major holders of land: any alteration of property law would have had implications for monasteries, just as the survival of the religious houses would have had major implications for land use. The relationship of the dissolution to the intent of the statute of uses is circumstantial, but the disablement of wills from handling beneficial use interests was potentially as significant to monasteries as it was to the laity; and the merging of most "equitable" titles with "legal" titles resolved tangled issues that would otherwise inevitably have arisen in the course of the dissolution. The statute of uses made the

59. Statute 27 Henry VIII, c. 10.
60. Haigh, *English Reformations*, 146.
61. Statute 32 Henry VIII, c. 1.

dissolution easier; the question really is only whether that desirable effect could have been a portion of the reason for the statute, whether public law and private law stood in completely insulated spheres for Henry VIII and Cromwell.

This section is necessarily technical. The explanation is, hopefully, as clear as the technicality will permit, but property law is not simple. The careful reader who is inexperienced in law will be able to understand this section, but the more casual reader may prefer simply to exercise a Reformation-style faith that the crown transformed property law in part to facilitate the dissolution and thus skip to the conclusion of this section.

Most of the large estates in England were held in use by the early sixteenth century. Uses were the antecedent of the modern trust: owners of property could put legal title into the hands of trusted individuals (now called trustees, then called feoffees to uses) to avoid inconveniences that accompanied legal title.[62] The use thus allowed owners to increase the effective value of their landed wealth. One of the inconveniences they sought to avoid was wardship. The legal guardian of an underage military tenant with legal title (title at common law and not as a beneficial use interest) had a profitable wardship: he took care of the ward, but took the profits of the land for himself. Putting the legal title into the hands of trustees ensured that the legal tenant never actually died, because the feoffees, the tenants at common law, would grant to other feoffees to prevent an inheritance by their own heirs. The revenue from the tenements during the time that otherwise would have been a wardship could be diverted from the guardian's hands into the minor heir's hands or to the deceased parent's specified uses: increasing family wealth, paying debts, controlling family members after death with financial incentives, or providing for prayers and alms. Since the widow's portion of her husband's lands (dower) came only from land he had held heritably at common law at some point during their marriage, prospective husbands could limit a widow's guaranteed benefit by putting the land in use prior to the marriage. He would retain full benefit of the land and could reward wife or children as he saw fit at any time down to his death without the encumbrance of dower law or the law of primogeniture. The advantages in terms of male power in the family as well as value made the use extraordinarily attractive.[63] Since wills concerning land were not legal in England (except for lands in boroughs), uses were the only mechanism that allowed the wealthy actively to manipulate their landed holdings for longer than

62. Appendix 6.
63. Palmer, *ELABD*, 110–32; Ives, "Genesis of the Statute of Uses," 673–74.

their life. Indeed, the clear line between uses and wills had blurred, because decedents often made their feoffees the same people as their executors or willed the beneficial interest of the use to the executors to be used in the performance of the will.[64] By 1529 the simple statement that one could not devise land in England was still true, but only technically.

The statute of uses overtly sought to simplify the complicated world created by the uses. In a use the feoffees to uses (trustees) held the legal title recognized and protected by the common law, but the chancellor enforced the benefit of the lands for a different individual. The statute did not prohibit anyone from setting up a use, from making a grant to feoffees to hold to his own or another's use. Rather, it simply decreed that, whenever feoffees were seised to the use of another party, that other party would henceforth have his estate at common law as the chancellor would have protected it before 1536 in the chancellor's court. The most simple case was that in which the feoffees were seised of a fee simple to be held to the use of the beneficiary as a fee simple. Prior to the statute, the common law would have protected only the interest of the feoffees; the chancellor in his own, noncommon law court, would have protected the beneficiary's interest as a matter of the feoffees' conscience. After the statute the common law courts would have protected the interest only of the beneficiary as a common law ("legal") fee simple, and the chancellor would no longer be involved. The feoffees, without having done anything and thus purely by operation of the

---

64. Ives, "Genesis of the Statute of Uses," 688. In 1509 king's bench at first allowed pleading on the content of instructions to feoffees to uses in a will; after a verdict, the court decided to replead in a way that avoided reciting the contents of the will. KB27/993, m. 20. In 1513 William Arnold enfeoffed a knight of two acres in Kent to the use of Arnold himself; he then devised his interest to Edward White so that when Arnold died the knight would hold to the use of White. When Arnold died, however, his cousin and heir maintained that Arnold had been only seventeen when he made his will so that the will would be invalid. King's bench in 1529 put the case to a jury on the issue of Arnold's age when he made the will, thus involving itself in the validity of wills. KB27/1073, m. 78. In 1480 there was a feoffment of land in Waldron, Sussex, to seven people to fulfil the will of Richard Heggyngworth; the executor after Richard's death was "seised of the abovesaid tenements to the use of fulfilling the last will of the abovesaid Richard Heggyngworth." The executor then enfeoffed six people to the same use and then bargained and sold to others. The church wardens of Waldron claimed that the executor should have held the land for the church for services for Heggyngworth's soul. CP40/1004, mm. 448, 456. For other instances (which seem not at all unusual), see CP40/978, m. 454; CP40/1002, m. 426; CP40/1005b, m. 538; CP40/1120, m. 506. One could reinforce wills also by using a performance bond, such as the bond for £700 dependent on Christopher Wroghton, knight, delivering over certain goods and chattels given in a woman's last will. CP40/1006, m. 437.

statute of uses, would have no protected interest, either at common law or before the chancellor. The statute thus merged the two interests into the hands of the beneficiary. The statute, however, was very precise. It only applied when the feoffees were seised. Since one could be "seised" only of a "free tenement," the statute only applied when the feoffees held the legal estate for life or heritably, not when they held a lease, no matter the length of the lease. Likewise, it soon became clear, unsurprisingly, that beneficiaries received only their proportional interest. When the feoffees held to the use of more than one person (a life tenant, with the benefit going thereafter to someone else by virtue of the grant and not by inheritance from the life tenant), the beneficial life estate became a "legal" life estate, and the remainder in fee simple likewise became a "legal" interest, an interest before the common law. What happened with future interests more complicated than such a simple remainder remained to be worked out over the decades.[65]

The statute of wills cut back on the effect of the statute of uses, ostensibly because of great public dissatisfaction. Since the statute of uses sought to transfer the common law interest of the feoffees into the hands of the beneficiaries and thus eliminate the feoffees from the equation, the wealthy could no longer utilize the use to operate as a substitute for a will. The statute of wills redressed that problem. In 1540, the statute of wills reversed the common law prohibition of wills relating to land, but in such a way as to preserve the king's most important rights of wardship. After 1540 the landed classes could use wills regarding land just as they had always been able to utilize wills for the disposition of goods and chattels. The statute of wills thus remedied much of the detriment the landed classes experienced from the statute of uses.

That "simple" explication of the relationship between the statute of uses and the statute of wills, however, glosses over major problems with the statute of uses. The most obvious problem is the inconsistent application of the statute. The statute on its face would seem to apply to all uses. Apparently, however, despite the lack of express language to this effect, no one intended for the statute to apply against the so-called active uses: only passive uses were affected.[66] A passive use was a use in which the feoffees were simply under the instructions of the beneficiary and had no independent duties: those were the target of the statute. Active uses were uses in which the feoffees had specified duties, such as feoffees who were charged with collecting the revenues of the

65. Baker, *IELH*, 321–27.
66. Ibid., 329.

land and dispensing them to so many of the needy local parishioners every year. Active uses were primarily charitable, and even in the statutes of 1529 the needs of "hospitality" had often generated exceptions. Despite the comprehensive words of the statute of uses, the original and continuing understanding was apparently that active uses, thus largely charitable uses, were immune from the statute of uses.

A different anomaly came with early applications of the statute. The court of common pleas between 1536 and 1540 should have been wrestling with thorny problems about beneficiary interests that had been set up to secure certain marriages, to care for widows but only under certain circumstances, with all kinds of future interests that were in fact typical of the ways in which the wealthy had been creating uses. The future interests most problematic should have thus been "springing" or "shifting" interests: interests that would "spring" from the grantor at a future date or at a particular future event by virtue of a present grant or that would terminate a preceding estate prematurely and "shift" the possessory right to a third party. Both of those had been possible with uses before 1536; both would present difficult intellectual problems for the common law courts. An inspection of the plea rolls from 1537 and 1538, however, reveals applications of the statute limited to the absolutely most simple cases: (a) when the feoffees had stood seised to the use of the beneficiary as a fee simple, the beneficiary now had a legal fee simple; (b) when the feoffees had stood seised to the use of the beneficiary as a life estate, the beneficiary now had a legal life estate. Neither of these dealt with future interests; neither was at all complicated. The complicated situations under the statute of uses seemingly came up only after the statute of wills.

A third anomaly in the statute of uses is the difference between the supposed motivation for legislative action and the statute's actual coverage. The initial crown strategy that finally resulted in the statute of uses had concentrated on securing the feudal incidents for the crown. The crown had begun its effort in 1529 by an agreement with the magnates that ripened in 1532 into a bill to preserve the feudal incidents: the bill of primer seisin.[67] That bill faced an extraordinarily difficult audience in the House of Commons. Faced with opposition, the crown, apparently Henry VIII himself, decided to pursue the matter through the courts, by getting the common law justices to undermine the use as a legitimate device. The case that presented itself was Lord Dacre's Case. The jury assembled to examine Lord Dacre's will in January 1534. That

---

67. Ives, "Genesis of the Statute of Uses," 680–82; Baker, *IELH*, 290.

will had contained instructions to feoffees that would have avoided royal wardship rights; and the jury, taken in the presence of Thomas Cromwell, returned
that there was intent to defraud the king. All the justices debated the issue, with
personal intervention by the king. The resolution of the case was against Lord
Dacre's will. The king was now assured, one way or the other, of retaining his
feudal incidents. That process, first with the attempt to pass the bill of primer
seisin and then to preserve the feudal incidents through voiding Lord Dacre's
will in the courts, focused exclusively on feudal incidents such as wardship.[68]
The initial suggestion for a bill of primer seisin, however, was substantially the
same as the statute of wills that finally resulted in 1540. The intervening statute
of uses (1536) was much broader. Feudal incidents could have been preserved
simply by treating the beneficiary *as if* the beneficiary were seised at common
law. Such an approach would have left the venerable structure of bifurcated
rights in place and thus continued to allow uses to serve the main purpose of
wills. The disruption to lay estates would have been minimal. Other avenues for
protecting the king's feudal incidents were available. The king certainly had the
power to protect his feudal incidents from tenants-in-chief because his permission was required for alienations by such tenants. The feudal incidents that
came from subtenants both by regular seigneurial rights and by prerogative
rights could likewise be protected. In the 1530s that problem prompted the
routine addition in common recoveries[69] of a recognizance that would protect
the king's feudal incidents.[70] Since common recoveries were necessary to un-

---

68. Ives, "Genesis of the Statute of Uses," 682–90.

69. The common recovery was a fictitious suit routinely used to remove limitations on
heritable estates, that is, to change a fee tail (limited in alienability and the breadth of heirs) into
a fee simple.

70. CP40/1073, m. 211 (1533), a recognizance by Henry Doyle of Hadleigh, gentleman, to the
king in the amount of £300, with the addition of the condition: "The condition of this
recognisaunce is suche that where the abovebounden Harry Doyle and on Robert Veysy &
Thomas Veysy have suyd a wrytt of entre in the post out of the Kynges Court of Chauncery
ageynst Rychard Clifton and Richard Aystheton of the manor of Toppesfeld Hall with the
appurtenaunces and of three meases one watermyll one dosehous three hundred acres of lande
fyfty acres of medowe thre hundred acres of pasture fyfty acres of wodde and tenne poundes of
rent with thapurtenaunces in Hadley in the countye of Suffolk to thentent to recovere the same
maner meses lands tenements and other the premisses with thappurtenaunces to the use of the
said Harry and of hys heyrez for ever yf the same Harry ne his heyrz ne any other persone or
persones to whose use the seid recoverers shall stond and be seasid of and in the premissez ne
ther heyrez do nothyng herafter that shalbe in any wyse preiudiciall or hurtfull to the kyngs
grace his heyrez or successours of or for any tytle or interest that the kyngs grace hys heyrez or

tangle property settlements and thus allow the establishment of uses, this device, with others, could have handled much of the problem of feudal incidents. The statute of uses in 1536, however, actually merged those bifurcated rights and had the beneficiary hold at common law instead of treating the beneficiary *as if* he held at common law. The edifice of property law suffered an earthquake instead of a reform.

These three anomalies in the statute of uses—the exclusion of active uses, the apparent unwillingness of the courts before 1540 to deal with the more complicated issues of uses, and the breadth of the statute—indicate that the motivations for the statute were much more complicated than current historiography allows. Current historiography chooses a single-cause model, focusing solely on the crown's problem securing its feudal incidents. That version, of course, is completely congruent with the easiest, most tempting, and most simplistic historical hypothesis: major decisions were made for only a single reason, and that single reason was economic in nature. Even a contemporary analysis of the problems of uses stressed the issue of feudal incidents. Nevertheless three complaints appear in that analysis that were completely irrelevant to the feudal incidents but directly relevant to religious questions. Uses brought more lands into mortmain "and to Fyndyng of prestes." Uses also encouraged lands to be disposed by testamentary instructions to feoffees (at a time when wills were primarily within the domain of church courts), although many people were incompetent to understand the complexities of property law when making wills. And finally, the use of wills for disposing of lands held in use left determinations concerning land to spiritual courts, where the provisions could be voided by testimony of two witnesses.[71] Beyond even these stated concerns, there were several obvious problems with uses. Clerics who sought to circumvent the statutes of 1529 tried to employ uses.[72] Earlier than that, king's bench had objected to church courts handling various matters mixing uses and wills.

---

successours myght or shuld have or be intitled to have the premissez by reason of the nonage of any heyre prymer season or any other profytt that herafter myght or shulde come or growe unto the kyngs grace hys heyrez or successours that then this recognisaunse to be voyd and of none effect and ells to stond and abyde in hys full strenght and effect." There were many of these in the 1530s, even after the statute of uses: CP40/1093, mm. 271–80, 562–66.

71. "The Evil Consequences of Uses," printed in Holdsworth, *History of English Law*, 4:577–80. The preamble to the statute of uses did not directly refer to either the monasteries or the church, referring only to "gredye covetous persones lyeng in a wayte" around those dying. One would not expect anyone to advertise its relationship to the monasteries. Statute 27 Henry VIII, c. 10.

72. CP40/1072, m. 410.

In 1509 Fyneux had issued premunire writs when church courts handled instructions to feoffees to uses who were also executors.[73] In 1526 the court likewise issued a premunire for church court involvement in forged wills, since that conflicted with the subject matter of an English statute.[74] Moreover, borough courts already handled wills, and king's bench entertained litigation against a prior who sought in church court to upset a determination of the London mayor's court on a devise.[75] Those concerns picked up not only more general concerns of the Reformation, but also the concerns of the 1531 statute that had limited parish endowments to uses that endured no longer than twenty years.[76] The problem of uses was not restricted to the issue of feudal incidents, but implicated also the complex of religious issues involved in the Reformation.

All those concerns had a decided bias against ecclesiastical courts and can account for the expansion from the proposals in the bill of primer seisin to the provisions in the statute of uses. The bill of primer seisin would have treated the beneficiary *as if he were* seised; the statute of uses put the beneficiary in seisin. The bill of primer seisin would have only put a third of an inheritance into wardship, as would the statute of wills finally in 1540; the statute of uses in fact worked on the whole of the estate, ensuring that the whole of an inheritance would fall into wardship. The bill of primer seisin concerned only persons; the statute of uses concerned, as regards beneficiaries, also bodies politic, that is, corporations like religious houses. Making bodies politic seised of their beneficial interests would have no conceivable affect on wardships since bodies politic did not die anyway, although they could be suppressed. The broader concerns about uses can account for the differences between the statute of uses on the one hand and the bill of primer seisin and the statute of wills on the other.

The fate of the religious houses dictated that the statute of uses be broader than was required by the crown's interest in feudal incidents. Religious houses, after all, had been the beneficiaries of uses since the fourteenth century, because such uses were much more effective for securing prayers for the dead.[77] Religious houses were clearly, as bodies politic, going to be covered by the statute of uses. Moreover, the crown could see a clear benefit to making the statute apply in certain ways to the religious houses. The chancellor enforced the

73. KB27/993, m. 33; KB27/995, m. 37.
74. Appendix 7. For a common law action on a forged will: KB146/10/16/4 (1500).
75. KB27/998, m. 8d.
76. Statute 23 Henry VIII, c. 10.
77. Palmer, *ELABD*, 118–19.

feoffees' duty to the beneficiaries as a matter of the feoffees' consciences. If a religious house was dissolved, conscience might have dictated directing the benefit to the same persons who had been members of the houses, to institutions of similar purposes or educational institutions, or, most likely, back to the original donors and their heirs. The problem was not insuperable or even novel: monasteries had been suppressed and their assets confiscated before. Prior suppressions in England, even under Wolsey, had often resulted in the assets being used for founding a college. Lay feoffees for uses in favor of monastic houses might have become adamant about such a usage as the more appropriate use according to both their conscience and English tradition. Problems of conscience were multiplying anyway in the Reformation; the crown did not need to create new moral dilemmas. Eliminating the feoffees completely from the equation by giving the monasteries the legal interests in which previously they had had only a beneficial interest simply avoided a substantial nuisance to confiscation that otherwise might have arisen.

Likewise, the statute of uses did not cover active uses because the dissolution of religious houses removed the only objectionable purposes of active uses. To the extent that the crown was intent on suppressing all religious houses, to that extent religious houses would clearly not be recipients of active uses. The beneficiaries of active uses would only have been colleges, charitable organizations, parishes, and lay people involved in transactions that required feoffees to undertake real management. Any potential problems with parish endowments had already been handled by the statute of 1531, which limited parish endowments by use to endure for no more than twenty years.[78] Colleges and charitable organizations were favored institutions, and the statutes of 1529 had repeatedly insisted on using ecclesiastical resources for hospitality. Active uses worked in tandem with the main purposes of the statutes of 1529; the only problem would have arisen had the religious houses not been dissolved. The 1531 statute addressing parish endowment by uses rapidly followed the 1529 reform of the parish; the statute of uses similarly accompanied the dissolution. By the sixteenth century any manipulation of substantial social institutions involved uses.

The dissolution was not the reason for the statute of uses, nor was one a precondition for the other, but the dissolution does explain otherwise perplexing aspects of the statute of uses. The dissolution accounts not only for the breadth of the statute but also for the decision of the crown to proceed with such a radical statute at the same time that it was heavily embroiled in social

78. Statute 21 Henry VIII, c. 14, section 3.

reorganization. The relationship between the dissolution and the statute of uses also explains the statute's early narrow implementation as well as the willingness of the crown to retrench to the position of the early bill of primer seisin, but only after 1540, when the religious houses no longer complicated the issues. Religion and property law often interacted, particularly in a world in which the ecclesiastical sector of society held great landed resources. It is unlikely, although admittedly not completely impossible, that Henry VIII and Cromwell would not have noticed or planned those interactions.

Regulating Reform

Managing drastic reform demanded large-scale continuity. The English Reformation in the 1530s had in reality transformed the context for the exercise of governmental power. For nearly four centuries crown and church had operated legal systems that were theoretically independent of each other. Nevertheless, to one degree or another, and increasingly after 1495, the crown legal apparatus had exercised a strong supervisory role over the church courts. When the king of England became head of the church in England, he simply became head of the church court system: he did not dissolve the church courts as he had done with the religious houses. The survival of the church courts was one of many forms of the continuity of particular institutions in a dramatically transformed context. Since courts were a primary mechanism of governance for asserting policy and regulating society, all the old assumptions about the relationships between the church courts and the king's court had to be tested, because now the king controlled both. No more could the church courts seem like the arm of an external power, but likewise subjects could no longer expect to play one system off against the other quite so easily, even though the old forms of litigation survived. The new distribution of power within the parishes had to cope with the new ordering of legal authority over the spiritual life of England. King and subject discovered a changed environment for exercising power, as much in the parish as at Westminster. The forms of continuity, however, cloaked and familiarized the new realities of a laity regulating the clergy, of a changed ordering of property right, of a church without religious houses, and of unified and centralized governmental power.

The new environment put rectors in a context so changed that disputes were inevitable. Rectors, now largely resident on the parish and restricted from overt commercial activity, certainly had to focus intently on tithes to protect their economic position. Moreover, with the dissolution, about 3,300 parishes that had had an absentee rector with an institutional history with the parish now had an absentee rector who, with or without a lessee of the rectorial profits, had no institutional record with the parish. The tithe arrangements that religious houses had struck with vicars and with other religious houses had to be settled: would those arrangements lapse or bind rectors and vicars now in very different circumstances? Similar difficulties would arise with the diminished number of pluralists. The pluralists who had been grandfathered in by the statutes of 1529 had suffered a decade of mortality by 1540. Death had reduced the absolute number of pluralists and thus increased the total number of different rectors. Some of these rectors had to survive on a living that had been reduced in resources to the point of serving best only as a supplement to a pluralist's income. Rectors who had been newly resident in the 1530s might have been too threatened to enforce their rights fully; by the 1540s, if they were willing to submit to the crown in fact, they were in a stronger position, although in a less certain context. Parishioners were aware of the reductions in clerical exactions and the alterations in ecclesiastical authority. Even though a statute mandated the continuance of tithing,[79] people might legitimately wonder whether tithing was as mandatory as in the past or to whom they should pay tithe. These parishioners, moreover, had found themselves newly empowered to enforce obligations on their clergy and had seen massive transfers of wealth away from the clergy. Tithes in kind were increasingly precious because England since the 1520s had experienced substantial inflation. That inflation would only accelerate.[80] As far as was possible, the regulation of the clergy did not change the traditional handling of the agrarian surplus of the country. Clergy faced a new role and new restrictions; parishioners regulated their own clergy; the handling of foodstuffs was traditional but dominated by the laity. Reform inevitably produced confusion, and tithe disputes in particular were inevitable.

Making rectors reside on the parish must have generated substantial problems with lay lessees whose leases were still protected at common law.[81] Auxili-

79. Statute 27 Henry VIII, c. 20.

80. Outhwaite, *Inflation*, 10–11.

81. In 1536 a statute further secured leaseholds of parishes since the handling of agrarian surplus could not be allowed to be disrupted. Traditionally, lessees had to have special provisions in the lease to protect against the lessor who resigned his benefice. The 1536 statute continued a parish lease for up to six years after an incumbent's resignation, but limited by the resigning incumbent's life. Protection for six years included the leases of virtually all benefices not held by religious houses. Only benefices worth at least £2 annually were protected. The incoming rector

ary incomes (particularly stipends for praying for the dead) that absentee rectors had accumulated were now not possible, so a rector's efforts to maintain his economic position would have included recapturing the margin that represented the lessees' profits from managing the parish as well as recapturing the rectory buildings themselves for his own use. Rectors and vicars seemingly did not return to the practice of managing the parish by bailiff.[82] The lessees were unlikely simply to give up a profitable leasehold, although a decent compromise may often have been a reduction in the lessee's rent in return for the rector's use of the rectory building and service as the parish priest in fact. How these tensions actually were resolved, however, remains speculative. Confusion in many parishes, however, must have been substantial, even in those rare situations in which all parties had good intentions.

Confusion for both rectors and parishioners in the parish melded with the uncertainty produced by the new royal control over the church courts, for the crown now controlled both the secular and religious lives of its subjects. Part of that control was direct. The bishops in their ecclesiastical courts had never been completely independent of the crown, but they had been the representatives of the separate ecclesiastical order that responded more to the pope than to the king. After the statutes of the 1530s, the bishops responded to the king, so the ecclesiastical courts were now also royal courts. Part of the royal control, however, was indirect, control exercised by private litigation. Like all regulation through litigation, this control depended on local conflict that brought a disappointed or outraged party to the king's court complaining of an injustice. The source of these conflicts probably derived by and large from the new order of residency, regulation, and loopholes established by the statutes of 1529 and by the dissolution of the religious houses. In handling those disputes so much rooted in local facts but given context also by royal court willingness to intervene, the king's bench implemented royal control over church matters throughout the parishes of England by using traditional writs and legal doctrine. The justices rapidly adapted those writs and doctrines to a new reality of a crown-controlled church. Religious houses disappeared rapidly; the objectives of surviving institutions continued. The common law's orientation to regulate or

would be bound by the current lease and capable of claiming the proceeds of the lease, but could not eject the leaseholders. The provision thus resembled the kind of protection lessees occasionally had managed to stipulate in their leases. Statute 28 Henry VIII, c. 11, section 5.

82. Examination of cp40/1102 (T1539), cp40/1122 (T1544), and cp40/1141 (T1549) indicates no significant resort by clerics to actions of account against bailiffs.

absorb ecclesiastical jurisdictions conflicted with continuing ecclesiastical convictions about the appropriate powers of church courts. Inevitably, these tensions played out both in the central courts and in parishes, where the litigants lived, disputes arose, and both rector and parishioner had to secure the economic resources necessary for their own personal aspirations.

After the king became supreme head of the church, however, the same regulation would be regulation not of a separate court system, but of a court system that derived its power from the king in as full measure as did the king's bench. Premunire, obviously, was no longer appropriate. A plaintiff in church court could not plausibly be an enemy of the king simply because he had sued in the king's church court instead of in the king's common law courts. King's bench handled that difficulty by abandoning the premunire procedures that had proliferated after 1495 and adapting prohibition procedures that salvaged as much as possible from the premunire forms. Prohibitions, of course, carried more reasonable penalties than premunire: prohibition procedure was merely regulatory and more respectful to church courts. In moving from premunire to prohibition petitions, however, king's bench modified the prohibition forms to regulate tithes. The resulting prohibition petitions read much like premunire, with broad jurisdictional preambles, descriptions of circumstances, and imputations of bad intentions, but avoided the penalties now inappropriate because of the new status of the church courts. The modified prohibition procedure monitored the boundaries between the king's common law courts and the king's church courts.

The new prohibition procedures incorporated a different element that both discouraged frivolous suits and pushed petitioners into litigation. King's bench had often compelled defendants to find mainprise for their appearance. Mainprise was surety for the appearance of the defendant; if the defendant thus found mainprise, the court was sufficiently sure that the defendant would appear that it released the defendant from prison. In these prohibition hearings, however, the court insisted that the *petitioners* find mainprise to pursue their complaint if the defendants chose to contest. Petitioners no longer had an easy way to back down, because those people who had gone mainprise for them would be penalized. Petitioners thus could not use prohibition simply to harass an enemy, because their allies would suffer. When defendants contested the prohibition, the plaintiffs had to pursue their complaint and show why the church court should not have jurisdiction. King's bench thus not only established the power to filter the petitions and make the initial decisions about jurisdiction, but also developed a structure to push the case forward into formal pleading expeditiously. King's bench not only wanted those jurisdictional boundaries to be defined, but it also wanted to be in control of that definition.

The subject matter of the prohibitions showed a parish-oriented concentration. The cases tied together the problems of the 1530s: the dissolution of the religious houses, the increasing inflation, concerns about tithes, and supervision of the clergy. The court dealt with the complexity of tithe arrangements that had been thrown into confusion by the dissolution of the religious houses.[83] It also had to handle the difficulty of commutation of tithes at a time when rectors or vicars, because of inflation, would have greatly regretted any agreement to receive a money payment instead of produce.[84] Predictably, king's bench still rebuffed old clerical desires to tithe great trees, a nexus of dispute that seemed never to disappear.[85] The justices, as well as the king's council and Parliament,

83. KB27/1121, m. 121 (William Pulter had been the lessee of the parish of Great Wymondley, Hertfordshire, from the abbess of Elstow. When the convent surrendered, the king confirmed his lease, but Pulter required a prohibition in 1541 to stop the new rector of the parish from proceeding in ecclesiastical court for the tithes from twelve and a half acres of land); KB27/1123, m. 111d (Robert Cosyn, lessee of a house from Charterhouse Priory; the house was located in the London parish of St. Peter the Poor. By 1542 Cosyn was paying his tithes to the rector of St. Peter the Poor, but had to get a writ of prohibition to stop the rector of St. Benet's Wharf in an ecclesiastical court case for tithes worth £2). KB27/1122, m. 107 (H1542); KB27/1123, m. 126d (The vicar of Huish, Somerset, went to the official of Canterbury claiming that Pitney was anciently annexed to his parish so that he could claim those tithes also. The patron, the rector, and a parishioner of Pitney asserted their independence as a parish, but the vicar of Huish continued with his suit, even against the prohibition from king's bench. In 1542 they sued the vicar for £266.67 damages, but were still trying to assemble their jury late in 1547).

84. KB27/1132, m. 68 (Anthony Coope had commuted his tithes to the rector of Banbury for £5 annually for the rector's life in 1534. The rector tried to circumvent the agreement by suing in the Court of Arches for the tithes from grain and from 1,500 ewes. The church court proceeded despite the prohibition issued out of king's bench, and Coope prosecuted vigorously); KB27/1121, m. 125 (The free chapel of Rock, Northumberland, was part of the parish of Embleton. The chaplain received the tithes of parishioners in Rock and compensated the vicar with a monetary payment of £0.67. The inhabitants of Rock got a prohibition in 1541 to prevent the vicar from reversing that custom by resort to the bishop of Durham).

85. KB27/1122, m. 78; KB27/1125, m. 137 (1541) (the parishioners of Stansted Mountfitchet, Essex, brought a prohibition against their vicar when he sued in the Court of Arches for tithes from great trees); KB27/1122, m. 113 (1541) (William Bennet v. the vicar of Kea and Kenwyn, Cornwall; the vicar had sued in the consistory court of Exeter); KB27/1125, m. 116 (1542) (Thomas Felton with a writ of prohibition for trees in Minster, Kent); KB27/1125, m. 104d (1542) (John Peede and William Felde v. the vicar of Kimpton, Hertfordshire); KB27/1131, m. 23d (1544) (Christopher Sandy and Agnes Seamys v. the official of the bishop of Gloucester (who had sued on behalf of the lay lessee of the parish of Cherington, Gloucestershire); KB27/1133, m. 136d

became involved in the sensitive matter of tithes in London,[86] as well as tithing from the fishing in the Severn.[87] Even the tithing of ale in the Southwest merited attention more than once.[88] King's bench asserted itself also in matters concerning wills,[89] uses,[90] and defamation.[91] The justices were clear even that matters of repair obligations on the parish belonged to the common law.[92] Only

---

(1544) (John Potten v. John Santon rector of Wittersham, Kent; the rector sued for tithes from three acres of trees); KB27/1134, m. 113 (1545) (John Hacche v. William Egerton, rector of Wormshill, Kent: the prohibition, followed by litigation on KB27/1135, m. 111); KB27/1136, m. 40 (1545) (John Pratt & Henry Fyson v. Cristofer Threder, vicar of Wood Ditton); KB27/1138, m. 69 (1546) (Henry May & Edward Crosse v. Oliver Browne, rector of Rattlesden, Suffolk); KB27/1140, m. 157 (1546) (Lawrence Eden, Alexander Clerk, and Simon Waren v. Thomas Butler, vicar of Barkway, Hertfordshire); KB27/1143, m. 94 (John Crofte v. Elizabeth Heron, widow, lessee of rectory of Croydon).

86. Robert Shaw, Edward Morlay, and John Bush (alias Colyns), all of London, raised the issue of enforcement squarely in 1542. In addition to the normal assertions of jurisdictional control of the common law, they went further, citing additional official acts. A statute of 1534 had enacted that no canons, institutes, ordinances, or uses contrary to the king's prerogatives, the common law, and the statutes of the realm should be put into execution. Statute 25 Henry VIII, c. 14. The implications of that statute for the common law courts would have been both welcome and obvious. On 25 February 1534 the chancellor and the king's counselors had arbitrated between the London inhabitants and the London curates concerning tithes: the customary rate of tithing in London would remain the same for the poorest ranks of inhabitants, but for everyone else the rate was reduced by more than 20 percent. The rate cited for those who received rents was 2s9d/£1 and proportionally for each £0.50. KB27/1124, m. 102. The former rate was 3s5d/£1. Brigden, *London and the Reformation*, 49–50. There are a series of dates for the council decision. This case lists the decision as occurring on 25 February. Brigden dates the proclamation on 30 March and confirmation by letters patent on 2 April. Brigden, "Tithe Controversy," 298. This rate was later confirmed by statute in 1536. Furthermore, it had been decreed that the mayor should enforce tithing, by committing to jail anyone who refused to pay until agreement was reached with the curate. Finally, they cited a general injunction of the king's council of 12 July 1540 prohibiting ecclesiastical courts from vexing any London inhabitant for tithes. Apparently this injunction has not been otherwise recorded. Brigden, in her thorough recounting of the London tithe controversy, thus attributed the absence of London tithe litigation in consistory court in the 1540s to Londoners' preference for secular courts. Such an injunction, however, makes sense not only of the church court records but also of the London clergy's worry about premunire. Brigden, "Tithe Controversy," 298–300. Nevertheless, the vicar of St. Dunstan in the West, London, in his controversy with his own rector concerning tithes, had sued them in the court of Arches, not only claiming the tithes from rent of houses, but also claiming from Robert Shaw a customary tithe for the brewing of beer. That customary tithe, they alleged, had begun by a papal bull obtained without royal license and thus against the custom of the realm. The judge of the court of Arches, despite their arguments, had proceeded to judgment and excommunication, exercising ecclesiastical coercion in the matter of tithes despite the statute of 1540. King's

one or two prohibitions appeared each term: the volume of litigation certainly did not overwhelm the court. Each prohibition granted, however, staked out the court's territory, and a couple cases each term was the same as the frequency of the premunire suits that had originally diminished the jurisdiction of the church courts around 1500.

---

bench granted the petition for a prohibition against both the vicar and the official of the court, but in this instance did not require any mainprise from the plaintiff: the matter must have seemed to them a priority. The rate cited for those who received rents was 2s9d/£1 and proportionally for each £0.50. KB27/1124, m. 102. For earlier tithing problems in London, see Thomson, "Tithe Disputes," 1–17. London was particularly sensitive about tithes, but the solution arrived at was secular control. For a case concerning tithes in Oxford, see KB27/1135, m. 122 (1545) (Thomas Maleson v. William Whyte master of Balliol College; the master had sued for tithes of a rented tenement). For part of the background to the problems, see Pontsbury v. Foxford, a suit by a cleric against the chancellor of the bishop of London for delaying judgment in a church court case to enforce tithing obligations in London, the delay allegedly because such cases were difficult to bring to a successful conclusion (*sciens huiusmodi causarum sectas absque magnis laboribus et expensis ad bonum effectum minime perveniri sive produci posse*). CP40/1076, m. 450.

87. KB27/1132, m. 68d (1544) (John Wyntle and William Hyett v. Richard Sheryff, vicar of Westbury, Gloucestershire, where the parishioners had a custom to pay 3d for each line; the vicar sued for particular tithes of the fish caught for five years).

88. KB27/1128, m. 38. (1543) (Thomas Fox and William Cole v. vicar of Buckfastleigh, Devon: vicar alleged a custom exercised for the preceding sixty years and before time of memory dictating payment of a gallon of ale or equivalent money for every brewing of tavern ale). Shortly thereafter John Hynde of Stokenham, Devon, complained that his vicar was claiming that traditionally (also alleging sixty years usage and time out of mind) each tavern brewing would yield to the vicar or his lessee a gallon of beer or at least 1 ½d by judgment of the vicar at Easter each year. KB27/1129, m. 33.

89. KB27/1122, m. 112. Elizabeth Tunkyns had sued Thomas Habrehale and Margery, his wife, before the commissary general in spiritualities of Canterbury, alleging that they had wrongfully and without authority administered the goods of John Tayler, sr. They promptly sought a writ of prohibition, explaining their version of events. Margery had been married to John Tayler, jr. John Tayler sr. had apparently retired, handing over his goods, including a malt quern, tables, a couple vessels of fat, and other named goods, to John Tayler, jr. and Margery in 1521 under an agreement that they would provide him with sufficient food and clothing for the remainder of his life: this was thus not a will, but an agreement for care. John Tayler, jr. did make out a will, constituting Margery his executrix, and died before John Tayler, sr. Both before and after her husband's death, Margery had provided for the food and clothing for her father-in-law. Thus, after John Tayler, sr. died, Elizabeth Tunkyns's claim, based on the allegation of a will of John Taylor, sr., was completely unfounded. Margery and her husband thus received a writ of prohibition in 1542. KB27/1133, m. 136 (1544) (Edward Sandes v. Elizabeth wife of Thomas Wawton and late wife of John Sandes; Elizabeth had sued Sandes in court Christian for expending goods of the estate instead of suing the taking of goods and chattels at common law); KB27/1136, m. 170 (1545)

The court itself was interested in these cases. Richard Heywood was usually the petitioner's attorney.[93] Heywood, as it happened, was no ordinary attorney. He was a filazer in king's bench and in 1548 joined William Rooper as chief clerk of king's bench in 1548: he was thus part of the Rooper dynasty in king's bench that apparently assisted in the revitalization (if revitalization was necessary) of

---

(William Wellys v. Henry Alen, who had alleged fraudulent cancellation of obligatory bonds by the Wellys acting as successor executor of Thomas Orwell).

90. KB27/1122, m. 115 (1542) (John Bosynger, a Cambridgeshire yeoman, received king's bench help in the form of a prohibition in 1542. He complained of a matter involving a use. The feoffees, both yeomen, had held a messuage and an annual rent of £0.25 for the use of William Ayleff, Katherine his wife, and the heirs of William. In 1526 William had granted the reversion of the lands [that is, the heritable interest that would remain after both William and Katherine died] to John Bosynger, the petitioner in this case. William then died, and Katherine made out her will instructing her feoffees to use the rent to celebrate an obit for her soul. The interest in that rent after her death, however, had already been granted to John so that at law the feoffees would have had to take John's interest to fulfil Katherine's will: that would have been improper, because Katherine had tried, perhaps in ignorance, to use something that would no longer be hers after her death. Nonetheless, William Brauncewell and Thomas Hawes, the church wardens of Gamlingay, sued John before the official of the bishop of Ely to compel him to use the rent to perform Katherine's will. Since this litigation came after the statute of uses, the feoffees were probably now inactive: John was the right person to sue, but as a matter of property law the church wardens had no right to insist that he use his property to perform the terms of a will that specified the use for property no longer belonging to the testator. The king's bench granted John's petition for a prohibition directed to the bishop's official).

91. KB27/1138, m. 102 (1546) (Richard Sterkey and Elizabeth his wife v. Elizabeth Daye, wife of Richard Daye; allegation of suit before the official of Canterbury for defamatory words ["Hyes wyffe (innuendo, said Elizabeth Daye) is a harlett and a pocky harlett, for both she and her husband (innuendo, said Richard Daye) hath the poxes"]); KB27/1139, m. 125 (1546) (John Percy rector of St. Edmund the King and Martyr in London v. Agnes Grave, who sued the rector before the archdeacon of Surrey for saying, "She [innuendo the said Agnes] ys an arrant hore and she [innuendo the same Agnes] had a chyld by a doctour yt was a prysts byrde," whereas she should have sued under a statute of 1540 concerning sexual misconduct of ecclesiastical men and women).

92. KB27/1122, m. 103; KB27/1125, m. 109 (1542) (suit against the executor of the late rector of Pilton, Somerset, claiming £80 in repairs; the justices issued the writ of prohibition on the executor's assertion that all the buildings were customary tenures or leaseholds); KB27/1125, m. 155 (1542) (Elizabeth was the wife of Humphrey Aunsley, but had been before that Elizabeth Lynde and before that Elizabeth Hewster, wife of John Hewster. John Hewster had been, allegedly, the executor of Matthew David, late rector of Cound, Shropshire. When the new rector sued Elizabeth in court Christian as the executor of Hewster in his capacity as executor of Matthew David for an £8 debt, £8 adjudged as costs, and £10 owed for necessary repairs to the chancel and various buildings of the Cound rectory, she presented two defenses. On the one

king's bench.[94] With him as their attorney, petitioners had foreknowledge of the viability of their petition and thus of the court's likely stand in the matter. It seems that the court did not enroll denied prohibitions: those that made it to enrollment had already been vetted. To the extent that a court could, king's bench took a proactive role in the redefinition of the jurisdictional boundaries between the common law courts and the now-royal church courts.

Conclusion

The dissolution of the religious houses carried a strong financial incentive for the crown, but the intent, execution, and effect of the dissolution were far more than just financial events. Dissolving the religious houses eliminated about 3,300 absentee clerical rectors (many of them, of course, not different people) that canon law had allowed to be absent. The lay impropriators who replaced them were often likewise absentee, but they were not clerics and were expected to be more commercial. The dissolution, moreover, occasioned a reorganization of governance that largely abolished the franchises that the religious houses had held: governance was the prerogative of the king. The dissolution also added religious reform incentives to the crown's desire to protect its feudal incidents and thus shaped the statute of uses, a statute that still seems a critical watershed in Anglo-American property law. The major statutory initiatives of the 1530s were an interwoven complex, not neatly insulated into the categories either of public and private law or of governance and religion.

The content of religious culture certainly includes personal piety and dogma, but it also includes popular perceptions about the appropriate role of church people and church institutions in social life and governance. With the monasteries dissolved the religious culture could not remain the same. About 837

---

hand, she produced a document acquitting her late husband of all liability from his executorship. On the other hand, she denied having received any goods belonging to Matthew David from which she could pay his debts. The clerical judge refused to recognize such defenses and tried to compel her to pay. She and her new husband had to find mainprise worth £10 to get a prohibition against the clerical judge and three other people. The record did not expressly note that the prohibition had been granted).

93. KB27/1121, m. 121; KB27/1121, m. 125; KB27/1122, m. 115; KB27/1124, m. 102; KB27/1128, m. 38; KB27/1128, m. 116; KB27/1129, m. 33; KB27/1131, m. 23d; KB27/1132, m. 68; KB27/1122, m. 112; KB27/1132, m. 68d; KB27/1133, m. 136d; KB27/1135, m. 122; KB27/1136, mm. 40, 170; KB27/1138, m. 69; KB27/1139, mm. 125, 126; KB27/1140, m. 157; KB27/1143, m. 94.

94. Baker, Introduction to *Spelman*, 2:55–56.

religious houses had populated a relatively small country. They were visible assertions that the perfect life was not the married life, that celibacy, prayer, and some kind of separation from the world—even though some of the religious houses did not live up to their ideals—were the highest aspirations of the religious person. Monasteries also were a physical embodiment, visible and tangible in nearly every locality, of the separate order espoused by the church. Augustinians, Benedictines, Franciscans, and Dominicans stood for different emphases of Catholic culture, but they all represented in the local communities a physical and influential pronouncement about what religion was. They were also physical representations of a church that was wealthy and exercised governmental rights and prerogatives over both ecclesiastical and secular matters. When they were swept away in a brief five years, secular priests were left as the sole representatives of the clerical order. That order could never be as strong or the Catholic message as powerful as it had been with the religious houses. Although personal piety did not change until later in the century, local religious culture changed immediately: the job of the clergy was now a spiritual life in service to the aristocracy, the parish, and scholarship, not involvement in the governmental or commercial sphere and not simply the search for personal salvation in a clerical society.

Conceiving the Reformation

The English Reformation was a composite of central governmental reform, a reformation of piety, and a reformation of parish life. That part of the Reformation involving the parish began in 1529: it struck rapidly and with continuing and lasting effect, and not only altered who was in the parish but also empowered the laity. The statutes of 1529 transformed the exercise of power in the parish; clerics could not exercise the same authority or independence, once it was clear that their parishioners regulated them. The succeeding portions of that parish reformation derived from the dissolution of the religious houses and the reassessment of tithe obligations in the king's court. The parish reformation altered the local religion in ways so mundane and comprehensive as to be truly revolutionary; that reformation changed the context but not the mechanism for handling a major part of the agrarian surplus of the parish, reallocated vital positions of local patronage, abolished the religious houses and thus eliminated primary symbols of Christian ideals, and reshaped forms of local influence.

The Commercial Parish

The late medieval parish that this Reformation reformed was a commercial entity. Rectors and perpetual vicars had gone far beyond leasing out tithes. They leased out parishes, both the economic and spiritual aspects, as complete economic enterprises. The ecclesiastical arrangements concerning the parish became a facade after the Black Death, while leasehold law and lease provisions governed parish life in fact. Parishes constituted the bulk of upper-end lease-holds, and thus occupied a central position in agrarian, legal, and church affairs. The lessees received the whole parish, in both its material and spiritual elements, with all its perquisites and responsibilities for taxes and building maintenance. Whether the parishioners thereafter actually tithed properly, the rector got his rent. The lessees, often themselves not clerics, determined the clerical curate who actually provided the religious services. Parish leasing impeded effective episcopal regulation of the parish.

Parish leases made tithing more a mere financial exaction than parishioner support of local spiritual services. Parishioners in that commercial society were not ignorant about economic relations and would have realized that scrupulous payment of tithes only contributed to the lay lessee's profit margin. Sophisticated parishioners might have realized that present full tithe payments supported the ability of the rector to get full value in his next leasehold negotiation. For most parishioners, however, tithing lost the aspect of a direct contributory participation in the provision of their own church services and retained only the questionable edification of having paid a tax ordered by the church. The lessees ran the parish: they were responsible for hiring a priest to say religious services, for maintaining the chancel and church buildings, and for paying both ecclesiastical and royal taxes.

The English parish from the Black Death in the mid-fourteenth century to 1529 was thus completely commercialized. Payment of religious dues was not particularly connected to the provision of religious services. Bishops' control over parish life was difficult to maintain. Lay people were often in de facto control of the parish, although the lay people involved were more precisely investors, not parishioners. The proliferation of church wardens from the fourteenth century was seemingly one reaction to this situation, a rational response to provide stability to counter absentee rectors, short-term lessees, and chaplains of parishes hired for even shorter terms. Pluralities in this social context were likewise simply not as objectionable: how much difference did pluralism make in a system in which physical residence was only the normative ideal and not the actual norm?

The commercial revolution of the Middle Ages[1] was thus a comprehensive cultural phenomenon transforming the church as much as the merchants. In England at least the parish was an essential part of the economic structure. The agricultural surplus was not completely dispersed in the hands of innumerable free and villein tenants, but already accumulated in the hands of manorial lords and parish rectors, ready for the provisioning of the towns or for shipment abroad. The parish thus was a node for automatic resource accumulation and integral to the efficiency of the economic structure of England. The common law not surprisingly thus became involved in its management; and English common law, of course, was the archetypical "local custom" to which the canon

---

1. Lopez, *Commercial Revolution of the Middle Ages*.

CONCLUSION   [249]

law often deferred. Working through performance bonds and ordinary informal leasehold agreements, the common law had enabled rectors to disassociate
themselves from the parish. Rectors became landlords to parishes managed
wholly by lessees who were predominately lay and interested primarily, from all
we can tell, in the parish as an economic enterprise—a commercial revolution
indeed. The local churches of late medieval England were, quite simply, up for
sale for terms of years.

The Spiritual Parish

By statutory action, the commercialized parish changed in 1529, or, perhaps
better, in 1530. The statutes of 1529 in fact reformed the parish. Legislative
fiat accomplishes little, of course, but legislation sufficiently cunning to meld
strong economic self-interest with traditional religious ideals accomplished
much more than could any administrative bureaucracy that sixteenth-century
England could have afforded or tolerated. The direction of the change was away
from the commercialized parish to a parish focused on spirituality: priests were
cast out of the commercial life of the country. The individual parishioner and
priest may or may not have actually been more spiritual after 1530, but the rector
was certainly more strictly limited to spiritual matters than had previously been
the case.

The statutes of 1529 related to prominent practices of the late medieval
church and propounded consistently a spiritual instead of a commercial vision
for the parish and its clergy. The relevant provisions compelled rectors to reside
in the parish, at university, or with aristocrats as personal chaplains, prohibited
spiritual persons from being lessees, limited pluralism, and prohibited clerics
from running commercial operations. Nothing prohibited parishes from being
leased to lay people; that practice continued and received even further statutory
protections. The frequency of leased parishes nevertheless declined. As the
great pluralists died, the number of parishes actually served by a rector in
residence increased. The dissolution of the religious houses further reduced the
number of lawfully absent clerical rectors. Although lay rectors were at least as
likely to be absentee as their clerical predecessors, the specifically clerical abuse
received a remedy. Clerical rectors and vicars were now almost prisoners on the
parish unless they were in service to the magnates or were involved in education.

The statutes would have meant nothing without enforcement, and it was the
method of enforcement that changed parish politics by empowering the laity.

The new role for the laity was neither a doctrinal concern nor even the intent, but only the means chosen to implement a governmental mandate of clerical reform. Regardless of intent, however, the effect was indeed a reallocation of power within the parish, a result pregnant for English religion. Enforcement came through *qui tam* procedures: anyone could sue and would receive half the judgment penalty. Parishioners thus drew on royal power to enforce traditional ideals about the clergy: residency and dedication to spiritual, rather than commercial, endeavors. Personal advantage reinforced the initiative: parishioners could measure the time of infraction and the accumulating penalty and would realize that the first to sue would reap the profit. The lessor or anyone observing a harvest going unexpectedly to the rectory could sue; country people do have a reputation for being observant. The result was a vicious set of statutes that enlisted the aid of common people. Litigation to enforce traditional values about the clergy led parishioners to buy into a different vision of both church and state, of a church subject to a king who regulated it by recruiting the laity to sue the clergy.

The response from the countryside was impressive. Local people flocked to enforce these statutes. The enforcement cases are astounding from two different perspectives. The first is that the statutes were designed to maximize voluntary compliance. The effective date for most of the prohibitions was from six months to a year after passage. Priests thus had sufficient time to consult, realize the dynamics and the danger, assess the determination of the government, liquidate their leaseholds, and move back onto their parishes in sufficient time to avoid the forfeitures. Two pardons provided further opportunities to comply without loss. The defendants in the cases thus represent not a realistic cross-section of the beneficed clergy, but the obstinate, the naive, the desperate, or, indeed, the innocent poor clergy harassed for attempting to use the exceptions allowed by the statutes.

The dynamics of *qui tam* litigation made enforcement particularly effective. Plaintiffs had little incentive to push the litigation to verdict and judgment, nor did the priest defendant who was guilty. All kinds of *qui tam* cases were abandoned without royal inquiry about the expected forfeiture due the king, thus encouraging plaintiffs and defendants to compromise to mutual advantage. At this point the king was not interested in generating revenue, but in securing compliance. The cumulative nature of the penalties placed an increasing temptation before potential plaintiffs. The traditional nature of the statutory prohibitions meant that plaintiffs would feel more comfortable with their self-interest: they were, after all, only enforcing what the church had always believed should be ecclesiastical practice. The prosecutions in the exchequer facilitated prosecution of the innocent taking appropriate advantage of the statutory exceptions; harassing the innocent was necessary to instill such caution that even the legitimate exceptions would only be used sparingly.

Enforcement accomplished extraordinarily diverse results. The litigation almost certainly transferred, covertly by compromise and overtly by reallocation of commercial opportunities, significant wealth from the parish clergy to the laity. At the same time, to the extent that the regulation reduced the leasing of parishes and pluralism, the reform reconnected religious dues with the provision of local religious services. Sending the rectors back to the parishes gave the parishes access to some of the more educated and wealthy clergy, possibly laying the foundation for the teaching and preaching that would finally result in the reformation of personal piety later in the century. At the same time, the process of regulation itself empowered the laity. A laity that regulated the clergy had been a part of the agenda of the Lollard movement and would be an element of radical Protestantism in England. The statutes of 1529 did not derive directly from Lollardy. They did not draw more hostility on this issue, in part because the statutes did not explicitly state a new lay role, in part because such a role for the laity was already a current in English culture. The lay experience in enforcing the statutes also laid the practical foundation for later Protestants who would further diminish the role of the clergy and exalt the regulatory role of the laity. In 1529, however, the empowerment of the laity was only a pragmatic strategy that recruited reformers and allowed the government to enforce very traditional elements of clerical conduct without an elaborate administrative bureaucracy.

The statutes reconnected parish revenue to the provision of religious services, but two concerns limited that attempt to bring the payment of tithes into accord with the theoretical justification for tithing. The parish reformation was very careful not to prejudice lay interests, even if that preservation of lay interest violated the traditional ideas that the statutes otherwise enforced. Lay persons continued to lease parishes as complete economic units from lawfully absent rectors, such as personal chaplains and scholars. Moreover, the dissolution of the religious houses eliminated many absentee clerical rectors, but did not reconnect those rectors' tithe income to the parish. The old appropriated parishes had been leased out at long terms; by 1536 the lessees would have been lay. Parliament protected those leaseholds specifically, so that *clerical* absenteeism was reduced, even though that protection overtly disconnected the tithes from underwriting the provision of the spiritual needs of the parish. The other concern that continued a separation of the resources of some rectors from the provision of religious services in the parish was the emphasis on service to the aristocracy. King and Parliament were content to allow both pluralism and absenteeism to continue if they provided personal chaplains for the powerful and positions for aristocratic sons and brothers. Mere aristocratic economic motives might have justified the provision of positions for their relatives. A more aristocratic clergy, however, would have seemed to be a more learned and loyal clergy; priests familiar with aristocratic expectations and habits would have also been prime candidates to serve as personal chaplains. Many more parishes now had their tithes command the rector's services in fact; for many others, the parish resources now supported not a separate clerical order but a clergy that served the upper lay orders and education. The parish reformation incorporated a perspective on the clergy that assumed that its proper role was service to the laity, and particularly to the aristocracy. The continuation of parish leasing was also pragmatic: such leases accumulated the agrarian surplus. Restructuring the economic patterns of the countryside that were central to the supply of food would have been dangerous; it might also have seemed beyond the practical capacity of Parliament, particularly when it was already reforming the parish and clergy, the institutions of religion and of local governance, and property law.

The participation of the clergy in the commercial sector declined substantially in fact. The enforcement litigation leads to such a deduction. Clerical participation in litigation generally reinforces that deduction. Admittedly, over long periods of time such analysis is difficult. Litigation in 1386, for instance, might be taken to indicate much higher clerical commercial activity then than around 1500,[2] but the comparison may be completely flawed: litigation was spread among many different courts by 1500 and there had been important changes in both substantive and procedural law as well as an apparent decline in the ease with which people resorted to litigation. Comparison of litigation frequencies confined to the reigns of Henry VII and Henry VIII, however, yields more reliable conclusions. An initial foray in this direction might indicate a decline of clerical commercial activity by half, if litigation frequency can be related to commercial activity. In three Trinity terms before 1529, an average of 173 different clerical plaintiffs who were not heads of religious corporations were involved as plaintiffs in the court of common pleas. After 1529, the average number of different clerics, likewise in Trinity terms, was 121 (70 percent of the

2. See above, Chapter 3.

FIGURE 9. Clerical (Noninstitutional) Plaintiffs in Common Pleas

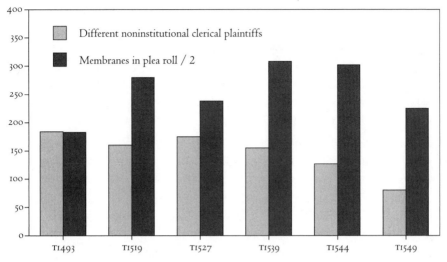

Sources: CP40/925 (1493); CP40/1025 (1519); CP40/1055 (1527); CP40/1102 (1539); CP 40/1122 (1544); CP40/1141 (1549).

pre-1529 average), but the number declined finally to only 80 (46 percent of the pre-1529 average) in 1549. The size of the plea rolls actually increased after 1529 so that a decreasing absolute number of clerical litigants represented a seriously smaller percentage of all plaintiffs in the court of common pleas.[3] Clerical litigation would never disappear, because the clergy retained the tithes and glebe lands and legally sold that produce, as long as they simply sold and did not buy produce for resale. In the 1540s, however, clerics less frequently participated in those activities that would lead them to bring cases of debt or to protect property interests with actions of trespass. As older pluralists with more than two benefices died, fewer clerics found it necessary to litigate at common law. Ambitious clerics still struggled mightily to maximize their income and position, but the new order dictated different avenues for advancement.

In the reformation of the English parish, the local and the national were inextricably related. More than four hundred different parishioners the length and breadth of England invoked the royal powers available under the statutes of 1529 even in the first few years. They were direct participants in the local reformation. The parishioner's perception of the parish changed. The statutory enforcement cases were not private events that were concealed from the public

3. Figure 9.

view, but prolonged public confrontations that educated whole localities into the new order. The dissolution of the religious houses was, in a similar way, 837 local events, most of which carried immense implications for local parish life. Each dissolution was an assertion of royal power over religion, a change in the parishioner's possibilities for spiritual expression, a change in local power and sources of alms, and a dramatic change of life for about nine thousand people who had relatives and friends in the parishes: a broad reformation in the locality that touched and changed individuals. When a parishioner observed the problems of Catharine of Aragon, Anne Boleyn, and, in general, Henry VIII's marital affairs and the great affairs of the realm, he or she would have had difficulty putting those events in any other context than the reformation through which he or she was living in the practical world of the parish.

Despite the fundamental local changes occurring in the 1530s, the parish church was still occasionally up for sale. The dissolution left long-term lessees securely in possession of their leases of parish churches. Exempted pluralists continued to let out their parishes. Statute even fortified the position of lay lessees against rector landlords. Still, the parish in 1540 was a more spiritual parish than the parish of 1528. The new regime had established new expectations for clerical conduct in fact: they were supposed to reside on their parish and to refrain from commercial activity. Commercial activity was now necessarily nonclerical. Religious dues in many parishes had become more related to the provision of local religious services. Radical statutory action had reduced clerical wealth and circumscribed clerical avenues for enrichment. The dissolution of the religious houses dramatically diminished the involvement of the clergy even as lessors of land and constructed a society in which economic resources were much more decisively controlled by the laity. The actual late medieval parish, of course, had not been abandoned completely. Henry VIII's local reforms, nevertheless, had implemented to a surprising extent the ideals of the late medieval church for the clergy. The king had erected a separate priestly order by isolating the clergy from commerce. This reformation broke with late medieval practice and directed the clergy away from seeking their own economic interests or their own personal salvation in a clerical society and instead to service of the spiritual needs of the aristocracy and the parish.

Bailiff Style of Parish Management

Parsons in Account Cases, Michaelmas 1338 (CP40/316)

The common pleas plea rolls contain many account cases, most of which disappear before pleading. The following table provides the information in this plea roll that covers a quarter of the year 1338 for those account cases brought by a parson against his bailiff. The record only describes the plaintiff as a parson except in those instances below in which the entry describes the plaintiff as a vicar. The instances important for this study are those in which the parson's parish and the bailiff's bailiwick are the same: those are instances in which the parson mostly likely was using a bailiff approach to managing the parish. Where the parish and the bailiwick are different, one suspects only that the priest had acquired or inherited wealth that gave him a different estate requiring management.

PARSON	PARISH	BAILIFF	BAILIFF'S BAILIWICK
Thomas de Radclyve	Olney, Bucks	John son of William le Colier of "Thurstyngton," cleric	Olney
Ralph de Brok	"Gosberkyrk"	Philip atte Sloo of Chesham	Chesham, Bucks
John de Croudecote	Lamorran, Corn	John de Trebelek	Lamorran
Simon Stiria, vicar	Brixham, Devon	Thomas atte Barre	West Leigh and Brixham
John de Briggewater	Chapel of Clifton, Dors	Ralph son of Ralph de Seghull	Clifton and Beer Hacket
John son of Robert de Lokeswell	Chadwell, Essex	John Cut, cleric	Chadwell
Robert	Layer Marney, Essex	Thomas Hockele of Layer Breton	Layer Marney

PARSON	PARISH	BAILIFF	BAILIFF'S BAILIWICK
Richard de Ragenhull	Burghclere, Hants	Roger Cloppe of Ragnall	Ragnall and "Bernelby"
Geoffrey de Clare	Kimbolton, Hunts	William son of Humfrey de Clare	Kimbolton
William de Baumburgh	Little Gidding, Hunts	Ranulf le Persoun-serjaunt of Little Gidding	Little Gidding
William Giffard	Half of Hallaton, Leics	Walter le Chaumberleyn of "Glaptorp"	Hallaton
Richard	Boothby, Lincs	William Hocy of Corby	Boothby
Richard de Amcotes	Scawby, Lincs	Walter Carter of Luddington	Waddingham, Lincs
Roger	Stamford St. Peter, Lincs	William de Durem of Selby	Stamford
Henry de Ingelby	Brumstead, Norf	John de Sleford	Brumstead
Ralph de Toftes[1]	Hackford, Norf	Thomas Chauntecler	Hackford
Edward de Stowe	Roughton, Norf	Adam de Thorplond	Roughton
William	Sloley, Norf	Roger son of John de Bouk	Sloley
William de Undele	Upwell, Norf	Robert de Botulnesdale	Upwell
John le Warde	Woodton, Norf	William son of John the Bailiff of Framlingham	Hoo
John le Warde	Woodton, Norf	Geoffrey le Sormour	Woodton
John de Bassingburn	Benefield, Northants	Reginald Rote of Huntingdon	Benefield
John de Macclesfeld	Litchborough, Northants	John Smart of Wick	Litchborough

1. Toftes alleged that Chauntecler was bailiff of a messuage and twenty-four acres in 1337 with care of all matters and goods (oxen, cows, wheat, barley, oats, beans, peas, and hay worth in all £60, and as receiver of money took £20 delivered by Robert Gylot of Thornham). Chauntecler produced a quitclaim of actions, on which they went to issue. CP40/316, m. 59d. The twenty-four acres here could have been the glebe.

PARSON	PARISH	BAILIFF	BAILIFF'S BAILIWICK
Henry, vicar	Nassington, Northants	John le Warenner, John Gernoun	Warenner in Nassington; Gernoun in Newton
Thomas de Vaux	Attenborough, Notts	John Torel	Attenborough
Thomas de Somerton	Steeple Aston, Oxon	Richard Noreys	Steeple Aston and Somerton
Steven de Shrewsbury	Oldbury, Salop	Richard le Shepeherdesone of Abbots Eyton	Oldbury
John de Eysy	Cadbury, Som	Richard Dygoun	Cadbury
John de Pykeslegh	Marksbury, Som	Hamond de Marksbury	Marksbury
John Ryvers	Hanbury, Staffs	Henry de Hertham	Hanbury
John de Malton	Cockfield, Suff	Robert de Boxford	Cockfield
William de Reppes	Dennington, Suff	Geoffrey Trympe	Dennington
Richard de Barton	Sutton, Surrey	Adam Gad of Sutton, John de BernardCastel of Scarborough	Sutton
Hamo de Ceszay	Blatchington, Sussex	William Bruneby of Ford	Blatchington
Master Robert de Worth	Bradford, Wilts	Thomas Hamond of "Farendone"	Bradford, Melksham, Winterbourne, Dauntsey
Roger de Chipham	Heddington, Wilts	John Poyntz of Farley	"Haghe"
Master Robert de Warenna	Steeple Langford, Wilts	William Pyke of Marden	Steeple Langford
William de Swyndon	Trowbridge, Wilts	Robert le Foundeur	Trowbridge
Hugh	Ombersley, Worcs	John Sampson of Eastham	Ombersley

PARSON	PARISH	BAILIFF	BAILIFF'S BAILIWICK
John de Percy	Quadring, Yorks	Richard Bailiff	Lambton, Pelton, and Chester (Durham)
William de Hillum	Thorner, Yorks	John son of Roger le Clerk of Barnby	Thorner

Parsons in Account Cases, Michaelmas 1390 (CP40/519)

PARSON	PARISH	BAILIFF	BAILIFF'S BAILIWICK
John Benet	Hydon, Devon	Thomas Torre; Robert Torre	Hydon
William Dere	Croft, Lincs	William Skipse of Bradley	Somercotes
Nicholas	Firsby, Lincs	John North of Firsby	Firsby
Roger Stoke, vicar	Shirburn, Oxon	John Sclatter of Shirburn	Shirburn
Nicholas Slake	Yeovil, Som	Henry Whyte	Yeovil
John James	Glemsford, Suff	Robert Moyse, jr.	Coddenham
William Saxy	Mancetter, Warw	Richard Campeden, chaplain; Thomas Warde, chaplain	Mancetter
Ralph de Yedynham	Brigham, Yorks	John de Synderby, chaplain	Middleham

Incidence of Nonparish Leaseholds in Common Pleas

Appendix 2a.
Nonparish Leaseholds in Common Pleas, Easter 1397–Hilary 1398

LEASEHOLD PROPERTY	TERM	ANNUAL RENT	REFERENCE
Fordingbridge manor, Hants	20 yrs.	£39.67	CP40/545, m. 184
Letton manor, Heref.	6 yrs.	£18.67	CP40/548, m. 84
Lands and tenements in Essex and Middlesex	10 yrs.	£22	CP40/547, m. 413
Denver manor in Norfolk	2 yrs.	£19.5	CP40/547, mm. 430, 640, 657
"Sentlyng" manor in St. Mary Cray, Kent	5 yrs.	£16.67	CP40/546, m. 105d
Toft manor in Cambs.	4 yrs.		CP40/546, m. 111d
Dower lands, Nottinghamshire	20 yrs.	£10.67	CP40/547, m. 439
Croxton manor, Norfolk	4 yrs.		CP40/547, m. 241
One-third manor of Fetcham, Surrey	10 yrs.		CP40/546, m. 326
Guthlaxton hundred, Leics	1 yr.	£8	CP40/545, m. 50
120 acres of land in Hockley, Essex	1 yr.	£5.35	CP40/546, m. 108d
Buckland manor, Kent	8 yrs.	£4.33	CP40/548, m. 231
1 messuage, Norwich	1 yr.	£2.33	CP40/545, m. 238d
1 messuage in London	1 yr.	£2.33	CP40/547, m. 332
Water mill and wind mill in Wingham, Kent	1 yr.	£3.33 for water mill; 9 quarters of barley for wind mill	CP40/548, m. 399d
1 messuage, one acre of land in New Borough, Crediton, Devon	20 yrs.		CP 40/545, m. 422d

Appendix 2a. *continued*

LEASEHOLD PROPERTY	TERM	ANNUAL RENT	REFERENCE
Messuage in Wilberfoss, Yorks.	100 yrs.		CP40/546, m. 280
1 messuage and 40 acres in Latham, Yorkshire	20 yrs.	£0.5	CP40/547, m. 520
1 messuage, 200 acres in Great Greenford, Middlesex	12 yrs.		CP40/545, m. 111
40 acres in yorkshire	30 yrs.		CP40/547, m. 507d
1 messuage with croft, 24½ acres of land, 3 rods of meadow in Biddenham, Beds.	12 yrs.	£1.33	CP40/547, m. 658
31 acres in Swalecliffe, Kent	4 yrs.	£1	CP40/547, m. 620
2 gardens in Myllysworth, Surrey	10 yrs.		CP40/546, m. 421d
4 acres of land in Beckering, Lincs.	½ yr.	£0.18	CP40/548, m. 305d
20 acres of marsh in Latchingdon, Essex	3 yrs.		CP40/545, mm. 118, 228

Appendix 2b. Nonparish Leaseholds in Common Pleas, Trinity 1513–Easter 1514

LEASEHOLD PROPERTY	TERM	ANNUAL RENT	REFERENCE
Amys manor with all rents and services, Kent	7 yrs.	£14.67	CP40/1004, m. 534
Somerton manor, Suff	1 yr.*[1]	£13.33	CP40/1004, m. 503d
3 messuages, 52 acres of land, 20 acres of meadow, 8 acres of pasture in Hackney, Midd	1 yr.*	£10	CP40/1004, m. 435d
1 messuage, a sheepcote, 49 acres of land, 100 acres of salt marsh in Bobbing and Iwade, Kent	1 yr.*	£6.83	CP40/1006, m. 552
Willoughby's Farm, Wardington, Oxon: a messuage and 100 acres of land	20 yrs.	£6.67	CP40/1004, m. 192

1. Asterisks indicate a periodic tenancy.

Appendix 2b. *continued*

LEASEHOLD PROPERTY	TERM	ANNUAL RENT	REFERENCE
1 messuage, an apple orchard, and 1 acre of woods in Langford, Notts	12 yrs.	£6.33	CP40/1005b, m. 330d
A field or pasture containing 100 acres of land and meadow in "Stretton by the Strete," Warw	1 yr.*	£5	CP40/1004, m. 538d
1 messuage, 100 acres of land in Alderton, Suff	1 yr.*	£4.33	CP40/1007, m. 203d
1 messuage called "le brewhous within le blakhert" in parish of Mary Magdalene	7 yrs.	£4	CP40/1006, m. 533d
3 tenements lying together in the parish of St. Augustine, London	5 yrs.*	£3.60	CP40/1005a, m. 120d
1 messuage, 80 acres of land in Berking, Essex	1 yr.*	£3.50	CP40/1007, m. 566d
1 messuage and 7 bovates of land in Middleton on the Wolds, Yorks	1 yr.*	£3.17	CP40/1004, m. 507d
100 acres of land, 40 acres of pasture in Holbeach, Lincs	1 yr.*	£3	CP40/1004, m. 370d
A fulling mill in Belstead, Suff	10 yrs.	£3	CP40/1004, m. 167d
24 acres in Bonnington, Kent	2 yrs.	£2.40	CP40/1006, m. 415
2 messuages, 2 virgates of land, a croft with 24 acres of land, 8 acres of meadow, and common of pasture for 200 sheep in Dodington, Gloc	1 yr.*	£2	CP40/1004, m. 418d
40 acres of land in Great Plumstead, Norf	3 yrs.	£2	CP40/1007, m. 179d
1 messuage, 1 garden, 15 acres in Chalk, Kent	7 yrs.*	£1.67	CP40/1007, m. 531
1 marsh in Southtown, Suff	5 yrs.	£1.53	CP40/1007, m. 171
1 messuage, 4 acres called Halstroppys in Worstead, Norf	3 yrs.	£1.12	CP40/1006, m. 401d
1 messuage, 20 acres of land in Tadcaster, Yorks	1 yr.*	£1	CP40/1006, m. 21d

Appendix 2b. *continued*

LEASEHOLD PROPERTY	TERM	ANNUAL RENT	REFERENCE
1 messuage, 40 acres in Thormanby, Yorks	1 yr.*	£1	CP40/1006, m. 105d
All of "Cowtotemershe" with courts and letes	30 yrs.	£1	CP40/1006, m. 513d
7 acres in Algarkirk, Lincs	5 yrs.	£1	CP40/1005a, m. 45
1 messuage, 1 garden in Milton by Sittingbourne, Kent	1 yr.*	£1	CP40/1006, m. 415
1 messuage in Norwich	1 yr.	£1	CP40/1006, m. 519
1 croft, 10 acres of land in Tring, Herts	4 yrs.	£0.67	CP40/1005b, m. 449
1 messuage, 1 virgate in Finstock, Oxon	1 yr.*	£0.60	CP40/1005b, m. 521
1 messuage, 2 acres of meadow in Stanstead, Herts	1 yr.*	£0.50	CP40/1005a, m. 50
20 sheep and 1 cow in Sittingbourne, Kent	1 yr.*	£0.43	CP40/1005b, m. 493
2 tofts in Kent	1 yr.*	£0.40	CP40/1007, m. 502

Parish Leases from the Plea Rolls[1]

Abbreviations.

AG = attorney general; r = rector; rec = rectory; v = vicar; vic = vicary;
cl = cleric; cpn = chaplain; psn = parson; gen = gentleman; kt = knight;
hus = husbandman; 10a = ten acres.

1. CP40/476, m. 254. William de Ketilwell TO Katherine de Barneby: rec of York St. George, Ebor; 1 yr. at £21, made 1370. * 2. CP40/499, m. 193. Walter de Ashebury psn of Todenham TO John atte Hide of Todenham, Peter de Stodele cpn: rec of Todenham, Gloc; 4 yrs. at £26, made 1375. * 3. CP40/500, m. 124; CP40/501, m. 297d. William de Cawode psn of Beelsby TO John Grymesby of Burton Pidsea, John Cusays cpn: rec of Beelsby, Lincs; 3 yrs. at £40. * 4. CP40/501, m. 234; CP40/503, m. 132; CP40/504, m. 119d. Thomas prior of Launde TO Henry Buckingham of Northampton: rec of Ashby St. Ledgers, Northt; 6 yrs. at £13.33. * 5. CP40/501, m. 303. Phillip Kelleseye psn of Nutfield TO Roger de Lincoln, Robert de Kingston citizen of London: rec of Nutfield, Surrey; 4 yrs. at £20 made 1379. * 6. CP40/501, m. 303. Roger de Lincoln, Robert de Kingston citizen of London TO Henry Grenecobbe citizen dyer of London: rec of Nutfield, Surrey; 2 yrs. made 1381. * 7. CP40/501, m. 344. John Moubray prebendary master TO William Reyson: rec of Cropredy, Oxon. * 8. CP40/502, m. 307. Robert Outheby sr, Thomas Outheby psn of Stonton Wyville TO John de Abyndon psn of Cranoe, Thomas Spencer; Richard son of Richard de Welham: deanery of Gartree, Leics made 1381. * 9. CP40/502, m. 312d. John de Tathewell psn of Stoke Dry TO Henry Byweston cpn, Norman Charneus, William Whytheved of Marcott: rec of Stoke Dry, Rutland; 3 yrs. at £16. * 10. CP40/503, m. 629d. Prior of Watton TO John Slaghterman: rec of Skerne, Ebor; 6 yrs., made 1389.

11. CP40/505, m. 316. William de Retford subdeacon of cathedral TO Walter Frost of Kingston upon Hull, Henry de Bristowe cpn, and John de Wilflet of Preston in Holderness: rec of Preston, Ebor; 5 yrs. at £100, made 1366. * 12. CP40/507, m. 121d. John Broune psn of Hareby TO John Carneby cpn: rec of Hareby, Lincs; 1 yr. at £10.67, made 1385. * 13. CP40/507, m. 627d. Prior of Thetford TO John Chevere of Sustead, Thomas

---

1. Some of these rolls were searched thoroughly for parish leasing cases; others, done earlier, only noted the occasional case as something I considered at the beginning as just an interesting oddity.

Dorel of Sustead, and Ralf Cat of Great Barningham: rec of Sustead, Norf; 7 yrs. at £8.67, made 1378. * 14. CP40/508, m. 110. John Cokerell of Dunham psn of Bradford Peverell TO Richard Jurdan, John Jurdan, and Richard Foul: rec of Bradford Peverell, Dorset; 3 yrs. at £20, made 1382. * 15. CP40/510, m. 407. Nicholas de Aquila master of Writtle All Saints v general r procurator of hospital of order of St. Faith in Rome TO Lawrence John merchant of Florence, Zanabius notary of Benosia of Florence, and Walter Malewayn cpn: rec of Writtle, Essex, with chapel of Rockwell; 5 yrs. at £80, made 1387. * 16. CP40/510, m. 410. Lincoln Cathedral as prebendary during vacancy TO John Gotebed: rec of Biggleswade, Beds; 1 yr. at £58, made 1382. * 17. CP40/511, m. 115. Henry Wynterton prebendary of Woodford and Widford TO John Drury: prebend of Woodford and Widford, Gloc; 3 yrs. * 18. CP40/511, m. 523d. John Glasiere v of Shilton TO Gilbert de Drayton cl: vic of Shilton, Oxon; 4 yrs. at £5.33, made 1386. * 19. CP40/518, m. 101. psn TO cl: rec of Great Staughton, Hunts; 1 yr. at £80. 20. CP40/519, m. 328. dean and chapter of Exeter Cathedral TO Thomas de Holbroke: rec of Clyst Honiton, Devon; 10 yrs. at £8, made after November 1387.

21. CP40/520, m. 391d. William Hyndele psn of Bardfield TO John Esthalle cpn, William Alman of Thaxsted barker: rec of Bardfield, Essex. * 22. CP40/520, m. 399. Geoffrey Purchas cl TO Robert Warande, William Salmon cl: rec of Tofts Monks, Norf; 5 yrs. * 23. CP40/521, m. 395. John Yernemouth psn of Sutton Courteney TO George Roudene, Richard Marmeon, and John Marmeon: rec of Sutton Courteney, Berks and chapel of Appleford. * 24. CP40/545, m. 114d. r TO John Copleston: rec of East Luccombe, Som. * 25. CP40/545, m. 182d. Brigit prioress of Usk TO Robert Sage armiger, Robert Sage of Caerleon cpn: rec of Rangeworthy (?), Gloc; 20 yrs. * 26. CP40/546, m. 39. John Lilbourne r of Worth TO John Alfray, William Chelsham cpn: rec of Worth, Sussex; 3 yrs. made 1394. * 27. CP40/548, m. 278. Richard Wildebrigg v Portsmouth TO John Lynne v Portsea: profits of vic of Portsmouth, Hants; 1 yr. at £6.67 made 1395 (all profits whatsoever on lands and oblations of church and 2 chapels, tithes of wool, hay, lambs, sheaves, demesne land, with Richard serving as priest in church and chapels). * 28. CP40/599, m. 375. John Colley psn of Kelshall TO Thomas Shane cpn: rec of Kelshall, Herts; 3 yrs. at £17.33, made 1407. * 29. CP40/599, m. 428. Henry Winchester cl TO Thomas Dyer of Lindfield: rec of Lindfield, Sussex; 1.5 yrs. at £10.67, made 1406. * 30. CP40/623, m. 307. John Wodham psn of Middleton TO John Knapton of Cambridge chapman: rec of Middleton, Norf; 3 yrs. at £20, made 1410.

31. CP40/623, m. 395. Dean and Chapter of Exeter Cathedral TO Robert Poyer of Topsham yeo: rec of Topsham, Devon; 5 yrs. at £16.67, made 1410. * 32. CP40/799, m. 137d. Thomas Thowe cl TO Thomas Stikbuk of Lichfield cpn: precentory in cathedral of Lichfield, Staffs; 5 yrs. at £2, made 1448. * 33. CP40/806, m. 316. prior of Repton TO Richard Bray v of Great Baddow: rec of Great Baddow, Essex; 2 yrs. at £10, made 1455. * 34. CP40/816, m. 280. William Alexander psn of Leigh TO William Ewkeston cpn: rec of Leigh, Staffs; 5 yrs. * 35. CP40/844, m. 515d. Richard Mielis TO Walter Howard of Buntingford cpn v Rushden: rec of Rushden, Herts; 7 yrs. at £1.33, made 1465. * 36.

CP40/844, m. 583. William Sutton prior New Hospital outside Bishopsgate TO Edward Warde yeo: rec of Wonersh, Surrey; 1 yr. at £6.67, made 1471. * 37. CP40/845, m. 168d. John Tram cl TO Alexander Fayreclough of Skirbeck: rec of Linwood, Lincs; 3 yrs. at £8, made 1468. * 38. CP40/846, m. 146. William Chaddeworth sr. armiger, Mr. John Chaddeworth prebendary TO Stephen Somerton gen, John Attewell of King's Sutton: prebend of King's Sutton, Northt; 5 yrs. at £40, made 1465. 39. CP40/848, m. 38d. Thomas prior of Norwich Cathedral TO Henry Bozoun of Hopton cpn: rec of Manor Hopton, Norf; 5 yrs. at £5.33, made 1467. * 40. CP40/848, m. 419. John Shyrwyn cl TO Richard Hadylsey of Langham cl: rec of Little Langham, Norf; 4 yrs. at £3, made 1470.

41. CP40/850, m. 76d. Henry Vernon armiger TO John Pole jr. armiger: rec of Hartington, Derbs; 4 yrs. at £24, made 1468. * 42. CP40/874, m. 143. Prior of Merton TO Edward Luke citizen brewer of London: rec of Tregony, Cornwall; 7 yrs. at £8, made 1475. * 43. CP40/874, m. 400. William abbot of Gloucester TO John Tasker of Coln St. Aldwyn hus and Alice his wife: rec of Coln, Gloc; 21 yrs. * 44. CP40/874, m. 401. Robert prior of Breadsall TO John Couper psn of half of Muggington: rec of other half of Muggington, Derbs; 9 yrs. at £5.33, made 1470. * 45. CP40/897, m. 235. Adrian de Bardys prebendary of Thame TO Thomas Padnale, William Leynthale: prebend of Thame, Oxon. * 46. CP40/898, mm. 33, 336. William prior of Butley TO Robert Barr of Gissing cl: rec of Gissing, Norf; 1 yr. at £4, made 1481. * 47. CP40/898, m. 338. John Bonaunter cl r of Chiselborough and West Chinnock TO William Abbot cl, John Abbot: rec of Chiselborough and West Chinnock, Som; 3 yrs. at £12, made 1482. * 48. CP40/899, m. 117. Henry prior of Coxford TO Richard Ode of Thorpe Market spicer: rec of Bradfield, Norf; for life at £0.83, made 1480. * 49. CP40/910, m. 358. Walter Hert r of Wheathampstead TO Richard Lawdy of Wheathampstead gen: rec of Wheat-hampstead, Herts; 3 yrs. at £20, made 1483. * 50. CP40/912, m. 121d. Thomas Cart-wryght cl psn of Folksworth TO John Styvecley of Ramsey gen: rec of Folksworth, Hunts; 5 yrs. at £4, made 1488.

51. CP40/912, m. 154d. Prior of Merton TO Thomas Pomeray of Berry Pomeroy armiger: rec of Berry Pomeroy, Devon; 20 yrs. at £16, made 1480. * 52. CP40/915, m. 207. John Ardern cl TO Edmund Brycham of Sharrington cpn: rec of Brinton, Norf; 1 yr. at £6.67, made 1476. * 53. CP40/922, m. 233d. John Edmond cl TO John Carlighan of Helland cpn: vic of St. Winnow, Cornwall; 1 yr. at £6.67, made 1485. * 54. CP40/922, m. 311d. John prior of St. Mary Overy TO David Walton of Wendover hus: rec of Wen-dover, Bucks; 2 yrs. at £24, made 1490. * 55. CP40/922, m. 355d. Edward Poole arch-deacon of Richmond TO John Lynche of Westbury clothier: rec of Westbury, Wilts; 5 yrs. at £63, made 1481. * 56. CP40/933, m. 156. John Weston prior of Hospital of St. John of Jerusalem TO John and Edward Palmer: preceptory of Poling, Sussex; 20 yrs. at £2.67(?), made 1485. * 57. CP40/934, m. 326. John fitzHugh dean Lincoln cathedral TO Gervase Lyfton of Clifton armiger: rec of Bingham, Notts; 3 yrs. at £40, made 1492. * 58. CP40/934, m. 334d. Robert Stoke prior of Breamore TO Thomas Haynowe, Joan his wife, Joan Hymerford his daughter: rec of Brading, Hants; for lives of the three

grantees, made 1437. * 59. KB27/939, m. 35. Richard Walsyngham abbot of North Creake TO Thomas Smetherst cpn: rec of Hapton, Norf; 30 yrs., made 1492. * 60. KB27/937, m. 62. Peter abbot of Notley TO William Snath, William Lammyng: rec of Choseley, Norf; 5 yrs., made 1488.

61. CP40/935, m. 237. William abbot of Peterborough TO William Spenser of Stamford gen, John Benell: rec of Bringhurst with Easton and Chapel of Drayton, Leics; 30 yrs. at £10, made 1486. * 62. CP40/935, m. 312. John abbot of Thornton TO Thomas Gilby of Wyham: rec of Kelstern, Lincs; 60 yrs. at £3, made 1472. * 63. CP40/935, m. 330. Richard abbot of Battle TO John Hore: rec of Exning, Suff; 20 yrs., made 1493. * 64. CP40/942, m. 211. James bishop of Norwich TO John Elsy of Cley next the Sea yeo: rec of Langham, Norf; 3 yrs. at £12, made 1493. * 65. CP40/950, m. 126d. Thomas Shenkwyn doctor of law TO Edward Newenham of Everdon gen: rec of Stuchbury, Northt; 1 yr. periodic at £5.67, made 1489. * 66. CP40/950, m. 423. Richard Hatton cl v of Yeovil TO John Bush cpn: vic of Yeovil, Som; 2 yrs. at £15, made 1495. * 67. CP40/950, m. 520. Hugh Oldom prebendary of Colwich (?) TO Ralph Wolsey of Wolseley armiger, Thomas (sic): prebend of Colwich, Staffs; 5 yrs. at £21, made 1495. * 68. KB146/10/15/1, no. 7; KB27/954, m. 29. Adrian Castelleus r of St. Dunstan in the East, London TO John Arnold cl, Robert Rydon, Benjamin Dygby, Thomas Elderton: rec of St. Dunstan in the East, London; 5 yrs. at £50, made 1497. * 69. CP40/962, m. 151d. John abbot of Bermondsey TO William Wright of Cobham yeo: rec of Cobham, Kent; at will at £10, made 1497. * 70. CP40/962, m. 184d. Nicholas Goldwell master of Hospital Norwich St. Giles TO Robert Barton of Attleborough yeo: r of Coltishall, Norf; 1 yr. at £6, made 1497.

71. CP40/962, m. 353d. William Russell cl TO John Predy of Marshfield yeo: rec of Cold Aston, Gloc; 2 yrs. at £6.83, made 1497. * 72. CP40/962, m. 363. Henry abbot of Missenden TO William Wycle and Alianora his wife with sublease to Edward Brudenell armiger: rec of Chalfont St. Peter, Bucks; 21 yrs. at £10.50, made 1484/1498. * 73. CP40/962, m. 554. John Denham r TO Robert Frankyshe of London cl: rec of Great Brickhill, Bucks; 3 yrs. at £13.33, made 1498. * 74. CP40/962, m. 565d. Thomas abbot of Cirencester TO Abbot of Pipewell: rec of Rothwell, Northt; 21 yrs. at £16, made 1480. * 75. CP40/962, m. 67. Elias Garnet of Tillington cl TO Roger, Robert Webbe cpn: rec of Tillington, Sussex. * 76. CP40/966, m. 316d. Richard Charnok prior of London St. Trinity TO George Boteler of Broomfield gen: rec of Broomfield, Essex; 10 yrs. at £13.33, made 1496. * 77. CP40/966, m. 489. Robert prior of Spalding TO Richard Geryng of Sibsey gen: rec of Sibsey, Lincs; 10 yrs., made 1500. * 78. CP40/966, m. 549. William Pykering cl TO Ingincius Ditton of Paston by Peterborough gen: rec of Paston, Northt; 3 yrs. at £13.33, made 1500. * 79. CP40/970, m. 601. John Weston prior of St. John of Jerusalem TO Henry Colet alderman citizen London merchant: rec of Greenham, Berks; 31 yrs. at £64, made 1479. * 80. CP40/970, m. 601. Henry Colet alderman citizen London merchant TO Richard Bedford clothier, William Pynman of Newbury: rec of Greenham, Berks; 28 yrs. at £64, made 1482.

81. KB27/970, m. 29d. r proprietors TO Roger Amyas, Richard Woderove knight: rec of Dewsbury, Ebor; 16 yrs. at £50. * 82. KB27/973, m. 35d. Thomas Dalton r of Cottesmore TO William Dalton: rec of Cottesmore, Rutland; 3 yrs. at £18, made 1488. * 83. CP40/974, m. 102. Richard abbot of Notley TO Nicholas Brightwell of Chearsley gen: rec of Chearsley, Bucks; 1 yr. at £8, made 1504. * 84. CP40/974, m. 286. John Frense master of Hospital of Bury St. Edmunds St. Peter TO Thomas Man of Lakenheath yeo: rec of Elveden, Suff; 1 yr. at £16, made 1504. * 85. CP40/974, m. 354. Ralf abbot of Kenilworth TO John Pappe (Collys) of Stewkley hus: rec of Stewkley, Bucks; 21 yrs. at £16, made 1495. * 86. CP40/974, m. 446. Henry Carnebull cl TO Richard Gelston of Newark yeo: rec of Langford, Notts; 1 yr. periodic at £10, made 1502. * 87. CP40/974, m. 530. William Middelton succentor of Lichfield and vs of Lichfield TO Richard Cook of Coventry merchant alderman: rec of Chesterton, Staffs; 10 yrs. at £6. * 88. CP40/978, m. 242d. William Cook cl TO John Baxter of Garboldisham yeo: rec of Garboldisham, Norf; 2 yrs. at £18.67, made 1502. * 89. CP40/978, m. 620. Peter Swyllyngton cl TO Thomas Ordwey: rec of Belton, Suff; 3 yrs. at £16, made 1498. * 90. CP40/982, m. 113d. Nicholas Goldwell archdeacon of Suffolk TO Richard Scote of Wootton cl: rec of Knoyle, Wilts; at £5.33, made 1503.

91. CP40/982, m. 310. Nicholas Goldwell archdeacon of Suffolk master TO Thomas Cusnet of North Newnton cl: prebend and rec of North Newnton, Wilts; 2 yrs. at £6.33, made 1503. * 92. CP40/982, m. 408d; CP40/986, m. 431d. William Wode cl TO Giles Talbot of Wisbech gen: rec of Elm, Cambs, 0.58 yr. at £30 (annual rate), made 1504. * 93. CP40/982, m. 496. John Dale cl TO William Heron of Weston Turville cpn: rec of Weston Turville, Bucks; 0.42 yr. at £7.50 (annual rate), made 1503. * 94. CP40/982, m. 511. John Chambre prebendary of Corringham r of Willingham, Lincs TO Thomas Burgh of Stowe armiger, Hugh Childyng of Upton v of Upton, Robert Humberston of Braceby yeo: rec of Stow, Northt; 3 yrs. at £16, made 1502. * 95. CP40/982, mm. 414, 512. William Crawne papal notary TO William Throkmerton cl psn of Great Houghton: rec of Great Houghton, Northt; 3 yrs. at £20, made 1507. * 96. KB27/985, m. 102. John abbot of Westminster TO Thomas Nycolys of Ashwell hus: rec of Ashwell, Herts; 10 yrs., made 1503. * 97. CP40/986, m. 160. Thomas Wyse cl TO John Leke of Kingston cpn: chapel of Kingston, Devon; 5 yrs. at £20, made 1501. * 98. CP40/986, m. 618d. Godfrey Foliambe armiger TO Henry Wylloughby of Walton knight: rec of Lowdham, Notts; 1 yr. periodic at £20.33, made 1506. * 99. CP40/993, m. 121. Edward Scott doctor of laws TO William Weston of Sutton Coldfield yeo: rec of Sutton Coldfield, Warw; 3 yrs. at £22, made 1501. * 100. CP40/993, m. 435. Richard prior of Leeds TO Richard Goddyn of Rochester St. Margaret citizen: rec of Chatham, Kent; 1 yr. periodic at £22, made 1508.

101. CP40/993, m. 550. Thomas Hobbys dean of free chapel of St. Stephen Westminster TO Walter Bulstrode of Shifford: rec of Steeple Aston, Oxon, 30 yrs., made 1508. * 102. CP40/993, m. 638. William Grene prior of Bisham TO John Langeford, John Carewe: rec of Montalt, Wales; 15 yrs. at £22, made 1506. * 103. CP40/997, m. 264;

CP40/999, m. 237d. Richard Gryffyn of Chipping Warden cl TO Edmund Haselwode: rec of Chipping Warden, Northt; 3 yrs. * 104. CP40/997, m. 57d. Richard Salter of Standlake cl TO Simon Harcourt armiger, Thomas Skynner cpn: rec of Standlake, Oxon. * 105. CP40/1000, m. 268d; CP40/1002, m. 235d (latitat for London). Thomas Chanon r of Great Dunham TO John Wyngfeld cl: rec of Great Dunham, Norf; 5 yrs. * 106. CP40/1000, m. 354; CP40/1002, m. 355. John Hogekyns r of Harbridge v of Ringwood TO Walter Pryochet of Fordingbridge yeo, James Barre of Fordingbridge cl: rec of Harbridge, Hants; 3 yrs. at £10, made 1509. * 107. CP40/1001, m. 544. John Hadynham cl r of Fobbing TO William Goldwyn of Woolwich yeo, John Redehede cl: rec of Fobbing, Essex; 3 yrs. at £11, made 1508. * 108. CP40/1001, m. 604. John Hardyng prebendary of Longridge in Penkridge TO William Fyncheley: prebend of Longridge, Staff; 3 yrs., made 1512. * 109. CP40/1001, m. 608. Robert prior of Norwich Holy Trinity TO Richard Couper cl, William Neve of Beetley yeo, John Taverner hus: rec of North Elmham, Norf; 10 yrs. at £16, made 1505. * 110. CP40/1001, m. 652. John Baptist Boerio king's physician prebendary TO John Hopwood v of Romsey: rec of Timsbury, Hants; 5 yrs. at £5, made 1508.

111. CP40/998, m. 404. William Cooke cl TO Walter Wolmere of Wickham Market yeo: rec of Rougham, Suff; 3 yrs. at £22, made 1503. * 112. CP40/998, m. 484. William prior of Merton TO William Woderove master of Clare College: rec of Barton, Cambs; 16 yrs. at £12, made 1507. * 113. CP40/999, m. 216; CP40/1000, m. 204d. John Herrys prebendary of Denys in Chumleigh TO John Gyll of Chumleigh cl, William Cruys of Chumleigh gen: rec of Denys in Chumleigh, Devon; 5 yrs. at £2.33. * 114. CP40/999, m. 513. William Reson prior of Barnwell TO George Nicholles: rec of Hinxton, Cambs; 20 yrs., made 1502. * 115. CP40/999, m. 536. Christopher Braunche cl TO John Cowper of Thorndon hus: rec of Thorndon, Suff; 7 yrs. at £12, made 1510. * 116. CP40/1002, m. 224d. r of Rousham TO John Archer of Rousham hus: rec of Rousham, Oxon. * 117. CP40/1002, m. 261. Gamaliel Clifton cl r of Wistow TO Thomas Pigot coiner: rec of Wistow, Ebor; 2 yrs. at £14, made 1511. * 118. CP40/1002, m. 293. Abbot of Selby TO William Ascoghe armiger: rec of Stallingborough, Lincs; made 1511. * 119. CP40/1002, m. 350. John Fetherby r Oxted TO John Wodeward of Oxted hus: rec of Oxted, Surrey; made 1511. * 120. CP40/1004, m. 191d. John Dale cl TO William Heron of Weston Turville cl: rec of Weston Turville, Bucks; 0.38 yrs. at £7.50 (annual rate).

121. CP40/1004, m. 30d; CP40/1007, m. 504d. Thomas Halewell cl TO Thomas Otley: rec of Harbledown, Kent; 2 yrs. at £8, made 1509. * 122. CP40/1004, m. 521. Robert Norbourne (alias Frevill) v of Appledore TO William Marchall cl, Richard Upton: vic of Appledore, Kent; 4 yrs. at £10, made 1508. * 123. CP40/1004, m. 524. Edward Belcher lessee of rec TO John Chylderley of Guilsborough v of Guilsborough: rec of Guilsborough, Northt; 1 yr. periodic at £2.33, made 1504. * 124. CP40/1004, m. 532; CP40/1006, m. 550. John Pykeryng canon of Westminster v of Burneston TO James Parker cpn: vic of Burneston, Ebor; 3 yrs. at £29, made 1510. * 125. CP40/1004, mm. 132d, 322d. John abbot of Reading TO Richard Hall of Leominster cl: rec of "Westharnes," Heref; 1 yr. at £11,

made 1508. * 126. CP40/1002, m. 499d. William Horne of Tattersett r of Tattersett TO John Thurloke hus: rec of Tattersett, Norf. * 127. CP40/1005b, m. 119. William Woode cl TO Robert Hopkynson of Emneth hus: rec of Elm, Cambs; 1 yr. at £30 made 1510. * 128. CP40/1005b, m. 310d; CP40/1006, m. 401d. Thomas Walshe prior of Bradenstoke TO John Anne armiger, Alexander Anne cl: rec and manor of North Aston, Oxon; 30 yrs. at £8, made 1484. * 129. CP40/1005b, m. 317. Humfrey Stanley cl r of Clifton Campville TO John Stanley: rec of Clifton Campville, Staffs; 3 yrs. at £28.33, made 1509. * 130. CP40/1005b, m. 367d. Thomas Love prebendary of Stowford TO Gilbert Gale of Kenton hus: prebend of Stowford, Devon; 7 yrs. at £11, made 1510.

131. CP40/1005b, m. 558; CP40/1006, m. 305. Richard Nele r of South Pickenham TO Thomas Sylesdon of London gen: rec of South Pickenham, Norf; 3 yrs. at £8, made 1514. * 132. CP40/1005b, m. 574; CP40/1006, m. 334d. Richard Wylkynson TO Thomas Mynskyp of Denton cpn: rec of Denton, Lincs; 1 yr. at £22, made 1512. * 133. CP40/1006, m. 276d; CP40/1007, m. 335. John abbot of Notley TO Thomas Kyrkeby r of Fringford, Lawrence Worthington gen: rec of Stoke Lyne, Oxon; 21 yrs., made 1502. * 134. CP40/1006, m. 334d. Richard Wilkynson TO Thomas Mynskop of Denton cpn: rec of Denton, Lincs; 1 yr. at £22, made 1512. * 135. CP40/1006, m. 413. Gregory Mawer of Ipswich cl TO John Chapman of Swannington cl: rec of Swannington, Norf; 3 yrs. at £4.17, made 1510. * 136. CP40/1006, m. 486. Abbot of Leicester TO Robert Wryght: rec of Clifton, Warw. * 137. CP40/1006, m. 491. Roland Messenger r of Knapwell TO William Bonde of Boxworth cl, Robert Bonde cpn, John Lune yeo: rec of Knapwell, Cambs; 3 yrs. at £7.50, made 1509. * 138. CP40/1006, m. 550. John Pickering v of Burneston TO James Parker of Leeming cpn: rec of Burneston, Ebor; 3 yrs. at £29, made 1510. * 139. CP40/1007, m. 268. John Yotton professor Dean of Cathedral of Lichfield TO Henry Flemyng of Brewood v Brewood: rec of Brewood, Staffs; made 1509. * 140. CP40/1007, m. 346. Cuthbert Tunstall v Kirkby in Kendal TO Thomas Dalby of London archdeacon Richmond: vic of Kirkby; 1 yr. at £10, made 1511.

141. CP40/1007, m. 566; CP40/1008b, m. 633. John Sheffeld of Scotton, John Chalonerm, William Sheffeld TO William Dalyson of Scotton armiger: rec of Laughton and Blyton, Lincs; 3 yrs. at £23, made 1508. * 142. CP40/1008a, m. 124d. Thomas Halywell TO Thomas Otley: rec of Harbledown, Kent; 2 yrs. at £8, made 1509. * 143. CP40/1008a, m. 343d. John Cumblys cl TO Robert Myllys of Whitestone cl: rec of Bradford, Devon; 1 yr. at £6, made 1504. * 144. CP40/1008b, m. 602. Thomas Goodwyn prior of Ipswich St. Peter TO William Wyght of Cambridge cl: vic of Cambridge Holy Trinity; 4 yrs. at £8, made 1510. * 145. CP40/1008b, m. 634. John Robynson cl r of Fawkham TO William Swan of Southfleet gen: rec of Fawkham, Kent; 3 yrs. at £1.33, made 1508. * 146. CP40/1008b, m. 638. Peter abbot of Notley TO Thomas Kyrkeby r, Lawrence Worthington gen: rec of Stoke Lyne, Oxon; 21 yrs. at £6.50, made 1492. * 147. CP40/1012, m. 656. Elias Bell cl r of Dean TO Richard Holland, Richard Hemur chapman: rec of Dean, Cumb; 3 yrs. at £22, made 1511. * 148. CP40/1014, m. 382. Thomas Randolf cl prebendary of Brampton TO Robert Lammot: prebend of Brampton, Hunts; 3 yrs. at £31, made 1516. * 149. CP40/

1016, m. 131. Robert Woderove master of House of Ospringe TO Roger: rec of Headcorn (?), Kent; 1 yr. periodic at £15, made 1514. * 150. CP40/1016, m. 510. Thomas Gybon master TO John Pulverteste: rec of Wyberton, Lincs; 2 yrs. at £26.67, made 1505.

151. CP40/1018, m. 401. Henry Skelton cl r of Bowthorpe TO Edward Reynold of Mattishall cpn: rec of Bowthorpe, Norf; 5 yrs. at £4.67, made 1506. * 152. CP40/1018, m. 436d. John Maltby cl r of Bonsall TO Richard Cley of Grindon, Staffs cl r of Grindon, Staffs: rec of Bonshall, Derbs; 3 yrs. at £10.50, made 1510. * 153. CP40/1018, m. 99. William Aby v of Bromham TO John Wyne of Bromham: vic of Bromham, Beds. * 154. CP40/1026, m. 420. John Mesyngham prior of Baswich TO John Egerton: rec of Ilam (?), Staffs; 1 yr. periodic at £11, made 1510. * 155. CP40/1026, m. 438. Brian Sanford of Escrick cl r of Escrick TO Sir Simon Thompson cl, William Grigge yeo, Robert Gregge: rec of Escrick, Ebor; 3 yrs. at £18, made 1513. * 156. CP40/1026, m. 438. Brian Sanford of Escrick cl r of Escrick TO Alvered Rawson, Cuthbert Cotes cl: rec of Escrick, Ebor; 3 yrs., made 1516. * 157. CP40/1026, m. 676d. Simon Yates of Beckingham cl TO James Plumtre: rec of Beckingham, Lincs; 3 yrs. * 158. CP40/1026, m. 850. John Veysey dean of Windsor St. George chapel TO Robert Pulvertoft: rec of Exbourne, Devon; 10 yrs., made 1515. * 159. CP40/1034, m. 603d. Robert Hoode cl r of Acton Burnell TO Henry Knight armiger: rec of Acton Burnell, Salop; 3 yrs., made 1519. * 160. CP40/1034, m. 634. dean and chapter of Exeter Cathedral TO John Saunder of Buckerell hus: rec of Buckerell, Devon; 90 yrs., made 1501.

161. KB27/1044, m. 77. John Robynson r of Eastham TO Thomas Hanley gen: chapel of Over Hanley, Worcs; 0.85 yrs., made 1512. * 162. CP40/1041, m. 430. Christopher Tamworth cl r of Ingoldsby TO Leonard Thompson, John Markall: rec of Ingoldsby, Lincs; 3 yrs. at £17, made 1510. * 163. KB27/1053, m. 63d. William Darlyngton cl r of Barnham TO John Palmer gen: rec of Borsham, Sussex; 1 yr. periodic at £10.33, made 1522. * 164. CP40/1051, m. 221. Roger Clarke cl TO William Walton of Emley cl: rec of Rushock, Worcs; 0.75 yrs. * 165. CP40/1052, m. 145d. Richard Blynsham cl TO Robert Rassheley of Eggesford hus: rec of Eggesford, Devon; 2 yrs. at £8.08, made 1523. * 166. CP40/1052, m. 507d. Thomas Qarret TO John Palmer of Barnham gen: rec of Barnham, Sussex; 0.5 yrs. at £5.40, made 1524. * 167. CP40/1052, m. 534. William Isbellys cl r of Tacolneston TO William Came of London, James Holt of London, John Braynforte abbot of Wymondham: rec of Tacolneston, Norf; 5 yrs. at £10, made 1523. * 168. CP40/1052, m. 628d. Thomas Lubsed citizen goldsmith of London TO Thomas Coke of Hilborough r of Hilborough; Thomas Leeman of Swaffham r of Swaffham: chapel of London St. Margaret; 1 yr. periodic at £2, made 1520. * 169. CP40/1052, m. 722. John Wastell prior of Dunstable TO Anthony Babington: rec of Bradbourne, Derbs; 7 yrs. at £24, made 1519. * 170. KB27/1061, m. 67. John Lacy prior of Merton TO Edward Pomeroy knight: rec of Berry Pomeroy, Devon; 21 yrs., made 1513.

171. KB27/1066, m. 17. Thomas Hall of Halberton TO Nicholas Turner, Thomas Weer: vic of Halberton, Devon; 5 yrs., made 1526. * 172. KB27/1073, m. 116d. Alan Percy cl TO William John ap Thomas: rec of "Layhern," South Wales; at £44, made 1524. * 173.

CP40/1067, m. 108. Roger Walkott v TO Richard Cotton of Graveney fishmonger and Richard Watkyns cl to the use of Richard Cotton: v of Graveney, Kent; 3 yrs. at £12, made 1527. * 174. CP40/1067, m. 302. John Veysy cl TO Thomas Rendale of Lychett Matravers hus, Thomas Rendale of Lychett Matravers jr. hus: rec of Lychett Matravers, Dorset; 3 yrs. with renewal for 3 yrs., made 1525. * 175. CP40/1067, m. 528. Prior of Canwell (suppressed 1524) TO Robert West cl: rec of Ragdale, Leics; 40 yrs. at £1.67, made 1516. * 176. CP40/1067, m. 629. William prior of Thetford TO George Denby: rec of rec and manor of Ousden, Suff; 21 yrs. * 177. CP40/1067, m. 718. John prior of Maxstoke TO Thomas Est and Anne his wife: rec of Yardley, Worcs; 99 yrs., made 1489. * 178. CP40/1067, m. 738. Felix Massarosa of Tredington cl r of Tredington TO Richard Cartwright, Anne Middelmore, William Willington: rec of Tredington, Worcs; 5 yrs. at £60, £65, £80x3, made 1524. * 179. CP40/1068, m. 411d; CP40/1069, m. 104d. John Vyall canon of Hereford Cathedral TO James Ravynhyll of Woolhope yeo: vic of Woolhope, Heref. * 180. CP40/1068, m. 428. Thomas abbot of St. Albans TO John Boston, Richard Wyllons, with sublease to Henry Wattys gen: rec of Winslow, Bucks; 24 yrs., made 1524/1530.

181. CP40/1068, m. 529; CP40/1069, m. 133. Henry Robynson cl r of Clapham TO John Borowe of Water Lambeth yeo: rec of Clapham, Surrey; 1 yr. periodic at £7, made 1523. * 182. CP40/1069, m. 217. John Roo of Gussage cl TO Thomas Wallys: vic of Gussage, Dorset; made 1528. * 183. CP40/1069, m. 553d. Elias Birche cl r of Sturmer TO John Reve of Haverhill hus clothmaker: rec of Sturmer, Essex; 3 yrs. at £12, made 1528. * 184. CP40/1070, m. 406. John Prestall cl TO William Wode of Gravesend yeo, John Baylle of Wrotham cl: rec of Ash next Ridley, Kent; 5 yrs. at £13.33, made July 1530. * 185. CP40/1070, m. 205. Lawrence Waterhouse of Braithwell v of Braithwell TO Robert Otys, Gilbert Otys: vic of Braithwell, Ebor; Jan. 1530 at Braithwell (not necessarily a lease; this could be a compromise with lessees because of statutes of 1529). * 186. CP40/1070, m. 419. Arthur Chadwyke cl r of Clifford TO John Turnour of Clifford yeo, John Hobbyns: rec of Clifford, Gloc; 1.5 yrs. at £15, made August 1529. * 187. CP40/1071, m. 111d. William Boleyn prebendary of Strensall TO Tristram Teske of York gen: prebend of Strensall, Ebor; made February 1530. * 188. CP40/1071, m. 424. Robert Burnell r of Tilbrook TO William Kyng of Kimbolton, Hunts yeo, Henry Grene v of Riseley, Edward Pell of Great Staughton: rec of Tilbrook, Beds: 3 yrs. at £6.67, made 1503. * 189. CP40/1071, m. 502. John Burton abbot of Osney TO William Gadbury: rec and manor of Weston, Oxon; 41 yrs. at £31.33. * 190. CP40/1071, m. 512. William Burbank master of Hospital of Wilton Sts. Giles and Anthony TO John Burgchier of Durnford: hospital of Wilton, Wilts; 4 yrs. periodic up to 20 yrs., at £5.33, made 1528.

191. CP40/1072, m. 406. John Roydon master of two chapels in the weald of Kent TO Walter Herenden of Maidstone gen master: two chapels in Kent; 7 yrs. at £5, made June 1530. * 192. CP40/1072, m. 421d. Richard Parker of Lincoln cl TO Richard Dudley cl: rec of Leicester St. Margaret; 3 yrs. at £31.33, made 1523. * 193. CP40/1072, m. 439. Margaret abbess of Godstow TO John Wellyburn of Hughendon gen: rec of Chepping Wycombe,

Bucks; made March 1529. * 194. CP40/1073, m. 421d; CP40/1075, m. 624. Richard abbot of Notley TO Thomas Cade of St. Albans cl, Thomas Garrard of Swell yeo: rec of Lower Swell, Gloc; 21 yrs. at £6.67, made 1521. * 195. CP40/1074, m. 407. Edward Fynche cl r of Ross TO Robert ap Gwyllym gen: rec and manor of Ross, Heref; 3 yrs. at £43, made March 1529. * 196. CP40/1074, m. 454d. Robert Brudenell armiger and Philippa his wife TO William Barton yeo: rec of Chesham, Bucks; 14 yrs. at £16.50, made 1516. * 197. CP40/1075, m. 119. John Clarke cl master r of Hothfield TO Thomas Harlakyngden of Hothfield clothmaker: rec of Hothfield, Kent; 3 yrs. at £10, made 1525. * 198. CP40/1075, m. 119. William Hollyn TO James Chadwyke of Bramfield hus: rec of Bramfield, Herts; 3 yrs. at £12, made 1528. * 199. CP40/1075, m. 444. George Byllyngton of Grafton Flyford cl r of Grafton Flyford TO John Wheler of Droitwich gen: rec of Grafton Flyford, Worcs; 5 yrs., made October 1530. * 200. CP40/1075, m. 448. William prior of Bridlington TO Richard Brandly: rec of Witham, Lincs, 1 yr. periodic at £14.67, made 1527.

    201. CP40/1075, m. 509. George Grey of London cl r of Ilfracombe TO Thomas Harrys registrar of archdeaconry of Cornwall: rec of Ilfracombe, Devon; 5 yrs. at £60, £0; £40 x 3, made June 1529. * 202. CP40/1076, m. 150. William prior of Bridlington TO William Broun: r of Witham, Lincs; 1 yr. periodic at £14.67, made 1518. * 203. CP40/1076, m. 435. Philip Frere TO William Lottesham of Midsomer Norton hus, Thomas Shepard of Babington hus: rec of Midsomer Norton, Som; 1 yr. at £6.33, made September 1530. * 204. CP40/1077, m. 402d. Thomas Thornton cl r of Elsenham TO John Longman yeo: vic of Elsenham, Essex; 3 yrs. at £15.17, made May 1529. * 205. CP40/1077, m. 528. Thomas Yaxley r of Addington TO Anthony Furthoo of Addington gen: rec of Addington, Northt; 3 yrs. at £14.33, made March 1531. * 206. CP40/1077, m. 630. Thomas Webster master v of Tetford TO Thomas Cope of Langtoft hus: vic of Tetford, chapel of Baston, Lincs; 3 yrs. at £10, made September 1529. * 207. CP40/1078, m. 422. William Vaughan cl TO Thomas Fowler of Bugbrooke gen: rec of Bugbrooke, Northt; 1 yr. periodic at £28, made April 1530. * 208. CP40/1080, m. 426; CP40/1081, m. 339. Milo Wyllen of Windsor cl psn of Willingham TO William Wood gen, Alexander Tayllour gen: rec of Willingham, Lincs; 5 yrs. at £13.33, made March 1531. * 209. CP40/1080, m. 521. Richard Reston master of College of Putney St. Lawrence TO John Clever of Napton on the Hill hus: rec of Napton on the Hill, Warw; 13 yrs. at £20, made 1520. * 210. CP40/1081, m. 445. Thomas Hyckett v of Offton TO Richard Cooke of Somersham: vic of Offton with Little Bricett, Suff; 5 yrs. at £13.50, made 1528.

    211. CP40/1081, m. 453. Robert Shorton master of Pembroke College Cambridge TO John Passewater and Margaret his wife: rec of Waresley, Hunts; 21 yrs., made 1525. * 212. CP40/1081, m. 548. Thomas Lililowe of Lincoln cl r of Matlock and Bonsall TO Ralph Shawe cl v of Lowdham, Notts: rectories of Matlock and Bonsall, Derbs; 3 yrs. at £40, made 1522. * 213. CP40/1083, m. 435d. Henry Slyfeld cl TO John Myller of Bapchild yeo: chapel in Bapchild, Kent; 1 yr. period at £2, made September 1529. * 214. CP40/1084, m. 504. Lawrence Stubbys cl TO John Daryngton of Stafford draper, Agnes Barington

widow: chapel of St. Nicholas, Stafford castle, Staff; 5 yrs. at £2.65, made 1523. * 215. CP40/1084, m. 522. John Elton cl r of Staunton TO John Deyn of Staunton cl; Anthony Staunton of Staunton armiger: rec of Staunton, Notts; 1 yr. at £10.33, made March 1529. * 216. CP40/1085, m. 170. John prior of Hospital St. John of Jerusalem TO William Cordall gen: rec of Burham, Kent; 40 yrs., made 1528. * 217. CP40/1085, m. 170. William Cordall gen TO John Fowle of Halling gen: rec of Burham, Kent; 25 yrs. at £15.33, made December 1529. * 218. CP40/1085, m. 321; CP40/1086, m. 124. Henry Carbott v of Heversham archdeacon of Richmond TO James Bolkescale of Kirkby Lonsdale yeo, James Metcalf: vic of Heversham, Westmor; 5 yrs. at £33.33, made May 1529. * 219. CP40/1086, m. 406. John Metham v of Hornsea TO Richard Wylkynson cpn: chapel of Rolston, Ebor; 3 yrs. at £9.17, made 1524. * 220. CP40/1087, m. 514d; CP40/1088, m. 657. Thomas Lowe cl TO Anna, who became wife of John Dycas: chapel of St. Thomas (Worcester?), Worcs; 1 yr. periodic at £3.33, made September 1531.

221. CP40/1093, m. 197. John Williams cl v of Bristol St. Nicholas TO Thomas Wynsmore mercer: vic of Bristol St. Nicholas, Devon; 3 yrs. at £18, made 1535. * 222. CP40/1093, m. 521d. William Bulleyn of Aylsham archdeacon of Winchester v of Aylsham TO James Hawe of Cromer gen: vic of Aylsham, Norf; 3 yrs., made 1533. * 223. CP40/1113, m. 343. John Roberts cl r of Fovant TO Thomas Rendall of Fovant hus: rec of Fovant, Wilts; for £20, made 1540. * 224. CP40/1113, m. 691. Dean of collegiate church of Warwick and chapter TO Dame Alice Belknapp widow: rec of Wolfhamcote, Warw; 21 yrs. at £31, made January 1529.

Enforcement Suits under the Statutes of 1529

The entries in this appendix are arranged first by statutory concern, then by term (Hilary, Easter, Trinity, and Michaelmas respectively), then by court, and then by county. Entries list county margination, plaintiff (alias in parentheses), plaintiff status, defendant, defendant status, amount claimed, and document references. The lessor appears last in recitation ("Lease . . . from lessor"). A plea of "insufficient glebe" had to include an assertion that the profit was not used for personal advantage, as in use solely for household and hospitality. The attorney general regularly assumed the prosecution of the case; note was taken of his participation irregularly for that reason and thus appears here less frequently than in the documents. This appendix relates my database and is not as comprehensive as a calendar. Dates are designated month/day/year.

Abbreviations as in Appendix 3.

Leaseholding

HI531

L1. Cornub. John Martyn v. William Rowe of Poundstock cl. £40. CP40/1068, m. 617d. * L2. Devon. Anthony Harvy v. William Sheppard of Ashreigney cpn. £10. CP40/1068, m. 68. * L3. Devon. Anthony Harvy v. William Sheppard of Ashreigney cpn. £10. CP40/1068, m. 68d. * L4. Ebor. William Vinler v. Percival Sykerwham of Ebberston cl. £40. CP40/1068, m. 628; CP40/1069, m. 624d. Lease: land. D appeared. * L5. Ebor. Edward Gower kt v. William prior of Malton. £40. CP40/1068, m. 227; CP40/1074, m. 350. Lease: land. Issue: extent of priory's lands. * L6. Warw. Edward Rydge v. Henry Hykys cpn cl v of Burton. £40. CP40/1068, m. 274.

EI531

L7. Ebor. William Gyrlyngton of Kippax v. Thomas Jaxson of Kippax cpn of Kippax chantry. (along with allegation of buying and selling for profit) E159/310, m. 22. Lease of enclosure. Issue: application of profits; whether he bought or sold after 9/29/29. MI538: jury acquits. * L8. Oxon. John Richard v. Hugh Thomas r of Kencot.

£70. E159/310, m. 28. Lease of land. Issue: surrender of interest in a copyhold lease to his cotenants on 9/26/30. MI533: jury acquits. * L9. Oxon. Henry Sare v. John Heydon r of Edgcote (Northt). £70. E159/310, m. 34. Lease of closes. AG joins issue: application of profits. HI535: AG withdraws suit. * L10. Salop. John Reynolds of Bridgnorth v. Edward Mychell (= Smythyman) parson of Broseley. £70. E159/310, m. 27. Lease of pastures and tenements. AG joins issue: the taking or retaining of any profits. MI532: jury acquits. * LI1. Wilts. Robert Temes of Ashton v. John Dene v of Bradley. £62. E159/310, m. 23. Lease of rec. Issue: holding the lease after divestiture on 9/29/30. MI533: jury convicts with costs of £0.67. Justices excuse £44 because of the pardon. Forfeiture: £18. * L12. Beds. William Marcham gen v. George Bolles of "Martin Abbey, Surrey" cl. £10. CP40/1069, m. 380d. * LI3. Kent. Rex v. John Morys of Hawkhurst cpn. £30. CP40/1069, m. 257. Lease: land. * LI4. Lincs. John Foster v. Richard Oxman of Kirton in Holland cl. £40. CP40/1069, m. 27d.

TI531

L15. Suff. Robert Cove gen v. John Burton cpn. £20. KB27/1080, m. 3. * L16. Gloc. Richard Dangerfield of Bedford hus v. Richard Brown v of Stonehouse. E159/310, m. 16. Lease of rectory of Stonehouse from abbess of Elstow. Issue: the lease of the rec. E1533: jury acquits. Deliberation until MI535; sine die. * L17. Heref. Ralph Eton valet of the chamber of Mary princess of England v. Richard Vaughn v of Marcle. £26. E159/310, m. 13d. Lease: rec of Marcle from prior and convent of Sheen. Plea: denial of lease. AG joins issue. E1535: jury acquits. * L18. Oxon. Edward Willmott of Witney v. Bartholomew Gunson (= Gunston) v of Horley. £68. E159/310, m. 20. Lease: rectory of Horley from abbot of Hailes. AG joins issue: holding the rec against the form of the statute. Jury still being summoned in E1545, and thereafter by a lost cedula. * L19. Salop. Peter Hyggyns v. William Hall v of Cardington. £90. E159/310, m. 11. Lease: meadow. Plea: insufficient glebe. HI536: jury acquits. * L20. Ebor. Henry Wethereld v. Richard Beke of Os-motherley cl. £40. CP40/1070, m. 218. Lease: pasture and meadow. D appears.

MI531

L21. Gloc. John Richard v. John Lorde cl v of Southrop. £130. E159/310, m. 20. Lease: messuage from dean and college of Leicester. Plea: insufficient glebe. HI534: AG withdrew king's suit. * L22. Gloc. Thomas Edmond v. Edward Watton v of Lechlade. £120. E159/310, m. 22. Lease: land. Plea: insufficient glebe. AG joins issue. 1534: AG withdraws kings's suit. Court deliberates until T1534; sine die. * L23. Gloc. Thomas Edmondes v. Edward Watton v of Lechlade. £120. E159/310, m. 23. Lease: land and pasture from Catherine queen of England. Plea: insufficient glebe. AG joins issue. 1534: AG withdraws king's suit. Court deliberates until T1534; sine die. * L24. Kent. AG v. John Crosse cl v of

Hadlow. £130. E150/310, m. 30. Lease: Shipbourne chapel from prior of Hospital of St. John of Jerusalem in England. The court committed Crosse to prison on 11/21/31. Plea: insufficient glebe. AG joins issue. T1532: jury returned that he did not keep household and hospitality there. M1534: forfeiture of £130 adjudged for the king. 11/11/34: a writ of error came from king's bench. On 5/20/36 reported that Crosse was dead. * L25. Norf. Gregory Castell v. William Duffyng r of Burnham Thorpe. E159/310, m. 25. Lease: pasture and land. Process at least until E1532. * L26. Northt. Maurice Wogan gen v. Hugh Myllyng cl r of Farthingstone. £24. E159/310, m. 27. Lease: rec of Towcester. D died 9/-/31. * L27. Northumb. Henry Colyngwode and Robert Colyngwode v. Cuthbert Ogle r of Ford and Bothal and Stanhope and v of Ilderton. £140. E159/310, m. 19. Lease: lordships or manors of Bolton and Branxton. Plea: divestiture of interest to lay persons before 9/29/30. Court deliberates until M1636. * L28. Oxon. John Richard v. Edward Watton r of Westwell. £130. E159/310, m. 21. Lease: tenement. Plea: insufficient glebe. AG joins issue. Court deliberates until E1534: AG withdraws king's suit. T1534: sine die. * L29. Salop. Nicholas Hely of Wheaton Aston yeoman v. William Colbrand r of Astley. E159/310, m. 29. Lease: messuage and land. Plea: denial of lease. AG joins issue. E1536: jury acquits. * L30. Staffs. Gerard Chauncey valet of king's crown v. Ralph Alen of Alrewas cl. £120. E159/310, m. 24. Lease: lands and pastures. Plea: Alen guards a house looking to his chantry in Alrewas and has a family of 6 persons with insufficient glebe. Process continues at least until E1536. * L31. Staffs. Richard Lee v. Ralph Snelston prior of Calwich. £16.70. E159/310, m. 28. Lease: subleased meadow. Plea: admission of receipt of previous debts; denial of receipt of annual benefits against the statute. Nothing after plea. * L32. Suff. Simon Toppefeld one of two clerks of the exchequer v. William Whight v of Fressingfield. £120. E159/310, m. 26. Lease: rec of Fressingfield from dean of college of Norwich Blessed Mary. Plea: denial of holding by self or others to his use and issues sold for profit. AG joins issue. E1534: jury convicts. Forfeiture: £60 immediately, further process to assess forfeiture from profits. * L33. Bucks. John Appryce v. Thomas Watson of Bierton cpn. £40. CP40/1071, m. 767. * L34. Ebor. William Danby gen v. John prior of Mount Grace. £40. CP40/1071, m. 267. Lease: manor. D appeared. * L35. Ebor. Robert Mennel gen v. John prior of Mount Grace. £40. CP40/1071, m. 267d. Lease: rec of Ingleby from prior of Guisborough. * L36. Ebor. William Burton v. Launcelot Claxton of Stratton cl. £40. CP40/1071, m. 671. * L37. Ebor. William Burton v. John Johnson of Thirsk cpn. £40. CP40/1071, m. 671. * L38. Ebor. William Burton v. John Johnson of Fleetham cpn. £50. CP40/1071, m. 1071, m. 671; CP40/1072, m. 196. * L39. Ebor. William Burton v. Steven Levechyld of Aldborough cpn. £40. CP40/1071, m. 671; CP40/1072, m. 194d. * L40. Ebor. William Burton v. William Mansell of Little Langton cpn. £40. CP40/1071, m. 671d; CP40/1072, m. 196. * L41. Ebor. William Burton v. Robert Messynger cpn. £40. CP40/1071, m. 671. * L42. Ebor. William Burton v. Richard Pratt of Dalton by Swale cpn. £40. CP40/1071, m. 671. * L43. Ebor. William Burton v. John Richardson of Watlowe cl. £40. CP40/1071, m. 671. * L44. Ebor.

William Burton v. William Stevenson of Knayton cpn. £40. CP40/1071, m. 671. * L45. Ebor. William Burton v. Robert Whysehed of Barton cpn. £40. CP40/1071, m. 671; CP40/1072, m. 191d. * L46. York City. Nicholas Fairfax kt v. Edward abbot of Rievalux. £40. CP40/1071, m. 20d. * L47. Hants. Henry Warner v. Robert Cresseler of West Tisted cl. £50. CP40/1071, m. 18d. * L48. Heref. John Habrehale v. John Phelpottys of Peterstow cl. £40. CP40/1071, m. 486d. * L49. Lincs. John Corde v. William Haryson of Stamford cl. £40. CP40/1071, m. 33d; CP40/1072, m. 432. Lease: cottage, meadow, pasture from dean and chapter of Stamford. D appeared. * L50. Lincs. John Lyndesey v. John Freshemar of Huttoft cl. £40. CP40/1071, m. 33d. * L51. Norf. William Day v. Thomas Falke of Mundford cl. £20. CP40/1071, m. 749. * L52. Norf. William Day v. Thomas Falke of Mundford cl. £40. CP40/1071, m. 378d. * L53. Westmor. Roland Thornburgh v. Thomas Wursley of Windermere cl. £40. CP40/1071, m. 661d; CP40/1072, m. 270; CP40/1073, m. 178d. * L54. Worcs. Lawrence Robynson v. William Hull of Waresley by Hartlebury cl. £20 (£40). CP40/1071, m. 488d; CP40/1072, m. 396; CP40/1073, mm. 361d, 464d; CP40/1075, m. 558d; CP40/1082, m. 198. Lease: messuage, land. Issue: denial of lease.

H1532

L55. Cheshire. Percival Creswell gen and Ralph Grey yeoman v. Richard Orneshawe v of Acton. £160. E159/310, m. 16. Lease: messuage, pasture from abbot and convent of Combermere. E1532 plea: fee or lease. AG joins issue. Jury process into M1532. * L56. Ebor. Anthony Bayles of Bielby yeoman v. John Olyver v of Hayton. £150 (?). E159/310, m. 15. Lease: pasture, enclosure, land, the tithes of Bielby and Millington. Plea: vic of Hayton is not worth more than £7, did not hold most; did not convert the profits to his own use. * L57. Ebor. Roger Wytherton v. James Thwayte prior of Pontefract. £90. E159/310, m. 11. Lease: land from master of Hospital of Burton Lazars. Plea: denial of holding in the mode and form alleged. AG joins issue. M1533: jury acquits. H1534: sine die. * L58. Kent. John Hastlyn of Meopham v. Christopher Ayrresom parish priest of Meopham. £160. E159/310, m. 25. Lease: messuage, land, tithes, and oblations in Meopham pertaining to the vic. H1532 plea: never beneficed so that he leased the vic of Meopham to support his family. AG demurs. * L59. London. Gerard Chauncey v. John Stokesley bishop of London. £170 + £260. E159/310, m. 53. Lease: tenements with shops, cellars. E1533² plea: complete alienation of term. Process for jury into E1535. * L60. Norf. Robert Foster gen v. Lawrence Blaclock v of Attlebridge. £80. E159/310, m. 26. Lease: rec of Attlebridge from prior of Norwich. Process without appearance until H1533, with reference to further process in the files. * L61. Notts. Thomas Milner (Rouge Dragon) v. Ralph Edworth r of Stanford. £100. E159/310, m. 8. Lease: pasture from Abbot of Dale. Plea in E1532: fee or lease for part; insufficient glebe. Margination indicates that Edworth died. * L62. Notts. Thomas Milner (Rouge Dragon) v. Robert Holt v of Wysall. £100. E159/310, m. 9. Lease: tenements with lands and pastures. Plea: insufficient glebe.

Court deliberated until H1540 when AG joined issue. Process for jury into M1541. * L63. Notts. Thomas Milner (Rouge Dragon) v. Ralph Hout v of Rempstone. £100. E159/310, m. 10. Lease: land. Plea in H1532: insufficient count. Court deliberates into M1539 when AG joins issue; jury process into M1541. * L64. Suff. William Cowper, William Skynner of Bury St. Edmunds hus, Robert Gilmyn of Bury St. Edmunds weaver, and John Cokeyn of Bury St. Edmunds pinner v. William Eglyng r of Hawstead. £90. E159/310, m. 12. Lease: lands. Plea in H1532: insufficient glebe. Court deliberates into H1540. * L65. Suff. William Cowper, William Skynner of Bury St. Edmunds hus, Robert Gilmyn of Bury St. Edmunds weaver, and John Cokeyn of Bury St. Edmunds pinner v. John Gyttour r of Horningsheath. £90. E159/310, m. 18. Lease: land from abbot of Bury St. Edmunds. Issue by AG T1537: holding the lease. E1538: jury acquits. * L66. Suff. William Cowper, William Skynner of Bury St. Edmunds hus, Robert Gilmyn of Bury St. Edmunds weaver, and John Cokeyn of Bury St. Edmunds pinner v. John Redman r of Little Whelnetham. £90. E159/310, m. 17. Lease: land. Plea: insufficient glebe. H1533: AG withdraws suit. * L67. Suff. William Cowper, William Skynner of Bury St. Edmunds hus, Robert Gilmyn weaver, and John Cokyn of Bury St. Edmunds pinner v. John Kele cl master of chapel of St. Nicholas in Bury St. Edmunds. £90. E159/310, m. 14. Lease: land. Issue by AG T1532: holding the lease. Jury process into E1540. * L68. Worcs. Edward Porter v. Richard Sponer r of Knightwick. E159/310, m. 13. Lease: lands from Prior of Little Malvern. Plea: insufficient glebe. M1539: AG joins issue. Jury in T1541 acquits. * L69. Cumber. Oswald Bethom v. Edward Penrith of Penrith cl. £40. CP40/1072, m. 410. Lease: messuage from John bishop of Carlisle. D denies holding. * L70. Devon. Henry Adams v. Thomas Thomson of Lifton cpn. £40. CP40/1072, m. 250d; CP40/1073, m. 505; CP40/1075, m. 102; CP40/1076, m. 654. Lease: messuages. Issue: whether he occupied. * L71. Devon. Benedict Glub v. Richard Alyn of Clayhidon cl. £40. CP40/1072, m. 565. * L72. Devon. John Hoskyns cl v of Colaton Raleigh v. Richard Alyn of Clayhidon cl. £40. CP40/1072, m. 565; CP40/1073, m. 131. * L73. Ebor. Ralph Ward v. Thomas Teshe of York cl. £20. CP40/1072, m. 188d. * L74. Ebor. Thomas Hardwyk v. Robert Word of Ilkley cpn. £40. CP40/1072, m. 199. * L75. Ebor. James Langley v. Robert Buttill of Handsworth cpn. £20. CP40/1072, m. 200; CP40/1073, m. 33d. * L76. Ebor. James Langley v. John Reynold of Handsworth cpn. £40. CP40/1072, m. 200; CP40/1073, m. 33; CP40/1074, m. 273. * L77. Hants. Henry Warner v. Richard Crosswal [= Crosweler] of West Tisted cl v of Alfriston (Sussex). £50. CP40/1072, m. 382; CP40/1073, m. 481; CP40/1075, m. 360. Lease: rec of West Tisted. Issue: whether he held. M1533: jury convicts, costs of £1.33. * L78. Heref. Richard Moreton v. Roger Wylcokyan of Acton Beauchamp (Worcs) cl. £40. CP40/1072, m. 324. * L79. Lincs. Hugh Grantham v. John Baker of Thorpe in the Fallows cl. £40. CP40/1072, m. 29. * L80. Lincs. John Starky v. Andrew Weyde of Thornton cl. £40. CP40/1072, m. 30. * L81. Lincs. John Lyndesey v. Simon Maltby of Withcall cl. £40. CP40/1072, m. 333. Lease: land. D appeared. * L82. Lincs. John Webster v. John Davy of Deeping St. James cpn. £40. CP40/1072, m. 25d. * L83. Norf. Gregory Whyte v. William Newton of Hoxne,

Suffolk cl. £40. CP40/1072, m. 172. * L84. Norf. Robert Wellys v. George Waryng [= Waren] of Upton cl v of Upton. £40. CP40/1072, m. 504; CP40/1073, m. 408. Lease: rec of Upton, from prior of Butley. Issue: insufficient glebe. M1532: jury convicts. H1533 judgment: £40 forfeiture; damages £0.33; costs £2. * L85. Norf. James Boleyn kt v. Vincent Halman of Erpingham cl. £40. CP40/1072, m. 537d. * L86. Oxon. John Grove v. John abbot of Bruern. £160. CP40/1072, m. 650. * L87. Suff. Richard Fulmerston gen v. Hugh Burbanke of Tunstall cl (cpn). £40. CP40/1072, m. 373d; CP40/1073, m. 389d; CP40/1075, m. 656; CP40/1076, m. 593. * L88. Worcs. John Stokedale v. Richard Adney of Overbury cl. £40. CP40/1072, m. 514d. * L89. Worcs. John Stokedale v. Thomas Phoppes of Stockton cl. £40. CP40/1072, m. 514d.

E1532

L90. Heref. Walter Prowde v. Thomas Apowell cl v of Withington. £170. E159/311, m. 20. Lease: messuages. Issue T1532: insufficient glebe. Asked for release. * L91. Kent. Desiderius Tomson v. William Gateman cpn. £100. E159/311, m. 15. Lease: messuage in Hernhill with all oblations, tithes, profits, emoluments, and advantages pertaining to the vic. Judgment: £100 forfeiture; inquest for forfeiture of 10x the profits. * L92. Kent. Thomas Cock v. David Reynolds r of Betteshanger. £104. E159/311, m. 21. Lease: vic of Minster in the Isle of Thanet. Plea T1532: functioned as vicar's bailiff. Asked for release. * L93. Kent. Thomas Packkarde v. Thomas Hewys cl v of Thurnham. £110. E159/311, m. 22. Lease: rec of Milsted. Process without appearance into H1533. * L94. Oxon. Anthony Cotismore v. Richard Mook cl r of Swyncombe. £90. KB27/1083, m. 23. Lease: rec of Nettlebed from abbot of Dorchester. Plea: took as servant to lessee without taking profits for self. M1534: jury acquits. * L95. Salop. Roger Pole gen v. William Marshall r of Hodnet. E1532: E159/311, m. 12d. (enrolled with H1533) Incomplete allegation. * L96. Suff. Arthur Lowe v. John Wilkynson cl v of Mildenhall. £110. E159/311, m. 17. Lease: land Plea: insufficient glebe. Issue: took the lease by fraud and covin to sell the proceeds for profit. Process into M1532. * L97. Sussex. Marmaduke Darrell gen v. Alexander Shaw cl v of Pagham. £110. E159/311, m. 18. Lease: messuages from prior of Christ Church Canterbury. Issue by AG in T1532: holding against the statute. T1534 verdict: he had an annual profit of £1 above the annual rent. Forfeiture: £120. * L98. Sussex. Marmaduke Darrell v. Alexander Shaw. £170. E159/311, m. 19. Lease: tenement from prior of Bruton. Issue by AG T1532: holding against the statute. H1534 verdict: divested before 9/29/30 but took £1.33 in profits afterwards. Forfeiture: £13.33. Writ of error: 11 May 1535, KB27/1092, m. 33 (T1534). The relevant challenges were based on the statute limiting the time for forfeitures in *qui tam* actions, the facts that the profits had not been specified in the pleading, that the profits found by the jury were not allocated as between the time covered by the pardon and the time not so covered, that AG had taken over the case so that it might seem that Darrell had withdrawn from the suit, that there was a problem with the enrollment concerning Shaw's attorney. Successively continued through to

H1549. * L99. Sussex. Marmaduke Darrell gen v. Alexander Shaw parson and v of Pagham. £138. E159/311, m. 23. Lease: rec of Pagham from prior of Christ Church Canterbury. Plea T1532: surrender of lease. Asked for release. Court adjourned to be advised to E1534. Verdict T1534: he held the rec and took annual profits of £0.33 from 9/29/30 to 3/10/31 and of £2.67 from 3/10/31 to 5/16/31. Court applies statute 7 Henry VIII, c. 3 time limitation on *qui tam* suits: forfeiture of £102 plus 10x the relevant profits (£26.67). Writ of error on 10/28/34, KB27/1094, m. 65 (H1535). Challenges were based on the lack of certitude in the amount of land leased; that AG had taken over the case; that the profits had not been specified; that there was a problem with Shaw's attorney's warrant. * L100. Warw. Richard Walker v. Thomas Hawkyns cl v of Welles-bourne Hastings. £120. E159/311, m. 16. Lease: tenements from abbot of Kenilworth and another. Plea M1532: insufficient glebe and application of proceeds to household and hospitality. Court to be advised into H1536. * L101. Westmor. Richard Jaxson v. Richard Broun cl r of Burton. £110. E159/311, m. 14. Lease: Clawthorpe Hall from abbot of York. Plea T1532: tenement was traditionally endowment of the vic, not a lease. M1532: jury acquitted. * L102. Devon. John Thomas v. John Beauple of Marwood cl. £100. CP40/1073, m. 641d; CP40/1075, m. 233. Return that Beauple is beneficed in Marwood. * L103. Ebor. Richard Brandeley v. Oliver Blak of Ottringham. £40. CP40/1073, m. 39d. * L104. Ebor. Milo Fairfax v. Thomas Smythe of Kirkby in Cleveland cl. £40. CP40/1073, m. 493d; CP40/1074, m. 278. * L105. Lincs. William Betkuyse v. John Tharold of Holton cl. £40. CP40/1073, m. 206d; CP40/1074, m. 24. * L106. Lincs. William Betkuyse v. Henry Harwyk of Waithe cl. £40. CP40/1073, m. 207; CP40/1074, m. 24. * L107. Lincs. John Crowde v. Robert Luddington of Barnoldby, cl. £40. CP40/1073, m. 206d. * L108. Lincs. John Crowde v. John Creke of Wootton cl. £40. CP40/1073, m. 207. * L109. Norf. William Leve v. Thomas Kelke of Worstead cpn. £40. CP40/1073, m. 298. * L110. Norf. William Dey v. Thomas Draper of Wootton cl. £20. CP40/1073, m. 671. * L111. Sussex. John Gyttowe v. John Frankwell of Kirdford cl. £100. CP40/1073, m. 76d.

T1532

L112. Heref. Richard Caple v. John Dyrram cl v of Birley. £100. E159/311, m. 20. Lease: messuage. * L113. Staffs. John Smyth of Waterfall v. Richard Hall v of Ilam. £200. E159/311, m. 19. Lease: pasture. Plea M1532: insufficient glebe. M1533: AG joins issue. * L114. Worcs. Francis Graunt gen v. Thomas Adams cl v of Feckenham. £110. E159/311, m. 21. Lease: rec of Feckenham from prior of Sheen and other lands. Plea M1532: insufficient glebe. E1535: AG relinquishes the issue. Court deliberates into T1535. * L115. Cambs. John Grene v. Richard Marvyn of Castle Camps cl. £40. CP40/1074, m. 96d. * L116. Devon. Thomas Cullyng v. Richard Alyn of Clayhidon cl. £175. CP40/1074, m. 561d. Lease: land of vic of Colaton Raleigh. D appears. * L117. Ebor. Matthew Oglethorp v. Oswald Benson master of house of St. Robert of Knaresborough. £40. CP40/1074, m. 271d. * L118. Ebor. Richard Brandeley gen v. Richard Carter of Withernwick cl. £40. CP40/

1074, m. 278d; CP40/1076, m. 593d. * L119. Ebor. John Newton v. William Asheton of Nidd cl r of Nidd. £40. CP40/1074, m. 279d; CP40/1075, m. 450. Lease: chapel of Nidd from chapter of collegiate church of Ripon. Plea: rec is not worth £8. * L120. Ebor. Richard Brandeley v. William abbot of York. £40. CP40/1074, m. 280d. * L121. Ebor. Robert Foster v. Richard Hogeson of Hunsingore cl. £40. CP40/1074, m. 280d; CP40/1075, m. 261d; CP40/1076, m. 591. * L122. Ebor. John Wethereld v. Richard Beke of Osmotherley cl. £40. CP40/1074, m. 280d. * L123. Ebor. Richard Lassels v. William Roye of Yafforth cpn. £40. CP40/1074, m. 263d. * L124. Kingston. Robert Kemsey gen v. Prior of North Ferriby. £40. CP40/1074, m. 262. * L125. Leics. Richard Sherrard gen v. Thomas Derneley of Edmondthorpe cl r of Edmondthorpe. £40. CP40/1074, m. 198; CP40/1076, m. 357; CP40/1077, m. 157; CP40/1078, m. 483d. Lease: messuage. Issue: holding against the statute. E1534: jury acquits. * L126. Norf. Richard Brandeley v. Thomas Barnesdale of Riddlesworth (?) cpn. £30. CP40/1074, m. 691d. * L127. Norf. Richard Brandeley v. John Crofte of Riddlesworth (?) cpn. £30. CP40/1074, m. 691d. * L128. Norf. Richard Brandeley v. John Purpett of Riddlesworth (?) cl. £30. CP40/1074, m. 691d. * L129. Som. Robert Hyll v. John Alger of Bagborough cl. £178. CP40/1074, m. 353d; CP40/1079, m. 391. Lease: rec of Bishop's Lydeard from dean of Wells. D appears.

MI532

L130. Essex. John Lawrence v. John Pogmer of Farnham. £120. KB27/1085, m. 34. Lease: rec of Farnham. D was undefended. Full forfeiture plus £0.67 costs. * L131. Cheshire. John Cowstoke of London merchant tailor v. Richard Smith cl r of Bury (Lancs). £243.33. E159/311, m. 32. Lease: rec of Bangor from archdeacon of Richmond. Plea H1533: acting as agent of William Knight. Asked for release. H1534: issue joined. Process continued at least until H1535. * L132. Derbs. John Bugby of Edgerley (?) v. George Savage v of Castleton. £180. E159/311, m. 34. Lease: mill and land from the king. Plea H1533: as master of the hospital called Spitalhouse in the High Peak; hospital does not have lands to the value of £533.33; the lease is for maintenance of household and hospitality. Enrollment ends. * L133. Essex. Richard Plommer of London clothworker v. John Smyth cl resident canon of St. Pauls Cathedral. £210. E159/311, m. 29. Lease: manor of Chingford Hall from dean and chapter of St. Pauls Cathedral. Plea MI532: divestiture. Jury in H1533 with AG present acquits. * L134. Kent. John Otterbury king's messenger v. George Taylour cl v of Burham. £120. E159/311, m. 36. Lease: land and meadow, including land of rec of Burham. D dead in E1533. * L135. Sussex. John Cole of Bishopstone v. John Butler cl r of South Heighton. £150. E159/311, m. 30. Lease: land and meadow. Plea H1533: insufficient glebe. MI533: AG withdrew the suit. * L136. Sussex. Robert Duffeld yeoman v. Thomas Spere r of Stedham v of Cocking. £96. E159/311, m. 31. Lease: rec of Selham. Issue by AG in MI532: denial of holding. H1533: AG withdraws king's suit. * L137. Sussex. Robert Duffeld v. John Frankwell v of Kirdford. £96. E159/311, m. 35. Lease: rec of Kirdford from master and college of Arundell. Plea MI532: insufficient glebe. Court deliberates into H1533. * L138. Ebor. Robert Gybson v. George Lambe of Copgrove cl. £40. CP40/1075, m. 262; CP40/1079, m. 61. * L139. Ebor. Richard Brandeley gen v. William abbot of York. £40. CP40/1075, m. 665d. * L140. Ebor. Henry Nordaill v. Giles Parcor of Croft cl. £40. CP40/1075, m. 272d; CP40/1078, m. 201d. Lease: all tithes at Stapleton. D appears. * L141. Ebor. Richard Brandeley gen v. William abbot of York. £40. CP40/1075, m. 265d. * L142. Leics. John Stanesby gen v. John Johnson of Sewsterne cpn chantry priest of Sewsterne. £40. CP40/1075, m. 708. * L143. Lincs. Robert Arther v. Robert Luddyngton of Barnoldby cl. £40. CP40/1075, m. 30. * L144. Norf. Richard Brandeley v. Robert Webster of Roudham cl. £40. CP40/1075, m. 726. * L145. Norf. Christopher Heydon kt v. Peter Page of Saxthorpe cl. £230. CP40/1075, m. 736; CP40/1076, m. 686. * L146. Norf. Richard Heydon armiger v. Robert Waller of Burston cl. £230. CP40/1075, 736. * L147. Suff. Robert Asshefeld armiger v. John prior of Ixworth. £240. CP40/1075, m. 219d; CP40/1077, m. 605. Lease: pasture, meadow, woods. Plea: denial of holding against the statute. * L148. Suff. John Fyshe v. John Knoll of Earl Stonham cpn. £120. CP40/1075, m. 627d; CP40/1081, m. 436. Lease: rec of Elmswell. Issue: holding lease.

H1533

L149. Essex. Robert Brownyng of Gravesend (Kent) v. Robert Downys parish priest of Clavering. (maximum forfeiture for term would be £120). E159/311, m. 23. Lease: messuage, all tithes, oblations, and other profits of vic of Clavering. Process without appearance to T1533, reference to further process in files. * L150. Kent. John Foule of Halling gen v. Richard Lytylford v of Teynham. (maximum forfeiture for term would be £104). E159/311, m. 24. Lease: vic of Lynstead. Issue by AG in E1533: denial of lease. E1534 jury acquits. * L151. Essex. William Germen v. Henry Crosse cl r of Great Wigborough. £200. E159/311, m. 25. Lease: land. Issue by AG in T1533: holding against the statute. Verdict in E1535 with AG present: Crosse did not have or occupy, but took profits of £2. Judgment: forfeiture of £20. * L152. Norf. Gregory Castell gen v. Richard Roberts cl r of Burnham Norton. £24. E159/311, m. 26d. Lease: all tithes of grains pertaining to the church of Burnham Norton. Issue by AG in E1533: holding the lease. M1535: jury acquits. * L153. Devon. Peter Cole v. Thomas Thomson of Lifton cpn. £40. CP40/1076, m. 231. * L154. Ebor. William Lovett v. William Dybbe of Conisbrough cl. £40. CP40/1076, m. 216; CP40/1077, m. 572. Lease: land from prior of St. Pancras Lewes. Plea: denial holding against the statute. * L155. Ebor. Leonard Warcop v. Alvered prior of Nostel. £40. CP40/1076, m. 216; CP40/1077, m. 201d; CP40/1078, m. 210d. * L156. Ebor. Anthony Shorthose v. William abbot of York. £40. CP40/1076, m. 593d. * L157. Leics. Richard Bythemore gen v. Nicholas Page of Buckfastleigh cl v of Buckfastleigh. £120. CP40/1076, m. 448; CP40/1079, m. 660; CP40/1082, m. 188d. Lease for life: messuage abbot of Buckfastleigh. Plea: insufficient glebe. Issue: application to needs of household. * L158. Norf. Henry Dengayn v. John Bemont cl. £40. CP40/1076, m. 451. Lease:

land. * L159. Norf. Robert Langewade v. William Dale prior of St. Olave's Herringfleet. £40. CP40/1076, m. 501d; CP40/1077, m. 677d; CP40/1078, m. 319d. Lease: manor. D appeared. * L160. Norf. Francis Payn v. John Wynter of Tattersett cl. £40. CP40/1076, m. 663; CP40/1078, m. 502. Lease: land. D appeared. * L161. Norf. John Manser v. Adam Elward of Dersingham cl. £24. CP40/1076, m. 514; CP40/1079, mm. 160, 394. Lease: land. Issue: insufficient glebe. * L162. Som. Humfrey Walrond v. William Bassett of Mark cpn. £120. CP40/1076, m. 642d. [CP40/1078, m. 383d: Perhaps the continuation of the suit against Bassett.] * L163. Som. Thomas Arthur v. Thomas Dey of Lockyng cl. £100. CP40/1076, m. 231d. * L164. Som. Richard Bythemor v. John Conde of South Brent cl. £120. CP40/1076, m. 231d. * L165. Som. Humfrey Walrond (and John Hayne) v. William Vyncent [= Garnesby] of Creech cl v of Creech. £120. CP40/1076, m. 642d; CP40/1077, m. 224; CP40/1078, m. 78d. * L166. Staffs. William Rugeley v. Henry Hunte of Shenstone cl. £40. CP40/1076, m. 50d; CP40/1077, m. 628. Lease: messuage. D appeared. * L167. Suff. William Bumpsted v. Thomas Alkyn of Mutford cl. £80. CP40/1076, m. 681. Lease: messuage. D appeared. * L168. Suff. William Bumpsted v. Robert Lyngath of Corton cl. £80. CP40/1076, m. 69d; CP40/1078, m. 74.

E1533

L169. Essex. John Barker v. John Laurence v of Rainham. £83.33. E159/312, m. 19. Lease: land. T1532 demurrer; asked to be released. * L170. Essex. Robert Crawley v. Richard Glover v of Little Wakering. £104. E159/312, m. 16d. Lease: rec of Little Wakering from Hospital of St. Bartholomew in West Smithfield, London. Plea T1533: insufficient glebe. Asked for release. * L171. Staffs. John Brereton v. John abbot of Hulton. (maximum forfeiture). E1533: E159/312, m. 18. Lease: woods. Issue by AG in T1533: holding against the statute. Jury process into E1535. * L172. Worcs. John Whyler of Hallow tailor v. Walter Colyns v of Hallow. £100. E159/312, m. 20. Lease: tenements. Plea T1533: insufficient glebe. Court deliberates into M1533. * L173. Dorset. John Huchyns v. John Fletcher of Stockland cl. £20. CP40/1077, m. 230d; CP40/1078, m. 397d. * L174. Ebor. Richard Gilbert v. John Inglott cl. £40. CP40/1077, m. 613. Lease: land. Issue: holding against the statute. Apparently repleaded in M1533. * L175. Lincs. John Roberts v. Thomas Cur of Fleet cl. £40. CP40/1077, m. 30d; CP40/1079, m. 755; CP40/1082, m. 187. Lease: land. Issue: occupation in mode and form alleged. * L176. Norf. Henry Hubberd armiger v. William Curson of Garboldisham cl. £40. CP40/1077, m. 517; CP40/1083, m. 480d. Lease for life: lands. Issue: holding against the statute. * L177. Norf. Edward Beaupre armiger v. William Curson of Garboldisham cl. £40. CP40/1077, m. 517d; CP40/1083, m. 480d. Lease for life: lands. Issue: holding against the statute. * L178. Norf. John Davy v. Henry Taylour of Bressingham cl. £40. CP40/1077, m. 671d. * L179. Norf. Edward Wryght v. Ralph Butfeld of Roydon cpn. £80. CP40/1077, m. 673d. * L180. Norf. Humfrey Tyndall v. Thomas Chester of Little Fransham cl. £70. CP40/1077, m. 677. * L181. Som. William Brent armiger v. John Stayner of Puriton cl. £80. CP40/1077, m. 223; CP40/1078, m. 431. Lease: rec of Puriton from College of St. George of Windsor. D appeared. * L182. Som. Humfrey Walrond and John Hannam v. John Marlar of Ash Priors cl v of Nynehead. £120. CP40/1077, m. 223. * L183. Som. Humfrey Walrond v. William Mere of Heathfield farmer of Heathfield. £40. CP40/1077, m. 223d; CP40/1078, mm. 383d, 433d. Lease for life. D appeared.

TI533

L184. Surrey. Ralph Bayl v. Henry Hand of Morden cl v of Morden. £40. KB27/1088, m. 13; KB27/1089, m. 83. Lease: lands. Plea M1533: insufficient glebe. Issue joined. * L185. Middx. Thomas Byrde of the king's chapel gen v. Thomas Okborne one of the cpns of the chantry in Edmonton. £110. E159/312, m. 13. Lease: vic of Edmonton. Issue M1533: holding the lease. M1534: jury acquits. * L186. Northt. Edward Chamberleyn of Little Creaton yeoman v. Robert Palmer r of Great Creaton. £130. E159/312, m. 12. Lease: pasture. Plea M1533: insufficient glebe. M1535: jury acquits. * L187. Som. William Baker v. John Rowsewell cpn v of Marston Magna (?). £100. E159/312, m. 14. Lease: messuages from prioress of Polsloe. Plea T1533: insufficient glebe. Process into H1535. * L188. Devon. Robert Fyrebaron v. Thomas Brampford of Ermington cl chantry priest in Ermington St. Peter. £40. CP40/1078, m. 369d; CP40/1079, m. 659; CP40/1080, m. 173d. Lease: half rec of Ermington. Issue: application of profits only for household and hospitality. * L189. Dorset. John Locke v. Thomas Walterboye of Bryanston cl. £80. CP40/1078, m. 390; CP40/1079, m. 192. * L190. Dorset. Thomas Locke v. John Cleke of Stour Weston cl. £80. CP40/1078, m. 390; CP40/1079, m. 192. * L191. Gloc. Arthur Kemys v. John Barlowe dean of college Holy Trinity at Westbury-on-Trym. £40. CP40/1078, m. 434. Lease: park and farm from bishop of Worcester. D appeared. * L192. Norf. John Colvile v. George Nuby of Repps cl. £40. CP40/1078, m. 188; CP40/1079, m. 744. * L193. Norf. William Bradford v. Henry Threkston of Middle Harling cpn. £80. CP40/1078, m. 193. * L194. Norf. Stephen Shurdlowe v. Robert Ferrand of Wilby cpn. £40. CP40/1078, m. 193. * L195. Norf. John Manser v. Aldam Elward of Dersingham cl. £80. CP40/1078, m. 662. * L196. Som. Humfrey Walrond v. Peter Lane of Over (Lower?) Weare cpn. £120. CP40/1078, m. 598d. * L197. Som. Thomas Locke v. Irranus Nasshe of Fivehead cl. £80. CP40/1078, m. 667d. * L198. Suff. Thomas Bakon v. John Sponer of South Cove cl. £40. CP40/1078, mm. 61, 78; CP40/1082, m. 183d. Lease: land. Process to a jury summons.

MI533

L199. Som. Henry Grenfelde and William Bursey v. Nicholas Gillet v of Muchelney. £230. E159/312, m. 36. Lease: pasture from abbess of Muchelney. Plea M1533: insufficient glebe. Issue by AG in M1534: application of profits for household and hospitality. M1535: jury acquits. * L200. Som. Henry Grenfelde and William Bursey v. Nicholas Gillet v of Muchelney. £38. E159/312, m. 37. Lease: rec of Muchelney. Plea M1533: insufficient glebe;

denial that he did not take the proceeds for his own use for the period of a month. H1534: AG demurs. E1534: plea insufficient in law. Forfeiture: £38; order for inquest to ascertain the profits. * L201. Suff. William Baker gen v. Richard Iden of Sudbury archdeacon of Middlesex. £238.33. E159/312, m. 35. Lease: watermills from Catherine dowager princess. Process without appearance into M1534. * L202. York city. Ralph Sympson v. John Dean. £50. E159/312, m. 34. Lease: parish church of York St. Mary Bishophill Senior. Issue by AG in H1534: holding the lease. M1536: jury acquits. * L203. Dorset. Giles More gen v. Richard Martyn of Winfrith cl. £60. CP40/1079, m. 191d. * L204. Ebor. Richard Thomson v. Richard Moer of Rillington cl. £40. CP40/1079, m. 205. * L205. Ebor. John Ingram v. John Lygtseite of Ripon cl. £80. CP40/1079, m. 695. L206. Ebor. John Mawde v. Robert Ward of Ilkley cpn. £40. CP40/1079, m. 699; CP40/1080, m. 155. Lease: close. Issue joined. * L206. Lincs. Edmund Wright v. William Smyth of Washingborough cpn. £80. CP40/1079, m. 28. * L207. Norf. Thomas Wellys v. James May of Walpole cpn. £80. CP40/1079, m. 746. * L208. Norf. Richard Gilbert v. John Inglott of Burlingham. £40. CP40/1079, m. 599. Lease: land. D appeared. * L209. Suff. Henry Parker v. John Burton of Nedging cl. £40. CP40/1079, m. 804. * L210. Suff. Henry Parker v. John Cley of Whatfield cl. £40. CP40/1079, m. 804. * L211. Suff. John Fyshe v. William Wright of Rickinghall Inferior cpn. £120. CP40/1079, m. 805d. * L212. Suff. Peter Broun v. Alan Chenerey of Cockfield cpn. £80. CP40/1079, m. 602d. Lease: land. D appeared. * L213. Suff. Richard Clerke v. Robert Thompson of Copdock cl. £40. CP40/1079, m. 649. Lease: land. D appeared. * L214. Wilts. Nicholas Hamond v. William Stevyn of Codford St. Mary cl. £80. CP40/1079, m. 279. * L215. Worcs. John Stokedale v. Thomas Wolaston of Pershore cpn. £40. CP40/1079, m. 551; CP40/1082, m. 187. Lease: pasture. Issue: taking profits. M1534: jury acquits.

H1534

L216. Norf. Milo Groose gentleman v. John Wryght r of half of Scarning. £200. KB27/1090, m. 69. Lease: land. Plea: insufficient glebe. M1534: jury acquits. * L217. Devon. William Symons yeoman v. John Pawle cl. £120. E159/312, m. 17. Lease: manor. Issue by AG: holding the lease. M1535: jury acquits. * L218. Kent. Roger Holford v. Elizabeth prioress of Dartford. £600. E159/312, m. 20. Lease: manor and rec of Dartford from bishop of Rochester. Demurrer on total value of lands held by priory and long holding of the lease. Court to be advised into H1535. * L219. Norf. Robert Moseley v. John Adkok r of Hingham. £340. E159/312, m. 19. Lease: pasture. Plea T1534: insufficient glebe. Court deliberates into T1535. * L220. Norf. Edward Ferrour gen v. Robert Elvered (= Skynner) r of Gressenhall. E159/312, m. 22. Lease: portion of tithes from Gressenhall, Hoe, and Bittering from prior of Castle Acre. Issue M1534: holding the lease. E1536 verdict: he held the tithes for 6 wks. taking issues of £0.05. Forfeiture of £12.50. * L221. Wilts. Robert Cowslad v. John Dowce v of Whiteparish. £60. E159/312, m. 21. Lease: rec of Whiteparish. Issue by AG in T1534: holding the lease. In M1534 AG withdraws the king's suit. * L222. Worcs. Richard Bradeley of Bromsgrove v. John Clerk r of Belbroughton. £360. E159/312, m. 18. Lease: lands, pasture. Issue E1534: insufficient glebe. E1535: jury acquits. * L223. Berks. John Blaste v. Richard Heley of Stratfield Mortimer cl. £60. CP40/1080, m. 71d. * L224. Derbs. Robert Dingley v. John Barrett of Bradbourne. £240. CP40/1080, m. 674d. * L225. Devon. John Wychehalse and John Redgate v. Thomas Valans cl v of Heavitree. £40. CP40/1080, m. 280. * L226. Ebor. James Robinson v. Edward Person of Skipwith cl. £40. CP40/1080, m. 203d. * L227. Ebor. William Levet v. Henry abbot of Roche. £40. CP40/1080, m. 208; CP40/1081, m. 202; CP40/1082, m. 211. Lease: messuages from prioress of Arthington. D appeared. * L228. Ebor. James Rokeby v. Robert Elesyng of Kirkby Ravensworth. £40. CP40/1080, m. 209. Incomplete enrollment. * L229. Ebor. Roland Tode v. John Wod of Kilvington cl. £40. CP40/1080, m. 220. * L230. Hants. William Smythwyke v. William Douned of Stratfield Saye cl. £120. CP40/1080, m. 513. * L231. Herts. Nicholas Norres v. Henry Johnson cl v of Amwell. £20. CP40/1080, m. 635. * L232. Norf. Hugh Bryket v. Nicholas Bothe cl r of Saxlingham. £40. CP40/1080, m. 418; CP40/1081, m. 409. Lease: lands from prior of Mount Grace. Issue: use of all proceeds for household and hospitality. * L233. Norf. Christopher Herward v. Nicholas Bothe cl r of Saxlingham. £40. CP40/1080, m. 418d; CP40/1081, m. 502. Lease: lands from prior of Mount Grace. Issue: application of all proceeds to household and hospitality. * L234. Norf. Thomas Coke v. William Stratwayth of Narford cl r of Narford. £100. CP40/1080, m. 518; CP40/1081, m. 519; CP40/1082, m. 191d. Lease: lands from prior of West Acre. Issue: application of all proceeds only for hospice and hospitality. * L235. Suff. Christopher Wylkynson v. William Towneshend of Finningham cl. £100. CP40/1080, m. 474. * L236. Suff. Henry Parker v. John Hudson of Brettenham cl. £40. CP40/1080, m. 475. * L237. Sussex. John Herberd v. William Childe of Goring (?) cl. £80. CP40/1080, m. 186. * L238. Sussex. William Paye v. Alexander Harryson r of Ford. £60. CP40/1080, m. 195; CP40/1081, m. 511. Lease: Cudlow chapel. Issue: application of all proceeds to household and hospitality. * L239. Wilts. John Arnold v. Edward Elys of Sherston. £80. CP40/1080, mm. 18d, 350; CP40/1082, m. 197; CP40/1083, m. 475; CP40/1086, m. 376d. Lease: "rec" of Pinkney. Issue: holding against the statute. * L240. Wilts. Thomas Chafyn v. John Swynnerton of Mere cl. £80. CP40/1080, m. 247; CP40/1081, m. 176; CP40/1082, m. 199. * L241. Worcs. John Stokdale v. Richard More of Inkberrow cl v of Inkberrow. £40. CP40/1080, m. 297d; CP40/1085, m. 101d. Lease: pasture. Issue: application of all proceeds to household and hospitality.

E1534

L242. Notts. William Frenshe v. William Stanley. £40. KB27/1091, m. 62. Lease: fishery. Issue: holding against the form of the statute. E1536: jury convicted. Forfeiture of £40, damages of £0.33, costs of £1. Statutory pardon eliminated the £20 due the king. * L243. Cornub. John Wayte of Exeter v. Richard Robyns cl r of Warleggan. £120.

E159/313, m. 16. Lease: lands. Issue by AG in T1534: insufficient glebe. Jury process into MI535. * L244. Ebor. Thomas Boswell of "Buknam Castle" (Norf) gen v. Leonard Lynley v of Beighton (Derbs). £460. E159/313, m. 15. Lease: pasture. Issue by AG in T1534: insufficient glebe. E1536: jury acquits. * L245. Essex. John Grene of "Reddeswell" v. William Hebbys v of Great Maplestead. E159/313, m. 21. Lease: rec of Maplestead from abbot of Statford Langthorne. MI534: D demurs. Asked for release. * L246. Kent. James Brascha v. Hugh Fryssyll r of Kenardington. E159/313, m. 12. * L247. Lease: meadows and pastures. Plea T1534: insufficient glebe. He asked release. * L248. Norf/Suff. Edward Todd v. James Calvord v (or r) of Whitlingham (?). £102. E159/313, m. 20. Lease: rec of Great Waldingfield (Suff). Issue by AG in MI534: holding the lease. Jury process into E1540. * L249. Northt. Thomas Knight gen v. John Smyth r of Brackley. £160. E159/313, m. 19. Lease: messuage. Issue by AG in T1534: holding against the statute. E1536: jury acquits. * L250. Notts. Randolf Jaxson (= Chester) and Simon Cales v. John Fynnys cl guardian of the chantry in Clifton. £110. E1534: E159/313, m. 17. Lease: messuage. Issue by AG in T1534: holding the lease. MI536: jury acquits. * L251. Suff. William Welham of Horningsheath hus v. John Gryffith r of Great Horningsheath. £120. E159/313, m. 14. Lease: meadow, pasture. Issue T1534: insufficient glebe. He asked release. * L252. Warw. Robert Sheperd of Chilvers Coton yeoman v. John Kelderman v of Chilvers Coton. £110. E159/313, m. 18. Lease: pasture, tenement, part from Hospital of St. John of Jerusalem in England. Plea T1534: insufficient glebe. Asked for release. * L253. Worcs. Nicholas Robynson v. Thomas Calcott of Hampton Hampton Lovett chantry priest of Hampton Lovett. £300. E159/313, m. 13. Lease: meadow. Plea T1534: insufficient glebe. Asked for release. * L254. Suff. Edward Todd v. John Lyes v of Acton. £102. E159/313, m. 22. Lease: rec of Acton. Issue T1534: holding against the form of the statute. MI539: jury acquits. Sine die. * L255. Berks. Robert Sobyn v. Richard Heldy of Stratford Mortimer cl. £60. CP40/1081, m. 163d. * L256. Essex. Thomas Josselyn v. Robert Knokstubbe of High Roding cpn. £40. CP40/1081, m. 377; CP40/1082, m. 12. D appeared. * L257. Norf. William Candeler v. Edmund Clerke of Tofts Monks cpn v of Tofts Monks. £80. CP40/1081, m. 447; CP40/1083, m. 478; CP40/1084, m. 22. Lease for life: rec of Tofts Monks from prior of Lewes. Issue: insufficient glebe. * L258. Suff. Edward Bullen kt v. John Alye of Acton cl. £80. CP40/1081, m. 194; CP40/1082, m. 105. Lease: rec of Acton from prior of Hatfield Peverel. Issue: holding against the statute. * L259. Wilts. Robert Temmys v. Thomas Baker (= Horton) of Calne cl. £80. CP40/1081, m. 177d; CP40/1085, m. 101. Suit withdrawn. * L260. Worcs. John Walsyngham v. John bishop of Poletensis abbot of Pershore. £120. CP40/1081, m. 487. Case started earlier than this term.

T1534

L261. Cornub. William Carvannell valet of the guard of the king v. James Gentyll cl provost of college of St. Thomas near Penryn. £120. E159/313, m. 10. Lease: pasture. * L262. Staffs. Gabriel Joslyn v. Hugh Sheldon. £110. E159/313, m. 11. Lease: lands. Plea

MI534: insufficient glebe. EI535: AG joined issue. MI536: jury acquits. * L263. Gloc. John Kyrkeby of Lechlade yeoman v. Edward Watton v of Lechlade. £20. EI59/313, m. 5. Lease: tenements from church wardens of Lechlade and from Anne queen of England; tithes of hay of rec of Alvescot. Issue by AG in MI534: denial of holding most; insufficient glebe. EI535: jury acquits. * L264. Staffs. Francis Stedeman yeoman v. Henry Flemyng cl v of Brewood. £120. EI59/313, m. 6. Lease: pasture, tenement. Plea EI534: insufficient glebe. Asked to be released. * L265. Cheshire. William Holynzed gen v. John Trafford cpn. £110. EI59/313, m. 7. * L266. Lease: rec of Barrow. Issue by AG in MI534: holding against the statute. The order for a jury was incomplete. * L267. Cornub. William Carvannell valet of the king's household v. James Gentyll cl provost of college of St. Thomas near Penryn. £120. EI59/313, m. 8. Lease: lands. Plea TI534: insufficient glebe. Asked to be released. MI534: AG joined issue. Jury process into EI545. * L268. Suff. Edward Todd v. John Lyes cl v of Acton. £110. EI59/313, m. 9. Lease: lands. Plea TI534: insufficient glebe. Asked to be released. * L269. Lincs. John Starky v. Martin Roos of High Toynton cl. £80. CP40/1082, m. 23d. * L270. Lincs. Anthony Porter v. Martin Rouse of High Toynton cl. £100. CP40/1082, m. 30; CP40/1083, m. 630. Lease: house, barn, lands. Issue: holding the lease. * L271. Northt. Edward Phillips v. Richard Leycetur of Preston Capes cl. £80. CP40/1082, m. 51. * L272. Nørf. George Castell v. William Isbellye of Tac-olneston cl. £26.67. CP40/1082, m. 609. * L273. Norf. Thomas Pakeman v. John Lodge of Hanworth cl. £80. CP40/1082, m. 609d; CP40/1083, m. 704. * L274. Norf. Edward Warner gen v. Thomas Falke of Mundford cl. £80. CP40/1082, m. 393d. * L275. Norf. Roger Goslyng v. Thomas Draper cl. £40. CP40/1082, m. 368. Lease: pasture from abbot of Langley. D appeared. * L276. Norf. Edward Warner gen v. Thomas Falke of Mundford cl. £80. CP40/1082, m. 393d. (second suit). * L277. Staffs. Thomas Rowley v. John Nevall of Brewood cpn. £40. CP40/1082, m. 44; CP40/1083, mm. 43d, 720. The case began somewhat earlier. * L278. Worcs. John Freman v. William More prior of Worcester. £80. CP40/1082, 403d.

MI534

L279. Cheshire. Robert Jonys of the king's chapel gentleman v. John abbot of Chester. £110. EI59/313, m. 22. Lease: pasture from Hospital of St. John in Chester. Plea MI534: denial of holding or taking profits against the statute. * L280. Ebor. William Thompson of Owthorne v. Richard Bolton v of Owthorne. £96. EI59/313, m. 21. Lease: rec of Owthorne from abbot of Kirkstall. Issue by AG plea EI535: occupation in mode and form. MI535: jury acquits. * L281. Ebor. John Barton of Whenby armiger v. William Franklyn prebendary of Stillington. £110. EI59/313, m. 23. Lease: pasture and enclosure from prior of Merton. Issue by AG in HI535: insufficient glebe. MI535: jury acquits. * L282. Ebor. John Barton of Whenby v. Launcelot Colynson treasurer of York cathedral. £110. EI59/313, m. 24d. Lease: close. Plea HI535: insufficient glebe. Asked to be released. * L283. Heref. John Peryll of Hereford v. Miles Jeffes v of Yersland. £102. EI59/313, m. 27d.

Lease: rec of Yersland (*sic*) from prior of Sheen. Issue by AG in E1535: holding against the statute. H1536: jury acquits. * L284. Heref. John Peryll of Hereford gen v. David Richards v of Lugwardine. £112. E159/313, m. 28. Lease: rec of Lugwardine. Plea E1535: denial of holding against the statute. E1537: jury acquits. * L285. Heref. John Peryll of Hereford gen v. David Richards v of Lugwardine. £120. E159/313, m. 29. Lease: land. Plea E1535: insufficient glebe. Asked for release. * L286. Notts. Thomas Milner (Rouge Dragon) gen v. Jullian Crosby r of Leike. £110. E159/313, m. 31. Lease: tenement. * L287. Oxon. William Marten v. Thomas Robynson. £34. E159/313, m. 22. Lease: rec of Minster Lovell from college of Eton. * L288. Suff. Richard Thurston, Walter Sydaye, John More v. Richard Iden master or provost of Sudbury College. £100. E159/313, m. 25. Lease: mills and house from Anne queen of England. Plea H1535: denial of holding in the mode and form. * L289. Wilts. Nicholas Udall of Milborne Port yeoman v. Simon Hyll of Bulbridge in suburb of Wilton v of Bulbridge. £50. E159/313, m. 31. Lease: pasture. Plea M1534: insufficient glebe. Asked to be released. Court to be advised into H1535. * L290. Berks. Robert Stevyn v. Richard Hely of Stratford Mortimer cl v of Stratford Mortimer. £60. CP40/1083, m. 793; CP40/1084, m. 581d; CP40/1086, m. 363d. Lease: rec of Stratford Mortimer. Issue: holding against the statute. * L291. Devon. Thomas Redgate v. Thomas Valance of Heavitree. £40. CP40/1083, m. 603. Lease: pasture from abbot of Tavistock. Issue: holding against the statute. * L292. Dorset. Oliver Lubbons v. John Poskyn of Stalbridge cl. £80. CP40/1083, m. 191d. * L293. Ebor. Thomas Craven v. John Hastynges of Bainton cl. £40. CP40/1083, m. 216. * L294. Ebor. Thomas Leton v. Lawrence Wright of Crathorne cl. £40. CP40/1083, m. 220d. * L295. Ebor. Ralph Babthorp v. George Peryn parson of Skellow cpn. £50. CP40/1083, m. 683. * L296. Gloc. Thomas Bell v. John Carter of Alderton cl. £20. CP40/1083, mm. 555d, 645; CP40/1084, m. 568. Lease: messuage. * L297. Hants. Fulk Walwyn v. John Lee of Stratfield Turgis cl. £80. CP40/1083, m. 243; CP40/1086, m. 527. Suit started earlier than this term. Lease for life: close. D appeared. * L298. Heref. Thomas Leyghton v. Henry Walker of Hereford cl. £40. CP40/1083, m. 268d. * L299. Kent. Andrew Swayne v. Richard Forde of Okeryge cl. £40. CP40/1083, m. 760d. * L300. Kent. John Barham v. John Edward of Challock cpn. £40. CP40/1083, m. 283d; CP40/1084, m. 537d; CP40/1085, m. 56d. * L301. Kent. John Foule v. John Lytylford of Kingsdown. £40. CP40/1083, m. 289d. Suit started earlier than this term. * L302. Norf. John Dey v. John Percival of Grimston cl. £40. CP40/1083, m. 315; CP40/1084, m. 569d; CP40/1086, m. 369d. Lease: messuage. Issue: holding against the statute. * L303. Norf. William Hubberd v. Henry Aleyns of Aylsham Burgh cl. £300. CP40/1083, m. 705. * L304. Northt. John Webster v. William Sherman of Maxey cl. £40. CP40/1083, mm. 50d, 722d. * L305. Som. Nicholas Walrond v. William Bery of Taunton v of Taunton St. Mary Magdalene. £80. CP40/1083, m. 552. Lease: rec of Taunton St. Mary Magdalene from prior of Taunton. Issue: holding after the statute. * L306. Som. Nicholas Waldron v. William Bery of Taunton cl v of Taunton St. Mary Magdalene. £80. CP40/1083, m. 353. D appeared. * L307. Suff. Thomas Barnes gen and Thomas Audeley gen v. John Coppyng cl. CP40/1073, m. 756. Suit withdrawn.

H1535

L308. Dorset. John Perkyns v. William Peson of Closworth cl. £30. cp40/1084, m. 275; cp40/1088, m. 261d. Lease: prebend of Lyme from college of Leicester rendering £14 annually. * L309. Gloc. Reginald Jevyns v. Robert Jones of Eton cl r of Eton. £100. cp40/1084, m. 505; cp40/1085, m. 406d. Lease: rec of Longhope from prior of Monmouth. Issue: holding against the statute. * L310. Gloc. Roland Long v. Robert Jones of Eton cl r of Eton. £20. cp40/1084, m. 508d.; cp40/1085, m. 406 (2nd). Lease for life: rec of Longhope from prior of Monmouth. Issue: holding against the statute.

E1535

L311. Norf. John Dey of Gressenhall v. Nicholas Marche (= Marshall) r of East Bilney. £50. e159/314, m. 8. Lease: pasture. Issue by AG in T1535: holding against the statute. M1536: jury acquits. * L312. Notts. Thomas Milner (Rouge Dragon) gen v. Julian Crosby r of Leake. £60. e159/314, m. 12. Lease: land. Issue by AG in T1535: holding the lease. Jury process into H1536. * L313. Notts. Thomas Milner (Rouge Dragon) gen v. William Stanley cl r of Sutton Bonington St. Anne. £12. e159/314, m. 17. Lease: half rec of Sutton Bonington St. Anne. Issue by AG in T1535: holding in mode and form. Jury process into E1536. * L314. Notts. Thomas Milner of London (Rouge Dragon) gen v. Robert Holt cl v of Wysall. £60. e159/314, m. 12d. Lease: lands from various people. Plea T1535 for part he did not hold against the statute; for part insufficient glebe. Asked to be released. E1536: AG joins issue. Jury process into T1545. * L315. Oxon. William Weston of Banbury mercer v. John Bradford of Bodicote spiritual person. £60. e159/314, m. 10. Lease: lands from bishop of Winchester. Issue in T1535: holding against the statute. E1541: jury convicts. * L316. Cornub. John Lenne v. Richard Benett of St. Teath cl r of St. Teath. £40. cp40/1085, m. 112; cp40/1086, mm. 371d, 570l; cp40/1088, m. 630. Lease: messuage. Issue: application of all to household and hospitality. E1536: plaintiff withdrew suit after the jury came back but before delivery of verdict. * L317. Essex. William Gaywod v. William Ward of Fordham cpn. £80. cp40/1085, m. 24. * L318. Heref. Alexander Whyttyngton gen v. Thomas Wotton of Marden cl v of Marden. £40. cp40/1085, m. 495d (2nd); cp40/1086, m. 576; cp40/1088, m. 658. Lease: rec of Marden from dean and chapter of Hereford. Issue: holding against the statute. * L319. Kent. John Wyllote v. John Harryson of Hackington. £40. cp40/1085, m. 295d (2nd).

T1535

L320. Devon. John Witherigge of Pilton v. John Belamy r of Kentisbury. £80. e159/314, m. 21. Lease: enclosures. Plea M1535: insufficient glebe and that he is r of both Kentisbury and Heanton Punchardon and he keeps hospitality at Heanton Punchardon; AG joins issue. Jury process into E1546. * L321. Dorset. Robert Coke of Rye sherman

v. Matthew Crosse v of Coombe Keynes. £70. E159/314, m. 22d. Lease: rec of Coombe Keynes from prior of Merton. Issue by AG in MI536: holding against the statute. Jury process into HI536. * L322. Durham. George Whelplay v. Richard Gasby cl. £66. E159/314, m. 22. Lease: rec of Gateshead. MI535: D demurs. Asked to be released. * L323. Kent. Thomas Derby v. Elizabeth prioress of Dartford. £113.33. E159/314, m. 16. Lease: manor of Dartford with rec from bishop of Rochester. Plea MI535: she does not have any rec with care of souls; the priory had that lease long before the statute and does not have over £533.33 in revenue. * L324. Norf. Thomas Cok of Weasenham v. William Sterthewayth of Narborough v of Narborough and Narford. £80. E159/314, m. 18. Lease: land from prior of West Acre. Plea MI535: insufficient glebe. Asked to be released. Margination: he is dead. * L325. Suff. Walter Sydaye of Sudbury wax chandler v. Richard Iden master or provost of Sudbury College. £70. E159/314, m. 20. Lease: house. HI536: D demurs. * L326. Bucks. John Compton v. Robert Hansom of Little Missenden cl. £60. CP40/1086, m. 478d. * L327. Dorset. John Lovell v. John Steyner of Tarrant Gunville cl. £80. CP40/1086, m. 672d. * L328. Norf. Anthony Callibut v. Thomas prior of Castle Acre. £240. CP40/1086, m. 506. Lease: lands. Plea: exception for religious houses with proceeds under £533.33. Issue: application of all proceeds only for household and hospitality. * L329. Oxon. Robert Squyer v. John Pereson of Stanton Harcourt cl v of Stanton Harcourt. £40. CP40/1086, m. 465. * L330. Salop. John Heley v. William Colbrond of Astley Abbots cl. £40. CP40/1086, m. 46. * L331. Staffs. Richard Forster v. John Couper of Wolverhampton cl. £40. CP40/1086, m. 56. Lease: land. D appeared. * L332. Suff. John Holmes v. William Bergh of Little Saxham cl r of Little Saxham. £80. CP40/1086, m. 670; CP40/1087, mm. 392, 607; CP40/1088, m. 510. Lease: portion of rec of Fornham All Sts. Issue: holding against the statute.

MI535

L333. Cumber. John Senhouse of Frizington gen v. Robert Symm of Camerton. £120. E159/314, m. 24. Lease: lands. Issue by AG in HI536: holding against the statute. * L334. Cumber. John Senhouse of Frizington gen v. Charles Martendale r of Moresby. £120. E159/314, m. 25. Lease: enclosure. Issue by AG in EI536: insufficient glebe. Jury process into TI545. * L335. Cumber. John Senhowse of Frizington gentleman v. Edward Metcalf r of Egremont. £120. E159/314, m. 24d. Lease: land. Issue by AG in EI536: holding the lease. Jury process into MI536. * L336. Hants. Thomas Parry gen v. Henry Broke prior of St. Swithins Winchester. £120. E159/314, m. 21. Lease: pasture from bishop of Winchester. Appearance in HI536; process into EI536. * L337. Hants. Thomas Parry gen v. Henry Broke prior of St. Swithins Winchester. £120. E159/314, m. 28. Lease: pasture from bishop of Winchester. Appearance in HI536. * L338. Lincs. Robert Bell of North Witham v. John Comberige r of Colsterworth. £360. E159/314, m. 27. Lease: enclosures from various lessors including prioress of Catley and master of college of Fotheringhay. Issue by AG in HI536: insufficient glebe. Process into TI545. * L339. Middx. Thomas

Greyngham v. William Maior prior of house or hospital of St. Mary Spittle. £120. E159/314, m. 20. Lease: pasture from bishop of London. Issue by AG in T1536: application of all proceeds for maintenance and sustenance. Process into T1545. * L340. Staffs. John Thorley yeoman v. Nicholas Whelocke cl v of Biddulph. £110. E159/314, m. 16d. Lease: pasture. 21 May 1536: Issue by AG on not guilty plea to assaulting person delivering the writ and insufficient glebe defense. Process into T1545. * L341. Suff. Edward Hygham v. John Wryghtington cl v of Gazeley. £120. E159/314, m. 29. Lease: land. Issue in E1536: for most denial of holding; insufficient glebe. E1537: jury acquits. * L342. Sussex. Rex v. Alexander Shaa v of Pagham. £236. E159/314, m. 36. Indictment from 10/29/32 for lease of rec of Pagham from prior of Christ Church Canterbury and sale of various goods at markets and fairs taking the profits for himself. Plea: divestiture. * L343. Sussex. Rex v. Robert Wylson v of Washington. £328. E159/314, m. 36d. Indictment from 10/29/32 for lease of rec of Washington and sale of grain for profit. Wylson is reported dead. * L344. Ebor. Lawrence Norton v. John Robynsson of Knaresborough cl. £40. CP40/1087, m. 90; CP40/1088, mm. 199d, 206. Suit began earlier than this term. * L345. Heref. John Williams v. John Beale of Ullingswick cl r of Ullingswick. £40. CP40/1087, m. 551. Lease for life: messuage and lands in part from abbot of Gloucester. Issue: application of all proceeds to household and hospitality. * L346. London. William Saule v. Thomas Smyth of Kirkham cl. £40. CP40/1087, m. 636d. * L347. Wilts. Anthony Bonham v. William Breton of Nettleton cl. £60. CP40/1087, m. 371. * L348. Wilts. James Smith v. Nicholas Hobbys of Chirton cl. £40. CP40/1087, m. 371. * L349. Suff. Edward Higham gen v. John Wrightyngton of Gazeley cl. £80. CP40/1087, m. 392; CP40/1088, m. 507d. Lease: land. D appeared.

H1536

L350. Ebor. William Walker of London v. John Stowtheley v of Ledsham. £110. E159/314, m. 21. Lease: lands from prior of Pontefract. Issue by AG in T1536: insufficient glebe. M1537: jury acquits. * L351. Ebor. Osward Wilstrop kt v. William Collyn of Bickerton cl. £120. E159/314, m. 26. Lease: enclosure. * L352. Gloc. Richard Snappe v. William abbot of Gloucester. £120. E159/314, m. 23d. Lease: lands and tenements. Plea E1537: the abbey did not have more than £533.33 in revenue; the abbot keeps hospitality at Brynknashe manor in Gloucester and does not have sufficient glebe. Asked to be released. Margination that he is dead. * L353. Heref. Thomas Ambler yeoman v. Robert Bawdwyn of Brimfield cl and spiritual person. E159/314, m. 22. Lease: lands and tenements from abbot of Reading. Suit still active in T1545. * L354. Heref. Phillip Scarlett of Leominster (?) yeoman v. Henry Carres v of Lingen. £120. E159/314, m. 25. Lease: tenement and lands. D jailed for contempt. Plea T1536: he is not v of Lingen mode and form. * L355. Kent. Alexander Hyll v. Robert Frankeshe v of All Saints in Hoo. £110. E159/314, m. 23. Lease: land. Issue by AG in E1536: holding lease. T1537: AG abandoned the issue and demurred on the sufficiency of the plea. Suit still active in T1545. * L356. Leics. Jerome Lynne gen v. Thomas Ratclyff master of St. Burton Lazar. £120. E159/314, m. 24. Lease: lands from abbot of Vaudey in 1492. Margination that Ratclyff is dead. M. 31: a letter patent to Ratclyff for holding the lease and for all breaches of the 1529 statutes sealed with the private seal and with the authority of parliament, signed by Cromwell. * L357. Beds. Thomas Grendon v. Roland Clerke of Langford cl. £40. CP40/1088, m. 668d. * L358. Bucks. John Poley v. Edward Skynner of Sherington cpn. £40. CP40/1088, m. 668d. Suit started earlier than this term. * L359. Hants. William Cheke v. Roland Ferrer of Hannington cl. £80. CP40/1088, m. 448d. * L360. Lincs. John Jamys v. Christopher Spencer of Heningby cpn. £40. CP40/1088, m. 36. * L361. London. Nicholas Fytton v. William Peers of Little Hereford cl. £40. CP40/1088, m. 617. * L362. Norf. Robert Mathewe v. John Makyn of Clippesby, cl r of Clyppesby and Billockby. £40. CP40/1088, m. 423; CP40/1093, m. 506. Lease: lands. Issue: application of all proceeds to household and hospitality. T1537: jury returned that he had sufficient glebe and demesne and he took £0.05 in profits, that is, 3d each month for 4 mos. Forfeiture £40.50. * L363. Norf. William Boleyn cl v. Edmund Skyte of Blickling cl. £80. CP40/1088, m. 574d. * L364. Norf. Gregory Catell gen v. Brian Lucas of Holme Hale cl. £40. CP40/1088, m. 575d. * L365. Norf. William Boleyn cl v. Henry Aleyns of Aylsham Burgh cl. £8 (sic). CP40/1088, m. 577d. * L366. Staffs. Thomas Smalley v. William Sylfeld of Barre cpn. £40. CP40/1088, m. 53. * L367. Suff. John Heydon v. Robert (?) Whityng of Cowlinge cpn. £40. CP40/1088, m. 680. * L368. Wilts. Anthony Bonham v. William Creton of Nettleton cl. £40. CP40/1088, m. 199d.

Residence

H1531

R1. Cambs. Richard Flower v. Robert Johnson r of Wentworth. £30. E159/309, m. 19d. Absence: 9/29/30 1530 to 2/18/31. AG active. E1536: jury acquits.

E1531

R2. Essex. John Williams v. Thomas Green cl r of Ginge at Stone. £50. E159/310, m. 21. Absence: 9/29/30 for 5 mos. by residing at St. Albans. Pardon for Canterbury province claimed for offenses up until 3/10/31. Ad judicium. * R3. Warw. John Byrtt valet of king's ward v. Richard Ryle cl v of Honington. £60. E159/310, m. 20d. Absence: 11/11/31 to 3/21/32; 4/12/32 to 5/17/32. Continued into E1532. * R4. Norf. Alan Ryce v. William Pratt cl r of Cantley. £40. KB27/1079, m. 28d. Absence: 9/29/30 for 4 mos. by residing at Stratford Bow St. Mary (Middx). Issue: residence.

T1531

R5. Norf. Richard Holbroke v. Thomas Clerk r of Diss. E159/310, m. 18. Absence: 10/1/30 to 11/18/30. Claim pardon for province of Canterbury; request for release. * R6. Salop. Peter Hyggyns v. John Hogeys r of Hanwode. E159/310, m. 10. Absence: 9/29/30 to 7/6/31 from Hanwode and also from rec of Cardeston and prebend of St. David in Shrewsbury. Denial of being r of Cardeston and prebendary of St. David. Issue by AG: continual residence at Hanwode. Jury in E1533 verdict: continually resident at Shelton in collegiate church of St. Chad. No forfeiture mentioned. * R7. Salop. Peter Hyggyns v. John ap David r of St. Nicholas de la More. T1531: E159/310, m. 15. Absence: 9/29/30 to 7/6/31 (?). Plea: he was v of Cleobury St. Swithin and r of St. Nicholas de la More; he was continually resident at Cleobury. E1534: jury acquits. * R8. Suff. Robert Cove gen v. Robert Towar of Scottow cl. £20. KB27/1080, m. 3. * R9. Surrey. William Brokett of Dorking yeoman v. Alan Maunsel v of Dorking. £40. E159/310, m. 13. Absence: 4 mos. Plea: absence by injunction to attend the king's council from day to day, wherefore he asked to be sent away.

M1531

R10. Chester. Thomas Wayne v. Nicholas Savage r of Moston St. Mary. E159/310, m. 39. Absence: 9/29/31 to 11/7/31. Process to T1532 without appearance. * R11. Derbs. Edmond Mody and William Armourer v. Robert Emonson r of Somersal. £120. E159/310, m. 35. Absence: 10/1/30 to 9/29/31. Issue by AG in E1534 on residence. Process for jury into M1536. * R12. Northt. Maurice Wogan v. Hugh Myllyng r of Farthingstone. £60. E159/310, m. 36. Absence: 3/10/31 to 10/9/31. Plea: he was both r of Farthingstone and provost of college of Towcester; he resided at Towcester. Myllyng died in September 1531 (before complaint was filed). * R13. Oxon. Anthony Wood v. Richard Moreys of Salford cl. £80. CP40/1071, m. 780d; CP40/1074, m. 436. * R14. Salop. William Smalle v. John Pole v of Alberbury St. Michael. E159/310, m. 34. Absence: 9/29/31 (?) to 11/7/31. Plea H1531: not absent against statute. Nothing further entered. * R15. Salop. Richard Bawdwyn v. Thomas Townge (= Tonge) r of Myddle. E159/310, m. 37. Absence: 4/1/31 to 11/6/31. Plea E1532: he is prebendary in collegiate church of Shrewsbury St. Mary; absent only 4/23/31 to 5/9/31; 6/12/31 to 6/24/31; and 10/16/31 to 12/6/31 when he was a defendant at court of arches. Asked for release. * R16. Salop. Richard Bawdwyn v. John Lyttilton r of Munslow. £40. E159/310, m. 72. Absence in February, May, July, and August 1531 for 4 mos. Plea: residence. * R17. Som. Edmond Mody and William Armourer v. William Tattourne r of Spaxton. £80. E159/310, m. 38. Absence: 10/12/30 to 6/24/31. Plea H1532: claim of pardon for everything up to 10 March; he was also r of Rowney (Herts) where he was resident. Plaintiffs protest that there is no parish church of Rowney in Hertfordshire and join issue on whether he was r there. T1532: received benefit of the pardon up to 10 March but admitted the offense after 10 March and thus forfeits £30. Court deliberates to M1532.

H1532

R18. Norf. Evan Fludd servant of Edward Peckham cofferer of king's household v. Robert Blith cl r of Hellesdon. £100. E159/310, m. 20. Absence: 4/9/31 for 10 mos. Issue by AG in E1532: residence. H1536: jury acquits. * R19. Salop. John Sennoke v. John ap John cl r of Tederthowe. £100 (?). E159/310, m. 21. Absence: 3/20/31 to 2/3/32. Process without appearance into H1533. * R20. Salop. John Carter v. John Peers cl r of Alhyerne. E159/310, m. 22. Absence from 3/20/31. Process until H1533, with reference to more process in files. * R21. Worcs. Richard Averey of Kidderminster felmonger v. William Thomas cl v of Stone. £100. E159/310, m. 19. Absence: 3/10/31 for 10 mos. Plea: resignation on 11/16/30. Asked for release. * R22. Devon. Richard Garland v. Edward Arosmyth of Battadon cl. £40. CP40/1072, m. 564d.

E1532

R23. Cornub. John Stoyle cpn v. John Escott cl v of St. Anthony. £100. E159/311, m. 28. Absence: 9/22/31 to 12/19/31 by residing at Buckland, Devon. Issue T1532: residence. M1538: jury acquits. * R24. Ebor. John Nicolson v. Thomas Russell v of Beverley St. Mary. £20. E159/311, m. 61. Absence: 5/18/31 for 1 month; from 12/13/31 for 1 month. Plea T1532: claim was insufficient in law; asked for release. * R25. Kent. Thomas Cock v. David Reynolds r of Betteshanger. £100. E159/311, mm. 10, 24. Absence: 4/1/31 for 10 mos. Issue by AG in T1532: continual residence. T1534: jury convicts. Courts applied statutory time limitation: forfeiture of £90. M1534: error procedure. * R26. Kent. Hugh at Fenne v. Amphibelus Note cl v of Halstow by Upchurch. £140. E159/311, m. 25. Absence: 3/10/31 for 14 mos., residing at Upchurch. Issue by AG in T1532: residence. In H1533 Barons and serjeants at law: mispleading results in repleading that reached similar issue. * R27. Som. Humfrey Walround v. James Carter r of Brean. £110. E159/311, m. 27. Absence: 5/18/31 for 11 mos. Process without appearance into H1533. * R28. Suff. Robert Power of Lambeth v. Robert Bond cl r of Carlton. £100. E159/311, m. 26. Absence: 4/9/31 for 10 mos. T1532: suit withdrawn by both king and Power because king had pardoned Bond as a king's chaplain. * R29. Worcs. Avery de Kydermynster v. William Thomas cl v of Stone. £20. E159/311, m. 29. Absence: 2/3/32 for 2 mos. Plea T1532: resignation of vicary. Asked to be sent away. * R30. Bucks. Edmund Wyndesore v. John Berlyswyke of Manchester cl. £60. CP40/1073, m. 3d; CP40/1074, mm. 391, 681d.

T1532

R31. Derbs. John Gough yeoman v. Thomas Donne cl r of Eyam. £80. E159/311, m. 23. Absence: from 9/29/31. Plea E1533: personal chaplain of George earl of Shrewsbury. H1534: AG and Gough withdraw king's suit. * R32. Kent. John Foule gen v. Richard Lytylford cl v of Teynham. £200. E159/311, m. 22. Absence: 9/29/30 for 20 mos. Plea T1532: residence. M1532: jury with AG present acquits. * R33. Kent. Robert Power gen v. William Showter r of Snave. £100+. E159/311, m. 26. Absence: 5/28/31 until 7/2/32. Process without appearance into H1534. * R34. Norf. Edmund Grey v. John Pory cl r of Merton. £130? E159/311, m. 24. Absence: 5/31/31. Issue in M1532: residence. M1533: jury acquits. * R35. Warw. John Hamond v. William Leyson cl r of Newton Regis. £200. E159/311, m. 25. Absence: 9/29/30. Plea H1533: advocate of the court of arches exercising his office. Court deliberates into T1533. * R36. Lincs. John Rede v. Thomas Compton of Stenigot cl. £60. CP40/1074, m. 28. * R37. Lincs. John Eston v. Thomas Wright of Conisholme cl. £40. CP40/1074, m. 29; CP40/1077, mm. 28d, 284. * R38. Norf. John Bosome armiger patron of church of Wetheringsett v. John Crowe of Wetheringsett (Suff) cl r of Wetheringsett. £40. CP40/1074, m. 608; CP40/1075, m. 420; CP40/1076, m. 174; CP40/1077, m. 312d. Absence: 10/8/31 for 4 months total at divers times. Issue: absence against the statute. * R39. Norf. Christopher Montney v. William Lupton of Stanford cl v of Stanford. CP40/1074, m. 690; CP40/1080, m. 226. * R40. Norf. Peter Pory v. John Pory of Merton cl. £200. CP40/1074, m. 361d. * R41. Suff. Nicholas Bohun gen v. Walter Skeggys of Brampton cl r of Brampton. £40. CP40/1074, m. 173; CP40/1076, m. 72; CP40/1077, mm. 404d, 488d; CP40/1078, m. 488d. Absence: 6/24/30 to 10/18/30. Issue: absence against the statute. * R42. Worcs. John Stokedale v. John More of Powick cl v of Powick. £40. CP40/1074, mm. 420d, 464d. Absence: 12/21/31 to 5/8/32 for 4 mos. at divers times. D appeared.

M1532

R43. Herts. Hugh Gethyn v. William Tattorn r of Rowley. £110. E159/311, m. 38. Absence: 10/6/31 for 11 mos. Plea M1532: he is the chantry priest in the free chapel of Rowley and not r. Asked for release. E1533: Tattorn dead. * R44. Warw. William Scarlett v. John Gee r of Leamington. £100. E159/311, m. 39. Absence: from 11/20/31. Plea M1533: resident in king's service in St. Stephen in Westminster Palace according to the letters patent granted to the dean and chapter of the chapel. Asked for release. * R45. Warw. Richard Dey v. Thomas Adams v of Radford. £110. E159/311, m. 40. Absence: 10/6/31 for 11 mos. Issue H1533: not the v of Radford. H1534: AG withdraws his issue. Court deliberates to T1534. Sine die. * R46. Oxon. Anthony Wood v. Richard Mores (Morys) of Salford cl r of Salford. £80. CP40/1075, m. 715; CP40/1076, m. 434. Absence by residence at Warwick. Recovery by default because attorney of defendant was not informed; full forfeiture plus £1 in damages.

H1533

R47. Herts. Thomas Russel gen v. William Ridale r of Radwell. £100. E159/311, m. 27. Absence: 4/9/31 for 10 mos. Plea T1533: from 3/29/31 he was personal chaplain of Thomas earl of Rutland; proffer of letters testimonial. H1534: AG withdraws king's suit. * R48. Salop. Richard Nicollys of Munslow yeoman v. Roger Walcotte cl r of Leighton. £100. E159/311, m. 27d. Absence: 5/3/32 to 2/1/33. Process without appearance into H1534. * R49. Wilts. Thomas Redgate yeoman v. John Wylloughby cl r of Semley. £90. E159/311, m. 26. Absence: 5/12/32 for 9 mos. Plea E1533: continuously resident until 10/29/32, when he left for Wood in Devon 44 miles away, intending to return within 26 days. On 11/11/32 he got "le Splene" whereby he could not return without dying before 1/21/33, when he did return. Court deliberates until H1534 when plaintiff demurred. * R50. Ebor. Ralph Barton v. John Deane of Middleham cl. £40. CP40/1076, m. 216d; CP40/1077, m. 201d; CP40/1078, m. 202. * R51. Ebor. Hugh Tyrgose v. John Deane of Middleham cl. £40. CP40/1076, m. 216d; CP40/1077, m. 201d; CP40/1078, m. 202. * R52. Sussex. William Pay v. Richard Wyatt of Slindon cl prebendary of Hurst in cathedral of Chichester. £10. CP40/1076, m. 525; CP40/1077, m. 539. Absence: 6/24/32 for 1 mo. by residing at Slindon. D appeared. * R53. Hants. Humfrey Walrond v. John Willoughby cl r of Kemble. £20. CP40/1076, m. 198; CP40/1077, m. 433. Absence: from 11/1/32 by continual willing residence at Wood in Devon 44 miles away. Issue: whether he was detained at Wood by such a grave attack of "le Splene" that he could not return to Kemble within the 26 days after 10/29/32. * R54. Suff. Osbert Echyngham kt v. Richard Patryck of Great Dunham r of Great Dunham. CP40/1076, m. 5. Suit withdrawn.

E1533

R55. Dorset. Robert Watkyns v. Nicholas Chauntrell r of Hawkchurch. E159/312, m. 21. Absence: 5/22/32 to 5/16/33. T1534: D appeared. M1534 Chauntrell reported dead. Inquest on death. * R56. Leics. Richard Holbroke v. Walter Hasilrigge r of Hallaton. £100. E159/312, m. 22. Absence: 7/1/32 for 10 mos. Issue by AG in M1533: residence. Jury process into E1534. * R57. Ebor. William Toty v. Richard Huchynson of Biggin. £80. CP40/1077, m. 572d. * R58. Hants. Christopher Waleson v. Richard Sharpe of Alton cl. £800. CP40/1077, m. 293. * R59. Hants. Christopher Walkeston v. Richard Sharpe of Lasham cl. £40. CP40/1077, m. 298. * R60. Herts. John Wilson v. William Rydall of Radwell cl. £40. CP40/1077, m. 12. D appeared. * R61. Norf. John Bosome armiger patron of Wetheringsett v. John Crowe of Wetheringsett cl r of Wetheringsett. £40. CP40/1077, m. 312. Absence: 2/5/32 until 5/12/32. Issue: absence against the statute. * R62. Suff. John Pytman v. Robert Tree of Westerfield cl r of Westerfield. £40. CP40/1077, m. 64.

T1533

R63. Dorset. John Durbar v. William Bretynton of Stour Provost cl. £80. CP40/1078, m. 390; CP40/1079, m. 192. * R64. Dorset. John Durbar v. John Dowdyng of Frawndreis Marsh cl. £80. CP40/1078, m. 390; CP40/1079, m. 192. * R65. Ebor. John Friston v. Richard Huchynson of Birkin cl. £40. CP40/1078, m. 208d; CP40/1079, m. 207; CP40/1080, m. 201d; CP40/1086, m. 288d. * R66. Som. John Locke v. Edward Sydgrove. £80. CP40/1078, m. 394d; CP40/1079, m. 189. * R67. Som. Robert Fairbaron v. Nicholas Coke of Compton Bishop cl. £80. CP40/1078, m. 667d; CP40/1079, m. 189. * R67. Wilts. Nicholas Cookys v. Thomas Skaylehorne of Easton Grey cl. £70. CP40/1078, m. 374 (*sic*, but positioned between mm. 481, 465).

MI533

R68. Salop. William Alcok yeoman v. Edward Strete r of Holdgate. £120. E159/312, m. 41. Absence: 11/1/32 for 11 mos. and more. Issue by AG in T1541: residence. E1545: jury acquits. * R69. Devon. George Hall v. William Dyskombe r of Belstone. £50. E159/312, m. 42. Absence: 12/1/32 for 5 mos. Issue by AG in H1534: residence. E1535: jury acquits. * R70. Lancs. Thomas Holecroft gen v. Milo Huddulston r of Withington. £120. E159/312, m. 43. Absence: 12/25/32 to 11/10/33. Issue T1534: residence. Jury process into E1535. * R71. Kent. Desiderius Thomson v. Richard Robert v of Preston next Faversham. £60. E159/312, m. 44. Absence: 5/2/32 for 6 mos. Plea M1533: he is both v of Preston next Faversham and r of Woodlands; residence first at Woodlands then at Preston. H 1534: AG acknowledges his two benefices but takes issue on residence. Jury from both parishes 10/7/35: resident on neither parish from 5/1/32 until 9/29/32 but resident at Preston from then until 11/1/32. Forfeiture: £50. * R72. Leics. John Stygham v. Edmund Barton r of Bruntingthorpe. £120. E159/312, m. 45. Absence: 9/29/32 for 12 mos. Issue by AG in M1534: residence. M1535: jury acquits. * R73. Som. William Rysdon v. William Warre of Otterhampton cl r of Otterhampton. £120. CP40/1079, m. 706d. The suit began earlier than this term.

HI534

R74. Som. John Hamond v. John Dovell r of Queen Camel. £40. E159/312, m. 24. Absence: 9/29/33 for 4 mos. Process without appearance into T1534. * R75. Wilts. Robert Ap Powell v. Henry Willoughby r of Wylye. £110. E159/312, m. 23. Absence: 3/1/33 for 11 mos. Plea E1534: at Oxford for study and learning. Asked for release. Court deliberates into M1534. * R76. Herts. Nicholas Norres v. Henry Bacon cl v of Bengeo. £40. CP40/1080, m. 635. * R77. Kent. Thomas Cookys v. James Bartlett cl v of Elmestone. £60. CP40/1080, mm. 187, 187d; CP40/1081, m. 384 (2x). * R78. Kent. Thomas Cookys v. James Turry cl v of West Hythe. £45. CP40/1080, mm. 187, 187d; CP40/1081,

m. 389d (2x). * R79. Suff. Christopher Wylkynson v. Robert Stylyard r of Finningham. £100. CP40/1080, m. 461d. * R80. Worcs. John Freman v. William More prior of Worcester. £40. CP40/1080, m. 288d; CP40/1081, m. 486d; CP40/1082, m. 403d; CP40/1084, m. 507d. Absence: 1/10/33 to 11/4/33 for 8 mos. at nine separate times while prior of monastery of Norwich cathedral. D protested that the act should not extend to abbots and priors, but pleaded the pardon of 11/3/34 for part; demurred on the other part. Pardon applied for part; for the remainder the court to be advised. * R81. Worcs. John Freman v. John Grey of Stoke Prior cl. £40. CP40/1080, m. 290d.

E1534

R82. Herts. Robert Ferneley v. John Sapcote r of Buckland. £40. E159/313, m. 23. Absence: 1/1/33 for 4 mos. Plea E1535: at the time of the information he was not 14 yrs. old. AG on inspection of the body and testimony withdraws suit. * R83. Sussex. Roger Holford v. Thomas Mekyn r of Bepton. £420. E1534: E159/313, m. 25. Absence: 9/29 1530 to Easter 1534. Plea in E1534: for part, statutory limitation for *qui tam* suits; for remainder, king's chaplain by letter patent. Court deliberates into H1535. * R84. Hants. Roger Sturston v. Thomas Hawthorn of Ludgershall cl. £80. E1534: CP40/1081, m. 174. * R85. Lincs. William Gedney v. William Burbanke of Oxford cl. £40. E1534: CP40/1081, m. 30d. * R86. Lincs. William Gedney v. William Hewton of Welton cl v of Welton. £20. E1534: CP40/1081, m. 30d; CP40/1083, m. 319. Absence: more than 3 mos. at 5 different times. D undefended. Forfeiture.

T1534

R87. Dorset. William Marten of London v. Thomas Carpenter (= Calbek) r of Stoke Wake. £40. E159/313, m. 30. Absence: 5/10/34 for 4 mos. Margination: pardoned. * R88. Kent. Roger Bexwell v. William Kempe of Ditton cl r of Ditton. £70. CP40/1082, m. 434; CP40/1084, m. 59. Absence: 7 mos. before 4/1/34 by residing in London St. Acons. Issue: admitted 7/21/33 to be the domestic cpn of baron John Zouche and thus allowed 2 benefices. * R89. Norf. Thomas Pakeman v. Thomas Gresham of Wiveton cl. £80. CP40/1082, m. 609d.

M1534

R90. Som. George Whelplay v. Robert Balfront r of Tellisford. £110. E159/313, m. 26d. Absence: 12/6/33 for 11 mos. 13 days. Plea M1534: residence. * R91. Hants. Arthur Clerke gen v. Thomas Rygby of Dogmersfield cl r of Dogmersfield. £240. CP40/1083, m. 619d. Absence: 24 mos. D appeared. * R92. Lincs. William Gedney v. William Burbanke of Welton by Lincoln cl prebendary of Westhall. £60. CP40/1083, m. 514; CP40/1084, m. 60d. Absence: 4/13/34 to 9/30/34. Plea: scholar residing for study at the university at Oxford (allegedly at monastery of London St. Catherine). * R93. Norf. Thomas Asketyll v. Robert Bysshop of Broadway (Worcs) cl. £5. CP40/1083, m. 381. * R94. Norf. Francis Payn v. William Bryan of Godwick cl. £40. CP40/1083, m. 708d. * R94. Norwich. William Hubberd v. Henry Aleyns of Aylsham Burgh cl. £80. CP40/ 1083, m. 709. * R95. Som. Robert Tymmys v. Robert Balefronte of Tellisford cl. £80. CP40/1083, m. 197. * R96. Suff. John Peynter v. Robert Thompson r of Sandcroft cl r of Sandcroft. £20. CP40/1083, m. 756d.

H1535

R97. Ebor. Robert Wyatt v. John Lyvett of Ryther cl. £30. CP40/1084, m. 205d.

E1535

R96. Calais. James Bourchier v. John Bradwey r of Campe in the march of Calais. £110. E159/314, m. 11. Absence: 11/3/34 for 6 mos. 7 days; (also lease of rectories of Balingham and Setles in march of Calais for 25 wks. [thus £60 + £50]). Plea H1536: for absence, a personal cpn of William Lord Sandys with letters testimonial; for lease, did not hold in mode and form. Asked for release. * R97. Calais. James Bourchier v. William Peterson r of Bonyng in march of Calais. £60. E159/314, m. 11d. Absence: 11/3/34 for 6 mos. 7 days. Issue by AG in T1535: residence. E1537: jury convicts. Writ of error: 7/9/37. * R98. Heref/Oxon. Roger Gratewych v. William Horwood v of Little Hereford. £50. E159/314, m. 13. Absence: 11/4/34 for 5 mos. Plea T1535: resident at the university at Oxford for study and learning. Asked to be released. E1536: jury acquits. * R99. Ebor. Roland Todde v. William Harison of Whitkirk v of Darton. £40. CP40/ 1085, m. 152. Absence: 11/4/34 for 4 mos. D appeared. * R100. London. Roger Bexwell, Ralph Tykhull, and Richard Sandell v. Simon Penne of London cl. £80. CP40/1085, m. 93d (2nd). * R101. Norf. Ralph Brike v. Rouland Johnson of Bixley cl r of Bixley. £60. CP40/1085, m. 475d (2nd).

T1535

R102. Ebor. Roland Todd of Wakefield gen v. William Haryson cl v of Whitkirk and Darton. £40. E159/314, m. 17. Absent: 11/4/34 for 4 mos. Plea M1535: suit already brought by Todd. Court deliberates into H1536. * R103. Essex. Gerard Chauncey v. Brian Appylby r of Sutton. £80. E159/314, m. 19. * R104. Absence: 11/3/34 for 8 mos. Issue by AG in M1535: residence. Jury process into T1545. * R105. Essex. Gerard Chauncey v. James Underwood r of Asheldham. £80. E159/314, m. 23. Absence: 11/3/34 for 8 mos. Issue by AG in M1546: residence. * R106. Essex. Gerard Chauncey v. John Mason cl r of Fambridge. £80. E159/314, m. 14d. Absence: 11/3/34 for 8 mos. Plea M1546: residence. * R107. London. Roger Bexwell, Ralph Tykhull v. Nicholas Dundy cl of London St. Margaret.

£80. CP40/1086, m. 639. * R108. London. Roger Bexwell and Ralph Tykhull v. John Smith of London cl. £10. CP40/1086, m. 639.

MI535

R109. Dorset. William Marten of London fletcher v. Walter Gardiner r of Stockland. £40. E159/314, m. 23. Absence: 7/3/35 for 4 mos. Issue by AG in E1536: residence. Jury process into T1536. * R110. Hants. John Baker v. James Mylner r of Farley. £110. E159/314, m. 26. Absence: 12/1/34 for 11 mos. Process without appearance into E1536. * R111. Hants. Richard Molyners buckle maker v. Thomas Brygis r of Shorwell. £120. E159/314, m. 23d. Absence: 11/7/34 for 12 mos. Issue by AG in M1536: residence. Jury process into E1537. * R112. Lincs. Anthony Porter v. John Pynder of Buckland cl r of Buckland. £40. CP40/1087, m. 433d. Absence: 11/3/34 by residing at Pilham. D appeared.

HI536

R113. Cornub. Jenkin Lloyd ap David and William David Williams v. Owen David Gryffyth r of Senghenydd (?). £120. E159/314, m. 17. Absence: 2/19/34 for 12 mos. Plea M1537: residence on Bishopton, his other benefice. Asked to be released. * R114. Notts. Robert Markham of South Collingham gen v. Robert Fludde r of South Collingham. £40. E159/314, m. 19. Absence: October 1535–January 1536. Plea E1538: on 4/8/33 retained as personal cpn of John Huse knight later attainted of treason; proffer of letters testimonial. Suit still active in T1545. * R115. South Wales. Jenkyn Lloid ap David and William David Williams v. Owen David Gryffyth r of Bishopston. £120. E159/314, m. 18. Absence: 2/19/34 for 12 mos. Process without appearance into M1536. * R116. Som. John Howell v. John Nosett of Berrow cl v of Berrow. £80. CP40/1088, m. 272. * R117. Wilts. Roger Stourton v. Thomas Hawhton of Ludgershall cl r of Ludgershall. £80. CP40/1088, m. 225. Absence: 4/26/32 to 11/20/32. D appeared.

Buying and Selling for Profit

1531

BS1. Ebor. William Gyrlyngton of Kippax v. Thomas Jaxson of Kippax cpn of Kippax chantry. (Along with lease claim) E159/310, m. 22. Lease of land used for pasturing animals for sale, with animals and grain purchased and then sold to butchers and others. Issue on commercial activity: did not buy or sell after 9/29/29. M1538: jury acquits. * BS2. Suff. Edward Arnold v. William Baron of Ipswich cpn. £9. KB27/1080, m. 3. * BS3. Oxon. Edward Stanbank v. Roger Smith abbot of Dorchester. E159/310, m. 12.

Purchase and sale of oxen. Plea: part covered by pardon; for rest, did not sell after 3/10/31. E1533: nonprosecution. * BS4. Salop. William Smalle v. Thomas Baker r of Myndtown. E159/310, m. 32. Purchase of 140 sheep and wool for resale; afterwards sold. Issue by AG: buying or selling all or any part. E1536: jury acquitted. * BS5. Worcs. John Page v. Richard Stone v of Cold Aston (Gloc). E159/310, m. 31. Purchase and sale of tallow; barley to be sewn in return for profits. Plea T1532: for the tallow, acting for father; denial of transaction with barley. * BS6. Ebor. Robert Conyers gen v. George Bynkes of Danby Wiske cpn. £10. CP40/1071, m. 672d; CP40/1073, m. 33d; CP40/1074, m. 615d.

1532

BS7. Salop. Fulk Raddoun v. Thomas Baker cl r of Myndtown. E159/311, m. 30. Purchase and resale of 140 sheep and wool. Process without appearance into H1533. * BS8. Suff. William Cowper and William Skynner of Bury St. Edmunds hus v. John Gyttour (= Gryffyth) r of Horningsheath. E159/310, m. 23. Purchase of barley then sold as malt. Issue by AG in T1357: did not sell. E1358: jury acquits. * BS9. Suff. William Cowper and William Skynner hus v. John Redman cl r of Great Whelnetham. E159/310, m. 24. Purchase of 4 horses thereafter sold. Issue by AG in T1535: did not buy and sell in mode and form. E1536: jury acquits. * BS10. Ebor. William Horsley v. William Johnson of Middleton by Bainton cpn. Buying and selling for profit, £40. H1532: CP40/1072, m. 61d. * BS11. Lincs. George Denton v. Richard Baynton of Horbling cl. £40. CP40/1072, m. 29; CP40/1073, m. 638. Purchase of horses, cows, and 180 sheep bought, leased out for profit. D appeared. * BS12. Ebor. William Frauncys v. John Boynton parish priest of Everingham. E159/311, m. 27. Purchase of barley and wheat thereafter sold. Process without appearance into H1533. * BS13. Staffs. Francis Bassett v. Richard Hall of Ilam cl. £20. CP40/1074, m. 52. * BS14. Salop. John Heyward yeoman v. Edward Gery cl in monastery of Shrewsbury St. Peter. E159/311, m. 37. Purchase of 56 quarters of malt and 40 measures of barley thereafter sold. Issue by AG in M1534: purchase and resale. E1538: jury acquits. * BS15. Ebor. John Symson v. John Potter of Keldholme cl. £20. CP40/1075, m. 663. * BS16. Norf. John Hacun gen v. George Washington of Narborough. £13.33. CP40/1075, mm. 432, 726d. Purchase of barley and oats then sold. D appeared.

1533

BS17. Kent. John Foule of Halling gen v. Richard Lytylford v of Teynham. E159/311, m. 22. Purchase wood, iron, tiles, and kitchen items from a kitchen, then sold. Issue by AG in E1533 on purchase. E1535: jury acquits. * BS18. Northt. Edward Chamberlayn of Little Creaton v. Robert Palmer r of Great Creaton. £5.50. E159/312, m. 23. Purchase of 20 sheep thereafter sold. Plea T1533: purchased for maintaining glebe and for household expenses; some died, others became less useful and were sold. Asked for release. * BS19. Devon. Richard Wychelhalse v. Richard Wykys of South Tawton cl. £40. CP40/1077, m. 412d; CP40/1078, m. 483. Purchase of tin afterwards sold. Plea: purchased for executors to perform last will. Issue on whether purchase was for resale. * BS20. Ebor. James Rokesby armiger v. Robert Blessyng of Kirkby Ravensworth cpn. £40. CP40/1077, m. 571. Purchase of victuals, grains, and malt (meats and spices). D appeared; enrollment ends before plea. * BS21. Kent. John Sawyer v. William Norcote of Great Mongeham cl. E159/312, m. 15. Purchase of different lots of barley sold as malt. Issue by AG in E1537 on purchase and sale. M1538: jury acquits. * BS22. Ebor. Robert Wood v. William Harryson of Whitkirk cl. £40. CP40/1078, m. 215d; CP40/1080, m. 202d. * BS23. Lincs. Michael Whyttyng king's valet v. Richard Barkeworth of Greetham cl. Buying and selling for profit, £50. T1533: CP40/1078, m. 28. * BS24. Norf. William Bradford v. Roland Cotney of Banham cl. £20. CP40/1078, m. 193. * BS25. Devon. John Cresse v. John Lill cl of Plymtree. E159/312, m. 40. Purchase of sheep and horses thereafter sold. Process without appearance into E1534.

1534

BS26. Ebor. Christopher Atkynson v. George Newton of Ripon cpn. £40. CP40/1080, m. 205d. * BS27. Ebor. Richard Penros v. John Long of Wheldrake. £40. CP40/1080, m. 218d. * BS28. Worcs. Richard Bradley yeoman v. John Clerk r of Belbroughton. E159/313, m. 38. Purchase of cattle sold to butchers and others. Plea M1534: cattle derived from the glebe and he sold them lawfully. Asked for release. * BS29. Essex. William Bull v. George Gowar r of Langenhoe. £3. E159/313, m. 16d. Purchase of a horse thereafter sold. Issue by AG in T1534: purchase, profit, or sale against the statute. Jury process into E1535. * BS30. Lincs. John Starky v. Thomas Skamon (?) of Dalderby cl. £20. CP40/1082, m. 30d. * BS31. Lincs. John Starky v. Martin Rouse of High Toynton cl. £20. CP40/1082, m. 31. * BS32. Norf. John Dey v. Nicholas Marche (= Marshall) of East Bilney cl. £40. CP40/1082, m. 578; CP40/1083, mm. 126d, 311d, 418; CP40/1084, m. 565d; CP40/1085, m. 311. Purchase of barley, hemp, and lead. E1544 jury convicts on purchase of part; had to be repleaded to allow for conviction on purchase of only part. * BS33. Kent. James Fitzwalter v. Richard Forde of Okeryge cl r of Okeryge. £40. CP40/1083, m. 281; CP40/1084, m. 543. * BS34. Kent. Andrew Swayne v. Richard Forde of Okeryge cl r of Okryge. £40. CP40/1083, m. 288. * BS35. Norf. Edmund Goodwyn v. John Marshalle of Necton cpn. £5. CP40/1083, m. 708d.

1535

BS36. Ebor. Robert Wyatt v. Michael Hercley of Kirkby cpn. £10. CP40/1084, m. 208d. * BS37. Dorset. Thomas Hall of London scribe v. Richard Charnock v of

Shapwick. E159/314, m. 15d. Purchase of 100 oak trees, 8 beech trees, sold the wood and bark. Process without appearance into H1536. * BS38. Oxon. Robert Squyer weaver v. John Pereson v of Stanton Harcourt. E159/314, m. 31. Purchase of 100 quarters of malt thereafter sold. Demurrer E1536: count did not specify days and places of purchase and sale. Asked for release. * BS39. Lincs. Humfrey Mysylden gen v. James Darby of Wood Enderby cpn. £20. CP40/1087, m. 31; CP40/1088, m. 34d. * BS40. London. Ralph Tykehull v. Richard Yong of Preston (Kent) cpn. £20. CP40/1087, m. 634d; CP40/1088, m. 101. Suit withdrawn in H1536.

1536

BS41. Lincs. Christopher Wylkynson v. John Richardson of Sedgebrook cl. £40. CP40/1088, m. 36d. * BS42. Lincoln city. James Curteys v. Nicholas Kendall of Lincoln cl. £40. CP40/1088, m. 37.

Stipend

S1. M1531. Salop. Richard Bawdwyn v. Hugh Geillys r of Fitz. E159/310, m. 33. Stipend of £6.67 to celebrate for a certain soul in Shrewsbury St. Chad. Plea: rec was worth only £6; stipend taken so that he can live a more honest, quiet life and still he always cared for his parish. Nothing entered after the plea. * S2. H1532. Bucks. William Tryppe v. William Stratton. £4. E159/310, m. 27. Stipend of £5.65 from church wardens of Princes Risborough. Process without appearance until M1532; further process in files. * S3. M1533. Suff. Richard Jermyn v. Edward Couper of Benacre cl r of Benacre. £40. CP40/1079, m. 806d; CP40/1080, m. 403d; CP40/1081, m. 419d. Stipend for 20 weeks. Issue: taking the stipend. * S4. H1534. Wilts. John Panter v. Thomas Skaylehorne of Easton Gray. (Along with residence claim.) £80. CP40/1080, m. 241d; CP40/1081, m. 12; CP40/1082. D appeared. * S5. E1534. London. Roger Bexwell v. William Kempe of London cl r of Ditton. £80. CP40/1081, m. 37; CP40/1082, m. 429; CP40/1084, m. 59. Stipend of £6, held for 40 wks. Plea: for most time, not r of Ditton; for rest, did not take pay. Issue joined. * S6. T1535. London. Roger Bexwell, Ralph Tykhull, and Richard Sandell v. Nicholas Dundy of London cl (r of Snave?). £36. CP40/1086, m. 460. Stipend held for 18 wks. from church wardens. Issue: taking stipend against the statute. * S7. London. Roger Bexwell and Ralph Tykhull v. Thomas Barard of London cl. £80. CP40/1086, m. 639. * S8. H1536. Kent. Thomas Hawkyns valet of the king's guard v. John Heth v of Borden. £98. E159/314, m. 20. Stipend of £3.33 held for 47 wks. Issue by AG in E1536: taking stipend mode and form. T1536: dead.

Mortuary

MI. MI530. Cambs. Nicholas Reder v. John Webster of Hinxton cl. £3. CP40/1067, m. 573. Gown worth £1 taken at wife's death. Issue: mortuary taken against statute. * M2. TI531. South Wales. Walter Havard v. Thomas ap David ap Morgan, David ap Guillam ap Thomas, and Howell ap Llen ap Thomas. EI59/310, m. 17. Defendants as lessees took ox worth £0.80 on estate not worth £6.67; took cow worth £0.50 from estate not worth £6.67. Issue by AG: taking the fees. Process continued into HI537. * M3. EI532. Dorset. Edward Willoughby knight v. John Hart prior of Horton. EI59/311, m. 6. Fee of £0.33 taken without decedent's body when moveables not worth £6.67. D appeared. EI535: dead. * M4. Sussex. Phillip Benett and Joan his wife v. Robert Wylson of Washington cl v of Washington. £2. CP40/1073, m. 553; CP40/1075. Vicar sought mortuary plus damages for withholding mortuary; v then refused mortuary without damages. Issue: whether v refused offer of fee. Jury convicts.

Probate

PI. TI531. Essex. John Bryklebank v. John Tenderyng clerk of the commissary general of John bishop of London in Essex. EI59/310, m. 9. Fee of £0.25 on estate worth less than £22.02. Issue: took only £0.13. TI532: D confessed. Forfeiture: £10. * P2. MI532. Norf. Thomas Palmer of Bishop's Lynn v. Robert Newman official of bishop of Norwich and Malech Gogley bishop's scribe. Probate fees, £50. EI59/311, m. 36. (A) taking £0.05 + £0.03 for commission of administration and commission on estate of £0.78; (B) taking £0.18 for probate and £0.60 for registration on estate of £12.75; (C) took £0.18 for probate on estate of £2. Issue by AG in MI533: taking those fees. EI534: jury acquits.

Citing outside the Diocese

CDI. HI533. Devon. Richard Jenyng v. Robert Johnson of London gen, John Hyndon of Lifton hus, and Elizabeth his wife. £10. CP40/1076, m. 232. * CD2. MI533. Beds. Robert Gurnell cl v. Thomas abbot of Abingdon. £10. CP40/1079, mm. 78d, 590.

Tannery

TI. MI535. Cumber. Richard Machell of Hesket v. Edward Penrethe of Penrith spiritual person. £120. EI59/314, m. 30d. Tanning house in Penrith. Issue by AG in HI536: denial of holding. Jury process into EI536.

Unspecified

U1. Kent. AG v. John Morys of Hawkhurst cpn. £1.13. H1531: CP40/1068, m. 687. * U2. Notts. Rex v. Robert Morton of Teversal cpn. £10. E1532: CP40/1073, m. 698d; CP40/1075, m. 878. * U3. Norf. Rex v. Robert Mortemer of Teversal cpn. £10. T1532: CP40/1074, m. 731; CP40/1075, m. 878. * U4. Suff. William Tryker v. John Hudson of Brettenham cl. E1534: CP40/1081, m. 195. * U5. Notts. Rex v. Robert Moreton of Teversal cpn. £10. T1534: CP40/1082, m. 638.

Request of a Feoffee

KB27 / 997, m. III–IIId: Humfrey Coningesby, JKB v. William Sandys, knight.

Middlesex. [Recitation of statute of 2 Richard II (scandalum magnatum)], and whereas the above Humfrey on 29 October 1510 and before and always and still is one of the justices of the said lord king assigned to hold pleas before the same king and one of the justices of the same lord king in the county of Lincoln and the city of Lincoln and the same Humfrey according to the exigencies of the abovesaid offices as are set out for the justices of the same lord king on the said 29 October 1510 at the vill of Westminster in Westminster Hall there was intendant upon and occupied with many and divers pleas and business touching both the same king and divers his subjects, certain of those pleas and businesses before the same lord king and certain of them before the afore- mentioned Humfrey and his companion justices of the same lord king assigned to take the assizes in the said county of Lincoln before the same Humfrey and his companion justices at the assizes abovesaid adjourned on account of divers ambiguities being in those assizes there into the said vill of Westminster in Middlesex in the chamber there called the Exchequer Chamber according to the form of the statute provided in such a case according to the exigencies of the law to be heard and determined, and as the same Humfrey then and there was walking across the said vill of Westminster in the abovesaid hall according to his office as before is prescribed for justices of the said lord king into the said camera called the Exchequer Chamber to hear and direct those assizes according to the 'exigency of the law, with many people both parties named in the assizes, pleas and businesses abovesaid and counselors and their friends and other subjects of the said lord king going with the same Humfrey then and there for that cause, the abovesaid William, little pondering the said statute edited in the said second year of the said Richard II late king of England or the other matters set out above, on the same 29 October 1510 in the vill of Westminster abovesaid in the abovesaid hall called the aforementioned Humfrey pleading with the same Humfrey in these English words:

"I wold speke with you"

and the same Humfrey granted there to do this freely to the same William there and then standing with divers his counselors, whereon a certain Guy Palmes one of the counselors of the same William as the same Guy then and there affirmed spoke to the same Humfrey in English words:

"Sir, here is master Sandys & he and master Edmund Bray be aggred for such londys as were Sir Reynold Brays and ye be a feoffe therin and he desireth you that ye will make such astate therof as the seid Guy then rehersed"

to which the abovesaid Humfrey responding said in these English words:

"Sir, ther be many honerable men feoffez as well as I and this matter was spoken of this last terme and ye were present and then I seid as I sey nowe, I woll be glad to doo therin as I shuld doo and ought to doo"

to which the abovesaid Guy then and there answering said in these English words:

"I was not ther"

whereon the abovesaid William then and there said to the same Humfrey in these English words:

"Will y make astate & noo"

to which the abovesaid Humfrey said there and then to the same William in these words:

"Sir, I woll be glad to doo as I ought to doo as my lord chauncellar or my lord of Wynchester or any oder honerable man will thynk I should doo and order me so will I doo"

whereon the abovesaid William forged then and there divers scandalous and horrible, false, new lies concerning the same Humfrey then and still one of the justices of the said lord king assigned to hear and determine pleas before the same king and to take the abovesaid assizes being then and there openly, publicly, and in a high voice before many persons being there and then said and retailed in these English words:

"I woll never axe the this question more; Thow are the falsest wrech alyve"

to which the abovesaid Humfrey responding for his faith then and there said to William:

"Nouther ye nor no man els shall prove me fals & I gaf ye never cause this to sey of me"

whereon the abovesaid Guy Palmes and John Newporte among other lieges of the said lord king then and there standing around and hearing these matters then and there said to the same William in these English words:

"Master Sandys, ye be to blame to sey this"

whereon the same William Sandys in greater scandal of the same Humfrey then and there with a great oath public and with higher voice forged other scandalous, seditious, and horrible false new lies concerning the aforementioned Humfrey then and there and said and retailed in these English words:

> "I sey he is the falsest Wrech alyve & so wold I sey to hym yf he sat yonder in his place and prove it and were almes to make a pylery yonder at the hall dore & set hym on it that all men myght knowe hym for a false wrech"

wherefore a great scandal arose to the same Humfrey then and there and afterwards in divers other vills and places in Middlesex and other counties and cities within the realm of England in contempt of the said lord king now and the grave damage of the same Humfrey and against the form of the abovesaid statute, wherefore he says that he is worse off and has damage to the value of £666.67, and thereof he produces suit etc.

[Sandys appeared and emparled into Hilary and then into Easter term.]

Premunire

KB27/1059, m. 20 (1526-Easter): William Clerk v. John Stevyn and William Parker of Billericay, Essex.

Essex. [Recitation of premunire statute of 16 Richard II]; and although pleas, complaints, and prosecutions of whatsoever trespasses of deceptions, falsities, counterfeits, and fabrications of whatsoever writings and muniments made, brought, or emerging within the realm of England specially pertains to the lord king now and his royal crown and dignity and not to the ecclesiastical forum and ought to be determined by the laws of the lord king of England and not elsewhere nor otherwise, nevertheless the abovesaid John Stevyn, not ignorant of the premises and not at all pondering the statute, and scheming to disinherit the said lord king now, and his crown and dignity of the cognizance of such pleas and unduly to burden, vex, and oppress the same William Clerk with divers labors and expenses on 12 November 1521 prosecuted the aforementioned William Clerk by the name of William Clerk alias Fuller of this that the same William together with a certain Agnes Steven fictitiously and falsely fabricated a certain clause of the last will of a certain William Wodham alias Gutter by sinister modes and means in this part of the same last will, viz., "and if it happen the seid William my son to dye or he cometh to his full age then the seid tenement to be sold by the best advice of my executors and of iiij of the best advysed men in the towne aforseid" in the court Christian before Thomas Wodyngton doctor of laws official of the court of Canterbury at London viz., in the parish of Blessed Mary of arches in the ward of Cordwainer Street, London, and made the same William Clerk to be summoned for the same cause and for circumstances and appendencies of the same cause afterwards, viz., 20 November 1521, by Thomas Brynkley constituted specially summonor or apparitor of the abovesaid official in this part at Billerica in Essex to appear before the aforementioned official in the abovesaid court Christian at the abovesaid church on the 15th day after that citation if it be a juridical day otherwise the very next juridical day thereafter to answer the aforementioned John Stevyn concerning the fabrication of the abovesaid clause of the abovesaid last will; by pretext of which certain citation the same William Clerk afterwards to wit on 9 December 1521 before the aforementioned official at London, viz., in the parish church and ward abovesaid, personally appeared and was compelled and forced to answer the aforementioned John Stevyn of and for the fabrication of the said clause of the last will by the same official then and there, and the same William Clerk in the same court for the same cause was greatly fatigued and weighed down with very many labors and expenses until Peter Leigham doctor of decretals now official of the court Christian before said afterwards, to wit, on 27 July 1523 at the petition and prosecution of the abovesaid John Stevyn in fact brought a definitive sentence contrary to and against the same William Clerk of and for the fabrication of the said clause of the abovesaid last will concerning the lands and tenements abovesaid in London, viz., in the church, parish, and ward abovesaid, and pronounced, decreed, and declared the same William Clerk by contemplation and cause of the fabrication of the said clause of the last will abovesaid to have fallen into and incurred the sentence of major excommunication and to have been involved in the same sentence of excommunication and excommunicated and ought to be denounced for such and as such; and he condemned the same William Clerk in the expenses by the part of the said John Stevyn in that part made and to be made and to be paid to him then and there by the definitive sentence or final decree abovesaid which he brought in and there promulgated in writing, and the same official afterwards, to wit, on 21 November 1525 at the prosecution and petition of the abovesaid John Stevyn taxed the expenses of the same John Stevyn in that part made and to be made at £7 at London, viz., in the abovesaid parish of Blessed Mary of Arches in the abovesaid ward, and the same official directed then and there certain monitory letters from the said court Christian to all and singular rectors, vicars, chaplains and clerics with and without cures and literate people whatsoever abiding wherever in the province of Canterbury mandating to them by the same that they warn or make to be warned or one of them warn or make to be warned peremptorily the abovementioned William Clerk that he pay or make to be paid to John Stevyn the abovesaid £7 for the abovesaid expenses before the Christmas next following under the penalty of excommunication or else that he appear personally before the same official or other presiding officer of the said court on the next juridical day after the feast of St. Hilary next following to see and hear himself excommunicated, by pretext of which certain letters a certain Hugh Gybson cleric at the petition and citation of the abovesaid John Stevyn warned the aforementioned William Clerk afterwards, to wit, on 25 November 1525 at Great Burstead in Essex peremptorily to pay the aforementioned John Stevyn the abovesaid £7 before the next following Christmas under the penalty of the abovesaid excommunication otherwise that he personally appear before the same official or other presiding officer of the said court on the juridical day next after the abovesaid feast of St. Hilary then next following to see and hear himself excommunicated. And the abovesaid William Parker procured, abetted, counseled, and maintained the aforementioned John Stevyn to prosecute against the same William Clerk in the court Christian before the aforementioned Peter Lygham official of that court in the abovesaid form of and for the fabrication of the said clause of the abovesaid last will concerning lands and tenements on 16 October 1525 and on divers days and places before and after at Great Burstead in Essex, whereof cognizance pertains to the said lord king and his royal crown and dignity and not to the ecclesiastical forum in the premises, and thus the abovesaid John Stevyn and William

Parker made the cognizance of the abovesaid plea which pertains to the said lord king now and his crown and dignity in the premises to be brought into an alien court, viz., into the court Christian abovesaid, deceitfully and tried to prosecute less justly in contempt of the lord king now and against the form of the statute abovesaid on the said 16th year edited and to the damage of the same William Clerk of £40. And thereof he seeks a remedy.

And thereon the same William Clerk seeks a writ of the lord king to be directed to the sheriff of Essex to warn the abovesaid John Stevyn and William Parker to be before the lord king to answer both to the same lord king and to the aforementioned William Clerk concerning the premises etc. And it is granted to him etc., wherefore the sheriff of Essex is ordered that by prudent etc., he should make to be warned the aforementioned John Stevyn and William Parker to be before the lord king at Westminster on the Friday after the octaves of Trinity. [Before which day there was a common adjournment to the morrow of St. John the Baptist. The sheriff of Essex then returned that he made them to be warned on 21 May 1526 by John Robynson and Simon May. On which day they came and emparled to Michaelmas term, obtaining mainpernors: Henry Parker of Billerica, husbandman; John Kyng of Billerica, yeoman; William Gyles of London, hatter; and Richard Wydoson of Codnor, Derbs, yeoman, obliged to have them in court each under a penalty of £13.67, and Stevyn and Parker put themselves under a similar obligation of £26.67 to be levied from their lands and tenements. In Michaelmas term they pleaded that they were not guilty. In Trinity term 1527 a jury found John Stevyn guilty with damages of £1 and costs of £2. The jury found William Parker not guilty. Judgment was adjourned successively into Hilary term 1528.]

Manuscripts

Public Record Office, London, England
  cp40. Plea rolls of the court of common pleas.
  e13. Plea rolls of the exchequer of pleas.
  e159. Memoranda rolls and enrolment books of the king's remembrancer.
  kb27. Plea rolls of the court of king's bench.
West Sussex Records Office
  Register of Robert Reade, bishop of Chichester, 1396–1415.

Printed Primary Sources

Councils and Synods with Other Documents Relating to the English Church, II. A.D. 1205–1313. Edited by F. M. Powicke and C. R. Cheney. Oxford: Clarendon Press, 1981.

An Episcopal Court Book for the Diocese of Lincoln, 1514–1520. Edited by Margaret Bowker. Lincoln Record Society, vol. 61. Lincoln, 1967.

"The Evil Consequences of Uses," printed in William S. Holdsworth, *A History of English Law*. Boston: Little, Brown, 1922–66.

Hall, Edward. *Henry VIII*. Edited by Charles Whibley. London, 1904.

Letters and Papers Foreign and Domestic of the Reign of Henry VIII (1529–1530). Edited by J. S. Brewer, J. Gairdner, and R. H. Brodie. London, 1862–1910.

The Notebook of Sir John Port. Edited by John H. Baker. Selden Society, vol. 102. London, 1986.

The Register of John Chandler, Dean of Salisbury, 1404–1417. Edited by T. C. B. Timmins. Wiltshire Record Society, vol. 39. Devizes, 1984.

The Register of John Kirkby, Bishop of Carlisle, 1332–1352 and the Register of John Ross, Bishop of Carlisle, 1325–32. Edited by R. L. Storey. Canterbury and York Society, vol. 79. Woodbridge, Suffolk, and Rochester, New York, 1993.

The Register of John Morton, Archbishop of Canterbury, 1486–1500. Edited by Christopher Harper-Bill. 2 vols. Canterbury and York Society. Boydell, 1991.

Registrum Thome Bourgchier, Cantuariensis Archiepiscopi, A.D. 1454–1486. Edited by F. R. H. Du-Boulay. Canterbury and York Society, vol. 54. Oxford, 1957.

Reports of Cases by John Caryll, Part I, 1485–1499. Edited by J. H. Baker. Selden Society, vol. 15. London, 1999.

The Reports of Sir John Spelman. Edited by John H. Baker. 2 vols. Selden Society, vols. 93, 94. London, 1977–78.

St. German's Doctor and Student. Edited by T. F. T. Plucknett and J. L. Barton. Selden Society, vol. 91. London, 1974.

Select Cases of Defamation to 1600. Edited by R. H. Helmholz. Selden Society, vol. 101. London, 1985.

Valor Ecclesiasticus temp Henrici VIII. Great Britain. Record Commission. 6 vols. London, 1810–34.

Visitations in the Diocese of Lincoln, 1517–1531. Edited by A. Hamilton Thompson. Lincoln Record Society, vol. 33. Hereford, 1930.

Secondary Works

Aston, Margaret. *Lollards and Reformers: Images and literacy in late medieval religion*. London: Hambledon Press, 1984.

Ault, Warren O. "The Village Church and the Village Community in Mediaeval England." *Speculum* 45 (1970).

Baker, John H. *Introduction to English Legal History*. 3rd ed. London: Butterworths, 1990. [*IELH*].

———. Introduction to *The Reports of Sir John Spelman*, edited by John H. Baker. 2 vols. Selden Society, vol. 94. London, 1978.

Bowker, Margaret. "The Henrician Reformation and the Parish Clergy." In *The English Reformation Revised*, edited by Christopher Haigh, 85–93. Cambridge: Cambridge University Press, 1987.

———. *The Henrician Reformation: The Diocese of Lincoln under John Longland, 1521–1547*. Cambridge: Cambridge University Press, 1981.

———. *The Secular Clergy in the Diocese of Lincoln, 1495–1520*. London: Cambridge University Press, 1968.

Brigden, Susan. *London and the Reformation*. Oxford: Clarendon Press, 1989.

———. "Tithe Controversy in Reformation London." *Journal of Ecclesiastical History* 32 (1981): 285–301.

Cam, Helen. *Law-Finders and Law-Makers in medieval England; collected studies in legal and constitutional history*. New York: Barnes and Noble, 1963.

Chaucer, Geoffrey. *The Canterbury Tales*. Edited by A. C. Cawley. London: J. M. Dent, 1975.

Chrimes, S. B. *Henry VII*. Berkeley: University of California Press, 1972.

Coke, Edward. *Institutes of the Laws of England*. Garland reprint. 1979.

Cooper, Helen. *Oxford Guides to Chaucer: The Canterbury Tales*. 2nd ed. Oxford: Oxford University Press, 1996.

Duffy, Eamon. *The Stripping of the Altars: Traditional Religion in England, 1400–1580*. New Haven and London: Yale University Press, 1992.

Dyer, Christopher. *Standards of Living in the Later Middle Ages: Social Change in England, c. 1200–1520*. Cambridge: Cambridge University Press, 1989.

Early Registers of Writs. Edited by Elsa de Haas and G. D. G. Hall. Selden Society, vol. 87. London, 1970.

Elton, G. R. *England under the Tudors*. 3rd ed. London: Routledge, 1991.

———. "Informing for Profit: A Sidelight on Tudor Methods of Law Enforcement." *The Cambridge Historical Journal* 11 (1954).

——. *Policy and Police: The Enforcement of the Reformation in the Age of Thomas Cromwell*. Cambridge: Cambridge University Press, 1972.

——. *Studies in Tudor and Stuart Politics and Government*. Cambridge: Cambridge University Press, 1974.

——. *The Tudor Constitution: Documents and Commentary*. Cambridge: Cambridge University Press, 1960.

——. *The Tudor Revolution in Government: Administrative Changes in the Reign of Henry VIII*. Cambridge: Cambridge University Press, 1954.

Emden, A. B. *A Biographical Register of the University of Oxford to A.D. 1500*. 3 vols. Oxford: Clarendon Press, 1957–59.

Garrett-Goodyear, Harold. "The Tudor Revival of Quo Warranto and Local Contributions to State Building." In *On the Laws and Customs of England: Essays in Honor of Samuel E. Thorne*, edited by Morris S. Arnold, Thomas A. Green, et al. Chapel Hill: University of North Carolina Press, 1981.

Guy, John A. Introduction to *Christopher St. German on Chancery and Statute*, edited by John A. Guy. Selden Society Supplementary Series, vol. 6. London, 1985.

——. *The Public Career of Sir Thomas More*. New Haven: Yale University Press, 1980.

——. *Tudor England*. Oxford: Oxford University Press, 1988.

Haigh, Christopher. "Anticlericalism and the English Reformation." In *The English Reformation Revised*, edited by Christopher Haigh. Cambridge: Cambridge University Press, 1987.

——. *English Reformations: Religion, Politics, and Society under the Tudors*. Oxford: Clarendon Press, 1993.

——. "The Recent Historiography of the English Reformation." In *The English Reformation Revised*, edited by Christopher Haigh. Cambridge: Cambridge University Press, 1987.

——. *Reformation and Resistance in Tudor Lancashire*. Cambridge: Cambridge University Press, 1975.

Heath, Peter. *The English Parish Clergy on the Eve of the Reformation*. London: Routledge, 1969.

Helmholz, Richard H. *Canon Law and the Law of England*. London: Hambledon Press, 1987.

——. *Roman Canon Law in Reformation England*. Cambridge: Cambridge University Press, 1990.

——. "Usury and the Medieval English Church Courts." *Speculum* 61 (1986): 364–80.

Historical Dictionary of Tudor England, 1485–1603. Edited by Ronald H. Fritze. New York: Greenwood Press, 1991.

Holdsworth, William S. *A History of English Law*. Boston: Little, Brown, 1922–66.

Hoyle, R. W. "Origins of the Dissolution of the Monasteries." *The Historical Journal* 38 (1995): 275–305.

Ibbetson, David. *A Historical Introduction to the Law of Obligations*. Oxford: Oxford University Press, 1999.

——. "Words and Deeds: The Action of Covenant in the Reign of Edward I." *Law and History Review* 4 (1987): 71–94.

Ives, E. W. "The Genesis of the Statute of Uses." *English Historical Review* 82 (1967): 673–97.

Jernigan, Scott Casart. "Law and Policy in the Reign of Henry VII." M.A. thesis, University of Houston, 1995.

Jewell, Helen M. *English Local Administration in the Middle Ages*. New York: Barnes and Noble, 1972.

Keir, Sir David Lindsay. *The Constitutional History of Modern Britain since 1485*. 9th ed. New York, 1966.

Knowles, David. *The Religious Orders in England*. 3 vols. Cambridge: Cambridge University Press, 1961.

Kumin, Beat A. *The Shaping of a Community: The Rise and Reformation of the English Parish c. 1400–1560*. Aldershot: Scolar Press, 1996.

Lambert, Malcolm. *Medieval Heresy: Popular Movements from the Gregorian Reform to the Reformation*. 2nd ed. Oxford: Blackwell, 1992.

Lander, Stephen. "Church Courts and the Reformation in the Diocese of Chichester, 1500–58." In *The English Reformation Revisited*, edited by Christopher Haigh. Cambridge: Cambridge University Press, 1987.

Lehmberg, Stanford E. *The Reformation Parliament, 1529–1536*. Cambridge: Cambridge University Press, 1970.

Loades, D. M. *Politics and the Nation, 1450–1660: Obedience, Resistance and Public Order*. London: Fontana/Collins, 1973.

Lopez, Robert. *The Commercial Revolution of the Middle Ages, 950–1350*. Cambridge: Cambridge University Press, 1976.

Mackie, J. D. *The Earlier Tudors, 1485–1558*. Oxford: Clarendon Press, 1952.

Martin, Diane. "Crown Policy and Anglo–Papal Relations: Premunire Prosecutions during the Great Schism, 1377–1381." M.A. thesis, University of Houston, 1992.

Midmer, Roy. *English Medieval Monasteries, 1066–1540*. Athens: University of Georgia Press, 1979.

Miller, Helen. "London and Parliament in the Reign of Henry VIII." *Bulletin of the Institute of Historical Research* 35 (1962): 128–49.

Milsom, S. F. C. Introduction to *Novae Narrationes*. Selden Society, vol. 80. London, 1963.

———. "Richard Hunne's 'Praemunire.'" In *Studies in the History of the Common Law*, edited by S. F. C. Milsom, 145–47. London: Hambledon Press, 1985.

———. *Studies in the History of the Common Law*. London: Hambledon Press, 1985.

Morris, Colin. *The Papal Monarchy: The Western Church from 1050 to 1250*. Oxford: Oxford University Press, 1989.

Musson, Anthony, and W. M. Ormrod. *The Evolution of English Justice: Law, Politics and Society in the Fourteenth Century*. Basingstoke and New York: Macmillan Press, 1999.

Orme, Nicholas. *English Schools in the Middle Ages*. London: Methuen, 1973.

Outhwaite, R. B. *Inflation in Tudor and Early Stuart England*. London: Macmillan, 1969.

Palmer, Robert C. "Contexts of Marriage in Medieval England: Evidence from the King's Court circa 1300." *Speculum* 59 (1984): 42–67.

———. *The County Courts of Medieval England, 1150–1350*. Princeton: Princeton University Press, 1982.

———. "Covenant, *Justicies* Writs, and Reasonable Showings." *American Journal of Legal History* 31 (1987): 97–117.

———. *English Law in the Age of the Black Death, 1348–1381*. Chapel Hill: University of North Carolina Press, 1993. [*ELABD*].

———. *The Whilton Dispute, 1264–1380: A Social-Legal Study of Dispute Settlement in Medieval England*. Princeton: Princeton University Press, 1984.

Pennington, Kenneth. *Popes and Bishops: The Papal Monarchy in the Twelfth and Thirteenth Centuries*. Philadelphia: University of Pennsylvania Press, 1984.

Rymer, Thomas. *Foedera, Conventiones, Literae et cujuscunque generis acta publica, inter reges angliae*. 17 vols. London, 1727–29.

Sayles, George O. *The King's Parliament of England*. New York: Norton, 1974.

Scarisbrick, J. J. "The Conservative Episcopate in England, 1529–1535." Ph.D. diss., Cambridge, 1955.

———. *Henry VIII*. Berkeley and Los Angeles: University of California Press, 1968.

Solt, Leo F. *Church and State in Early Modern England, 1509–1640*. New York: Oxford University Press, 1990.

Sutherland, Donald W. *Quo Warranto Proceedings in the Reign of Edward I, 1278–1294*. Oxford: Clarendon Press, 1963.

Swanson, R. N. *Church and Society in Late Medieval England*. Oxford: Blackwell, 1989.

Thomson, J. A. F. "Tithe Disputes in later medieval London." *English Historical Review* 78 (1963): 1–17.

Thomson, John A. F. *The Early Tudor Church and Society, 1485–1529*. London: Longman, 1993.

Warren, W. L. *Henry II*. Berkeley and Los Angeles: University of California Press, 1973.

Wunderli, Richard M. *London Church Courts and Society on the Eve of the Reformation*. Cambridge, Mass.: Medieval Academy of America, 1981.

Youings, Joyce. "Dissolution of the Monasteries." In *Historical Dictionary of Tudor England, 1485–1603*, edited by Ronald H. Fritze. New York: Greenwood, 1991.

———. *The Dissolution of the Monasteries*. London: Allen and Unwin, 1971.

Zell, Michael L. "The Personnel of the Clergy in Kent, in the Reformation Period." *English Historical Review* 89 (1974): 513–33.

English Reformation: and parish changes, 1, 3, 6, 7, 8, 9, 31, 212, 213, 216, 220–21, 228, 247, 249, 253; and Fyneux, 6; traditional historiography on, 8, 146–47; and advowson rights, 20; and governmental power, 23–24, 237, 247; and parish leases, 111; and evidence of anticlericalism, 150; and enforcement litigation, 182–83; and religious houses' dissolution, 211, 212; and problem of uses, 235

Entrepreneurial capital, 80

Estate executors: and tithes, 34; and common law, 55–56; and church court/common law court friction, 65–66; and church wardens, 72–73; and statutes of 1529, 151, 170; and property held in use, 230

Evolutionary change, 4

Exchequer of pleas: and statutes of 1529, 7, 147; and rectors, 12; and jurisdiction, 24; and enforcement litigation, 168, 173, 174–76, 177, 178, 179–81, 182, 188, 193, 219, 251; and religious houses, 175; and clergy's divestment, 186; and religious houses' dissolution, 219

Fee simple, 230, 231, 232

Feoffees, 229, 230–32, 233, 236, 307–9

Feudal incidents, 232–33, 234, 235, 245

Fiction of the lost grant, 224

Fisher, Bishop (Rochester), 153–54

Food distribution, 143

Forfeiture: and out-of-court settlements, 7, 250; and clergy as lessees, 165–66; and enticement to sue, 166, 188; and probate fees, 170; and royal pardons, 174–75, 186; and plaintiff's claims, 176–78; and prosecution of innocent clergy, 180; and clergy with small amounts of land, 192; and buying/selling for profit, 195; and mortuary fees, 199; and religious houses' dissolution, 216

Free tenements, 114, 123

Funerals: and king's court, 60–61

Fyncheley v. Creswall et al. (1512), 122

Fyneux, John: and church courts, 6, 25–26; and premunire process, 25–27, 28, 45, 62, 63, 64, 141, 235; and annuities, 60; and tithes, 62–63, 69; and debt litigation, 66; and parish leases, 87, 140; and ejectment, 120–21; and church governance, 149

Glebe lands: and rectors, 5, 11, 30, 40; and church courts, 26; and agricultural surplus, 30, 47; and agricultural produce, 32, 39, 41, 47, 160; management of, 39–40; and commerce, 39–41, 47; leasing of, 40, 41, 80, 188; value of, 40–

41; mortuary fees compared to, 42; and king's court, 73–74; and parish leases, 81; and clergy's leaseholding, 180, 189, 193, 194, 218; clergy's management of, 188; and buying/selling for profit, 196; and clergy's use of litigation, 253

Governmental power: and national life, 1–2; and local life, 2–3; assumptions concerning, 3; Henry VIII unified with, 4; and religious houses' dissolution, 7, 211, 215–16, 223–28, 245; and church, 10, 23–29, 48, 149, 225, 226, 237, 246; and Reformation, 23–24, 237, 247; and premunire, 23–29; and litigation, 113; and religious houses, 209, 211, 223; and crown, 224, 225–26; centralization of, 237. *See also* Parish government

Gray's Inn, 154

Great Schism, 13

Guilford, Henry, 152

Guy, John, 145, 151

Haigh, Christopher, 138, 146–47, 182–83

Hall, Edward, 153, 154, 155, 156

Henry V (king of England), 56

Henry VII (king of England), 25, 26, 28, 54, 183, 225, 226, 227

Henry VIII (king of England): as head of church, 1, 4, 5, 6, 28, 29, 48, 74, 174, 210, 212, 219, 223, 228, 237, 240; and Anne Boleyn, 1, 210, 254; use of law, 3; and parish leases, 7, 111; and clerical ideals, 10; and king's bench powers, 26; divorce of, 28, 29, 148, 150, 156, 158; and tithes, 31; and clergy's use of common law, 54; and absentee clerical rectors, 111, 112; and statutory reform of parish, 142, 143, 147, 148; and clergy, 148, 151, 153, 155, 156, 158; and origin of Reformation, 150; and church property, 151; and statutes of 1529, 153, 154, 155, 156; and royal debt remittance, 154–55; and clergy/laity separation, 164; and religious houses' dissolution, 209, 212, 213, 216, 217; and public/private law distinctions, 214, 229; and *quo warranto* procedures, 225; and sanctuary, 226, 227; and statute of uses, 232–33, 237

Heresy: and Wycliff, 13–14; and premunire, 27; and tithes, 39, 61; and Hunne, 45–46; and king's responsibility, 73; and bishops, 110; Henry VIII's diminished concern with, 151; and statutes of 1529, 154, 156

Heriot duty, 42–43, 46, 77, 203

Heywood, Richard, 244–45

Hoyle, R. W., 146

death duties, 30–31, 153; and commerce, 47; and parish leases, 81, 104; and rectors' stipends, 201; and religious services, 251

Parliament: and tithes, 33, 241–42; clerical representatives to, 54, 153; and priests' salaries, 56; and parish leases, 111, 142; alliances and dynamics of, 145; and fall of Wolsey, 148; and Cromwell, 150, 151, 152, 156, 157; and absentee clerical rectors, 152, 171–72, 252; and clergy, 152, 210; and royal debt remittance, 155; and religious houses, 209, 223, 227; and religious houses' dissolution, 219, 227

Parsons: and parish leases, 90, 106–7, 107n, 108, 111; and statutes of 1529, 169–70; and enforcement litigation, 183; and bailiffs, 255–58

Partnerships: and parish leases, 81, 92

Passive uses, 231

Penal bonds, 36

Penalties: and writ of prohibition, 21; and advowson rights, 22; and tithes, 35, 37; and performance bonds, 50, 51; and crown's regulation of church, 144; and statutes of 1529, 165–67, 173, 191–92; and clergy's opportunities to divest, 174, 186; and buying/selling for profit, 195, 196; and prohibition procedures, 240; and *qui tam* procedures, 250

Performance bonds: and commerce, 36; and tithes, 39; and mortuary rights, 44; church use of, 50–52; and morals, 51–52; and sexual regulation, 51–52, 54; and clergy, 53–54; and church wardens, 71, 72; and parish leases, 80, 82, 86, 110, 141; and leaseholds, 114, 116; and debt litigation, 116–17; and parish lease lessees, 116–18, 123; and parish lease lessors, 117–18, 125; and rent, 124–25; and church chancel/rectory building repair, 129, 130, 132, 133, 134

Periodic tenancy, 91, 123

Perpetual vicars: and parish leases, 1, 4, 87, 100, 221, 247; and absenteeism, 12, 75; and corporate rectors, 92; and advowson rights, 222

Personal conflicts: and parish changes, 2; and litigation, 4, 5, 8–9; and parish leases, 6; and law, 8, 15; royal remedies for, 48; and performance bonds, 51

Personal piety, 1, 8, 212, 245, 246, 251

Pilgrimage of Grace, 185, 218, 228

Pluralism: and absenteeism, 6, 12, 75, 102, 106, 172, 198, 248; and religious houses, 6, 217, 220; and statutes of 1529, 144, 145, 146–47, 156, 157, 158, 161–63, 165, 186, 202, 203, 206, 221, 222, 249; and Parliament, 152; and education, 162, 163, 206, 221, 222; and parish leases, 204, 254;

and religious houses' dissolution, 221; and rectors' income, 238; and clergy's use of litigation, 253

Pope and papacy: and state politics, 13; and church law, 15; and advowson rights, 16, 22, 23; and writ of prohibition, 21; and agricultural surplus, 30; and Henry VIII, 148, 210, 211; and religious house suppression, 217; and abolition of papal authority, 228, 239

Power allocation: in parish community, 5; and justices, 5, 6, 8; and litigation, 5, 8–9, 113; and church influence, 6, 28; and clerical ideals, 7–8; and law, 8; and parish government, 10; and church wardens, 14; and parish lease lessee, 137; and parish leases, 141; and statutes of 1529, 144, 159, 247, 250; and religious houses' dissolution, 223. *See also* Governmental power

Power relations: between laity and clergy, 1, 4, 7–8, 143, 144, 148, 152, 166, 167, 168, 172, 207, 208, 223, 237, 251; and statutes of 1529, 7, 148; between bishop and rector, 15–16; and advowson rights, 16, 17; and Henry VIII as head of church, 48; and parish leases, 112; and church power, 121. *See also* Governmental power

Prebendaries, 12, 92, 104, 122–23, 130

Premunire: and advowson rights, 23; and church governance, 23–29, 74; and tithes, 38, 62; and mortuary fees, 45, 46; and king's court jurisdictions, 62; and defamation, 63–65; and clergy, 155; and Wolsey, 210; and uses, 235; appropriateness of, 240; example of, 310–12

Prerogative courts: and national governance of localities, 2, 14; regulatory function of, 23; and litigation concerning statutes of 1529, 174

Priests: rectors as, 11; bishop's appointment of, 15; wages of, 54, 56–59, 61, 96, 98; and endowments for religious services, 59; hiring of, 66, 159; and bailiffs, 79; and parish leases, 85–86, 92, 102, 104, 108, 110, 194; as parish lease lessees, 108, 137, 158–59, 248; and statutes of 1529, 143; and enforcement of statutes of 1529, 168; and taxation, 218

Primogeniture, 229

Probate of wills: and church courts, 15, 56; and common law, 55–56; and church court/common law court friction, 65; and statutes of 1529, 146, 147, 151, 152, 153, 154, 155, 168–71, 210; enforcement of statutes of 1529, 305

Property distribution: and religious houses' dissolution, 220

Property law: and personal property, 14; and real property, 14; and religious houses' dissolu-